Railways Restored 2007

Edited by Alan C. Butcher

Ian Allan
PUBLISHING

Contents

Front cover: This former London & Southern Western Railway Class M7 0-4-4T, No 30053, will return to service this spring on the Swanage Railway.
Alan Barnes

Previous page: Dereham, on the Mid-Norfolk Railway must be one of the few locations where a level crossing is located under a bridge. Whilst on loan during 2006, GWR 0-6-0PT No 9466 is seen on the first day of steam operation over the full length of line following completion of a run-round loop at Wymondham Abbey station. No 9466 is booked for a return appearance this spring.
ACB

First published 1980
Twenty eighth edition 2007

ISBN (10) 0 7110 3216 5
ISBN (13) 978 0 7110 3216 3

Published by Ian Allan Publishing

an imprint of Ian Allan Publishing Ltd, Hersham, Surrey KT12 4RG
Printed by Ian Allan Printing Ltd, Hersham, Surrey KT12 4RG

Code: 0703/C3

The publishers, the railway operators and the Heritage Railway Association accept no liabiity for any loss, damage or injury caused by error or inaccuracy in the information published in *Railways Restored 2007*. Train services may be altered or cancelled without prior notice, and at some locations diesel traction may be substituted for scheduled steam workings.

Do you wish to advertise in *Railways Restored?*
If so contact David Smith, 01775 767184, for details

National Railway Heritage Awards

The Awards have been made annually since 1979 and were granted charitable status in 2004. The object remains the same: encouraging high standards of restoration of buildings, structures and signalling installations and of their environmental care, thus promoting public recognition and awareness of our historic railway and tramway heritage and its place in the environment. We aim to promote careful design and quality workmanship in restoration, modernisation, adaptation and maintenance, taking proper account of all relevant factors, particularly manpower and funding. In this way we encourage both public and heritage railways and tramways to present their operational premises as attractive 'shop-windows'. We also encourage owners and occupiers of former railway or tramway premises now used for other purposes to retain as much as possible of their original character.

The awards are organised by the National Railway Awards Committee. Our main sponsors are Ian Allan Publishing together with Westinghouse Invensys, Network Rail, London Underground and the Railway Heritage Trust. Judging is done from the beginning of May through to the end of August and those short listed are notified at the beginning of October. The Awards are presented in early December at a prestigious location by a well-known public figure, with full media coverage.

1992 saw the inclusion of Ireland in the Awards initially with the addition of a special Premier Award and up to three Certificates of Commendation in each sector.

The Ian Allan Independent Railway of the Year Award

The Ian Allan Judges pay incognito visits to each of the heritage railways around the county, buy tickets and spend the day travelling as members of the public. The judges look at the quality of service, presentation and helpfulness of the staff, the stations, the catering, the toilets and the day as a whole.

The 2007 winner was the West Somerset Railway.

The HRA Annual Award

This, the premier award made by the HRA, is for a group or organisation making an outstanding contribution to railway heritage during the year of the Award.

The Award takes the form of a Royal Train Headboard from the London, Brighton & South Coast Railway, which is on loan to the HRA from the National Railway Museum. The Award is held for one year and the winning group also receives a commemorative plaque. The Award is announced and presented at the Association's Annual General Meeting which is held on the last weekend of January each year.

The following projects are eligible:

1   Any building, structure or signalling installation, associated with railways or tramways since their inception in the United Kingdom, the Isle of Man and the Republic of Ireland.

2   An entry may comprise a whole station or any single structure or group of structures, which form, or once formed, part of railway or tramway premises.

3   Certain types of replica are eligible. These include:
- An historic building, structure or signalling installation re-erected at a new site
- An accurate reconstruction of a specfic building, structure or signalling installation, the original of which has been removed or demolished, rebuilt on or very close to its original site
- A completely new but authentic replica of a specific historic building, structure or signalling installation on a new site
- An entry comprising a combination of restored or adapted historic building, structure or signalling installation with modern additions
- Construction of a building in the general style of an historic building, structure or signalling installation with no specific or authentic basis for its design or location, would not be eligible.

Who can enter?

Entries are invited from the following:

Train and tram operating companies.

Companies owning track, structures and stations.

Urban underground and passenger transport authorities and companies.

Operators of heritage, tourist and private railways and tramways.

Residual property owning bodies.

Owners of eligible infrastructure, whether of not still in railway or tramway use.

Architects, engineers and contractors involved in restoration, new or maintenance work.

Local Amenity groups.

Private individuals.

Any group in Great Britain and Ireland involved in the railway industry, whether as a private railway company or as a less formal organisation. Network Rail, Irish Rail, Northern Ireland Railways (NIR). Other public or commercial organisations. Private individuals.

For application forms apply to:
Robin Leleux
12 Bilsdale Way
Baildon
Shipley
West Yorkshire
BD17 5DG
Tel/Fax: 01274 593235

Editor's Notes

On the following pages will be found a guide to the major heritage railways, railway museums and preservation centres in the British Isles. Information for visitors has been set out in tabular form for easy reference, together with a locomotive stocklist for most centres.

Many heritage centres and operating lines provide facilities for other groups and organisations to restore locomotives and equipment on their premises. It has not been possible to include full details of these groups, but organisations which own locomotives are shown under the centres at which they operate. In addition, a full list of member societies of the HRA is given elsewhere. In the case of most operating lines their length is given, but there is no guarantee that services are operated over the entire length.

Within the heading to each entry a heading block has been incorporated for easy reference as to what each site offers in the way of passenger service to visitors. These are as follows:

Timetable Service: Railways providing a passenger service between two or more stations with public access; eg Mid-Hants Railway.

Steam Centre: A railway or heritage site offering a passenger service on a short length of line, on a regular basis, with public access at only one point; eg Lavender Line.

Museum: A museum or site that does not offer a passenger service on a regular basis, if at all; eg Science Museum, London. Some sites may however offer rides on miniature railways.

Railway Centre: A catch-all for those centres which do not fall clearly into any of the other brackets. Generally those offering rides over short distances using non-steam motive power.

Attraction: Where the railway is an addition to the main attraction of the location (eg Bicton Woodland Railway).

As well as a guide as to what to expect on each site, this year's *Railways Restored* shows what, if any, particular professional body the Companies or Societies belong to. These are:

HRA: Indicates that the organisation is a member of the Heritage Railway Association (HRA).

TT: Indicates that the organisation is a member of the Transport Trust (TT).

Membership of the HRA and TT is open to both organisations and private individuals. Private members are able to take advantage of concessions offered to them by the organisations that subscribe to these two bodies.

The concessions range from a discount on the admission price to free entry. The TT's Travel Back leaflet provides details.

Details given under **Access by public transport** should be checked beforehand to ensure services shown are operating. Unless the Heritage Railway, Steam Centre or Museum has identified the privatised train company operating the service, the phrase 'by rail', or 'main line', has been used to identify access by train.

Visitors wishing to see specific items of rolling stock or locomotives are advised to check before their visit that the exhibit is available for inspection. It should be stressed that not all items are usually available for inspection due to restoration, operating or other restrictions.

Editor's Comment

Welcome to the 28th edition of *Railways Restored*. Once again a number of heritage lines have reported records being broken during 2006, both in terms of visitors and turnover. The railway sector of the heritage movement appears to be on an ever upward trend, this sadly is not reflected in some of the more 'static' forms of heritage. A number of attractions from Devon to Scotland have closed over the last few months, unable to break-even despite assistance by volunteers.

A couple of sites are missing from this edition due to major developments taking place on site: Dobwalls and Summerlee Heritage Park. At Bristol the railway remains operational, but please check dates/times before travelling, whilst the adjacent museum undergoes improvements.

After a traumatic period the Weardale Railway has re-opened and a number of other new entries are included.

The 2008 edition should see the inclusion of a few more heritage attraction as groups endeavour to re-open lines, some of these arre listed under the Applicant section in the HRA members list at the back of this book.

An additional item in a number of entries is the Special Facilities entry. This usually shows what additional arrangements can be offered for the more general events including marriage/civil paternership ceremonies, seminar accommodation, catering for larger party/corporate groups etc.

If you have enjoyed your visit to any of the attractions in *Railways Restored* why not join in the pleasure of becoming a member and may be volunteering. Not every 'job' entails years of training or physical work. Most operations now have a 'new volunteer' officer or hold an 'open weekend' when a behind the scenes tour gives an idea of how the prospective volunteer can get involved.

Allelys Heavy Haulage

Allely's Heavy Haulage Ltd. is part of the Allely Group running approximately 50 vehicles in total.

The Heavy Haulage side have been specialists in the movement of railway vehicles for the last 20 years and has undertaken numerous large contracts.

We offer a full service for the movement of railway rolling stock and trackwork and will consider any rail contracts.

We have extensive knowledge of all types of rolling stock and many rail locations throughout the U.K.

Contact Robert Ford
01527-857621 or email Robert@allelys.co.uk

Allely's Heavy Haulage Ltd
The Slough
Studley
Warwickshire
B80 7EN
Telephone 01527 857621
Fax 01527 857623

7

Standard Abbreviations

AEC	Associated Equipment Co
AEG	Allgemeine Elektrizitaets Gesellschaft
A/Barclay	Andrew Barclay
A/Porter	Aveling & Porter Ltd
A/Whitworth	Armstrong Whitworth
B/Drewry	Baguley/Drewry
B/Peacock	Beyer Peacock & Co
B/Hawthorn	Black, Hawthorn & Co
BRCW	Birmingham Railway, Carriage & Wagon
BTH	British Thomson Houston
Buch	23 August Locomotive Works
D/Metcalfe	Davies & Metcalfe
E/Electric	English Electric Ltd
F/Jennings	Fletcher Jennings & Co
F/Walker	Fox Walker
G&S	G. & S. Light Engineering Co
G/England	George England & Co
GRCW	Gloucester Railway, Carriage & Wagon
H/Barclay	Hunslet Barclay
H/Clarke	Hudswell Clarke & Co Ltd
H/Hunslet	Hudson-Hunslet
H/Leslie	Hawthorn Leslie & Co
K/Stuart	Kerr Stuart & Co Ltd
L/Blackstone	Lister Blackstone
M/Cam	Metropolitan Cammell
M/Rail	Motor Rail Ltd
M/Vick	Metrovick (Metropolitan-Vickers)
M/Wardle	Manning Wardle & Co Ltd
N/British	North British Locomotive Co Ltd
N/Wilson	Nasmyth Wilson & Co Ltd
O&K	Orenstein & Koppel
P/Steel	Pressed Steel Co Ltd
RSH	Robert Stephenson & Hawthorn Ltd
R/Hornsby	Ruston Hornsby
R/Proctor	Ruston Proctor
S. F. Belge	Société Franco Belge
SMH	Simplex Mechanical Handling
YEC	Yorkshire Engine Co
W&M	Waggon & Maschinenbau
W/Rogers	Wingrove & Rogers

Company abbreviations

BR	British Railways
DB	German Federal Railway
DSB	Danish State Railways
GWR	Great Western Railway
JZ	Yugoslav Railways
LBSCR	London, Brighton & South Coast Railway
LMS	London, Midland & Scottish Railway
LNER	London & North Eastern Railway
LSWR	London & South Western Railway
MoS	Ministry of Supply
MR	Midland Railway
NLR	North London Railway
NS	Netherlands State Railways
NSB	Norwegian State Railways
RR	Rhodesia Railways
S&DJR	Somerset & Dorset Joint Railway

SAR	South African Railways
SECR	South Eastern & Chatham Railway
SER	South Eastern Railway
SJ	Swedish Railways
SNCF	French National Railways
SR	Southern Railway
USATC	United States Army Transportation Corps
WD	War Department

Other abbreviations

BE	Battery-electric
DE	Diesel-electric
DH	Diesel-hydraulic
DM	Diesel-mechanical
DMU	Diesel multiple-unit
E	Overhead electric
EMU	Electric multiple-unit
F	Fireless
G	Geared
GH	Gas-hydraulic
IST	Inverted saddle tank
LRO	Light Railway Order
ParM	Paraffin-mechanical
PH	Petrol-hydraulic
PM	Petrol-mechanical
PT	Pannier tank
R	Railcar
ST	Saddle tank
STT	Saddle tank and tender
T	Side tank
VB	Vertical boiler
WT	Well tank
4w	Four-wheel

Multiple-unit Type abbreviations

B	Brake
C	Composite (First/Standard class seating)
D	Driving
F	First class
K	Corridor
LV	Luggage Van
M	Motor
O	Open (seating arrangement)
P	Pullman (ex-'Brighton Belle')
R	Restaurant
S	Standard ([or Second] class)
T	Trailer

Added together these give the vehicle designation, for example: DMBS — Driving Motor Brake Second.

The addition of an L indicates that the vehicle has a lavatory (may not be operational on some vehicles).

Some lines operate a Standard class only policy and the First class facility is downgraded. This may result in some vehicles having a different designation to that originally applied.

Keith & Dufftown
Strathspey
Alford
Royal Deeside
Caledonian Rly (Brechin)
Kerrs
Mull Rail
Almond
Prestongrange
PSPS
Bo'ness & Kinneil
EDINBURGH
Glasgow Museum
Scottish Ind
Leadhills
North Tyneside/Stephenson
Bowes
Tanfield
South Tynedale
Beamish
Monkwearmouth
Giant's Causeway
County Donegal
RPSI
Ulster
BELFAST
Weardale
Locomotion
Darlington
North Bay
Haig
Eden
Wensleydale
North Yorkshire Moors
Downpatrick
Ravenglass & Eskdale
Lightwater
Snaefell Mountain
Great Laxey
Groudle Glen
Manx Electric
I.O.M. Steam Railway
Lakeside & Haverthwaite
Keighley & Worth Valley
National Railway Museum
Cavan & Leitrim
Embsay & Bolton Abbey
Abbey Light
Derwent
VCT
Middleton
Leeds Museum
West Lancashire
Blackpool
Elsecar
DUBLIN
Windmill Farm
Ribble
Kirklees
Penrhyn
Lakeside
East Lancashire
Cleethorpes Coast
Rheilffordd Eryri
Rhyl
Museum (Manchester)
Astley Green
Lincolnshire Wolds
West Clare
Great Orme
Brookside
Peak Rail
North Ings
Poppy Line
Llanberis Lake
Crich
Barrow Hill
Snowdon Mountain
Convy
Churnet Valley
Midland/Golden Valley
Wells & Walsingham
Bure Valley
Llangollen
Railway Age
Ecclesbourne
Welsh Highland
Oswestry
Rudyard
Foxfield
Nottingham
Mid Norfolk
Ffestiniog
Cambrian
Amerton
Great Central
Irish Steam
Bala Lake
Chasewater
Silk Mill
Abbey
Fairbourne
Battlefield Line
Snibston
Rutland
Railworld
EATM
Corris
Ironbridge
Nene Valley
Irish Traction Group
Welshpool & Llanfair
Telford
Tyseley
Northampton & Lamport
Bressingham
Talyllyn
Kidderminster
Irchester
Mid-Suffolk
Waterford
Vale of Rheidol
Coventry
Northants Ironstone
Severn Valley
Evesham
Great Whipsnade
Gloucestershire Warwickshire
Leighton Buzzard
Audley End
Teifi
Brecon Mountain
Winchcombe
Buckinghamshire
Colne Valley
Gwili
Perrygrove
Didcot
Chinnor
Waltham Abbey
EARM
Swansea Vale
National Waterways
Ruislip
Epping
Mangapps Farm
Dean Forest
Cholsey
North Woolwich
Pontypool
Barry
Swindon & Cricklade
Steam
LONDON
Bristol
Great Cockcrow
Sittingbourne & Kemsley
CARDIFF
Avon Valley
Kew Bridge, LT Depot
Science Museum, Southall
Bredgar
East Kent
West Somerset
Midsomer Norton
Longleat
Spa Valley
Kent & East Sussex
Lynton
S&DJRT
East Somerset
Mid-Hants
Bluebell
Romney, Hythe & Dymchurch
Bideford
Yeovil
Gartell
Hollycombe
Lavender
Rother Valley
Devon Railway Centre
Moors
Amberley
Hayling
Volks
Launceston
Seaton
Swanage
Royal Victoria
Dartmoor
Beer
Bicton
Exbury
Eastleigh
Bodmin & Wenford
South Devon
Isle of Wight
Lappa
Paignton & Dartmouth
Plym Valley
Alderney

Rail TV - the new way to watch your favourite Railway DVDs

WWW.RAILTV.TV gives access to all your favourite DVD titles in one location at great prices.

WWW.RAILTV.TV allows you to rent your favourite Railway titles by downloading them in DVD quality ready to watch at your convenience on your PC, laptop or television. All you need is a computer and a broadband internet connection. For some titles we will give you the option to download to own, ensuring you can enjoy them forever.

With regularly updated content, we are confident there will be something for you to enjoy at WWW.RAILTV.TV. And with subscription and pay-as-you-go options you can watch as little or as much as you like.

Full Steam to Holyhead

Main line steam on the North Wales coast, including Flying Scotsman, Princess Margaret Rose, Duke of Gloucester and Union of South Africa.

Main line steam on the North Wales coast, including Pacifics from both the East Coast and Wrest Coast main lines such as Flying Scotsman, Princess Margaret Rose, Duke of Gloucester and Union of South Africa, seen hard at work on the route of the 'Irish Mail' from Crewe to Holyhead, past Conwy Castle.

Diesels in Action

Main line diesel action throughout Britain.

A detailed study of main line diesel action throughout Britain, particularly concentrating in the ten years leading to the privatisation of Britain's railway system, when the new train operating companies were established and the familiar classes still in operation on today's system became acquainted with their roles under privatisation.

Flying Scotsman - Part One: A Day in the Life

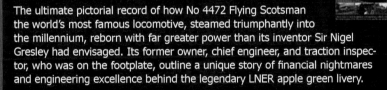

The story of the world's most famous steam engine and its return to the main line in 1999.

The ultimate pictorial record of how No 4472 Flying Scotsman the world's most famous locomotive, steamed triumphantly into the millennium, reborn with far greater power than its inventor Sir Nigel Gresley had envisaged. Its former owner, chief engineer, and traction inspector, who was on the footplate, outline a unique story of financial nightmares and engineering excellence behind the legendary LNER apple green livery.

A professional documentary crew intensively filmed the engine in action during its first year back on the main line in 1999 following restoration.

To see our full catalogue, visit

WWW.RAILTV.TV

2008 will celebrate 40 years since the end of British Railways steam traction on the main line. One on the locomotives to take part in the last day of action was No 70013 *Oliver Cromwell*. This locomotive is now at the Great Central Railway for restoration, it is seen here at Loughborough before work started. *Alan Barnes*

England

England

Member: HRA, TT

The Abbey Light Railway was founded in 1976. It is a family run operation supported by volunteers to restore and maintain vintage narrow gauge locomotives and stock. The railway takes visitors to the 11th century Cistercian Monastery of Kirkstall Abbey

Proprietor : Mr P. N. Lowe

Location: Bridge Road, Kirkstall, Leeds LS5 3BW

Telephone: (0113) 267 5087

Main station: Kirkstall Abbey

Other public station: Bridge Road (OS ref: SE 262356)

Car park: At Abbey and Bridge Road

Access by public transport: By train to Headingley station. Buses from City Square

Refreshment facilities: At nearby Morrisons supermarket

Souvenir shop: Badges on sale on the train

Industrial locomotives

Narrow gauge:

Name	No	Builder	Type	Built
Loweco	1	Lister (20779)	4wDM	1942
Atlas	2	Hunslet (2465)	4wDM	1943
Odin	3	Simplex (5859)	4wDM	1934
Vulcan	4	R/Hornsby (198287)	4wDM	1942
—	5	R/Hornsby (235654)	4wDM	1946
Druid	6	Simplex (8644)	4wDM	1941
—	7	O&K (5926)	4wDM	1935
Go-Go	8	Hudson (39924)	4wPM	1924
—	9	Muir Hill (110)	4wPM	1925
—	10	Baguley (736)	0-4-0PM	1917
—	11	Baguley (760)	0-4-0PM	1917
—	12	Greenbat (2848)	4wBE	1957

Depot: Workshops at Bridge Road

Length of line/gauge: Quarter mile, 2ft gauge

Period of public operation: Sundays and Bank Holidays (Sundays 13.00-17.00)

Special events: Kirkstall Gala in Abbey grounds — 7 July

Facilities for disabled: In Abbey grounds

Membership details: As above

Member: TT

Narrow gauge site railway (2ft gauge) formerly part of a sewage pumping station that now forms museum site. Railway relaid in concrete by MSC scheme during early 1980s to original track layout. New track layout as an extension to original laid with 35lb rail on wooden sleepers. All the railway system is now run by volunteers. Original Simplex locomotive kept on site in operational condition. Line originally used for transferring solid material from screens to tip (about 100yd). Demonstration skip wagon trains as well as passenger trains are run when the railway is operating

Industrial locomotives

Narrow gauge:

Name	No	Builder	Type	Built
Leonard	—	Bagnall (2087)	0-4-0ST	1919
—	—	Motor Rail (5260)	4wPM	1931
—	—	Hibberd (1776)	4wPM	1931
—	—	R/Hornsby (223700)	4wDM	1944
—	—	SMH (40SD515)	4wDM	1979
New Star	—	Lister (4088)	4wPM	1931

Stock

3 new passenger vehicles based on Leicester & Swannington coaches.
10 skip wagons, 2 mine tubs, 2 flats, bomb wagon, various miscellaneous.
All locomotives are restored to working order; *Leonard* returned to service in 2005 when restoration work was completed

Location: Abbey Pumping Station, Corporation Road, off Abbey Lane, Leicester LE4 5XP
Operating group: Leicester City Council Museum, Leicester Museums Technology Association
Telephone: 0116 299 5111
Fax: 0116 299 5125
Car park: Free on site
Access by public transport: Main line Leicester (London Road). First Bus route 54 from city centre (alight at Beaumont Leys Lane)
Length of line/gauge: About 300yd, 2ft gauge. Passenger carrying on special event days and railway running days (small fare payable on free-entry days)
Period of public opening: Daily 1 February to 31 November, Saturdays-Thursdays 11.00 to 16.30, Sundays 13.00 to 16.30. Open for special events only all year

On site facilities:
Museum/shop/toilets/car park. Refreshments only on special event days
Facilities for disabled: Access to museum lower floor and grounds. Lift to Engine House and refreshments on event days. Wheelchair access to railway
Volunteer contact: Tony Kendal, c/o Abbey Pumping Station
Museum contact: Mr C. Stevens, c/o Abbey Pumping Station (Tel: 0116 299 5111)
Other attractions: Museum holds various transport, steam navvy, beam engines. Some items only viewable by appointment or on special event days

Special events: Inventors & Inventions Steam Day — 15 April; Classics & Railway Running Day — 5 May; Teddy Bears' Picnic, Railway Running Day — 2 June; Urban Rally Weekend Steam Day— 23/24 Junc; Railway Running Day — 7 July; Pedal Power & Railway Running Day — 4 August; Steam Powered & Air Cooled Railway Running — 1 Stepember; Pastimes Steam & Crafts Day — 16 September; Train Rides & Miniatures Day — 6 October; Ghostly Engineer Running Event — 29 October; Christmas Toys, Steam Day — 9 December;
2008 dates include: Meccano Day — 13 January, Steam Toys in Action — 3 February

---

Steam Centre — Amberley Working Museum — West Sussex

Member: HRA, TT

Narrow Gauge & Industrial Railway Collection (incorporating the Brockham Museum of Narrow Gauge Railways)
The NG&IR Collection is part of an open air industrial museum set in 36 acres of the former Pepper & Co chalk pits. A 2ft gauge line has been constructed and this is used for carrying passengers in genuine workmen's vehicles
Museum Director: Howard Stenning
Location: Houghton Bridge, Amberley, West Sussex (3 miles north of Arundel) on B2139. Adjacent to Amberley main line station
OS reference: TQ 030122
Operating society/organisation: Amberley Museum Trust, Amberley Museum, Houghton Bridge, Amberley, Arundel, West Sussex BN18 9LT
Telephone: Bury (01798) 831370 (Museum office)
Internet address: Web site:

www.amberleymuseum.co.uk
e-mail (general museum enquiries): office@amberleymuseum.co.uk
e-mail (specific railway enquiries): info@amberleynarrowgauge.co.uk
Car park: Adjacent to Amberley station
On site facilities: Shop and audio-visual show. The 'Limeburners Restaurant' opened in 2004 (event booking details from 01798 839240)
Public opening: Wednesday to Sunday (inclusive) each week, and Bank Holiday Mondays, (open all week in school holidays) 10.00-last entry 17.00, 20 March-3 November
Special events: Spring Industrial Trains Day — 15 April; Mid-Summer Steam Show — 16/17 June; Railway Gala Weekend — 14/15 July; Miniature Steam & Model Weekend — 22/23 September; Autumn Industrial Trains Day — 21 October.
 Please see press for details of further activities
Special notes: Displays include working potter, blacksmith,

boatbuilder and printer, stationary engines, historic radio collection and vintage Southdown garage and buses. A 2ft 0in gauge industrial railway system is demonstrated when possible, and a 3ft 2.25in gauge line. In addition, a 2ft 0in gauge 'main line' has been constructed. The 500yd line was officially opened by HRH Prince Michael of Kent on 5 June 1984. The railway is operated every day the museum is open (subject to mechanical availability), with steam locomotive haulage on certain days — for details contact the museum office. Wheelchairs can normally be accommodated on the train.
 The 'Limeburners Restaurant' features a timber frame, cedar cladding and is floored with hand-made clay tiles
Membership details: Friends of Amberley Museum, c/o above address
Membership journal: *Wheelbarrow* — bi-monthly

Locomotives
(2ft or 60cm unless otherwise indicated)

Name	No	Builder	Type	Built	
Polar Bear	—	Bagnall (1781)	2-4-0T	1905	
Peter	—	Bagnall (2067)	0-4-0ST	1918	
Wendy	—	Bagnall (2091)	0-4-0ST	1919	
Townsend Hook	4	F/Jennings (172L)	0-4-0T	1880	(3ft 2.25in gauge)
Scaldwell	—	Peckett (1316)	0-6-0ST	1913	(3ft 0in gauge)
—	23†	Spence	0-4-0T	1921	(1ft 10in gauge)
—	—	Decauville (1126)	0-4-0WT	1947	
—**	—	Baldwin (44656)	4-6-0T	1917	
Monty	(6)	O&K (7269)	4wDM	1936	(3ft 2.25in gauge)
The Major	(7)	O&K (7741)	4wDM	1937	
—	2	Ransomes & Rapier (80)	4wDM	1937	
—	—	Hudson-Hunslet (3097)	4wDM	1944	
—	2	R/Hornsby (166024)	4wDM	1933	
—	3101	M/Rail (Simplex) (1381)	4wPM	1918	(Armoured)
Peldon	—	John Fowler (21295)	4wDM	1936	
Redland	—	O&K (6193)	4wDM	1937	
—	—	Lister (35421)	4wPM	1949	
—	—	M/Rail (Simplex) (872)	4wPM	1918	
—	27	M/Rail (Simplex) (5863)	4wDM	1934	
—	—	M/Rail (Simplex) (10161)	4wDM	1950	(2ft 11in gauge)
Ibstock	—	M/Rail (Simplex) (11001)	4wDM	1951	
Burt*	—	Simplex 9019))	4wDM	1959	
CCSW	—	Hibberd (1980)	4wDM	1936	
Thakeham Tiles	No 3	Hudson-Hunslet (2208)	4wDM	1941	
Thakeham Tiles	No 4	Hudson-Hunslet (3653)	4wDM	1948	
—	—	Hudson (45913)	4wP/ParM	1932	(2ft 6in gauge)
—	—	H/Clarke (DM686)	0-4-0DM	1948	
Star Construction	—	Hudson-Hunslet	4wDm	c1941	
—	18	R/Hornsby (187081)	4wDM	1937	
—	—	Lister (33937)	4wPM	1949	
—	—††	Hibberd 'Y-type Planet' (3627)	4wPM	1953	
—	WD 904	Wickham (3403/04)	2w-2PMR	1943	
—	2	Wingrove & Rogers (5031)	4wBE	1953	
—	—	Wingrove & Rogers (5034)	4wBE	1953	
—	—	Wingrove & Rogers (4998)	4wBE	1953	
—	—	Wingrove & Rogers (T8033)	0-4-0BE	1979	

†† not on site
** on loan to Leighton Buzzard Railway for restoration
* standard gauge
†includes hoist and 'haulage truck' for conversion to 5ft 3in gauge from Guinness Brewery

Stock
2 Penrhyn Quarry Railway 4-wheel coaches (2ft gauge, ex-1ft 10.75in gauge); RAF Fauld bogie coach (1940) (2ft gauge); Rye & Camber Tramway bogie (incomplete) (1895) (3ft gauge); Post Office Railway unit No 808 of 1930; 4 Groudle Glen Railway 4-wheel coaches (1896 and 1905) (2ft gauge); 60 other varied pieces of rolling stock of 12 different gauges ranging from 1ft 6in to 3ft 2.25in plus numerous miscellaneous exhibits including track, signals, etc

Owners
Wendy the Hampshire Narrow Gauge Railway Trust

Steam Centre	Amerton Railway	Staffordshire

The Amerton Railway is the home of the famous 1897-built Bagnall saddletank *Isabel*, the line having been built for it in the early 1990s. The railway has developed considerably over the years and

England

now consists of a mile-long line run through the countryside via a passing loop at Chartley Road. At Amerton station there is the locomotive shed, where items of rolling stock can be seen under restoration, the carriage shed and yard, the former GNR station building from Stowe and the Leek & Manifold Railway signalbox from Waterhouses, now under restoration

Location: Amerton Railway, Amerton Farm, Stowe-by-Chartley, Stafford ST18 0LA (situated between Stafford and Uttoxeter, signposted off A51 at Weston)

Operating company: Staffordshire Narrow Gauge Railway Ltd, c/o above address

Telephone:
(Railway only) (01785) 850965; Farm (01889) 270294

OS reference: SJ 993278

On site facilities: Car park at Working Farm. Museum under construction; licensed tea room and bakery (not operated by railway). Souvenir shop in railway ticket office. The railway is one of the main attractions at the farm, admission to most other attractions is free

Access by public transport: By rail to Stafford, then Stevenson's of Uttoxeter Ltd bus to Weston, then a mile walk to Amerton (no Sunday service)

Facilities for disabled: Wheelchairs can be accommodated in our 'Highland' coach where a wide door and access ramp is available

Period of public operation: Sundays from mid-March to end of October. Saturdays from Easter until August Bank Holiday. Bank Holiday Mondays. Trains run 12.00 until 17.00. Subject to availability

Industrial locomotives (2ft gauge)

Name	No	Builder	Type	Built
Isabel	—	Bagnall (1491)	0-4-0ST	1897
Lorna Doone	—	K/Stuart (4250)	0-4-0ST	1922
—	526	Henschel (14019)	0-8-0T	1916
—	746	M/Rail (40SD501)	4wDM	1975
—	—	M/Rail (7471)	4wDM	1940
Oakeley	—	Baguley (774)	0-4-0PM	1919
Golspie	—	Baguley (2085)	0-4-0DM/SO	1935
Dreadnought	—	Baguley (3024)	0-4-0DM/SO	1939
—	Yard No 70	R/Hornsby (221623)	4wDM	1943
—	—	R/Hornsby (506491)	4wDM	1964
Gordon	—	Hunslet (8561)	4wDH	1978

Rolling stock
4 toastrack coaches, 3 by Baguley, 1 ex-WHR, SNGRS-built passenger brake van and various wagons

Owner
Lorna Doone on loan from Birmingham Museum of Science & Industry

Isabel will be in steam Sundays and Bank Holidays. Diesel haulage generally on Saturdays

Special events: Summer Steam Gala, with visiting locomotives — 16/17 June (with at least two visiting locomotives); Santa Specials — December

Membership details: Membership Secretary, c/o above address

Membership journal: *Isabel Gazette,* quarterly

Astley Green Colliery Museum
Steam Centre   **Lancashire**

The museum occupies some 15 acres south of the Astley Green colliery site. The low-lying landscape ensures that the museum's 98ft high lattice steel headgear can be seen for many miles. Apart from the steam winding engine and headgear the museum houses many exhibits, not least of which is the collection of over 20 colliery locomotives, the largest collection of its type in the UK. The museum is now run and maintained, on behalf of the community, by the Red Rose Steam Society Ltd, a registered charity based in Lancashire. A railway is currently under construction with passenger-carrying expected to be available mid-2007

Location: Between the A580 and Bridgewater Canal in Higher Green

Industrial locomotives
(standard gauge)

Name	No	Builder	Type	Built
—	—	R/Hornsby (244580)	4wDM	1946

(3ft gauge)

Name	No	Builder	Type	Built
—	17	H/Clarke (DM781)	0-6-0DMF	1953
—	—	Hunslet (4816)	0-6-0DMF	1955
—	11	H/Clarke (DM1058)	0-6-0DMF	1957
—	20	H/Clarke (DM1120)	0-6-0DMF	1957
—	18	H/Clarke (DM1270)	0-6-0DMF	1961
—	BL/107	H/Clarke (DM1295)	0-6-0DMF	1962
—	DM1439	H/Clarke (DM1439)	0-6-0DMF	1978

(2ft 6in gauge)

Name	No	Builder	Type	Built
—	—	Hunslet (3411)	0-4-0DMF	1947
—	3	E/Electric (7936)	4wBEF	1957
—	4	H/Clarke (DM1173)	0-6-0DMF	1959
—	—	H/Clarke (DM1270)	0-6-0DMF	????
—	5	H/Clarke (DM1352)	0-6-0DMF	1967
—	6	H/Clarke (DM1413)	0-6-0DMF	1970
—	7	H/Clarke (DM1414)	0-6-0DMF	1970
—	—	H/Clarke (DM1439)	0-6-0DMF	1970
—	1-44-170	Hunslet (8575)	0-6-0DMF	1978

England

England

Lane, Astley Green, Tyldesley
Operating company: The Secretary,
Astley Green Colliery Museum,
Higher Green Lane, Astley Green,
Tyldesley, Manchester M29 7JB
Internet address: *e-mail:*
info@agcm.org.uk
For school parties *e mail:*
school.visits@agcm.org.uk
For other groups *e-mail:*
group.visits@agcm.org.uk
OS reference: SJ 705998
On site facilities: Car park, toilets
Access by public transport: Train to
Atherton, buses 551, 654
Facilities for disabled: Toilet
Period of public operation: Sundays
— 13.00-17.00
Tuesdays — 13.00-17.00
Thursdays — 13.00-17.00.
Closed Christmas and Boxing Days
Membership details: Membership
Secretary, Red Rose Steam Society,
Higher Green Lane, Astley Green,
Tyldesley, Manchester M29 7JB.
e-mail:
membership@rrss.agcm.org.uk

Name	No	Builder	Type	Built
—	1-44-174	Hunslet (8577)	0-6-0DMF	1978
Newton	—	Hunslet (8975)	0-6-0DMF	1979
Foggwell Flyer	—	Hunslet (8567)	0-6-0DMF	1981
Bullfrogs Bullet	—	Hunslet (8568)	0-6-0DMF	1981
—	—	Hunslet (8821)	0-6-0DMF	1978
(2ft 4in gauge)				
—	6	H/Clarke (DM??)	0-6-0DMF	'?'?
(2ft 1in gauge)				
Kestrel	2	H/Clarke (DM674)	0-6-0DMF	1954
(2ft gauge)				
Stacey	—	H/Clarke (DM804)	0-6-0DMF	1951
—	T1	H/Clarke (DM840)	0-6-0DMF	1954
George	14	H/Clarke (DM929)	0-6-0DMF	1955
—	8	M/Vickers (892)	4wBEF	1955
Warrior	14	H/Clarke (DM933)	0-6-0DMF	1956
—	—	H/Clarke (DM1164)	0-4-0DMF	1959
—	—	Hunslet (6048)	0-4-0DMF	1961
Sandy	—	M/Rail (11218)	4wDM	1962
Point of Ayr	—	R/Hornsby (497547)	4wDMF	1963
Roger Bowen	—	Hunslet (7375)	0-4-0DHF	1973
Calverton	9	Hunslet (7519)	4wDHF	1977
Mole	—	Hunslet (8834)	4wDHF	1978
Lionheart	—	Hunslet (8909)	4wDHF	1979
—	—R4	H/Clarke (DM1443)	0-6-0DMF	1980

Rolling stock (standard gauge)
1 Smith & Rodley steam crane, 1 Coles diesel crane

Miniature Railway	**Audley End Railway**	Essex

The Audley End miniature railway is a delightful ride on Lord Braybrooke's 10.25in gauge railway through estate woodland
Location: Audley End, Saffron Walden, Essex.
Headquarters: (Postal address) Audley End Estate Office, Brunketts, Wendens Ambo, Saffron Walden, Essex CB11 4JL
Contact:
General Manager: H. T. White
Telephone: (01799) 541354 or 541956

Internet address: *e-mail:* aee@farming.co.uk
Web site: www.audley-end-railway.co.uk
Car parking: On site
Access by public transport: Rail to Audley End (1 mile)
On site facilities: Ticket office, shop and light refreshments, toilets, large picnic area
Length of line: 10.25in gauge; 1.5 miles long
Period of public operation: Weekends 17 March-28 October

and 1-16 December.
Daily 1-16 April, 7, 28 May-3 June, 21 May-2 September, 20-28 October, 8-16 December
Trains from 14.00 to 16.00, except Bank Holidays, special events and Santa Specials when first train in 11.00
Special events: Santa Specials — 8-16 December (these can be booked by prior arrangement)
Facilities for disabled: Carriage built in 2002 to enable wheelchair access

---

Timetable Service	**Avon Valley Railway**	South Glos

Member: HRA
The Avon Valley Railway has now completed the first phase of its long-term aim to return steam trains, along the former Midland

Railway line, to the city of Bath. In May 2004 Avon Riverside station was opened in the heart of the Avon Valley, providing visitors with the opportunity to enjoy the riverside

walks, picnic areas and links to the River Avon scenic boat trips. For 2007 the rail/river trips will be operating every steam open day from April to the end of September,

England

except for 12/13 May and 29 July
Headquarters: Avon Valley Railway Company Limited, Bitton Station, Bath Road, Bitton, Bristol BS30 6HD
Telephone: (0117) 932 7296 for timetable information. (0117) 932 5538 enquiries
Internet address: *Web site:* www.avonvalleyrailway.org
Main station: Bitton
OS reference: ST 670705
Car park: Bitton
Access by public transport: Main line train service to Keynsham. Badgerline service No 332 (Bristol-Bath), No 558 (Bristol-North Common)
Access by bike: Bitton station is on the Bristol/Bath Railway Path (route 4 of the National Cycle Network)
Catering facilities: Buffet is able to provide hot and cold snacks, confectionery, hot and cold drinks and ice creams
On site facilities: Station buffet is open every day when the site is open; toilets, picnic area, children's play area close by
Public opening: Bitton station is open daily for viewing of its static collection of locomotives and rolling stock, except for the period between Christmas and New Year. Trains operate: 1, 6-12, 13*/14*, 15-18, 28*/29 April; 5*/6/7, 12/13, 20, 26*/27-31 May; 1,*, 3, 9*/10, 16*/17, 24 June; 1, 8, 14*/15, 21*/22, 28*/29, 31 July; 1/2, 4*/5, 7-9, 11*/12, 14-16, 18*/19, 21-23, 25*/26-30 August; 1*/2, 8*/9, 16, 23, 30 September; 6/7, 14, 21, 23-25, 28 October; 25 November; 1-3, 8/9, 15/16, 22-24, 30 December; 1 January 2008
*diesel-hauled
Special events: *Advance booking is essential for some of these events. Details from Bitton station —* (0117) 932 5538
Easter Steaming — 6-18 April; Day out with Thomas — 12/13 May; 4th Bitton Beer Festival — 9/10 June; Father's Day Lunch — 17 June; Teddy Bears' Picnic — 24 June; Murder Mystery Evening — 30 June; 1940s Day — 1 July, Polish Day — 15 July; Vintage Bus Rally — 12 August; Art Exhibition — 25-27 August; Railway Relics Valuation Day — 2 September; Teddy Bears Picnic — 9

September; Murder Mystery Evening — 15 September; Day out with Thomas — 6/7 October; Murder Mystery Evening — 20 October; Wizard Specials — 23-25 October; Murder Mystery Evening — 27 October; End of Season Gala — 28 October; Santa Specials — 25 November; 1-3, 8/9, 15/16, 22-24 December; Sherry and Mince Pie Specials — 30 December, 1 January 2008
   Steam 'N Cuisine (3 course dining trains) 22 April, 20 May, 17 June, 22 July, 19 August, 23 September, 14 October
   Bitton Bistro (2 course dining

trains) 1 April, 3 June, 8 July, 5 August, 2 September
   Driver experience courses — 21 April, 19 May, 2, 23, 30 June, 7 July, 15, 22, 29 September, 13, 20, 27 October
Special facilities: Carriage or train hire available for parties, staff outings or business functions
Facilities for disabled: Coach converted for disabled use (no toilet facilities)
Membership details: Membership Secretary, c/o Bitton station
Membership journal: *Semaphore* — every 6 months; *Ground Signal* newsletter every 2 months

Locomotives

Name	No	Origin	Class	Type	Built
Sir Frederick Pile	34058	SR	BB	4-6-2	1947
—	44123	LMS	4F	0-6-0	1925
—	48173	LMS	8F	2-8-0	1943
—	D2994	BR	07	0-6-0DE	1962
The Royal Alex	73101	BR	73	Bo-Bo	1965
*—	51909	BR	108	DMBS	1958
*—	56271	BR	108	DTC	1958

*stored off-site
Locomotive notes: D2994 and 73101 in service

Industrial locomotives

Name	No	Builder	Type	Built
Edwin Hulse	—	Avonside (1798)	0-6-0ST	1918
Karel	4015	Chrzanow (4015)	0-6-0T	1954
Phoenix	70	H/Clarke (1464)	0-6-0T	1921
Littleton No 5	—	M/Wardle (2018)	0-6-0ST	1922
—	7151	RSH (7151)	0-6-0T	1944
Meteor	1	RSH (7609)	0-6-0T	1950
Grumpy	WD70031	B/Drewry (2158)	0-4-0DM	1941
—*	Army 200	Barclay (358)	0-4-0DM	1941
Kingswood	—	Barclay (446)	0-4-0DM	1959
Western Pride*	D1171	H/Clarke (D1171)	0-6-0DM	1951
—†*	—	R/Hornsby (210481)	4wDM	1941
Basil*	—	R/Hornsby (235519)	4wDM	1945
—†*	—	R/Hornsby (252823)	4wDM	1947
—	429	R/Hornsby (466618)	0-6-0DH	1961
General Lord Robertson*	610	Sentinel (10143)	0-8-0DH	1961

*stored/undergoing restoration off-site
†chassis only

Locomotive notes: *Kingswood, Karel* and *Phoenix* are in service

Stock
22 ex-BR Mk 1 coaches (10 stored off-site); 1 ex-BR Mk 1 Restaurant coach; 1 ex-BR Mk 1 sleeper; 3 cranes; 1 Wickham trolley; numerous assorted wagons

Owners
44123 the London Midland Society
48173 the Bitton 8F Locomotive Group
73101 on loan from the Dean Forest Diesel Association

Barrow Hill Roundhouse Railway Centre

Member: HRA

In 1839 the North Midland Railway devised an arrangement of stabling locomotives around a turntable within a polygonal building with a conical roof, hence roundhouse. In 1864 locomotives began to be housed in buildings of a square nature (retaining the name) and in 1870 Barrow Hill was built to this design. Retained following the end of steam, Barrow Hill remained in use until 1991. Saved from demolition at the 11th hour, the Grade 2 listed building is unique in Great Britain as the last surviving working roundhouse.

The roundhouse can accommodate up to 24 main line locomotives, and includes maintenance pits and ancillary services

Location/headquarters: Barrow Hill Roundhouse Engine Shed, Campbell Drive, Barrow Hill, Nr Staveley, Chesterfield, Derbyshire S43 2PR.

Situated near junctions 29/30 on M1

OS reference: SK 4175

Project manager: Mervyn Allcock

Contact address: Barrow Hill Engine Shed Society, address as above

Telephone: 01246 472450

Fax: 01246 472450

Internet address: *Web site:* www.barrowhill.org.uk

Car park: Adjacent to site

Access by public transport: Train to Chesterfield, Stagecoach bus Nos 80/90/56

On site facilities: Refreshments, souvenir shop and museum. Toilets

Refreshment facilities: Drinks and light refreshments

Public opening: Open most weekends — 4 major open weekends a year

Special events: Easter, summer, autumn and Christmas open weekends

Membership details: Martyn Brailsford, 18 Queen Street, Brimington, Chesterfield, Derbyshire S43 1HT

Society journal: The Roundhouse — three times a year

Locomotives

Name	No	Origin	Class	Type	Built
Butler Henderson	506	GCR	'Director'	4-4-0	1920
Kolhapur	45593	LMS	'Jubilee'	4-6-0	1934
—	41708	MR	1F	0-6-0T	1880
—	D2868	BR	02	0-4-0DM	1961
—	03066	BR	03	0-6-0DM	1959
—	D2302	BR	04	0-6-0DM	1960
—	D2324	BR	04	0-6-0DM	1961
—	06003	BR	03	0-4-0DM	1959
—	07012	BR	07	0-6-0DE	1962
—	D3000	BR	08	0-6-0DE	1952
—	08492	BR	08	0-6-0DE	1958
—	08527	BR	08	0-6-0DE	1959
—	08818	BR	08	0-6-0DE	1960
Christine	D4092	BR	10	0-6-0DE	1962
—	D9500*	BR	14	0-6-0DH	1965
—	20092	BR	20	Bo-Bo	1961
—	20096	BR	20	Bo-Bo	1961
—	20119	BR	20	Bo-Bo	1962
—	20121	BR	20	Bo-Bo	1962
—	D8132	BR	20	Bo-Bo	1966
—	20138	BR	20	Bo-Bo	1966
—	20168	BR	20	Bo-Bo	1966
—	20901	BR	20	Bo-Bo	1959
—	20904	BR	20	Bo-Bo	1961
—	20905*	BR	20	Bo-Bo	1961
—	25067	BR	25	Bo-Bo	1963
—	D5300	BR	26	Bo-Bo	1958
—	26011	BR	26	Bo-Bo	1959
Spitfire	33035	BR	33	Bo-Bo	1960
—	33111	BR	33	Bo-Bo	1960
—	37079*	BR	37	Co-Co	1962
—	37100	BR	37	Co-Co	1962
—	37178†	BR	37	Co-Co	1963
—	37201	BR	37	Co-Co	1963
—	37667	BR	37	Co-Co	1963
—	37672	BR	37	Co-Co	1964
Andania	40013	BR	40	1Co-Co1	1959
—	47488	BR	47	Co-Co	1964
—	47707†	BR	47	Co-Co	1966
—	47744	BR	47	Co-Co	1966
—	47780	BR	47	Co-Co	1966
Sherwood Forester	45060	BR	45	1Co-Co1	1961
—	45105	BR	45	1Co-Co1	1961
Alycidon	D9009	BR	55	Co-Co	1961
Tulyar	55015	BR	55	Co-Co	1961
Gordon Highlander	55016	BR	55	Co-Co	1961
Royal Highland Fusilier	55019	BR	55	Co-Co	1961
—	56006	BR	56	Co-Co	1977
—	58001	BR	58	Co-Co	1983
—	E3003	BR	81	Bo-Bo	1960
—	82008	BR	82	Bo-Bo	1961
—	E3035	BR	83	Bo-Bo	1961
—	84001	BR	84	Bo-Bo	1960
Doncaster Plant 150 1853-2003	85101	BR	85	Bo-Bo	1961

England

Owners

*Harry Needle Railroad Co (for overhaul or stored)
†FM Rail
§stored off site
506, 55002 and 84001 on loan from the National Railway Museum
D3000 and D9500 Ian Goddard
03066, 03094, and 20096 Trevor Dean
33035, 45060 and 45105 the Pioneer Diesel Group
33111 the Class 33111 Group
55009 and 55019 the Deltic Preservation Society
E3003, 82008, 83012, 85101, 86401 and 89001 the AC Loco Group
The Welshman and 9 the National Mining Museum
41708 the Waterman Heritage Trust
47769 Riviera Trains

Name	No	Origin	Class	Type	Built
Sir William A Stanier	86101	BR	86	Bo-Bo	1965
—	89001	BR	89	Co-Co	1986

Industrial locomotives

Name	No	Builder	Type	Built
Henry	—	H/Leslie (2491)	0-4-0ST	1901
The Welshman	—	M/Wardle (1207)	0-6-0ST	1890
—	—	Peckett (2000)	0-6-0ST	1941
—	1	GEC	0-6-0	
—	9	YEC (2521)	0-4-0ST	1952
Harry	—	Drewry (2589)	0-4-0	1956
—	NCB 20	Barclay	0-4-0DE	—
—	RMS 10	GEC	0-6-0DE	—
—	—	Hunslet (63000316)	0-4-0DE	—
Coalite 7	—	Sentinel	0-6-0	—
Coalite 9	—	Vanguard	0-6-0	—

Stock

2 ex-BR Mk 1 BSK coach, 1 ex-BR Mk 2 coach, 1 ex-MR brake van, 1 Tunny wagon, 2 ex-BR bogie vans, 1 dynamometer car, 2 ex-BR Lowmac, 1 ex-LMS brake van, 2 ex-BR brake van, 1 ex-SR brake van, 1 ex-GWR Toad brake van

England

The Battlefield Line Railway

Member: HRA, TT

A quiet country railway operated by the Shackerstone Railway Society Ltd

Headquarters: Shackerstone station (3 miles north of Market Bosworth in Leicestershire)

Address: Shackerstone Station, Shackerstone, Nuneaton CV13 6NW

Telephone: Timetable enquiries: (01827) 880754

Internet address: *Web site*: www.battlefield-line-railway.co.uk

Operating Manager: D. Weightman

Main station: Shackerstone

Other public station: Shenton

OS reference: SK 379066

Car park: Shackerstone (free), Shenton (council car park)

Access by public transport: Bus service from Nuneaton weekends only. Ring Traveline 0870 6082608 for details

Refreshment facilities: Tea rooms on Shackerstone station. Buffet/bar on most trains

Souvenir shop: Shackerstone

Museum: Shackerstone

Depot: Shackerstone

Length of line: 4.75 miles (8km)

Passenger trains: Shackerstone-Shenton

Period of public operation: Easter to October

Special events: See leaflet and press for further details

Facilities for disabled: Special car park and toilets

Special notes: Family tickets available. Scenic countryside views including Ashby Canal. Shenton station is adjacent to Bosworth Battlefield (1485) Country Park. 20 minute walk along 'Battlefield Trail' to visitor centre, return by later train

Operating company/ preservation society contact: The Secretary, Shackerstone Railway Society, Shackerstone Station, Shackerstone, Nuneaton CV13 6NW

Membership journal: *Shackerstone News* — 2/3 times/year

Locomotives and multiple-units

Name	No	Origin	Class	Type	Built
Diane	D2867	BR	02	0-4-0DH	1961
—	03170	BR	03	0-6-0DM	1960
—	03180	BR	03	0-6-0DM	1962
—	11215	BR	04	0-6-0DM	1956
—	D2310	BR	04	0-6-0DM	1960
—	08818	BR	08	0-6-0DE	1960
—	12083	BR	11	0-6-0DE	1953
—	D9529	BR	14	0-6-0DE	1965
—	20105	BR	20	Bo-Bo	1961
Brush Veteran	D5518	BR	31	A1A-A1A	1958
Calder Hall Power Station	31130	BR	31	A1A-A1A	1959
—	31416	BR	31	A1A-A1A	1962
—	33008	BR	33	Bo-Bo	1960
Griffon	33019	BR	33	Bo-Bo	1960
—	33046	BR	33	Bo-Bo	1961
—	33053	BR	33	Bo-Bo	1961
—	37227	BR	37	Co-Co	1964
—	45015	BR	45	1Co-Co1	1960
—	47640	BR	47	Co-Co	1966
—	73105	BR	73	Bo-Bo	1965
—	73114	BR	73	Bo-Bo	1966
—	51131	BR	116	DMBS	1958
—	51321	BRCW	116	DMS	1959
—	55005	GRCW	122	DMBS	1958
—	59522	P/Steel	117	TC(L)	1959

Industrial locomotives

Name	No	Builder	Type	Built
Linda	—	Bagnall (2648)	0-4-0ST	1941
Waleswood	—	H/Clarke (750)	0-4-0ST	1906
Sir Gomer	—	Peckett (1859)	0-6-0ST	1932
Dunlop No 7	—	Peckett (2130)	0-4-0ST	1951
Richard III	—	RSH (7537)	0-6-0T	1949
Lamport No 3	—	Bagnall (2670)	0-6-0ST	1942
William	—	Sentinel (9656)	4wVBT	1956
—	—	Barclay (422)	0-6-0DM	1958
—	19	Barclay (594)	0-6-0DM	1974
—	—	E/Electric (8431)	0-4-0DH	1963
—	890445	GEC (5402)	0-6-0DM	1975
—	47	T/Hill (249V)	0-6-0DH	1974
—	—	R/Hornsby (263001)	4wDM	1949
—	44	Hunslet (6684)	0-6-0DH	1968
—	—	R/Royce (10254)	0-4-0DE	1966
—	—	Simplex (9921)	4wDM	1955

Stock

8 ex-BR Mk 1 coaches (including Griddle Car), 2 ex-BR Mk 2 coaches, 1 ex-BR Mk 3 sleeper; 5 passenger-rated vans; 1 rail-mounted steam crane; 2 rail-mounted diesel cranes; 35 wagons (inc 3 goods brake vans SR, MR, BR)

Owners

33019, 73105, 73114 and 47640 the administraters of FM Rail
20105, A/Barclay (594) and GEC (5904) on loan from Harry Needle Railroad Co

England

Member: HRA

The railway station, signalbox and goods shed have been completely re-created along with the other exhibits to show a way of life long past. There are some very old locomotives in the collection

Location: The North of England Open Air Museum, Beamish, County Durham DH9 0RG

OS reference: NZ 214548

Telephone: 0191 370 4000

Fax: 0191 370 4001

Internet address: *e-mail:* museum@beamish.org.uk

Web site: www.beamish.org.uk

Car park: At museum

Access by public transport: Bus service from Eldon Square, Newcastle upon Tyne; bus service Nos 775 and 778 from Sunderland via Chester-le-Street; bus service 720 from Milburngate, Durham City

On site facilities: This 300-acre open air museum vividly re-creates life in the North of England in the early 1800s and 1900s. The Town has dentist's surgery, solicitor's office, Co-op shops, garage, sweet shop and bank. The Colliery Village has pit cottages, village school and chapel, 'drift' mine and pithead. Home Farm with farm house, livestock and exhibitions. Railway station complete with goods yard and signalbox, rolling stock on static display. Pockerley Manor illustrates the lifestyle of a yeoman farming family in the early 1800s.

Early Railways — opened in 1999, near Pockerley Manor, a large stone engine shed with displays illustrating the development of railways in the early 1800s. New at Pockerley Waggonway in late May 2006 — a working replica of William Hedley's 1813 *Puffing Billy*. Visitors take a short ride in re-created carriages of the period pulled by the replica *Locomotion* or *Steam Elephant*

Locomotives

Name	No	Origin	Class	Type	Built
—	65033	NER	C	0-6-0	1889

On loan to Poppy Line until 2025

Industrial locomotives

Name	No	Builder	Type	Built
Locomotion*	1	LE (1)	0-4-0	1975
Twizell†	3	Stephenson (2730)	0-6-0T	1891
—††	14	H/Leslie (3056)	0-4-0ST	1914
South Durham Malleable Iron Co No 5	—††	Stockton Ironworks	0-4-0ST	1900
Coffee Pot§	—	Head Wrightson	0-4-0VB	1871
—††	E1	Black, Hawthorn (897)	2-4-0CT	1883
Jacob§	680	McEwan Pratt	0-4-0P	1916
—**	18	Lewin (693)	0-4-0WT	1877
Steam Elephant	—*	Wallsend Colliery	0-6-0G	2000
—	17	Head Wrightson (33)	0-4-0VB	1873
—	—	R/Hornsby (476140)	4wDM	1963
Puffing Billy	—	A/Keef (71)	0-4-0	2005

†on long-term loan to Tanfield ††on static display
§under repair **undergoing major rebuild
*replica

Locomotive notes: E1, 680 and R/Hornsby not usually on display. Others usually on display. 18 and *Coffee Pot* may be off site for overhaul during 2007

Owners
Locomotion the Locomotion Trust

Note
Not all exhibits on display
Twizell on long-term loan to Tanfield Railway

Public opening:
Summer (31 March-28 October) daily 10.00-17.00.
Winter (29 October-14 March 2008) 10.00-16.00.
Closed Mondays and Fridays.
Check for Christmas opening times.
Last admission always 15.00
  NB: A winter visit to Beamish is centred on the Town and Tramway; other areas of the museum are closed and admission charges are, consequently, reduced

Length of line:
Pockerley Waggonway, 1/4-mile — operational daily in summer. Rebuilt NER station, colliery sidings

Facilities for disabled: One carriage at 1825 Railway suitable for wheelchairs. Advance notice for parties to Bookings Officer preferred

Notes: Occasional visits by steam locomotives are planned to the NER station, Details of these will appear on the museum web site and in the railway press

Beer Heights Light Railway

An extensive railway in the landscaped grounds of publisher and model railway manufacturing group

Location/Headquarters: Pecorama, Underleys, Beer, Devon EX12 3NA

Managing Director: C. M. Pritchard,

Telephone: 01297 21542

Fax: 01297 20229

Internet address: *e-mail:* pecorama@btconnect.com *Web site:* www.peco-uk.com

OS reference: SY 223891

Car parking: Ample on site, free for our visitors

Access by public transport: By rail to Axminster station, then Axe Valley Bus to Beer. By rail to Exeter station, then First Bus to Weymouth via Beer.

On site facilities: Restaurant, shop, model railway exhibition and fully restored Pullman car 'Orion', extensive gardens, children's activities

Length of line: 1 mile, 7.25in gauge

Period of public operation: Easter to end October — Monday to Friday 10.00-17.30; Saturdays 10.00-13.00; Sundays open at Easter and then from late spring Bank Holiday to start of September

Locomotives

Name	No	Builder	Type	Built
Otter	1	WNG*	2-4-2	2004
Dickie	3	D. Curwen	0-4-2	1976
Thomas II	4	R. Marsh	0-4-2ST+T	1979
Linda	5	D. Clarke	2-4-0ST+T	1983
Jimmy	6	S/Lamb	Bo-Bo	1986
Mr P	7	Macdougall	2-4-2T	1997
Gem	8	Peco	0-6-0T+T	1999
Claudine	9	Macdougall	2-4-4†	2005
Alfred	10	Macdougall / Nation	Bo-Bo Tram	2003

*built by Western Narrow Gauge, privately owned
†single Fairlie

Rolling stock — coaches
3 x 4-seat bogie open coaches built by Cromar White; 9 x 4-seat bogie open 'Pullman' coaches built by BHLR; 8 x 4-seat quad-articulated coaches built by BHLR

Rolling stock — wagons
6 x 4-wheeled wagons; 1 bogie open wagon; 2 x 4-wheel bolster wagons, 2 x 4-wheeled tipper wagons; 1 generator wagon

10.00-17.30

Special events: PECO Annual Vintage/Classic Vehicle Rally — 27 May; DCC (Digital Command Control) Weekend — 9/10 June; Teddy Mac Days — 15-18 July; PECO Playgroups Week — 16-20 July; Thomas the Tank Engine Story Days — 19/20 July; PECO Garden Day — 22 July; August Bank Holiday Special Events —

26/27 August

Facilities for disabled: All toilet blocks with facilities for disabled, wheelchair access to Model Exhibition, gardens and restaurant (Note: some paths in the gardens are steep and wheelchair-bound will need assistance)

Membership details: Season ticket to Pecorama available, apply to above address

Bicton Woodland Railway

A passenger-carrying line of 18in gauge with stock mainly from the Woolwich Arsenal Railway and of World War 1 vintage

Location: Bicton Park, near Budleigh Salterton

OS reference: SY 074862

Operating society/organisation: Bicton Woodland Railway, Bicton Gardens, East Budleigh, Budleigh Salterton, Devon EX9 7BS

Telephone: Colaton Raleigh (01395) 568465

Fax: (01395) 568374

Internet addresses:

Locomotives (1ft 6in gauge)

Name	No	Builder	Type	Built
Bicton	2	R/Hornsby (213839)	4wDM	1942
Clinton	4	H/Hunslet (2290)	0-4-0	1941
Sir Walter Raleigh	—	Keef	4wDM	2000

Stock
5 closed bogie coaches

e-mail: info@bictongardens.co.uk
Web site: www.bictongardens.co.uk

Car park: On site

Access by public transport: Buses pass half-hourly from Exeter,

Exmouth, Sidmouth in season

On site facilities: Indoor and outdoor play areas, Glass Houses, Palm House, Grade 1 gardens, museum and restaurant

Length of line: 1.5mile (2.4km), 18in gauge
Public opening: Open all year (except 25/26 December), winter 10.00-17.00, summer 10.00-18.00
Trains operate: Winter 12.15 and 14.30, summer 6-8 trains a day. 25min trips
Facilities for disabled: Toilets, wheelchairs available. Special carriage for wheelchairs

Museum — Bideford Railway Heritage Centre — Devon

Member: HRA
Based at the former LSWR/SR station on the now closed Barnstaple-Torrington line, the site is undergoing restoration. The former signalbox has been rebuilt, double track laid throughout and signals erected. A growing collection of rolling stock is being gathered. Passenger railway rides returned to Bideford station during summer 2001 after a gap of 36 years. Diesel-hauled brake van rides on selected weekends during summer months. Long term aim of the Group is to reinstate the railway back to Barnstaple (9 miles)
Headquarters: Bideford Station, Railway Terrace, East-the-Water, Bideford, Devon EX39 4BB
Telephone: 01237 476769
Internet address: Web site: www.bidefordrailway.co.uk
OS reference: SS 456263
Operating society: Bideford & Instow Railway Group
Access by public transport: By train — Barnstaple 9 miles. Station is within walking distance of the town of Bideford and its bus stops

Multiple-units

Name	No	Origin	Class	Type	Built
—	76350	BR	423 / 4VEP	DTSO	1967

Industrial locomotives

Name	No	Builder	Type	Built
Kingsley	—	Hibberd (3832)	0-4-0DM	1957

Rolling stock
BR Mk 1 TSO No 4489, ex-SR Parcels Van No S2142, ex-BR brake van, ex-LMS closed box van, platelayers' trolley
2 18in gauge skip (ex Peters Marland Clay Works)

Owner
Kingsley the Torridge Diesel Loco Co Ltd

On site facilities: Museum, souvenir shop, book shop, refreshments, visitor centre, rolling stock under restoration
Period of public opening: Easter to end October — Sundays and Bank Holidays 14.00-17.00; November to Easter — Sundays and Bank Holidays only
Disabled facilities: Limited
Membership details: Mr R. Chapman, 17A Daneshay, Northam, Bideford, Devon EX39 1DG
Membership journal: Atlantic Coast Express (quarterly)
Special note: The group also manage Instow Signalbox, some three miles north. This all-equipped former LSWR box is open on Sundays, 14.00-17.00, throughout the year

Timetable Service — Blackpool & Fleetwood Tramway — Lancashire

The Blackpool & Fleetwood Tramway is the sole surviving traditional street tramway system in the United Kingdom and attracts visitors from all over the country. During the autumn the streets are illuminated and tours are available by historic or illuminated tram.
Operating organisation:
Blackpool Transport Services Ltd, Rigby Road, Blackpool, Lancashire FY1 5DD
Telephone: (01253) 473001
Managing Director: Steve Burd
Operations Director: David Eaves

Trams

No	Trucks	Builder	Date
Boat Cars			
§600	E/Electric	E/Electric	1930
602	E/Electric	E/Electric	1934
604	E/Electric	E/Electric	1934
605	E/Electric	E/Electric	1934
607	E/Electric	E/Electric	1934
Brush Cars			
§621	EMB	Brush	1937
622	EMB	Brush	1937
§623	EMB	Brush	1937
§625	EMB	Brush	1937
626	EMB	Brush	1937
§627	EMB	Brush	1937

Customer Services Officer:
Jean Cox
Length of line: 11.5 miles,
standard gauge
Period of public operation: Daily
throughout the year, except
Christmas Day, Boxing Day and
New Year's Day
Number of trams: 78 double and
single-deck trams.

No	Trucks	Builder	Date
630	EMB	Brush	1937
631	EMB	Brush	1937
§632	EMB	Brush	1937
§634	EMB	Brush	1937
636	EMB	Brush	1937
§637	EMB	Brush	1937

Centenary Cars

No	Trucks	Builder	Date
641	Blackpool	East Lancs	1984
642	Blackpool	East Lancs	1986
643	Blackpool	East Lancs	1986
644	Blackpool	East Lancs	1986
645	Blackpool	East Lancs	1987
646	Blackpool	East Lancs	1987
647	Blackpool	East Lancs	1988
648	Blackpool	East Lancs	1990

Towing Cars

No	Trucks	Builder	Date
671	E/Electric	E/Electric / Blackpool	1960
672	E/Electric	E/Electric / Blackpool	1960
673	E/Electric	E/Electric / Blackpool	1961
674	E/Electric	E/Electric / Blackpool	1962
675	E/Electric	E/Electric / Blackpool	1958
§676	E/Electric	E/Electric / Blackpool	1958
§677	E/Electric	E/Electric / Blackpool	1960

Ex-Towing Railcoaches

No	Trucks	Builder	Date
678	E/Electric	E/Electric / Blackpool	1961
§679	E/Electric	E/Electric / Blackpool	1961
680	E/Electric	E/Electric / Blackpool	1960

Trailer Cars

No	Trucks	Builder	Date
681	Maley & Taunton	MCW	1960
682	Maley & Taunton	MCW	1960
683	Maley & Taunton	MCW	1960
684	Maley & Taunton	MCW	1960
685	Maley & Taunton	MCW	1960
§686	Maley & Taunton	MCW	1960
§687	Maley & Taunton	MCW	1960

Balloon Cars

No	Trucks	Builder	Date
700	E/Electric	E/Electric	1934
701	E/Electric	E/Electric	1934
702	E/Electric	E/Electric	1934
703	E/Electric	E/Electric	1934
*704	E/Electric	E/Electric	1934
705	E/Electric	E/Electric	1934
706	E/Electric	E/Electric	1934
707	E/Electric	E/Electric	1934
708	E/Electric	E/Electric	1934
709	E/Electric	E/Electric	1934
710	E/Electric	E/Electric	1934
711	E/Electric	E/Electric	1934
712	E/Electric	E/Electric	1935
713	E/Electric	E/Electric	1934
715	E/Electric	E/Electric	1935
*716	E/Electric	E/Electric	1935
*717	E/Electric	E/Electric	1934
718	E/Electric	E/Electric	1934
719	E/Electric	E/Electric	1935
720	E/Electric	E/Electric	1935
721	E/Electric	E/Electric	1935
722	E/Electric	E/Electric	1935
723	E/Electric	E/Electric	1935
724	E/Electric	E/Electric	1935
726	E/Electric	E/Electric	1935

Jubilee Cars

No	Trucks	Builder	Date
761	Blackpool	E/Electric / Blackpool	1979

England

No	Trucks	Builder	Date
762	Blackpool	E/Electric / Blackpool	1982

Illuminated Trams

No	Trucks	Builder	Date
*632	EMB	from Brush 632	2001
*633	EMB	from Brush 633	2001
*734	E/Electric	from Pantograph 174	1962
*735	E/Electric	from Railcoach 222	1963
736	E/Electric	from Pantograph 170	1965

Engineering Vehicles

No	Trucks	Builder	Date
259	EMB	Blackpool	1937
260	EMB	Blackpool	1973
750	MRCW	Blackpool	1907
752	MRCW	Blackpool	1928
754	E/Electric	Blackpool	1992

Preserved Trams

No	Trucks	Builder	Date
5	?	D/Kerr	1901
40	Preston McGuire	United Electric Co	1914
66	Brill	Electric Railway & Carriage	1901
147	Preston McGuire	Hurst Nelson	1924
304	Maley & Taunton	Hurst Nelson	1952
§513	Maley & Taunton	Charles Roberts	1950
§619	E/Electric	Bolton Trams	1987
660	Maley & Taunton	Charles Roberts	1953

*out of service
§currently mothballed

Owners

5 the Stockport 5 Trust
40 the Tramway Museum Society
66 the Bolton 66 Group
304 and 632 the Lancastrian Transport Trust
513 Beamish Open Air Museum

Bluebell Railway

Timetable Service — **Bluebell Railway** — East Sussex

Member: HRA, TT

This famous steam railway was the first standard gauge passenger line to be taken over by enthusiasts. It derives its name from the bluebells which proliferate in the woodlands adjoining the line. A strong Victorian atmosphere pervades this branch line which has a large collection of Southern and pre-Grouping locomotives and coaches

Operations Manager: Mr Chris Knibbs

Headquarters: Bluebell Railway plc, Sheffield Park Station, A275, East Sussex TN22 3QL

Telephone:

For travel information (24hr talking timetable): Uckfield (01825) 720825.

General enquiries etc during office

Locomotives and multiple-unit

Name	No	Origin	Class	Type	Built
Stepney	55	LBSCR	A1X	0-6-0T	1875
Fenchurch	72	LBSCR	A1X	0-6-0T	1872
Birch Grove	32473	LBSCR	E4	0-6-2T	1898
—	27	SECR	P	0-6-0T	1910
—	65	SECR	O1	0-6-0	1896
—	263	SECR	H	0-4-4T	1905
—	323	SECR	P	0-6-0T	1910
—	592	SECR	C	0-6-0	1902
—	1178	SECR	P	0-6-0T	1910
—	96	LSWR	B4	0-4-0T	1893
—	120	LSWR	T9	4-4-0	1898
—	488	LSWR	0415	4-4-2T	1885
—	27505	NLR	2F	0-6-0T	1880
Earl of Berkeley	9017	GWR	90	4-4-0	1938
—	541	SR	Q	0-6-0	1939
—	847	SR	S15	4-6-0	1937
Stowe	928	SR	V	4-4-0	1934
—	1618	SR	U	2-6-0	1928
—	1638	SR	U	2-6-0	1931

Above: This Barclay 0-4-0ST dating from 1954 is seen at the reconstructed station at Beamish Open Air Museum during a visit from the Bowes Railway. *Beamish*

Below: Restored to as-built Southern Railway condition No 21C123 *Blackmoor Vale* at the head of a northbound service on the Bluebell Railway. *Alan Barnes*

England

Above: Ex-Great Western Railway No 5552, carrying BR green livery approaches Bodmin on the Bodmin & Wenford Railway. *Alan Barnes*

Below: Fowler 0-6-0T *Limpopo*, dating from 1930 crosses a road at the Bredgar & Wormshill Railway as the driver of Bean pick-up of 1927 vintage waits. *B&WR*

England

hours: (01825) 720800.
Golden Arrow Pullman,
reservations and Catering
Department: (01825) 720807.
Shop: (01825) 720803
Internet address: *Web site:*
www.bluebell-railway.co.uk
Main station: Sheffield Park
Other public stations: Horsted
Keynes and Kingscote
Car parks: Sheffield Park, Horsted
Keynes
OS reference:
Sheffield Park TQ 403238,
Horsted Keynes TQ 372293
Access by public transport: Bus
service 473 between main line East
Grinstead and Kingscote (2 miles).
See timetable brochure for details
of operation
Refreshment facilities: Sheffield
Park restaurant/bar/self-service;
Horsted Keynes – 1930s bar/ buffet.
The line's 'Golden Arrow' Pullman
operates a dinner service most
Saturday evenings and Pullman
luncheon service most Sundays.
   Telephone (01825) 720800 during
normal office hours for details.
Souvenir shops: Sheffield Park,
Horsted Keynes
Museum: Sheffield Park
Depots: Sheffield Park
(locomotives), Horsted Keynes
(stock)
Length of line: 9 miles
Passenger trains: Sheffield Park-
Horsted Keynes-Kingscote
Period of public operation:
Weekends all year round;
daily 12-16 February (half term),
April to October. Santa Specials
1/2, 8/9, 15/16, 22-24 December,
daily 26-31 December; 1 January
2008. Closed 25 December.
Museum. Locomotive sheds, buffet
and shop at Sheffield Park open
daily except Christmas Day
Special events: Goods Train Day
— 14/15 April; Toy and Rail
Collectors Fair — 22 April; Fish &
Chips Evening Special* — 27
April; Bluebell Specials — 1-3,
9/10 May; Southern at War
Weekend— 12/13 May; Fish &
Chips Evening Special* — 25 May,
8 June; Victorian Picnic — 15 June;
An Evening with the Yetties — 16
June; Fathers Day Ploughman's
Lunch — 17 June; Day out with
Thomas† — 23/24, 30 June, 1 July;

Name	No	Origin	Class	Type	Built
—	30064	SR	USA	0-6-0T	1943
Blackmoor Vale	21C123	SR	WC	4-6-2	1946
Sir Archibald Sinclair	34059	SR	BB	4-6-2	1947
Camelot	73082	BR	5MT	4-6-0	1955
—	75027	BR	4MT	4-6-0	1954
—	78059†	BR	2MT	2-6-0	1956
—	80064	BR	4MT	2-6-4T	1953
—	80100	BR	4MT	2-6-4T	1954
—	80151	BR	4MT	2-6-4T	1957
—	92240	BR	9F	2-10-0	1958
—	D3023	BR	08	0-6-0DE	1953
—	11201*	BR	4COR	DMBSO	1937

†purchased without tender, for conversion to tank engine, work in hand
*on static display at Horsted Keynes

Industrial locomotives

Name	No	Builder	Type	Built
Baxter	3	F/Jennings (158)	0-4-0T	1877
†*Stamford*	24	Avonside (1972)	0-6-0ST	1927
Sharpthorn	4*	M/Wardle (641)	0-6-0ST	1877
Britannia	—	Howard (957)	4wPM	1936

*On static display
†On long-term loan to the Rutland Railway Museum

Stock
Substantial collection of pre-Nationalisation coaches including SECR,
LSWR, Bulleid, Maunsell and Chesham vehicles. Also freight stock and
engineers' vehicles plus 45-ton steam crane

Owners
592 the Wainwright C Class Preservation Society
541, 847, 928 and 1618 the Maunsell Locomotive Society Ltd
96 and 21C123 the Bulleid Society Ltd
263 the H Class Trust
73082 the Camelot Locomotive Society
120 on loan from the National Railway Museum
80064 the 80064 Group
80151 the 80151 Group
D3023 on loan from the Heritage Shunters Trust
11201 the Southern Electric Group

Toy and Rail Collectors Fair —
21/22 July; Fish & Chips Evening
Special* — 3, 17, 31 August;
Bluebell 125 — 11/12 August; Fish
& Chips Evening Special* — 7,
21September; Sausage & Mash
Evening Special* — 14 September;
Grandparents' Day — 23
September; Curry Night* — 28
September; Autumn Tints Specials
— 1-5, 8-12, 15-19 October;
Giants of Steam — 20/21 October;
Vintage Bus Running Day — 11
November; 1920s Weekend —
17/18 November; Specials — 1/2,
8/9, 15/16, 22-24 December.
*Pre-booking essential.

†pre-booking recommended
Further details of events available
on request
Facilities for disabled: All station
facilities are on the level and ramps
available for placing wheelchair
visitors into trains. Special toilets in
buffet at Sheffield Park and at
Kingscote, 'multi-purpose vehicle'
for use by groups, please telephone
to confirm availability
Membership details: Membership
Secretary, c/o above address
Membership journal: *Bluebell
News* — quarterly

Bodmin & Wenford Railway

Member: HRA

The Bodmin & Wenford Railway typifies the bygone branch railways of Cornwall. The terminus, close to Bodmin town centre, has an interesting collection of standard gauge locomotives and rolling stock, and the operating line winds down to a junction with main line rail services at Bodmin Parkway. Passengers can alight at the intermediate Colesloggett Halt from where a footpath (not suitable for wheelchairs or the infirm) leads to Cardinham Woods (FC) with waymarked trails, picnic areas and a café. From the train there are scenic views across the beautiful valley of the River Fowey. A second line circles Bodmin to Boscarne Junction where it meets the Camel Trail, a recreational path for cyclists and walkers. A visit can be made to the nearby Camel Valley Vineyard (July and August only). Most trains are steam-hauled except Saturday

Location: Bodmin General station, on B3268

General Manager: Mr R. Webster

Operating society/organisation: Bodmin & Wenford Railway, Bodmin General Station, Bodmin, Cornwall PL31 1AQ

Telephone: Enquiries (01208) 73666

Internet address: *e-mail:* enquiries@bodminandwenfordrailway.co.uk

Web site: www.bodminandwenfordrailway.co.uk

Car park: Bodmin General

Access by public transport: Interchange at Bodmin Parkway arrivals by main line train; through tickets available from most stations. Local bus services to Bodmin

Refreshment facilities: Light refreshments at Bodmin General and bar on most trains. Café open daily at Bodmin Parkway

On site facilities: Railway shop, limited display of historic artefacts, toilets

Length of lines: 3.5 miles General-Parkway; 3 miles General-Boscarne

Passenger trains: 14, 18, 21, 24/25, 28 March; 1-15, 17/18,

Locomotives and multiple-units

Name	No	Origin	Class	Type	Built
—	30587	LSWR	0298	2-4-0WT	1874
—	4612	GWR	5700	0-6-PT	1942
—	4247	GWR	4200	2-8-0T	1916
—	5552	GWR	4575	2-6-2T	1928
Wadebridge	34007†	SR	WC	4-6-2	1945
Triumph	50042	BR	50	Co-Co	1968
River Fowey	20166	BR	20	Bo-Bo	1966
—	20197	BR	20	Bo-Bo	1967
—	33110	BR	33	Bo-Bo	1960
—	37142	BR	37	Co-Co	1963
—	D3452	BR	10	0-6-0DE	1957
—	08444	BR	08	0-6-0DE	1958
—	51947*	BR	108	DMBS	1960
—	52054	BR	108	DMCL	1960
—	53980	BR	108	DMBS	1960

*for spares

† may be away on loan during 2007

Industrial locomotives

Name	No	Builder	Type	Built
—	—	Bagnall (2766)	0-6-0ST	1944
—	19	Bagnall (2962)	0-4-0ST	1950
Judy	—	Bagnall (2572)	0-4-0ST	1934
Alfred	—	Bagnall (3058)	0-4-0ST	1953
—	—	Bagnall (3121)	0-4-0F	1957
Peter	—	Fowler (22928)	0-4-0DM	1940
Progress	—	Fowler (4000001)	0-4-0DM	1945
Lec	—	R/Hornsby (443642)	4wDM	1960

Stock

12 BR Mk 1 coaches; 1 BR Mk 2 coach; 1 Mk 3 Sleeper; 6-wheel 10-ton steam crane; 1 GWR coach; 1 GWR Siphon G; various freight wagons

Owners

34007 the Wadebridge 34007 Ltd

30587 on loan from the National Railway Museum

37142 the B&W Main Line Diesel Group

21/22, 24/25, 29 April; 1/2, 5-9, 13, 15/16, 20, 22/23, 26-31 May; daily — 1 June-30 September; 3, 7, 10, 14, 17, 20-28, 31 October; 1, 8 November.

Santa Specials 1/2, 8/9, 15/16, 22-24 December; Mince Pie Specials 26/27, 29/30 December and 1 January 2008

Special events: Diesel Weekend — 24/25 March; Easter 'Family Fun Weekend' — 6-9 April!; Steam at War Weekend — 5-7 May; Day out with Thomas — 26 May-1 June, 1-6 August; Steam Gala — 5-7 September; Diesel Gala — 22/23 September; Branch Line Weekend — 20/21 October; Ghost Night 27 October.

Murder Mystery Evening Specials most Tuesdays (and Fridays in August) from June to September; Vineyard Special (please phone for date); dining coaches on selected dates including 18 March, Mothering Sunday and 17 June, Father's Day. Please enquire for dates or see leaflet

Driving experience courses: Courses held in spring and autumn. Please apply for details

Facilities for disabled: Level access to platform, shop and buffet. Disabled toilet. Disabled section on train. Registered disabled travel at child fare, carers conveyed *free*

Membership details: Mr R. Holmes, Bodmin Railway

Preservation Society, c/o above address
Special notes: Reduced fares for families. Bicycles and dogs

conveyed *free*
Membership journal: *Bodmin & Wenford News* — 3 issues/year

Steam Centre — Bowes Railway — County Durham

Member: HRA

The railway includes the only heritage-operated rope-hauled standard gauge inclines, whose operation requires considerable skill and dexterity. You should not miss the opportunity of inspecting the inclines and winding house and haulage engine when you can. The Engineering Workshop has just been restored

Chairman: Phillip Dawe

Location: Bowes Railway, Springwell Village, near Gateshead (on B1288)

OS reference: NZ 285589

Operating society/organisation: Bowes Railway Co Ltd

Telephone: Tyneside (0191) 416 1847

Internet address: *Web site:* www.bowesrailway.co.uk

Car park: Springwell

Access by public transport: Northern Buses services Nos 184 Washington/Birtley, 187/188 Gateshead Metro/Sunderland, 189 Washington (Brady Sq)-Gateshead 638 Ryton/Sunderland

On site facilities: Exhibition of Railway's history, wagon exhibition, workshop displays. On operating days — shop, refreshments and guided tours. One of the last operational Strowger mechanical telephone exchanges still in daily use. Steam-hauled brake van rides. Rope haulage demonstration trains. Tarmac car park available for helicopter visitors (prior permission required, phone site)

Public opening: Site open Mondays to Fridays for static viewing. Please contact for operating details during 2007. Santa Specials week prior to Christmas. Guided tours Saturdays, out of season can be accommodated with prior notice (not trains)

Length of line: 1.25 miles of rope haulage incline railway.

Industrial locomotives

Name	No	Builder	Type	Built
WST	—	Barclay (2361)	0-4-0ST	1954
—	22	Barclay (2274)	0-4-0ST	1949
—	20/110/709	Barclay (613)	0-6-0DH	1977
—	—	Hunslet (6263)	0-4-0DH	1964
—	503	Hunslet (6614)	0-6-0DH	1965
—	101	Planet (3922)	4wDM	1959
—	2207/456†	E/Electric (2476)	4wBE	1958
Victoria	2216/286†	H/Clarke (DM842)	0-6-0DMF	1954
BO3	20/122/514*	Hunslet (8515)	Bo-BoDMF	1981
—	—*	EIMCO (LD2163)	Rockershovel	1959
—	—§	Clayton (5921)	4wBE	1971
—	—§	Clayton (B3060)	4wBE	1983

†2ft gauge *2ft 6in gauge §3ft gauge

Owners

WST on loan from British Gypsum Ltd and loaned to National Railway Museum
Barclay 0-6-0DH on loan from Mr P. Dawe

Stock

20 ordinary 10-ton wooden hopper wagons (Springwell built); 16 other wooden hopper wagons (of various pedigrees); 3 steel 14-ton hopper, 2 steel 16-ton hopper wagons; 7 wagons; 7 steel 21-ton hopper wagons; 1 reel bogie (for rope replacement); 1 drift bogie (for shunting by rope); 1 loco coal wagon; 7 material wagons; 2 tool vans; 3 brake vans; 4 flat wagons; 1 18-ton wooden hopper (ex-Ashington); 1 21-ton wooden hopper (ex-Seaham); 2 steel ballast hopper wagons; 1 tank wagon; 1 wooden side door coal wagon; 3 Londonderry Chaldron wagons, 2ft gauge 4-wheel manrider, 2ft 6in gauge R. B. Bolton-type bogie manrider, Easington Colliery weights wagon, 1 Pontop & Jarrow Railway flat bogie, 1 Dandy cart

Stationary haulage

Met-Vick/Wild, 300bhp electric (Blackham's Hill) 1950
BTH/Robey, 500bhp electric (Black Fell) 1950
Clarke Chapman, 22hp electric (Springwell Yard)
14ft diam, Gravity Dilly Wheel (Springwell)

1.5 mile line used for passenger trains as the Wreckenton extension is now open

Special notes: Preserved section of the Pontop & Jarrow Railway; designed G. Stephenson; opened 1826; largest collection of colliery wagons in country, the only preserved standard gauge rope-hauled incline railway in the world; Railway's own historic workshops preserved, with examples of all of the Railway's wagon types

Facilities for disabled: Toilet and refreshment room

Membership details: John Young, Railway Secretary, c/o above address

Disclaimer: The Bowes Railway Co Ltd wish to point out that all advertised facilities are subject to alteration without prior notice. The company can therefore not be held responsible for any loss or expense incurred

Bredgar & Wormshill Light Railway

Member: HRA

A short, 2ft gauge, private railway constructed and operated to a very high standard

Location/headquarters: The Bredgar & Wormshill Light Railway, The Warren, Bredgar, Nr Sittingbourne, Kent ME9 8AT

Contact: Bill Best, David Best

Telephone: (01622) 884254

Fax: (01622) 884668

Internet address: *Web site:* www.bwlr.co.uk

Access by public transport: Main line trains to Sittingbourne (5 miles) and Hollingbourne (3.5 miles). No taxis from Hollingbourne

OS reference: TQ 868579

Car park: On site (300 places)

On site facilities: Souvenir shop, museum, light refreshments, toilets, picnic sites, traction engines, 7.25in and 15in gauge model locomotives, working beam engine, model railway. Largest UK collection of Bean motor cars. Steam-hauled train rides from Warren Wood to Stony Shaw (1km).

Industrial locomotives

(2ft gauge)

Name	No	Builder	Type	Built
Bronhilde	1	Schwartzkopf (9124)	0-4-0WT	1927
Katie	2	Arn Jung (3872)	0-6-0WT	1931
Armistice	4	Bagnall (2088)	0-4-0ST	1919
Bredgar	5	B/Drewry (3775)	0-4-0DH	1983
Eigiau	6	O&K (5668)	0-4-0WT	1912
Victory	7	Decauville (246)	0-4-2ST	1897
—	8	O&K (12722)	0-4-0WT	1936
No 1	—	Hunslet (1429)	0-4-0ST	1922
—	—	Fowler (13573)	0-4-2T	1912
Limpopo	—	Fowler (18800)	0-6-0T	1930

(2ft 6in gauge)

Name	No	Builder	Type	Built
—	105	Henschel (29582)	0-6-0WT	1956

Stock

3 bogie coaches, 1 four-wheel coach, 6 four-wheel wagons, 2 four-wheel tank wagon, 4 four-wheel works trucks, 1 open bogie coach

Public opening: First Sunday in each month May to October (11.00-17.00). Also Easter Sunday. Admission: Adults £7.50, children £3

Special events: Steam locomotive driving courses, enthusiast days

Facilities for disabled: Generally good including toilets

Note: A private site with no 'out of hours' access, but groups by arrangement

Bressingham Steam Experience

Member: TT

Five miles of various gauges of railway running through extensive gardens, and a collection of well-maintained and impressive main line locomotives. All the fun of the fair, with something for everyone, a great day out for all the family

Location: Two miles west of Diss, and 14 miles east of Thetford on the A1066

OS reference: TM 080806

Operating society/organisation: Bressingham Steam Preservation Co Ltd, Bressingham Hall, Diss, Norfolk IP22 2AB

Charity number: 266374

Telephone: Bressingham (01379) 686900. Infoline (01379) 687382

Fax: (01379) 686907

Internet address: *Web site:*

Locomotives

Name	No	Origin	Class	Type	Built
Martello	662	LBSCR	A1X	0-6-0T	1875
Thundersley	80	LTSR	3P	4-4-2T	1909
Granville	102	LSWR	B4	0-4-0T	1893
—	490	GER	E4	2-4-0	1894
Henry Oakley	990	GNR	C2	4-4-2	1898
—	251	GNR	C1	4-4-2	1902
Royal Scot	6100*	LMS	7P	4-6-0	1927
Peer Gynt	5865	NSB	52	2-10-0	1944
King Haakon VII	377	NSB	21c	2-6-0	1919

*undergoing restoration

Industrial locomotives

Name	No	Builder	Type	Built
Beckton	1	Neilson (4444)	0-4-0ST	1892
Beckton	25	Neilson (5087)	0-4-0ST	1896
William Francis	6841	B/Peacock (6841)	0-4-0+0-4-0T	1937
Millfield	—	RSH (7070)	0-4-0CT	1942
Bluebottle	—	Barclay (1472)	0-4-0F	1916
County School	GET 1	R/Hornsby (497753)	0-4-0DE	1963

www.bressingham.co.uk
Car park: Steam Centre (free).
Access by public transport: Diss main line station (3 miles)
On site facilities: 10.25/15/24in and standard gauge lines, totalling nearly 5 miles. Museum, steam roundabout, souvenir shop and restaurant, extensive gardens and plant centre. 'Dad's Army' permanent exhibition open all year
Public opening: Open every day between Easter and end of October. Steam every day with narrow gauge rides and the Gallopers. 10.30-17.30. Education services for schools are available with pre-booking in March-October period
Special events: Please telephone (01379) 686900 for details
Special facilities: The corporate hospitality venue is available for events, from parties to conferences. Please telephone (01379) 686900 for details
Facilities for disabled: Wheelchair

Name	No	Builder	Type	Built
Bressingham	GET 10	T/Hill (163V)	4wDH	1966

2ft gauge locomotives

Name	No	Builder	Type	Built
Gwynedd	—	Hunslet (316)	0-4-0ST	1883
George Sholto	—	Hunslet (994)	0-4-0ST	1909
Toby	—	M/Rail (22120)	4wDM	1964

15in gauge locomotives

Name	No	Builder	Type	Built
Rosenkavalier	—	Krupp (1662)	4-6-2	1937
Mannertreu	—	Krupp (1663)	4-6-2	1937
Flying Scotsman	4472	W. Stewart (4472)	4-6-2	1976
Works Loco	—	Diss	0-4-0DM	1992
Replica	6353	—	Bo-Bo	—

10.25in gauge locomotives

Name	No	Builder	Type	Built
Alan Bloom	1	BSM	0-4-0ST	1995

Owner
80, 490 and 990 on loan from the National Railway Museum
GET 1 the Great Eastern Traction Group

access to majority of site including toilets. Able to take wheelchairs on Nursery Line Railway and Waveney Line
Special notes: Reduced rates for coach parties. Prices on application

---

Steam Centre	# Bristol Industrial Museum	Bristol

Member: HRA
Note: The museum is closed until autumn 2009 for redevelopment and transformation into the Museum of Bristol. The railway may operate occasionally (as well as the other working exhibits). Please see local press for details.
Location: Princes Wharf, Bristol
OS reference: ST 585722
Operating society/organisation: Bristol Industrial Museum, Princes Wharf, Bristol BS1 4RN
Telephone: (0117) 925 1470
Fax: (0117) 929 7318

Industrial locomotives

Name	No	Builder	Type	Built
Portbury	34†	Avonside (1764)	0-6-0ST	1917
Henbury	—†	Peckett (1940)	0-6-0ST	1937
—	3*	F/Walker (242)	0-6-0ST	1874
—	—	R/Hornsby (418792)	0-4-0DM	1958

*not on public display
†only on view when in steam

Car parks: Available nearby
Access by public transport: Buses to centre of city, 1km from Temple Meads station
Length of line: Half-mile, extension of one-mile open for a.m. trips
Membership details: Officer in charge — D. Martin, Bristol Harbour Railway c/o above address

---

Miniature Railway	# Brookside Miniature Railway	Cheshire

Member: Britain's Great Little Railways
A large extension will open in spring 2007
Location: Brookside Garden Centre
Headquarters: Brookside Garden Centre Ltd, Macclesfield Road,

Poynton, Cheshire
Contact:
Chief Executive: Mr C. Halsall
Telephone: (01625) 872919
Fax: (01625) 859119
Internet address: Web site: www.brookside-miniature-

railway.co.uk
Car parking: On site
Access by public transport: Main line stations: Hazel Grove (2.5 miles, Poynton (2 miles). Bus No 191 stops outside the Centre

England

On site facilities: Full restaurant/café facilities. Extensive museum of railwayana, large display of totems (c200) and advertising enamels

Depots: On site and visits may be made by prior arrangement

Length of line: 7.25in gauge, half mile

Period of public operation: Weekends throughout the year, plus Wednesdays April to September; every day mid-July and August. Summer — 11.00-16.30; winter — 11.00-16.00

Special events: Halloween Ghost Train Rides — 31 October; Santa Specials — weekends in December

Facilities for disabled: Disabled toilet facilities and access to all parts

Fare: Adults: £1.50; Child £1

Locomotives

Name	No	Builder	Type	Built
Jean	—	Exmoor	0-4-2T	2000
Jane	—	Exmoor	0-4-2T	2002
Billy May	—	Exmoor	2-4-2	1999
Mighty Max	—	Greatex	Bo-Bo	2000
Sandy River	—	D. Sims	2-4-2	1996
Callum	—	J. Horsfield	0-6-0T	2003
Annie	—	D McFarlane	Co-Co	1997
Gordon Highlander	—	—	4-6-0	1992

Steam Centre	**Buckinghamshire Railway Centre**	Bucks

Member: HRA

The Buckinghamshire Railway Centre is situated at Quainton Road on the freight-only Aylesbury-Calvert line, once part of the Metropolitan and Great Central line from London to Verney Junction. Quainton Road station is also the old junction for the Brill Tramway closed in 1935. The Centre is now home to the former LNWR Rewley Road station moved brick-by-brick from the centre of Oxford. Opened in 1851, this Grade 2* listed building is built in the same manner as the Crystal Palace Great Exhibition building of 1881 destroyed by fire in the 1930s. It is unique in its construction and provides a superb setting in which the pick of the Centre's locomotives and carriages are now displayed

Location: Adjacent to goods-only line to Aylesbury. Turn off A41 at Waddesdon 6 miles NW of Aylesbury, Bucks

OS reference: SP 738190

Operating society/organisation: Quainton Railway Society Ltd, The Railway Station, Quainton, Nr Aylesbury, Bucks HP22 4BY

Telephone: Quainton (01296) 655450

Internet address:
Web site: www.bucksrailcentre.org

Car park: Quainton Road — Free parking

Locomotives and multiple-units

Name	No	Origin	Class	Type	Built
—	1	Met Rly	E	0-4-4T	1898
—	30585	LSWR	0298	2-4-0WT	1874
Defiant	5080	GWR	'Castle'	4-6-0	1939
Wightwick Hall	6989	GWR	'Hall'	4-6-0	1948
—	7200	GWR	7200	2-8-2T	1934
—	7715	GWR	5700	0-6-0PT	1930
—	9466	GWR	9400	0-6-0PT	1952
—	41298	LMS	2MT	2-6-2T	1951
—	46447	LMS	2MT	2-6-0	1950
—	D2298	BR	04	0-6-0DM	1960
—	3405*	SAR	25NC	4-8-4	1958
—	51886	BR	115	DMBS	1960
—	51899	BR	115	DMBS	1960
—	59761	BR	115	TCL	1960

*3ft 6in gauge

Industrial locomotives

Name	No	Builder	Type	Built
Scott	—	Bagnall (2469)	0-4-0ST	1932
—	—	Baguley (2161)	0-4-0DM	1941
Swanscombe	—	Barclay (699)	0-4-0ST	1891
—	—	GF3 Barclay (1477)	0-4-0F	1916
—	—	Barclay (2243)	0-4-0F	1948
Osram	—	Fowler (20067)	0-4-0DM	1933
—	3	H/Leslie (3717)	0-4-0ST	1928
Sir Thomas	—	H/Clarke (1334)	0-6-0T	1918
—	—	H/Clarke (1742)	0-4-0ST	1946
—	—	Hunslet (2067)	0-4-0DM	1940
Arthur	—	Hunslet (3782)	0-6-0ST	1953
Juno	—	Hunslet (3850)	0-6-0ST	1958
—	65	Hunslet (3889)	0-6-0ST	1964
—	66	Hunslet (3890)	0-6-0ST	1964
—	26	Hunslet (7016)	0-6-0DH	1971
Redland	—	K/Stuart (K4428)	0-4-0DM	1929
Coventry No 1	—	NBL (24564)	0-6-0ST	1939
—	—	Peckett (1900)	0-4-0T	1936

Access by public transport: Main line Aylesbury station. Local bus Monday-Saturday only
On site facilities: Souvenir bookshop, light refreshments, toilets, steam-hauled train rides. Museum of small relics, secondhand bookshop, miniature railway
Catering facilities: Hot snacks and light refreshments available
Length of line: Two half-mile demonstration lines
Public opening: Open Wednesday to Sunday inclusive from April to October. Steaming days each Sunday and Wednesdays during school holidays, plus Bank Holidays.
Opening times: 10.30-16.30
Special events: Day out with Thomas — 6-9 April; Miniature Railway Gala — 6/7 May; Bus Rally — 28 May; Miniature Traction Engine Rally — 2/3 June; Day out with Thomas — 6-8 July; Classic Car Weekend — 26/27 August; Day out with Thomas — 8/9 September; Traction Engine Rally — 22/23 September; Steam Gala — 21 October
Facilities for disabled: Access to most of site including special toilets
Special notes: One of the largest collection of standard gauge locomotives, together with a most

Name	No	Builder	Type	Built
Gibraltar	—	Peckett (2087)	0-4-0ST	1948
—	—	Peckett (2104)	0-4-0ST	1948
—	—	Peckett (2105)	0-4-0ST	1948
—	T1	Hibberd (2102)	4wD	1937
Tarmac	—	Hibberd (3765)	0-4-0DM	1955
—	11	Sentinel (9366)	4wVBTG	1945
—	7	Sentinel (9376)	4wVBTG	1947
—	—	Sentinel (9537)	4wVBTG	1947
Chislet	9	Yorkshire (2498)	0-6-0ST	1951

Stock: *Coaches —*
1 LCDR 1st Class 4-wheeler; 1 MSLR 3rd Class 6-wheeler; 4 LNWR coach bodies; 2 GNR 6-wheelers; 3 LNWR; 3 LMSR; 1 BR(W) Hawksworth brake 3rd; 2 BR Mk 1; 1 BR Mk 2; 1 BR Suburban brake; 3 LNER; 1 LNWR full brake 6-wheeler; 1 LMSR passenger brake van; 1 GWR passenger brake van; 1 GCR Robinson brake third
Wagons —
A large and varied collection including 1 LNWR combination truck; 1 LSWR ventilated fruit van; 1 SR PMV; 1 BR(W) Siphon G; 1 BR horse box; 1 BR CCT
3 ex-London Underground coaches
1 2ft gauge post office mailbag car 803
Sentinel/Cammell 3-car steam railcar unit 5208 (ex-Egyptian National)
Numerous goods vehicles/wagons/vans

Owners
41298, 46447 and *Juno* the Ivatt Locomotive Trust
9466 the 9466 Group
Defiant on loan from Tyseley Locomotive Works

interesting collection of vintage coaching stock, much of which was built in the 19th century
General: The public area of the centre covers some 25 acres of land with views across the Buckinghamshire countryside. A picnic area is available at the miniature railway

---

Member: HRA, TT
Opened in 1990, the BVR runs over the old Great Eastern Wroxham-Aylsham line. It is paralleled throughout the entire 9 miles by the Bure Valley Walk and cycle path which offers excellent photographic opportunities
Headquarters: Bure Valley Railway (1991) Ltd, Aylsham Station, Norwich Road, Aylsham, Norfolk NR11 6BW
Chairman: Andrew Barnes
Telephone: (01263) 733858
Fax: (01263) 733814
Internet address: *e-mail:* info@bvrw.co.uk
Web site: www.bvrw.co.uk
Main public station: Aylsham (Norwich Road, NR11 6BW);

Locomotives

Name	No	Builder	Type	Built
Wroxham Broad	1	G&S/Winson	2-6-4T	1992
2nd Air Division USAAF	3	BVR	4w-4wDH	1989
—	4	H/Hunslet	0-4-0DH	1996
—	5	Lister	4wDM	
Blickling Hall	6	Winson*	2-6-2	1994
Spitfire	7	Winson*	2-6-2	1994
Thunder	8	BVR/Winson	2-6-2T	1997
Mark Timothy	10	Winson/Keef§	2-6-4T	2003

*based on Indian Railways 2ft 6in gauge 'ZB' class
§based on Leek & Manifold Railway design

Stock
19 fully enclosed saloons, 2 fully enclosed compartment coaches, 6 enclosed saloons designed to carry wheelchairs, 1 fully enclosed brake saloon, 2 guard's vans, generator car, miscellaneous wagons including a rail-mounted flail and weedkilling unit and purpose-built p-way tool vehicle arrangement

36   **England**

Wroxham (Coltishall Road, NR12 8UU)
Other public stations: Coltishall, Brampton and Buxton
Car and coach parks: Aylsham and Wroxham
OS reference:
Aylsham — TG 195264
Wroxham — TG 303186
Access by public transport:
By rail: Wroxham station is adjacent to main line Hoveton & Wroxham station (Norwich-Cromer/Sheringham line).
By bus: First and Sanders buses run between Norwich and Aylsham
Refreshment facilities: Restaurant at Aylsham with picnic area, light refreshments at Wroxham
Souvenir shops: Aylsham and Wroxham

Journey time: Approximately 45min each way plus turn round time
Length of line: 9 miles; 15in gauge
Passenger trains: Frequency depends on time of year, maximum frequency one per hour
Period of public operation: Weekends in March. Daily 31 March to 30 September. Weekends in October. Daily 20-28 October
Facilities for disabled: Toilets at Aylsham and Wroxham. Main stations are all on one level, special rolling stock to carry wheelchairs; advance notice would be appreciated
Special events: Please contact for full details. Day out with Thomas — 26-28 May and 22/23 September; Santa Specials 25

November, 1/2, 8/9, 14/16, 18-24 December (advance booking essential); Mince Pie Specials 27 December to 2 January 2008
Special notes: Steam locomotive driving courses. Group discounts available. Frequent Travellers Railcards. Children's Birthday Parties. Private charters by arrangement. Special combined train and Broads boat excursions run most days during the summer
Membership details: Friends of the Bure Valley Railway, Membership Secretary, c/o above address

Cambrian Heritage Railway

Diesel Centre

Shropshire

Member: HRA

This will be the third year of passenger operations, consolidating on the achievement of last year's full operating season of diesel trains between Llynclys (South) to Penygarreg Lane (Pant), a distance of two-thirds of a mile. It is also hoped to arrange occasional steam operation during 2007. The most exciting news is that spring 2007 should see the acquisition of the mothballed, but intact, line from Gobowen via Oswestry to Llynclys Junction. Agreement has also been reached that the Cambrian Railways Society will purchase the line from Llynclys Junction westwards to Blodwel — and that both bodies will co-operate with marketing, operations and development of the project. During the year, a start will be made on extending the Trust's line northwards from its current base, through the original Llynclys station to Llynclys Junction, then towards Oswestry

Location: Llynclys is situated on the B4396 about 5 miles south of Oswestry, just off the A483 Welshpool-Oswestry road

Locomotives and Multiple-units

Name	No	Origin	Class	Type	Built
Cogan Hall	5952	GWR	Hall	4-6-0	1935
—	D2094	BR	03	0-6-0DM	1960
—	D3019	BR	08	0-6-0DE	1953
—	51187	Met-Cam	101	DMBS	1958
—	51205	Met-Cam	101	DMBS	1958
—	51512	Met-Cam	101	DMC	1959
—	54055	Met-Cam	101	DTSL	1957

Rolling stock

9 ex-BR Mk 1 coaches, 4 ex-GWR coaches/bogie vans, 20 goods wagons
1 Plasser & Theurer maintenance vehicle No 73241

Telephone: 01691 831569
Internet address: *e-mail:* admin@cambrianrailwaystrust.com
Web site: www.cambrianrailwaystrust.com
OS reference: SJ 284239
Operating society: Cambrian Railways Trust, c/o Llynclys House, Llynclys, Oswestry, Shropshire SY10, 8LL
Access by public transport: Bus approx hourly from Oswestry to White Lion Inn, Llynclys crossroads (200yd from site), with connecting buses from Gobowen station and Shrewsbury. Also buses from Welshpool and Llanfyllin (Arriva Midlands / Tanat Valley Coaches)
On site facilities: Buffet and shop
Period of public opening: Generally weekends and Bank Holidays — April to October, but visitors welcome at other times
Disabled facilities: Level access to platforms, ramps onto trains
Membership details: c/o above address
Membership journal: Quarterly newsletter
Special note: Special trains can be arranged for parties at any time

Chasewater Railway

Steam Centre

Staffordshire

Member: HRA, TT

Founded in 1959 as the Railway Preservation Society (West Midlands District), the Chasewater Railway was re-formed in 1985 as a Registered Charity. The railway operates as 'The Colliery Line' to reflect its origins and location in the heart of the Cannock Chase coalfield. A regular timetabled service operates between Brownhills West station and Chasetown (Church Street), with intermediate stations at Norton Lakeside (which adjoins Chasewater's Wildfowl Reserve) and Chasewater Heaths.

Location: Chasewater Park, Brownhills (off A5 southbound, nr

Diesel locomotive and multiple-units

Name	No	Builder	Class	Type	Built
—	31203	BR	31	A1A-A1A	1960
—	37219	BR	37	Co-Co	1964
—*	73128	BR	73	Bo-Bo	1966
—	53160	BR	101	DMC	1956
—	53164	BR	101	DMBS	1957
—	W59444	BR Derby	116	TS	1958
—	W55922	Pressed Steel	117	TCL	1960
—	W59603	Pressed Steel	127	TSL	1959

*named O. V. S. Bulleid CBE
37219 on loan to Gloucestershire Warwickshire Railway during 2007

Industrial locomotives

Name	No	Builder	Type	Built
Colin McAndrew	3	Barclay (1223)	0-4-0ST	1911
British Gypsum No 4	3	Barclay (2343)	0-4-0ST	1953
Sheepbridge No 15	—	H/Clarke (431)	0-6-0T	1895
Whit No 4	—	H/Clarke (1822)	0-6-0T	1949

Above: Based on an Indian Railways 2ft 6in 'ZB' class design No 7 *Spitfire* is virtually a half-scale model as it runs on the 1ft 3in gauge Bure Valley Railway. *Andrew Barnes*

Below: Recently returned to service at the Buckinghamshire Railway Centre in this LSWR Beattie 2-4-0WT. This and sister locomotive No 30857, on the Bodmin & Wenford Railway date from 1874. *BRC*

jct A452 Chester Road). Brown tourism signs are provided on A5

OS Reference: SK 034070

Operating society/organisation: Chasewater Light Railway & Museum Co

Telephone: 01543 452623

Internet address: *e-mail:* info@chaserail.co.uk

Web site: www.chaserail.co.uk

Car park: Ample car parking within Chasewater Park

Access by public transport:
Nearest railway stations — Walsall and Birmingham New Street.
Bus services from Walsall Bus Station (St Paul's Street) —
Saturdays: 396A (Stand L) and 396C (Stand K), alight at Poole Crescent
Sundays: 362 (Stand K) and 395A (Stand L) to Brownhills West (Rising Sun Inn).
Bus services from Birmingham (Carrs Lane)
Saturdays and Sundays: 156 (Stand DH) to Brownhills West (Rising Sun Inn).
Brownhills West station is approx 15min walk from the Rising Sun Inn, 10min walk from Poole Crescent
For timetable information and details of services, contact Traveline 0870 608 2608

On site facilities: Refreshments, shop, lakeside walks and large grassed areas

Catering facilities: Hot and cold buffets at Brownhills West and Chasewater Heath stations

Length of line: Approx 2 miles

Public opening: Sundays and Bank Holiday Mondays throughout the year. Saturday and Wednesday

Name	No	Builder	Type	Built
Asbestos	4	H/Leslie (2780)	0-4-0ST	1909
Alfred Paget	11	Neilson (2937)	0-4-0ST	1882
—	6	Peckett (917)	0-4-0ST	1902
Sentinel	5	Sentinel (9632)	4wVBT	1957
Bass No 5	—	Baguley (3027)	0-4-0DM	1939
Hem Heath	—	Bagnall (3119)	0-6-0DM	1956
Dealer	—	Brush (3097)	0 4 0DE	1956
—	—	Fowler (4100013)	0-4-0DM	1948
Toad	37	Fowler (4220015)	0-4-0DH	1962
—	462	Hibberd (1891)	4wDM	1934
—	6678	Hunslet (6678)	0-4-0DH	1968
—	21	Kent Constr (1612)	4wDM	1929
—	1*	M/Rail (1947)	4wPM	1919
Ryan	—	R/Hornsby (305306)	0-4-0DM	1952
Fleet	11517	R/Hornsby (458641)	0-4-0DE	1963
—	—	R/Hornsby (544998)	0-4-0DE	1968

*currently dismantled

Rolling stock
A variety of passenger and freight vehicles are housed on site, including a number of considerable historical importance, together with an ex-LNER steam crane

Owner
Class 101 unit the East Pennine Class 101 Double Power Car Group

services operate during summer months and school holidays. Santa Specials during December.

Trains depart from Brownhills West station at 10.30, 11.45, 13.00, 14.15, 15.30, 16.45*.

*Service operates summer Sundays and Bank Holiday Mondays only.

Check web site for running dates and timetables.

Most services are with steam traction (subject to availability). Industrial diesel locomotives are normally used once a month and at off-peak periods.

All tickets give unlimited rides on day of issue. Family tickets (2 adults + 4 children available, under 4s free

Special events: Bus Rally — 17 June; Symphony Concert — 30 June; Steam & Diesel Gala — 8/9 September; Diesel Gala — 20/21 October; Halloween Specials — 28 October; Santa Specials — throughout December

Facilities for disabled: Disabled access to stations, trains and buffet

Membership details: Membership Secretary, Brownhills West Station, Chasewater Country Park, Pool Road, Nr Brownhills, Staffs WS8 7NL

(Steam Centre) **Chinnor & Princes Risborough Railway — 'The Icknield Line'** (Oxfordshire)

Member: HRA
The Chinnor & Princes Risborough Railway runs from Chinnor station, close to the beautiful Chiltern Hills and to the Vale of Aylesbury. Originally built in 1872 to connect the towns of Watlington in Oxfordshire to Princes Risborough

in Buckinghamshire, the line was closed to all traffic by British Railways in 1989. Since then a team of volunteers has rebuilt Chinnor station to its Victorian glory. The railway operates the 3.5-mile ex-Great Western Railway branch line as a tourist attraction for

both families and railway enthusiasts. A regular steam-hauled service is provided every Sunday from the end of March to October. Special events are a feature of the programme including Day out with Thomas weekends and Santa Specials. Cream teas are served on

40

selected afternoon trains during the summer months

Location: M40 junction 6 then B4009 north 4 miles towards Princes Risborough to village of Chinnor. Once in village follow brown tourist signs to station

Operating society/organisation: Chinnor & Princes Risborough Railway Co Ltd, Chinnor Station, Station Road, Chinnor, Oxon OX39 4ER

Contact: Brian Dickson, Press & Publicity Officer, 58 Grenville Avenue, Wendover, Bucks HP22 6AL. Tel: 01296 622569

Telephone: Talking Timetable 01844 353535. Thomas Booking Line: 01844 354117 (Weekends 10.00-17.00 only)

Internet address: *e-mail:* brian@dicksons.screaming.net
Web site: www.cprra.co.uk

OS reference: SP 756003

Access by public transport: Nearest main line station — Princes Risborough (4 miles) Chiltern Railways
By car: M40 junction 6 then B4009 north towards Princes Risborough to village of Chinnor, then follow brown tourist signs to station

Length of line: 3.5 miles

Journey time: 45min, steam and heritage diesel trains

On site facilities: Souvenir shop, small buffet on Chinnor station. Bar/buffet on most trains (cream teas on selected trains on summer Sunday afternoons). Toilets, free car park, picnic area

Passenger trains: Chinnor-Thame Junction-Chinnor

Public opening: 15, 25 March; 1, 6-9, 15, 22, 29 April; 5-7, 13, 20, 29 May; 3, 10, 17, 24, 29/30 June; 1, 7/8, 14/15, 21/22, 28/29 July; 4/5, 11/12, 18/19, 25-27 August; 2,

Locomotives

Name	No	Origin	Class	Type	Built
Haversham	13018	BR	08	0-6-0DE	1953
—	D8568	BR	17	Bo-Bo	1963
—	31113	BR	31	A1A-A1A	1959
—	D5581	BR	31	A1A-A1A	1961
—	55023	BR	121	DMBS	1958
—	9682	GWR	57xx	0-6-0PT	1949

Industrial locomotives

Name	No	Builder	Type	Built
Blue Circle	—	A/Porter (9449)	2-2-0TG	1926
Iris	459515	R/Hornsby (459515)	0-6-0DH	1952

Stock - coaches

1 ex-LNWR Mess coach, 1 ex-BR Mk 1 NDV, 1 ex-BR Mk 1 RMB, 1 ex-BR Mk 1 CK, 1 ex-BR Mk 1 BSK, 1 ex-BR Mk 2 FK, 16 various wagons, 1 Coles self-propelled crane

Owners

D8568 the Diesel Traction Group
9682 on loan from the Great Western Railway Preservation Group, Southall

9, 16, 23, 29/30 September; 7, 14, 21, 28 October; 2, 8/9, 15/16, 22/23, 29/30 December

Special events: Mother's Day — 18 March; Easter Egg Specials — 6-9 April; St George's Celebrations — 22 April; Teddy Bear Weekend — 27/28 May; Summer Diesel Day — 11 June; Father's Day — 17 June; 50th Year Commemoration of the Closure of the Line to Passengers — 29/30 June, 1 July; Senior Citizens' Day — 8 July; Teddy Bear Weekend — 26/27 August; Autumn Gala Day — 9 September; Senior Citizens' Day — 23 September; Halloween Spooks Express — 29 October
Afternoon Cream Teas — 18 March, 1, 15, 29 April, 20 May, 10, 17 June, 8, 29 July, 19 August, 2, 23 September, 7, 21 October. Other dates available for party bookings

Special note: Group charter hire and film and photographic facilities available, contact: 01844 353535. Advance booking is necessary for Day out with Thomas and Santa Special events

Driver experience courses: The railway will be offering steam driver experience days throughout the year. Gift vouchers are available for these courses. Please telephone 07784 189322 or visit the web site for details

Facilities for disabled: Ramp, toilet accessible parking area. All public areas accessible. Guide dogs welcome

Membership details: Mr Peter Harris, 12 Ann's Close, Aylesbury, Bucks HP21 9XG

Membership journal: *The Watlington Flyer* — quarterly

Timetable Service

Cholsey & Wallingford Railway

Oxfordshire

Member: HRA
The Barclay has now returned to steam and has been restored in the guise of GWR 701, a former Swansea Harbour Trust locomotive. Due to on going alterations/ improvements to Wallingford station and upgrading of the line to

Cholsey during 2005, the timetable is subject to revision without notice. Please check the web site or 24hr answerphone for up-to-date information

Location: 5 Hithercroft Road, Wallingford, Oxfordshire

Sales & Marketing: Denis Strange

Operating Society: Cholsey & Wallingford Railway Preservation Society, 5 Hithercroft Road, Wallingford, Oxon OX10 9GQ

Telephone: (01491) 835067 (24hr information line)

Internet address: *e-mail:* cwrail@yahoo.co.uk

Web site: www.cholsey-wallingford-railway.com

Disabled access: Access direct to Wallingford station from adjoining car park, access ramp to shop, platform and train, disabled toilet on site. No disabled facilities at Cholsey station

Access by public transport: Thames Travel Buses — X39 from Oxford, X40 from Reading. First Great Western Link trains to Cholsey station

Public opening: Trains depart every hour from Wallingford, 11.10-16.10; and from Cholsey platform 11.35-16.35

Length of line: 2.5 miles from Wallingford

Journey time: Approximately 14min (one way), 50min (return)

On site facilities: Souvenir shop, café and museum

Special events: No details available at press date

Locomotives

Name	No	Origin	Class	Type	Built
Unicorn	D3074	BR	08	0-6-0DE	1953
Lion	D3030	BR	08	0-6-0DE	1953
George Mason	D3190	BR	08	0-6-0DE	1955

Industrial locomotives

Name	No	Builder	Type	Built
—	701	Barclay (1964)	0-4-0ST	1929
Carpenter	3271	Planet (3270)	0-4-0DM	1949
—	803	Alco (77777)	Bo-Bo	1950

Rolling stock — coaches: GWR autocoach, Hawksworth brake coach, GWR full brake, 2 BR Mk 1 coaches

Special notes: Railway crosses new bypass (A4130) at a level crossing. The Society is running into Cholsey bay platform.

Membership details: Alan Saunders, at above address

Membership journal: *The Bunk* — 3 issues/year

Timetable Service		Churnet Valley Railway	Staffordshire

Member: HRA

This heritage railway is situated deep in the heart of the Staffordshire moorlands. Begin your journey at Cheddleton, a Victorian country station set in picturesque countryside complete with riverside parking and picnic island. The 10.5 mile return journey takes you to the idyllic hamlet of Consall Forge and onwards to the reinstated station Kingsley & Froghall

Main station/location: Cheddleton Station, Station Road, Cheddleton, Nr Leek, Staffs ST13 7EE

OS reference: SJ 983519

Operating society/organisation: Churnet Valley Railway (1992) plc

Telephone: 01538 360522

Fax: 01538 361848

Internet address: *e-mail:* mgtcvr@onetel.com

Web site: www.churnetvalleyrailway.co.uk

Other stations: Consall, Kingsley & Froghall

Car parks: Adjacent to Cheddleton and Froghall stations

Access by public transport: Main

Locomotives and multiple-units

Name	No	Origin	Class	Type	Built
—	5197	USATC	S160	2-8-0	1942
—	6046	USATC	S160	2-8-0	1945
Ditcheat Manor	7821	GWR	'Manor'	4-6-0	1950
—	80098	BR	4MT	2-6-4T	1954
—	92134	BR	9F	2-10-0	1957
—	D2334	BR	04	0-6-0DM	1961
—	D3991	BR	08	0-6-0DE	1960
—	20007	BR	20	Bo-Bo	1957
—	D8154	BR	20	Bo-Bo	1966
Tamworth Castle	D7672	BR	25	Bo-Bo	1967
—	33102	BR	33	Bo-Bo	1960
—	37009	BR	37	Co-Co	1961
—	37211	BR	37	Co-Co	1961
—	47192	BR	47	Co-Co	1965
—	47524	BR	47	Co-Co	1967
—	73110	BR	73	Bo-Bo	1966
—	53455	BRCW	104	DMBS	1957
—	53437	BRCW	104	DMBS	1957
—	53494	BRCW	104	DMCL	1957
—	53517	BRCW	104	DMCL	1957
—	59137	BRCW	104	TSL	1957
—	62351	BR	423	MBSO	
—	71032	BR	423	MTSO	
—	76529	BR	423	DTC	
—	76712	BR	423	DTS	

42

line Stoke-on-Trent (10 miles). A regular bus service (No 16) runs from Hanley and Leek to Cheddleton village

On site facilities: Refreshment facilities at Cheddleton and Froghall

Souvenir shop: Cheddleton and Froghall

Museum: Small relics museum and locomotive display hall at Cheddleton

Length of line: 5.25 miles

Tickets: Day rover tickets available

Public opening: Steam trains March-October inclusive: weekends and Bank Holidays.
Wednesdays in June and July. Daily in August.

Special events: Station at War, Day out with Thomas, Ghost Train and Santa Specials

Facilities for disabled: Access to station areas is possible by wheelchair, train travel by arrangement. Disabled toilet facilities at Consall and Froghall

Membership details: North Staffordshire Railway Co (1978) Ltd, Membership Secretary, c/o above address

Industrial locomotives

Name	No	Builder	Type	Built
Cammell	—	YEC	0-4-0DH	1960
Brightside	—	YEC	0-4-0DH	1960

Locomotive notes: Locos expected to be in service: 5197, 7821, 80097, D8154, D3991, 33102, 47192, 73110, 4-VEP and 104 DMU

Stock

Ex-BR Mk 1 coaches: CK (1), BSK (2), SO (3), TSO (2), FK (3), RMB (1), RK (1) and BG (2); ex-BR Mk 2 coaches: BFK (1); ex-BR suburban coaches: S (1), BS (2), SLO (1); 1 ex-NSR coach body; 1 ex-LMS 6-wheel full brake; 2 ex-LMS goods brake vans; 1 ex-LMS 6-wheel CCT; 2 ex-LMS box vans; 3 ex-BR box vans; 2 ex-LMS five-plank wagons; 1 ex-LMS hopper wagon; 1 Esso tank wagon; 1 ex-BR standard brake van; 1 ex-BR Oyster; 5 ex-BR General Utility Vans; 2 ex-BR Medfits; 2 ex-BR Catfish; 1 ex-GWR bogie bolster; 2 Flatrols; 1 Lowmac; 7-ton diesel rail-mounted crane; 75-ton rail-mounted diesel crane; 3 ex-BR QQX tool vans; 1 ex-BR QPX staff and dormitory

Owners

33102 and D7672 the NSR Diesel Group
20007, D8154, 37009, 37211, 73110, D3991 and *Cammell* the Churnet Traction & Rolling Stock Group
47192 and 47524 the Staffordshire Type 4 Ltd

Special facilities: Party bookings by arrangement, footplate experience courses, wine & dine dates on application. Licensed for weddings and civil partnerships at all three stations

---

Timetable Service	**Cleethorpes Coast Light Railway**	North East Lincolnshire

Member: HRA

The East Coast's award winning seaside 15in gauge steam railway. Built in 1948 as a 10.25in line, it was converted in 1972 to 14.25in and then to 15in gauge in 1994.

The railway has a good reputation for galas and events, and facilities continue to improve year on year. In 2005 a new 'Griffon Hall' museum was officially opened.

The railway is supported by the Light Railway Association, whose members assist in running the line, undertaking a wide range of duties. This small group provides volunteers from station staff to engine drivers.

2007 will again feature a spring gala, the 'Bakers Dozen' with other events planned throughout the year; two additional visiting engines are planned to visit the line for the main summer season

Locomotives (15in gauge)

Name	No	Built/rebuilt	Type	Date
—	7	Lister	4wDH Tram	—
The Cub/John	3	Minirail/CCLR	4w4DM	1993
—	24	Fairbourne	2-6-2	1989
—	—	A. Moss	4wDM	1995
Battison	—	Battison	2-6-4DH S/O	1958
Yvette	1	—	2-6-0	1946
Efie	—	Great Northern Steam	0-4-0	1999
—	—	Scarrott	4-4-0	1990
—	—	Massey/CCLR	0-6-4ST	2006/7

Rolling stock

10 coaches, 2 x 4-wheel wagons, 2 x 4-wheel box vans, 1 x 4-wheel goods brake van, 4 bogie flat wagons, 2 x 4-wheel ballast wagon

15in gauge Sutton Collection

Locomotives

Name	No	Built/rebuilt	Type	Date
Sutton Belle	1	BL/Cannon Ironfoundries/Hunt	4-4-2	1933
Sutton Flyer	2	Bassett Lowke/Hunt	4-4-2	1950
—	4	G&S Light Engineering	Bo-Bo	1946

Rolling stock

6 closed coaches, 4 open coaches, 4-wheel coal truck

43

Operating society/organisation:
Cleethorpes Coast Light Railway
Ltd, Lakeside Station, Kings Road,
Cleethorpes, Lincolnshire
DN35 0AG
Telephone: (01472) 604657
Fax: (01472) 291903
Internet address: *e-mail:*
office,cclr@btconnect.com
Web site:
www.cleethorpescoastlightrailway.c
om
Access by public transport: By
rail to Cleethorpes station (First
Transpennine South). Local bus
service Stagecoach services 9 (all
year) and 17 (summer only). Or
Coopers Seafront Open Top service
(summer only).
Alternative seafront roadtrain from
the pier to CCLR Kingsway station.
By car, Kings Road is the main
resort road, follow brown tourist
signs for Lakeside (look for the
train symbol)
On site facilities: Large 500 space
car park at Lakeside station (pay &
display, local authority operated).
Lakeside station — Brief
Encounters tea room; Model Box
model shop; Griffon Hall museum;
4-ways café.
Kingsway station — Station
Masters gift shop.

15in gauge Bushmills Railway Collection

Locomotives

Name	No	Built/rebuilt	Type	Date
Mountaineer	—	van Heiden/Severn-Lamb	0-4-0	1985
—	DA1		4wDM	

Rolling stock
5 closed coaches

Note
During the year visiting locomotives are based on the CCLR, and locomotives and rolling stock are under repair for other operators

Period of public opening: Please
contact for details
Special events: The Works Outing
(May). The new extension will be
open for the gala, an extra mile of
track and a new station called
Humberstone North Sea Lane.
Please see web site for details

Steam Centre — Colne Valley Railway — Essex

Member: HRA, TT
A completely reconstructed country
station and railway within sight of
a 12th century castle and
specialising in entertainment and
education. A complementary Farm
Park provides interest for all the
family (May to September).
Location: Castle Hedingham
Station, Yeldham Road, Castle
Hedingham, Halstead, Essex
CO9 3DZ
OS reference: TL 774362
Operating society/organisation:
Colne Valley Railway Preservation
Society Ltd
Telephone: Hedingham (01787)
461174
Internet address:
Web site:
www.colnevalleyrailway.co.uk
Car park: At the site (access from
A1017 road between Castle
Hedingham and Great Yeldham)
Access by public transport:
Eastern National bus services 88
Colchester-Halstead, 89 Halstead-
Hedingham and Hedingham
Omnibuses 4 Braintree-
Hedingham, 5 Sudbury-
Hedingham. Nearest main line
station — Braintree (7 miles)
On site facilities: Depot, museum,

Locomotives and multiple-units

Name	No	Origin	Class	Type	Built
Blue Star	35010	SR	MN	4-6-2	1942
—	45163	LMS	5	4-6-0	1935
—	45293	LMS	5	4-6-0	1936
—	D2041	BR	03	0-6-0DM	1959
—	D2184	BR	03	0-6-0DM	1962
—	D3476	BR	10	0-6-0DE	1957
—	31255	BR	31	A1A-A1A	1961
—	47771	BR	47	Co-Co	19??
—	54287	P/Steel	121	DTS	1961
—	55033	P/Steel	121	DTC	1960
—	68009	BR	MLV / 419	DMVL	1961
—	69318	BR	4-BIG / 422	TRBS	1965
—	E79978	AC Cars	—	Railbus	1958
—	55508	BR	141	DMS	1983
—	55528	BR	141	DMS(L)	1983

Industrial locomotives

Name	No	Builder	Type	Built
Victory	8	Barclay (2199)	0-4-0ST	1945
—	WD190	Hunslet (3790)	0-6-0ST	1952
Jupiter	60	RSH (7671)	0-6-0ST	1950
Barrington	—	Avonside (1875)	0-4-0ST	1921
—	1	H/Leslie (3715)	0-4-0ST	1928
—	—	Barclay (349)	0-4-0DM	1941
—	YD43	R/Hornsby (221639)	4wDM	1943
—	—	Hibberd (3147)	4wDM	1947
—	—	Unilok (2109)	4wDM R/R	1982
—	—	Lake & Elliot (1)	4wPM	1924
—	—	R/Hornsby (281266)	4wDM	1950

44

souvenir shop, buffet, 4-acre riverside picnic area, toilets, video carriage, exhibition centre, 30 acre farm park (May to September)
Catering facilities: Buffet carriage when trains operating. Pullman on-train service on selected days for Sunday lunch, private hire and evening wine and dine (pre-booking essential for all Pullman services)
Length of line: 1 mile
Public opening: Steam trains operate every Sunday from 14 April to 8 October, also Wednesdays and Thursdays during school summer holidays, every Bank Holiday (except Christmas & New Year), Wednesdays during other school holidays (except February). Diesel railcar on many other days. Phone for free timetable or visit web site
Special events: A Day out with Thomas, Santa Specials
Educational events: Diesel trains available every day for school visits (steam on certain days). Special steam school days in June. Victorian Special in October. All educational events must be pre-booked
Family tickets: Available —

Locomotive notes: *Barrington* and 190 will be operational during 2007. Diesels 31255 and 55033 also operational

Stock
2 ex-Pullman cars, *Aquila* and *Hermione;* 9 ex-BR Mk 1 coaches (2xTSO, SO, 2xCK, SK, 2xBSK); 1 ex-BR Mk 3 SLEP; 9 BR NPCCS, 2 ex-LNER — 1xBTO (16551) 1xTK (42240); 1 LMS BG, 1 GER BTK; 4 goods brake vans (GWR, LNER & 2 BR), 3 oil tank wagons, BR steam crane, LT ballast wagon, BR Sturgeon, BR Conflat, GER van, BR van, BR Medfit, LNER tube wagon, BR diesel crane, BR Flatrol, BR Lowmac

Owners
35010 and 45293 the British Engineman's Steam Preservation Society
54287 and 55033 Pressed Steel Heritage Ltd
31255 and 68009 the Colne Valley Railway Diesel Group
47771 the Class 47 Preservation Project
45163 the 45163 Preservation Group

2 adults and up to 4 children, giving unlimited train rides except on special events
Facilities for disabled: Access to most areas with disabled parking available. Ramps to trains, staff will help. Special carriage and toilets available
Special notes: The railway has been completely rebuilt on part of the original Colne Valley & Halstead Railway trackbed. It offers

much of educational value specialising in school party visits by appointment at any time of the year. 12 month season tickets available
Special facilities: Private or corporate hire of Pullmans is available.
Membership details: Membership Secretary, c/o Castle Hedingham Station

```
┌──────────┐  ╭─────────────────────╮  ┌──────────────┐
│ Museum   │  │  Coventry Electric  │  │ Warwickshire │
└──────────┘  │  Railway Centre     │  └──────────────┘
              ╰─────────────────────╯
```

Member: HRA
Originally commenced in 1983 as the Coventry Steam Railway Centre which was (and still is) is the only standard gauge line in the county of Warwickshire, The Centre has been developed on a six acre greenfield site with no prior railway use. In 2000 the Suburban Electric Railway Association (SERA) bought controlling interest in the operating company and used the site to locate its collection of vintage electric multiple-units (EMUs); with the SERA collection and some privately owned EMU vehicles and electric locomotives on site it has become home to the largest collection of DC electric traction in preservation. This prompted a change of name and direction in 2006 for the development of the site as the UK's only Electric Railway Heritage Centre. The site has witnessed some extensive development over

Electric multiple-units (complete)

Unit Nos	No	Origin	Class	Type	Built
4732	12795	BR	4SUB / 405	DMBSO	1951
	12354	BR	4SUB / 405	TS	1948
	10239	BR	4SUB / 405	TOS	1948
	12796	BR	4SUB / 405	DMBSO	1951
—	28690	LMS	503	DMBSO	1938
	29298	LMS	503	DTTO	1938
	29720	LMS	503	TCO	1938
5791/93	65321	BR	2EPB / 416/2	DMBSO	1954
	77112	BR	2EPB / 416/2	DTC	1954
4311	61287	BR	2HAP / 414	DMBSO	1959
	75407	BR	2HAP / 414	DTCL	1959
6307	14573	BR	2EPB / 416/3	DMBSO	1959
	16117	BR	2EPB / 416/3	DTS	1959
—	68008†	BR	MLV / 419	DMVL	1961

Electric multiple-units (from incomplete units)

From Unit No	No	Origin	Class	Type	Built
—	70186	BR	501	TS	
—	(7)	LOR*	—	TFO	1895
5176	15345	BR	415 / 4EPB	TSO	1954
1500	70345†	BR	4CEP / 411	TBCK	1958
2205	69339†	BR	4BIG / 411	TSRB	1970
7001	67300	BR	457	DMSO	1981
—	977349	BR	501	DMBSO	1957

the last couple of years
Location: At the boundary of Coventry Airport, south of the city centre and adjacent to the East Midlands Air Museum. Reached via Rowley Road, junction with A45/A46, Coventry Eastern Bypass — M6/M69/M1 link road. Follow signs to Coventry Airport and the entrance is on Rowley Road
Internet address: *e-mail:* info@emus.co.uk
Web site: http:/www.emus.co.uk
OS reference: SP 349750
Access by public transport: National Rail services to Coventry, West Midlands bus route 1 from overbridge at north end of station to Tollbar End — 10-15min walk up Rowley Road to site. Also 737 (hourly) from station forecourt to Tollbar roundabout
Operating society/organisation: Coventry Railway Centre/Suburban Electric Railway Association
Length of line: Third of a mile (under construction)
Public opening: Due to ongoing construction work at the site there is no regular opening, but groups or parties can be accommodated by

*Liverpool Overhead Railway, built by Brown Marshall & Co

Electric locomotives

Name	No	Builder	Type	Built
—	(1)	E/Electric (EE905)	4wBE/WE	1935
—	1	H/Leslie	Bo-Bo	1928

Diesel locomotives

Name	No	Builder	Type	Built
Mazda	—	R/Hornsby (268881)	0-4-0DE	1950
(Crabtree)	—	R/Hornsby (338416)	4wDM	1953

Petrol locomotives

Name	No	Builder	Type	Built
(C. P. May)	—	Hibberd (2895)	4wPM	1944

†may not be on site for all of 2006

Rolling stock
Coaches — Ex-City & South London Railway trailers Nos 135 and 163
Wagons — 1 bogie tool van (converted from Maunsell Ironclad coach), 1 LNER brake van
Rail-mounted cranes — 1 steam crane, 1 hand crane

prior arrangement. Please check web site and railway press for details of other public opening/events.
Please note that many items are tarpaulined for protection

Car park: On site, at main access gate
Facilities for disabled: Site is relatively flat, assistance will be given if requested by prior notice. There are no toilets on site

---

Tram Service	**Crich Tramway Village**	Derbyshire

Member: HRA, TT
An experience of living transport history with vintage horse-drawn, steam and electric trams running through a re-created townscape of authentic buildings, stone setts, iron railings and historic street furniture. The heart of the Museum is its collection of over 70 vintage trams and you can enjoy the thrill of travelling on the scenic mile-long track
Location: Crich, Nr Matlock, Derbyshire DE4 5DP
OS reference: SK 345549
Manager: Vacant
Operating society/organisation: Tramway Museum Society
Telephone: 01773 854321
Internet address: *Web site:* www.tramway.co.uk
Car park: Site; coach parking also available

Locomotives

Name	No	Builder	Type	Built
—	—	B/Peacock (2464)	0-4-0VB tram loco	1885
—	—	E/Electric (717)	4wE	1927
Rupert*	—	R/Hornsby (223741)	4wDM	1944
GMJ*	—	R/Hornsby (326058)	4wDM	1952
—*	—	R/Hornsby (373363)	4wDM	1954

*not on display

Trams

No	Operator	Built
1	Derby	1904
1	Douglas Head Marine Drive	1896
1	Leamington & Warwick	1881
1	London Transport	1932
2	Blackpool & Fleetwood	1898
4	Blackpool Corp	1885
5	Blackpool	*1972
5	Gateshead & District	1927
7	Chesterfield	1904
8	Chesterfield	1899
9	Oporto	1873

46

England

Access by public transport: By rail, nearest main line stations: Cromford or Alfreton then by bus; or Whatstandwell and steep uphill walk

On site facilities: Souvenir shop, play areas, bookshop and picnic areas. 1-mile electric tramway. Tramway period street, depots, displays, exhibitions and video theatre. Large exhibition hall with new interpretive display depicting the history of the tram and Turn of the Century Trade Exhibition plus other exhibitions/displays

Refreshment facilities: Hot and cold snacks and meals

Public opening: Daily 10-25 February (10.30-16.00). Weekends in March (10.30-16.00). Daily 31 March until 28 October (10.00-17.30). Weekends from November to 16 December (10.30-16.00).

Special events: Folk Weekend — 8/9 April; Morris Minor Day — 22 April; Models Weekend — 12/13 May; Dunkirk Spirit of 1940* — 27/28 May; Tramathon — 10 June; Jazz Years — 16/17 June; 1950s Day — 24 June; MiniMeet — 8 July; Edwardian Weekend — 14/15 July; Lancashire & Yorkshire Day — 22 July; 1940s Weekend — 11/12 August; Transport Extravaganza — 26/27 August; Ford Capri Day — 9 September; Beetle Drive — 16 September; Enthusiasts' Day — 29 September; Classic Ford Day — 30 September; Emergency Vehicles Day — 7 October; Starlight Halloween — 27 October; Red October Day — 28 October; Santa Special/ Christmas Street Fair — 8/9 December

Family tickets: Available

Facilities for disabled: Access to all public facilities, Braille guide book available, 1969 Berlin tram specially adapted to lift and carry people in wheelchairs. Also a 'wheelway', a smooth path routeing around and through cobbled areas

Special notes: Crich houses the largest collection of preserved trams in Europe and has a 1-mile working tramway on which restored electric trams are regularly operated. Special events are arranged at weekends and Bank Holidays throughout the season. Part of tram line occupies route of narrow gauge mineral railway built by George Stephenson

Membership details: From above address

Membership journal: *The Journal* — quarterly

No	Operator	Built
10	Hill of Howth	1902
14	Grimsby & Immingham	1915
15	Sheffield	1874
21	Dundee & District	1894
22	Glasgow	1922
35	Edinburgh	1948
40	Blackpool & Fleetwood	†1914
40	Blackpool	1926
45	Southampton	1903
46	Sheffield	1899
(47)	New South Wales Govt	1885
49	Blackpool	1926
52	Gateshead & District	*1901
59	Blackpool	*1902
60	Johannesburg	1905
68	Paisley & District	1919
74	Sheffield	1900
76	Leicester	1904
102	Newcastle	1901
106	London County Council	1903
132	Kingston-upon-Hull	§1910
166	Blackpool	1927
167	Blackpool	1928
180	Leeds	1931
180	Prague	1908
189	Sheffield	1934
264	Sheffield	1937
273	Oporto	—
298	Blackpool	*1937
331	Metropolitan Electric	1930
345	Leeds	*—
399	Leeds	1926
510	Sheffield	1950
600	Leeds	1931/54
602	Leeds	1953
674	New York 3rd Avenue Transit	1939
812	Glasgow	1900
869	Liverpool	1936
902	Halle	
1100	Glasgow	1928
1105	Glasgow	1929
1147	Hague	1957
1282	Glasgow	1940
1297	Glasgow	1948
1622	London Transport	1912
3006	Berlin	1969
—	London Tramways	c1895

*stored off-site
†on loan to Blackpool
§on loan to Hull Museum of Transport

Note: In addition to the trams (including examples from Czechoslovakia, Germany, The Netherlands, Portugal, USA and South Africa) — about a third of which have been restored to working order — there are a number of Works Cars not listed

England

Member: HRA

The site as a whole is known as the Darlington Railway Centre and Museum, and is owned by Darlington Borough Council. Within the site are four separate buildings. The former North Road Station is run as a museum by the council. Darlington Railway Preservation Society occupies the former Stockton & Darlington Railway North Road Goods and the former S&DR Hopetown Carriage Works is divided between the A1 Steam Locomotive Trust and the North Eastern Locomotive Preservation Group. Darlington Model Railway Club occupies the former Goods Offices.

All organisations except the Model Railway Club are members of the HRA.

The Ken Hoole Study Centre houses a collection of reference material on the railways of north-east England including the library of the North Eastern Railway Association (access by appointment).

Northern train services provide a link to Darlington's main line station and to Shildon, for 'Locomotion' and the Timothy Hackworth Museum

Museum Manager: Bob Clark

Location: North Road Station, Darlington, County Durham DL3 6ST. Approximately three-quarters of a mile north of town centre, off North Road (A167)

OS reference: NZ 289157

Telephone: (01325) 460532

Internet address: *Web site:* www.drcm.org.uk

Car park: At museum site

Access by public transport: Rail services to Darlington North Road station. Local bus services along North Road

Catering facilities: Buffet open 10.00-14.30 daily. Vending machines at other times

On site facilities: Souvenir and bookshop, toilets, meeting room

Public opening: Daily 10.00-17.00 (except 25/26 December and 1 January). Days and times may be subject to amendment

Locomotives

Name	No	Origin	Class	Type	Built
Locomotion	1	S&DR	—	0-4-0	1825
Derwent	25	S&DR	—	0-6-0	1845
—	1463	NER	1463	2-4-0	1885
—	910	NER	901	2-4-0	1875
Blue Peter	60532	LNER	A2	4-6-2	1948
—	2392	NER	P3	0-6-0	1923

Name	No	Builder		Type	Built
—	—	Bagnall (2898)		0-4-0F	1948

Stock

1 North Eastern Railway Coach body (c1860)
1 Chaldron wagon
1 BR Mk 1 BFK carriage, No 17023, built 1961

Owners

Locomotion, Derwent, and 1463 are all on loan from the National Railway Museum, along with the coach body
60532 and 2392 are on loan via the North Eastern Locomotive Preservation Group

Darlington Railway Preservation Society

Member: HRA

Internet address: *Web site:* www.drps.visit.ws

Locomotives

Name	No	Origin	Class	Type	Built
—	78018	BR	2MT	2-6-0	1954

Industrial locomotives

Name	No	Builder	Type	Built
—	2	RSH (7925)	0-4-0DM	1959
—	1	Peckett (2142)	0-4-0ST	1953
David Payne	185	Fowler (4110006)	0-4-0DM	1950
Smiths Dock Co Ltd	—	Fowler (4200018)	0-4-0DM	1947
—	—	GEC	4wE	1928
—	—	R/Hornsby (279591)	0-4-0DE	1949
—	—	R/Hornsby*	4wDM	—
—	—	R/Hornsby*	4wDM	—
—	—	R/Hornsby*	4wDM	—
—	—	RSH	0-6-0T	1938

*1ft 6in gauge

Stock

Various wagons, steam and diesel cranes

A1 Steam Locomotive Trust

Member: HRA

Locomotives

Name	No	Origin	Class	Type	Built
Tornado	60163	A1SLT	8P6F	4-6-2	Under construction

Special events: Contact for details, details will appear on the web site, or write or telephone
Facilities for disabled: Access to main museum building for wheelchairs. Disabled person's toilet. Parking spaces for disabled in forecourt
Membership details: Friends of Darlington Railway Museum, Darlington Railway Preservation Society, A1 Steam Locomotive Trust and North Eastern Locomotive Preservation Group.

All can be contacted via the museum. Members of these organisations and registered supporters of the A1 Trust, members of the Museums Association and holders of HRA InterRail passes all receive free admission except on Thomas and Santa days
Note: The A1 Steam Locomotive Trust's part of the Carriage Works, where they are building a new Peppercorn Pacific, *Tornado*, is generally open to the public on

Saturdays. The Goods Shed and part of the Carriage Works are occupied by the North Eastern Locomotive Preservation Group. Towards the end of 2007 they will start the heavy overhaul of No 2392. They are currently working on the J72. The workshop is open only by appointment. Visitors are welcome at all buildings on the site, but are strongly advised to make arrangements in advance for all buildings other than the main station itself

---

Timetable Service	Dartmoor Railway	Devon

Member: HRA

Dartmoor Railway is a very young railway as far as tourism is concerned although the railway has been in existence for 140 years as the Southern Railway main line from Waterloo to Plymouth. The line only survived because of ballast supplies from Meldon Quarry. Dartmoor Railway is now part of the ECT Group offering a unique experience which encompasses access to Dartmoor National Park for everyone including the disabled and cyclists. Views of Meldon Quarry and workings from the Cycle Route. Far reaching views at Meldon of DArtmoor, Exmoor and surrounding areas. Meldon visitor shows a history of the railways and tramways of Dartmoor. Okehampton station has been restored to the 1950s style

Headquarters: Dartmoor Railway Ltd, Okehampton Station, Okehampton, Devon EX20 1EJ

Telephone: 01837 55637

Fax: 01837 54588

Internet addresses: *E-mail:* info@dartmoorrailway.co.uk
Web site: www.dartmoorrailway.co.uk

General Manager: Stuart Farmer

Main station: Okehampton, access by road, rail (very restricted service), bus, or National Cycle Route 237 and other footpaths. Ample free parking, including coaches

Other public stations: Meldon for Meldon Viaduct and Dartmoor

Locomotives and multiple-units (in use as hauled stock)

Name	No	Origin	Class	Type	Built
Bluebell Mel	08937	BR	08	0-6-0DE	1962
—	31425	BR	31	A1A-A1A	1960
—	37198	BR	37	Co-Co	1964
—	37905	BR	37	Co-Co	1963
unit 205028	60146	BR	205	DMBS	1957
unit 205028	60673	BR	205	DMBS	1957
unit 205028	60827	BR	205	DTC	1957
unit 205032	60150	BR	205	DMBS	1957
unit 205032	60677	BR	205	DMBS	1957
unit 205032	60831	BR	205	DTC	1957
unit 1198	61736	BR	411 / 3CEP	DMSO	
unit 1198	61737	BR	411 / 3CEP	DMSO	
unit 1198	70573	BR	411 / 3CEP	DBC	
unit 412	70826	BR	438 / 4TC	DTSO	1967
unit 412	70860	BR	438 / 4TC	DTSO	1967
unit 412	76301	BR	438 / 4TC	DTSO	1967
unit 412	76302	BR	438 / 4TC	DTSO	1967
—	69332	BR	423 / 4VEP	TRB	1969
—	69310	BR	422	TRBS	1965
—	61742	BR			
—	61743	BR			
—	76812	BR	421 / 4CIG	DTCSOL	

Industrial locomotives

Name	No	Builder	Type	Built
—	S103*	H/Clarke (1864)	0-6-0T	1952
Darfield No 1	—	Hunslet (3783)	0-6-0ST	1953
Flying Falcon	MSC 0256*		Fowler 0-6-0DE	

*undergoing restoration, expected to enter service in 2007

Stock

ex-BR Mk 1s RBR: 1691; FO *Rosemary*
ex-BR Mk 2s TSO 5920, 6002, 6181; FO 3353, 3354, 3387, 3402, 3411, 3425; RBR 1213; BSO 9492, 9501
ex-BR Mk 3 sleeping cars 10518, 10595, 10611;
1 ex-BR sleeping car 10000; function coach, converted from 99622;
Selection of maintenance vehicles including horsebox S96300 converted to Generator coach for 'Dartmoor Belle'

National park, access only by rail and National Cyclepath. Sampford Courtenay has access by road or rail, limited free parking
Access by public transport: Bus all year, check with Traveline 0870 6082608 for availability. Trains from Exeter (Sunday Rover) late May to late September
Refreshment facilities: Okehampton buffet open daily all year. Meldon buffet open at weekends all year and other times when trains are running. Both buffets are fully licensed
Model & Gift shops: Extensive model and gift shop at Okehampton, some gifts also available at Meldon buffet (tel: 01837 55637
Depot: Meldon Quarry, no public access. Viewing only from National Cyclepath
Length of line: 15.5 miles from Coleford Junction-Meldon Quarry
Passenger trains: Services operate every weekend throughout the year,

Owners
Class 205 units stored on behalf of Porterbrook Leasing Co
31425, 37198 and 37905 the 37 Group
Unit 1198 the EMU Preservation Society
Unit 1399 Edward Lloyd
08937 and MSC 0256 Aggregate Industries
Darfield No 1 on loan from Llangollen Railway
61736, 61737 and 70573 the EMU Preservation Society
76301, 76302, 70812, 70860 and 70826 Rolltrack Trains
Groups and individuals own some of the rolling stock

bank holidays, summer half term and school holidays. Closed Christmas Day and Boxing Day. Sunday Rover trains operate between and Okehampton, Crediton and Exeter, late May to late September.
Special events: Wine & Dine trains, Santa and Mince Pie Specials, Halloween and Easter Bunnies. Tel: 01837 55667 for details
Special notes: Visits for special interest groups and education tours may be arranged. Trains are

available for private hire or corporate function. Trains have facilities to carry bicycles free, dogs also carried free
Facilities for disabled: Full disabled facilities and access at Okehampton, partial access to inside Meldon buffet. Toilets at Okehampton and Meldon are RADAR key operated
Membership details: Friends of Dartmoor Railway c/o Okehampton station. Various discounts available
Membership journal: Quarterley, also available to purchase

Timetable Service	Dean Forest Railway	Glos

Member: HRA, TT
Passenger services operate between Norchard and Lydney Junction (Severn & Wye Joint), and Norchard and Parkend.The line boasts five level crossings, three of which are manually operated
Location: Headquarters at Norchard station on the B4234. Signposted off the A48 Lydney bypass to town centre whence B4234 commences
OS reference: SO 629044
Operating society/organisation: Dean Forest Railway Society in conjunction with owning company, Forest of Dean Railway Ltd
Telephone: (01594) 843423 information line; (01594) 845840 (daytime)
Internet address: Web site:

Locomotives and multiple-units

Name	No	Origin	Class	Type	Built
—	28	TVR	O1	0-6-2T	1897
—	5538±	GWR	4575	2-6-2T	1928
—	5541	GWR	4575	2-6-2T	1928
—	9681	GWR	5700	0-6-0PT	1949
—	03128	BR	03	0-6-0DM	1960
Charlie	13308	BR	08	0-6-0DE	1956
—	08734	BR	08	0-6-0DE	1960
Gladys§	D3937	BR	08	0-6-0DE	1960
—	D9555	BR	14	0-6-0DH	1965
—	27066	BR	27	Bo-Bo	1962
—	D7633	BR	25	Bo-Bo	1965
—	D5634	BR	31	A1A-A1A	1960
—	37263	BR	37	Co-Co	1965
—	E6001	BR	73	Bo-Bo	1962
—*	73002	BR	73	Bo-Bo	1962
—§	E6005	BR	73	Bo-Bo	1962
—§	E6006	BR	73	Bo-Bo	1962
The Royal Alex	73101†	BR	73	Bo-Bo	1965
—	50619	BR	108	DMBS	1958
—	51914	BR	108	DMS	1960

50

England

www.deanforestrailway.co.uk

Car park: Norchard only, adequate for cars and coaches. No parking at other stations

Access by public transport: Main line station at Lydney. Stagecoach Red & White buses (service 73 Monday-Saturday) Gloucester-Lydney-Chepstow

On site facilities: Shop at Norchard with museum, riverside walk and forest walks

Catering facilities: Hot and cold meals at Coaches Café on Norchard platform on service days. Parties catered for by appointment. Sunday lunchtime service by 'Royal Forester' first class dining car service, runs on selected Sundays in season, advance booking essential

Length of line: 4.25 miles

Public opening: Daily for static display — shop and museum, open every Saturday and Sunday 11.00-16.00 and weekdays late March to Christmas.

Steam train rides (some supported by heritage DMUs). All Sundays 18 March then 1 April to 28 October; Good Friday, Easter Saturday and all Bank Holiday Sundays and Mondays (Christmas excepted). Wednesdays June to September. Thursdays in August.

Heritage DMU or main line diesel service operates alone most Saturdays June, July and September, plus Tuesdays in August

Special events: Day out with Thomas — 12-15 April, 31 May to 3 June, 30 August to 2 September; GWR Auto Train Days — 13 May, 10 June, 15 July, 4 August, 16 September (all tbc); Diesel days — 16 June, 14 July, 29 September; 1940 Wartime Weekend — 22/23 September; Santa Specials — 8/9, 15/16, 22-24 December

Facilities for disabled: Access to museum, shop, toilets and trains

Membership details: Mr R. Bramwell, 4 Poole Ground, Highnam, Gloucester GL2 8NA and web site

Membership journal: *Forest Venturer* — half yearly

Marketing name: The Friendly Forest Line — re-creating the railway heritage of the Royal Forest of Dean

Name	No	Origin	Class	Type	Built
—	56492	BR	108	DTC	1960
—	56495	BR	108	DTC	1960
—	62364	BR	421	MBSO	
—	62378	BR	421	MBSO	
—	70273	BR	411	TSOL	
—	76726	BR	421	DTCSoL	
—	76740	BR	421	DTCSoL	
—	76797	BR	421	DTCSoL	
—	76811	BR	421	DTCSoL	

§on loan to Severn Valley Railway
†on loan to Avon Valley Railway
*mobile stores vehicle
±dismantled awaiting restoration

Industrial locomotives

Name	No	Builder	Type	Built
—	—	Barclay (2221)	0-4-0ST	1946
Uskmouth No 1	—	Peckett (2147)	0-4-0ST	1952
Wilbert	—	Hunslet (3806)	0-6-0ST	1953
Warrior	—	Hunslet (3823)	0-6-0ST	1954
—	—	Hunslet (2145)	0-4-0DM	1940
—	—	Fowler (4210127)	0-4-0DM	1957
—	—	Hibberd (3947)	4wPM	1960

Stock

2 ex-GWR coaches; 10 ex-BR coaches; 1 DFR constructed Cafeteria coach (static at Norchard), 3 Wickham trolleys; 1 steam crane Thos Smith (Rodley) TS 5027 (10ton); Booth 15-24 tonne diesel-hydraulic crane, Cowans & Sheldon 30-ton diesel crane (ADRC 96101), Schöma p-way tram and trailer

Owners

28 the National Railway Museum
5541 the Forest Prairie Fund
9681 the Dean Forest Locomotive Group
03128, 13308, D3937, 08734, 27066, D5634, D7633, E6001, 73002, E6005, E6006 and 73101 the Dean Forest Diesel Association
37263 the 37362 Locomotive Group
Class 108 DMUs the Dean Forest DMU Group

Steam Centre — Derwent Valley Light Railway — North Yorkshire

Member: TT

The DVR's most notable fact about its history is that it was never nationalised. Private from its inception until the final section was closed in the late 1980s. The line was mothballed until 1989 when it was transformed into a cycleway by Sustrans. A half-mile section adjacent to the Yorkshire Museum of Farming was donated to the museum along with the most necessary Light Railway Order.

Location: Murton Park, Murton Lane, Murton, Nr York YO19 5UF

Operating society/organisation: Derwent Valley Light Railway Society

Telephone: (01904) 489966

Internet address: *e-mail:* jdunn@murphysden.karoo.co.uk *web site:* www.dvlr.org.uk

OS reference: SE 651537

On site facilities: Refreshments, souvenir shop (Yorkshire Museum of Farming)

Car park: Free, on site

Length of line: Half-mile

Access by public transport: York-Stamford Bridge and York-Hull bus services from York main line station. (Tel: 0870 608 2608 or

Locomotives

Name	No	Origin	Class	Type	Built
—	03079	BR	03	0-6-0DM	1960

Industrial locomotives

Name	No	Builder	Type	Built
—	8	A/Barclay (2369)	0-4-0ST	1955
—	65	H/Clarke (1631)	0-6-0T	1929
—	—	Fowler (4200022)	0-4-0DM	1948
Churchill	—	Fowler (410005)	0-4-0DM	1947
Jim	—	R/Hornsby (417892)	4wDM	1959
—	97088	R/Hornsby (466630)	4wDM	1962
British Sugar York	—	R/Hornsby (327964)	0-4-0DM	1953

Rolling stock

1 NER coach, 1 NER coach body, 1 Swiss-style coach (built in 2003), 12 various freight wagons, and 1 steam rail crane

www.yorkshiretravel.net)

Souvenir shops: Within the Yorkshire Museum of Farming, and a railway souvenir shop within the station (open when trains running). Once the entrance fee to the Yorkshire Museum of Farming has been paid train rides are free

Facilities for disabled: Toilets, ramped ways, etc

Public opening: Open daily mid-February-end October, for the Yorkshire Museum of Farming,

Danelaw (Viking) Village and the Derwent Valley Light Railway. Trains operate Sundays and Bank Holidays Easter-end September and for Santa Specials

Special events: Santa Special — weekends and certain weekdays in December

Membership details: Val Tasker, 28 St Anns Square, Headingley, Leeds LS2 2UF

Society journal: *DVLR News* (quarterly)

Railway Centre — Devon Railway Centre — Devon

The Devon Railway Centre features a lovingly restored Victorian Great Western Railway station together with historic locomotives, carriages and wagons as featured on TV. Unlimited passenger rides can be taken on the 2ft gauge railway and miniature railways. There is also a large model railway exhibition featuring 15 working layouts including Polchester and Chiltern Green. New for 2007 — Edwardian model village. All-inclusive admission price

Location: Alongside Bickleigh Bridge over the River Exe on the A396, four miles south of Tiverton

Industrial locomotives (2ft gauge)

Name	No	Builder	Type	Built
Pixie	—	K/Stuart (4260)	0-4-0ST	1922
—	—	O&K (5744)	0-4-0WT	1912
Horatio	—	R/Hornsby (217967)	4wDM	1942
Pen-yr-Orsedd	—	R/Hornsby (235711)	4wDM	1945
Ruston	—	R/Hornsby (418770)	4wDM	1957
Claude W. Lane	—†	R/Hornsby (435398)	4wDM	1959
Planet	—	Planet (2201)	4wDM	1939
Lister	—	Lister (6299)	4wPM	1935
—	—	Lister (34025)	4wDM	1949
—	—	Planet (2025)	4wDM	1937
—	—	Kent (1747)	4wPM	1931
Ivor	—	M/Rail (8877)	4wDM	1944
—	—	M/Rail (20073)	4wDM	1950
Sir Tom	—	M/Rail (40s273)	4wDM	1966
—	—*	M/Rail (105H006)	4wDM	1919
—	—	BEV	0-4-0BE	c1970

England

and 10 miles north of Exeter
General Manager: Matthew
Gicquel
Contact address: Devon Railway
Centre, Bickleigh, Nr Tiverton,
Devon EX16 8RG
Telephone: 01884 855671
Internet address: *Web site:*
www.devonrailwaycentre.co.uk
OS reference: SS 938074
Car park: On site
Access by public transport:
Regular bus service from Tiverton
and Exeter, routes 55 and 55A
On site facilities: Passenger-
carrying line, large model railway
exhibition, restored GWR station,
standard gauge static display,
historic narrow gauge collection,
miniature railway, refreshments and
souvenirs, crazy golf, drive your
own miniature railway. model
village
Length of line: Half mile, 2ft
gauge; half mile 7.25in gauge,
200yd standard gauge
demonstration line; 100yd 7.25in
gauge drive your own train
Opening times: 10.30-17.00.
6 April until 28 October. Daily 6-22
April, 23 May-9 September, 20-28
October (closed Mondays in June).
Wed-Sun 9-20 May, 12-
30 September. Sat/Sun in October.
Special events: Gala weekend —
4/5 August; Santa Specials —
phone for further details

Pixie on hire from Leighton Buzzard Railway for 2007, March until
September
†2ft 9in gauge
*3ft gauge

Industrial locomotives (standard gauge)

Name	No	Builder	Type	Built
Boris	1	Baguley (3357)	0-4-0DM	1952

Locomotive notes: In 2007 passenger trains will be hauled by either *Pixie*,
Ivor, Ruston or *Horatio*. It is expected the O&K will enter service in 2007.

Rolling stock: All 2ft gauge unless indicated. Two Alan Keef bogie
passenger coaches, Two Hudson bogie passenger coaches, Hudson 4-wheel
coach, Dinorwic Yellow Coach, 2 slate slab wagons, GWR slate wagon,
7 skip wagons, 4 mine tubs, RAF bomb wagon, Hudson 3-plank wagon,
2 bogie coach chassis. Lochaber incline wagon (3ft gauge), copper mine
tub (20in gauge), Cattybrook brickworks wagon (2ft 10in gauge), assorted
works wagons. Standard gauge: 2 ex-BR Mk 1 coaches, 1 ex-BR BG

Miniature railway locomotives (7.25in gauge)

Name	No	Builder	Type	Built
—	D7011*	Cromar White	Bo-BoBE	1969
—	D7029	Cromar White	Bo-BoPM	1972
(Intercity)	—	—	Bo-BoBE	c1995
—	—	Pfeiferbahn	4wPH	1993
—	—	Chandler	4wBE	1978
—	7	Parkside	4WBER S/O	2002

*rebuilt from petrol to battery power by DRC during 2002
7 is a drive your own train operated by coin in the slot

Rolling stock: 2 sit-in coaches built by DRC, 1 sit-astride coach

---

Steam Centre	**Didcot Railway Centre**	Oxfordshire

Member: HRA, TT
The Great Western Railway was
incorporated in 1835 to build the
railway from Bristol to London and
it was designed and engineered by
Isambard Kingdom Brunel to be
the finest in the land. At Didcot,
half way between Bristol and
London, members of the Great
Western Society have created a
living museum of the GWR. It is
based around the original engine
shed and depot, to which has been
added a typical branch line with a
country station, signalling
demonstrations and re-creation of
Brunel's broad gauge trackwork
and newly built replica of the
locomotive *Fire Fly* dating from
1840. There is a large collection of

Locomotives

Name	No	Origin	Class/Builder	Type	Built
Fire Fly	—†	GWR	'Fire Fly'	2-2-2	2005
	22	GWR	Diesel Railcar	1A-A1	1940
County of Glamorgan	1014§	GWR	'County'/GWS	4-6-0	
—	1338	GWR	Kitson (3799)	0-4-0ST	1898
			(Cardiff Rly)		
Trojan	1340	GWR	Avonside	0-4-0ST	1897
			(1380)		
—	1363	GWR	1361	0-6-0ST	1910
—	3650	GWR	5700	0-6-0PT	1939
—	3738	GWR	5700	0-6-0PT	1937
—	3822	GWR	2884	2-8-0	1940
Pendennis Castle	4079	GWR	'Castle'	4-6-0	1924
—	4144	GWR	5101	2-6-2T	1946
—	4866	GWR	4800	0-4-2T	1936
Lady of Legend*	2999	GWR	'Saint'/GWS	4-6-0	1929
Earl Bathurst	5051	GWR	'Castle'	4-6-0	1936
—	5322	GWR	4300	2-6-0	1917
—	5572	GWR	4575	2-6-2T	1927

GWR steam locomotives, carriages and wagons. On steamdays the locomotives come to life and you can ride in the 1930s trains on one or both of the demonstration lines. The present Didcot engine shed was built in 1932 and was taken over by the Great Western Society in 1967 when it arrived with just three locomotives, the start of what was to become the Didcot Railway centre, so this year we have a 40 75 celebration during the May Bank Holiday (5-7 May) with visiting locomotives from other railways

General Manager: Michael Dean

Location: Adjacent to main line station, Didcot, Oxfordshire. Access via station subway

OS reference: SU 525907

Operating society/organisation: Great Western Society Ltd, Didcot Railway Centre, Didcot, Oxon OX11 7NJ

Telephone: Didcot (01235) 817200

Internet address: *Web site:* www.didcotrailwaycentre.org.uk

Car park: Didcot station

Access by public transport: Entry is at Didcot Parkway rail station served by First Great Western trains from London (Paddington), the Thames Valley, Oxford, Birmingham, Bristol, etc.

On the A4130 road signed from the M4 motorway (jct 13) and A34

Refreshment facilities: Refreshment room open all days centre is open (lunches, snacks). Picnic area.

Lunch is available in the GWR super-saloon carriages on Mothering Sunday 18 March, Father's Day 17 June, or Victorian Pudding Evenings 19, 26 July (please contact the centre in advance)

On site facilities: GWR locomotive depot, replica GWR station, museum and broad gauge demonstration. Souvenir sales. Rides are available on the demonstration lines on Steamdays.

Admission prices vary according to events and included train rides on Steamdays. Party rates available for more than 15 persons, guided tours, evening visits and special menus for lunch or tea can be arranged. Private steamings when visitors can try their hand at driving locomotives can be arranged

Length of line: 1,000yd

Name	No	Origin	Class/Builder	Type	Built
Hinderton Hall	5900	GWR	'Hall'	4-6-0	1931
King Edward II	6023	GWR	'King'	4-6-0	1930
—	6106	GWR	6100	2-6-2T	1931
—	6697	GWR	5600	0-6-2T	1928
Burton Agnes Hall	6998	GWR	'Hall'	4-6-0	1949
—	7202	GWR	7200	2-8-2T	1934
Cookham Manor	7808	GWR	'Manor'	4-6-0	1938
—	D3771	BR	08	0-6-0DE	1959
Pontyberem	2	Burry Port & Gwendraeth Valley Rly		0-6-0ST	1900
Shannon	5	Wantage Tramway		0-4-0WT	1857

†broad gauge reconstruction of 1840 design
*under construction using frames of No 4942 *Maindy Hall*
§under construction using frames of No 7927 *Willington Hall*

Industrial locomotives

Name	No	Builder	Type	Built
Bonnie Prince Charlie	1	RSH (7544)	0-4-0ST	1949
—	26	Hunslet (5238)	0-6-0DH	1962

Locomotive notes: Locomotives available in 2007 should be: *Fire Fly*, 22, 1338, 1340, 3822, 4144, 5051. Locomotives under restoration include: 3650, 4079, 5322, 6023, 7202. 4079 was repatriated from Australia in 2000

Stock
Over 40 ex-GWR coaches are preserved along with numerous ex-GWR freight wagons

Owner
5 on loan from the National Railway Museum

Public opening: Saturdays and Sundays through out the year. Daily 31 March-15 April, 26 May-3 June, 23 June-2 September, 20-28 October, 27 December to 1 January 2008.
Weekends and Steamdays March to October — open 10.00-17.00 (10.00-16.00 midweek and January, February, November and December). Closed Christmas Day and Boxing Day.
Steamdays: Sundays 18 March, 1 April, 6-9 April, all Saturdays, Sundays and public holidays 28 April to 20 September, Wednesdays 25 July to 29 August and half term 24 October

Train rides: On Steamdays there is normally continuous operation of the passenger train, interrupted by Travelling Post Office demonstrations and turning of the locomotives on some days

Special events: Day out with Thomas — 2-4 March, 5-7 October; 40 75 Anniversary — 5-7 May; Family Activity Steamdays — 28/29 July; Broad gauge *Fire Fly* steamings — 30 June-1 July; 25 July, 1 August; Late Summer Holiday Victorian Weekend — 25-27 August; Artists and Modellers Weekend (with Pendon Museum) — 29/30 September; Halloween Steam — 27/28 October; Thomas Santa Special — 8/9, 14-16, 21-24 December; New Year Steaming — 1 January 2008

Facilities for disabled: Visitors are advised that there is an awkward flight of steps at the entrance, with level access within the centre (help can normally be given with prior advice)

Special facilities: Railway Experience days offer the chance to be an engine driver for a day and a Day at Didcot offers a guided tour on normal steamdays. Special steamings can be arranged for for group and party visits

Membership details: Charles Roberts, at above address

Membership journals: *Great Western Echo* — quarterly; *National Newsletter* — seven times annually

Note: Children under 12 must be accompanied by an adult

A head-on shot of one of the Great Western Railway's heavy freight locomotives. No 3822 stands at the head of a demonstration goods train at the Didcot Railway Centre. *Alan Barnes*

England

East Anglia Transport Museum

Member: TT

The East Suffolk Light Railway is the title given to the 2ft gauge railway, which winds its way 300yd or so along the northern perimeter of the museum site, between the stations of Chapel Road and Woodside. The railway commenced operation in 1973 and aims to re-create a typical passenger-carrying light railway of years gone by. Many aspects of railway interest can be found along its length. The track came from Leziate sand quarry and Canvey Island, as well as from the Southwold Railway, and signals from various local locations; all of which help to set the overall scene

Location: Carlton Colville, three miles south-west of Lowestoft in Suffolk

OS reference: TM 505903

Operating society/organisation: East Anglia Transport Museum Society Ltd, Chapel Road, Carlton Colville, Lowestoft, Suffolk NR33 8BL

Telephone: (01502) 518459

Internet address: *Web site:* www.eatm.org.uk

Car park: Adjacent

Access by public transport: First Eastern Counties 111, 112 and X2 (Monday-Saturday); First Eastern Counties X71 (Sundays and Bank Holidays) from Lowestoft. Main line rail, Oulton Broad South (1.5 miles) then Ambassador bus 606, 607, 608 or 609

On site facilities: Refreshments, picnic areas, souvenir and bookshop, toilets (including disabled), working transport museum, including trams, narrow gauge railway, trolleybuses, steamrollers and other commercial and public transport vehicles. Unlimited free rides

Public opening: Sundays and Bank Holidays (11.00-17.00) April until end of September. Also Saturdays (14.00-17.00) June to September. Midsummer opening, daily (except Mondays) 17 July to 31 August (14.00-17.00).

Last admission 1 hour before closing

Special events: Please phone for details

Special notes: Limited facilities for the disabled. Pre-booked party rates

Membership details: From the above address

Industrial locomotives

Name	No	Builder	Type	Built
Aldeburgh	2	M/Rail (5912)	4wDM	1934
Leiston	4	R/Hornsby (177604)	4wDM	1936
Orfordness	5	M/Rail (22209)	4wDM	1964
Thorpeness	6	M/Rail (22211)	4wDM	1964

Trams

No	Trucks	Body	Date	Operator
11	Maley & Taunton	E/Electric	1939	Blackpool Corp
14	Brill	Milnes	1904	Lowestoft Corp
159	Preston McGuire	Blackpool Corp	1927	Blackpool Corp
474	Beijnes	Beijnes	1929	Amsterdam
1858	EMB	E/Electric	1930	London Transport

Stock

Locally designed and built covered coach, plus combined coach and brake van, suitable for wheelchairs. Small selection of wagons. Van body ex-Southwold Railway

East Anglian Railway Museum

Member: HRA, TT, AIM, EETB, EATL

Adjacent to Chappel Viaduct which is the most spectacular railway structure in East Anglia

Location: Chappel & Wakes Colne Station, near Colchester

OS reference: TL 898289

Operating society/organisation: East Anglian Railway Museum, Chappel & Wakes Colne Station, Station Road, Wakes Colne, Essex CO6 2DS. Registered charity No 1001579

Locomotives and multiple-units

Name	No	Origin	Class	Type	Built
A. J. Hill	69621†	GER	N7	0-6-2T	1924
—	D2279	BR	04	0-6-0DM	1960
—	50599	BR	108	DMBS	1958
—	54223	BR	108	DTCL	1959
—	51213	BR	101	DMBS	1959
—	51505	BR	101	DMC	1959
—	56358	BR	101	DTC	1959
—	54365	BR	101	DTCL	1958

† on loan to North Norfolk Railway

Telephone: Colchester (01206) 242524
Fax: 01787 224473
Internet address: *e-mail:* information@earm.co.uk
Web site: www.earm.co.uk
Car park: On site
Access by public transport: 'one' Great Eastern Chappel & Wakes Colne station. Also Eastern National/Hedingham Omnibus service No 88 Colchester-Halstead (hourly). Sundays Eastern National No 88C Colchester-Halstead (every 2 hours)
On site facilities: Refreshments, bookshop, museum, signalboxes, souvenir shop, picnic area, miniature railway and toilets
Public opening:
Daily 10.00-16.30 or dusk
Special events: DMU Day, 40th anniversary of closure of Cambridge to Sudbury line — 10/11 March; Day out with Thomas — 6-9 April; Railway Experience Course — 5 May; Steam Day, Spanning the Century — 6/7 May; Ivor the Engine — 26-28 May; Railway Experience Course — 2 June; Steam Day — 3 June; 8th Cider Festival — 7-10 June; Railway Experience Course, plus Railwayana and book sale — 30 June/1 July; Railway Experience Course — 4 August; Steam Day — 5 August; Day out with Thomas — 24-27 August; 21st Chappel Beer Festival — 4-8 September; Railway

Industrial locomotives

Name	No	Builder	Type	Built
Jubilee	—	Bagnall (2542)	0-4-0ST	1936
Name	No	Builder	Type	Built
—	11	Barclay (1047)	0-4-0ST	1905
Belvoir	—	Barclay (2350)	0-6-0ST	1954
Jeffery	2039	Peckett (2039)	0-4-0ST	1943
Penn Green	54	RSH (7031)	0-6-0ST	1941
—	AMW144	Barclay (333)	0-4-0DM	1938
—	23	Fowler (4220039)	0-4-0DH	1965
—	2029	Simplex (2029)	0-4-0PM	1920

Stock
4 ex-BR Mk 1 coaches (TSO, BCK, SK, BS), 1 ex-LNER TSO coach; 1 fully restored GER 6-wheel full brake; 1 GER fully restored 4-wheel coach; 1 ex-GER bogie coach; 1 SR PMV; 1 ex-BR 13-ton open wagon; 2 ex-BR 16-ton mineral wagons; 1 Lowmac wagon; 1 ex-LMS 12-ton open wagon; 1 Wickham Trolley; 1 GWR Toad brake van; 1 ex-BR brake van; Somersham 'pump' trolley, 1 Grafton steam crane, 1 LMS 5 plank wagon, 1 BR cattle van (on loan ex-NRM), 1 BR special cattle van, 1 tube wagon, 1 Pooley van, 1 LNER fish van, 1 BR box van, 2 tank wagons, 1 Molasses tank wagon

Experience Course — 6 October; Steam Day — 7 October; Railway Experience Course — 27 October; Steam Day & Diesel — 28 October; Day out with Thomas with Santa — 15/16, 22/23 December
Family tickets: Available on all days (unlimited rides on steam days)
Special notes: Steam days as in Special Events list. Driver experience courses available on a number of dates throughout 2007; please phone for details or book online at http://www.earm.co.uk
Three restored signalboxes, large goods shed and restoration shed. Original Victorian country junction station. Schools days and Santa steamings. Disabled visitors welcome — prior advice appreciated. Guided tours by prior arrangement. Light refreshments daily
Membership details: Membership Secretary, 50 Ayr Way, Rise Park, Romford, Essex RM1 4UII
Membership journal: *Stour Valley Steam* — 3 times/year

Timetable Service	East Kent Railway	Kent

Member: HRA
The East Kent Light Railway Society was formed in 1985 with the aim of preserving the remaining 2-mile section of the Colonel Stephens light railway which originally ran from Shepherdswell to Wingham. Passenger-carrying operations between Shepherdswell and Eythorne started during 1995, and 1996 saw the first steam on the line for over 30 years. The extension to Wigmore Lane opened in August 2005 and is used on some special events
Location: Station Road, Shepherdswell, Dover, Kent CT15 7PD

Locomotives and multiple-units

Name	No	Origin	Class	Type	Built
—	09025	BR	09	0-6-0DE	1961
—	53256	M/Cam	101	DMBS	1957
—	54343	M/Cam	101	DTC(L)	1958
—	65373*	BR	2EPB/416	DMBS	1953
—	77558*	BR	2EPB/416	DTS	1953
—	68001	BR	MLV/419	MLV	1959
—	68002	BR	MLV/419	MLV	1959
—	61229†	BR	412/CEP	DMSO(A)	c1956
—	61230†	BR	412/CEP	DMSO(A)	c1956
—	69345†	BR	412/BEP	TSRB	c1956
—	70235†	BR	412/CEP	TBCK	c1956
—	60154§	BR	205	DMBS	1957
—	60800§	BR	205	DTCL	1957
—	10096	SR	4COR		
—	11161	SR	4COR		
—	11825	SR	4COR		

57

Internet address: Web site:
www.eastkentrailway.com
OS reference: TR 258483
Operating organisation: East Kent
Railway Trust
Car park: Shepherdswell and
Eythorne stations
Access by public transport: Main
line trains to Shepherdswell station
(adjacent) tel: 08457 484950
On site facilities: Light
refreshments, book and souvenir
shop, museum, plus 3.5/5in gauge
steam railway. Picnic area and
toilets. Restored signalbox.
Eythorne: Signalbox and small shop
Public opening: Most weekends
throughout the year for static
displays. Passenger trains — Easter
to September Sundays and Bank
Holidays
Special events: Please contact for
details
Events & site answerphone:
01304 832042
Facilities for disabled: Limited
access to buffet, and platforms at
both stations

§unit No 1101   *unit No 5759   †unit No 7105

Industrial locomotives

Name	No	Builder	Type	Built
Richborough Castle	—	E/Electric (D1197)	0-6-0D	1967
The Buffs	—	R/Hornsby (466616)	0-6-0DH	1961
Snowdon	—	Fowler (416002)	0-4-0DM	1952
St Dunstan	—	Avonside (2004)	0-6-0ST	1927

Rolling stock
Leyland Experimental coach, LMS brake third, LMS full brake (BG), BR
Mk 1s TSO, BR Mk 2 TSO and a selection of freight vehicles including an
SR GUV

Owners
St Dunstan and diesel multiple-units the East Kent Railway Trust
LMS brake third the Walmer Model Railway Group
Leyland Experimental Coach the Nene Valley Railway
EMU vehicles the EPB Preservation Group
4COR vehicles the Southern Electric Group

Membership details: EKR
Membership Secretary,
Shepherdswell Station, Dover, Kent
CT15 7PD
Membership journal: *East Kent
Railway News,* 3 times a year

Timetable Service	East Lancashire Railway	Lancashire

Member: HRA, TT
A very popular railway run by the
East Lancs Railway Society in
close co-operation with local
authorities, the line won the 1987
ARPS award. Visit the line to find
out the cause of the line's
popularity and success
Location: Bolton Street Station,
Bury, Lancashire BL9 0EY
OS reference: SD 803109
Publicity Director: Graham
Vevers
Operating society/organisation:
East Lancashire Railway
Preservation Society
Telephone: 0161 764 7790
Internet address: Web site:
www.east-lancs-rly.co.uk
Access by public transport: Main
line services to Manchester, Bolton,
Rochdale and Burnley. Metrolink
from central Manchester to Bury
Interchange. Various bus services
also operate to Bury, Ramsbottom
or Rawtenstall from the main line
stations listed

Locomotives and multiple-units

Name	No	Origin	Class	Type	Built
—	7229	GWR	7200	2-8-2T	1935
—	52322	L&Y	27	0-6-0	1896
—	42765	LMS	5P4F	2-6-0	1927
—	44871	LMS	5MT	4-6-0	1945
—	45337	LMS	5MT	4-6-0	1937
The Lancashire Fusilier	45407	LMS	5MT	4-6-0	1937
Leander	5690	LMS	'Jubilee'	4-6-0	1936
Princess Elizabeth	6201	LMS	'Princess'	4-6-2	1933
—	46428	LMS	2MT	2-6-0	1948
—	47324	LMS	3F	0-6-0T	1926
249 Squadron	34073	SR	BB	4-6-2	1948
Shaw Savill	35009	SR	MN	4-6-2	1945
Duke of Gloucester	71000	BR	8P	4-6-2	1954
—	76079	BR	4MT	2-6-0	1957
—	80097	BR	4MT	2-6-4T	1954
—	11506	BR	01	0-4-0DM	1956
—	D2062	BR	03	0-6-0DM	1959
—	D3232	BR	08	0-6-0DE	1956
—	08445	BR	08	0-6-0DE	1958
—	08479	BR	08	0-6-0DE	1958
—	08944	BR	08	0-6-0DE	1962
—	D9531	BR	14	0-6-0DH	1965
—	D8233	BR	15	Bo-Bo	1959
—	20087	BR	20	Bo-Bo	1961

On site facilities: Refreshments normally available when trains are running. Buffet car service on most trains. Souvenir shop, transport museum

Length of line: Approximately 12 miles

Public opening: Steam- and diesel-hauled services operate on Saturdays, Sundays and Bank Holidays throughout the year. Santa Specials (advance booking only) in December

Special events: Steam Theme Day— 31 March/1 April; Vintage Motor Bike Rally (at Heywood) — 8 April; Mini Meet (Heywood) — 15 April; Day out with Thomas — 5-7 May; 1940 Wartime Weekend — 26-28 May; Morris Minor Day at Heywood station — 17 June; Steam Event — 23/24 June; Diesel Event — 4-8 July; 20 Years of the ELR — 25-29 July; Day out with Thomas — 3-5 August; Shunter Weekend — 11/12 August; Nuttall Park Event - Teddy Bears' Picnic — 27 August; Diesel Event — 31 August/1 September; LMS Theme Day (all steam) — 8/9 September; Vintage Vehicle Day (Bury) — 9 September; Day out with Thomas — 6/7 October; Steam Event — 27/28 October; Steam Night Rider — 27/28 October; English Electric Theme Day (all diesel) — 10 November; Santa Specials — weekends in December; Irwell Valley Diner, Wine & Dine Trains (advance booking only — please apply for details)

Special Notes: The Society re-opened the Bury-Summerseat-Ramsbottom section in 1987 and the Ramsbottom-Irwell-Rawtenstall section in 1991 with the Bury-Heywood section following in September 2003

Membership details: D. Layland

Membership journal: *The East Lancashire Railway News* — twice yearly

Marketing name: East Lancs

Name	No	Origin	Class	Type	Built
—	D5054	BR	24	Bo-Bo	1960
—	D5705	BR	28	Co-Bo	1958
—	D5600	BR	31	A1A-A1A	1959
—	31467	BR	31	A1A-A1A	1960
—	31556	BR	31	A1A-A1A	1961
—	D7076	BR	35	B-B	1963
—	33109	BR	33	Bo-Bo	1960
—	33117	BR	33	Bo-Bo	1960
—	D335	BR	40	1Co-Co1	1961
—	D345	BR	40	1Co-Co1	1961
Onslaught	D832	BR	42	B-B	1961
3rd Carabinier	45135	BR	45	1Co-Co1	1961
Gateshead	47402	BR	47	Co-Co	1962
Valiant	50015	BR	50	Co-Co	1967
Western Prince	D1041	BR	52	C-C	1962
Royal Scots Grey	55022	BR	55	Co-Co	1961
—	51192	M/Cam	101	DMBS	1958
—	54352	M/Cam	101	DTC (L)	1959
—	51485	Cravens	105	DMBC	1958
—	56121	Cravens	105	DTC	1956
—	60130†	BR	207	DMBS	1962
—	60904†	BR	207	DTS	1962
—	65451	BR	504	DMBS	1958
—	70549	BR	207	TS	1958
—	77172	BR	504	DTS	1958

†unit 207202

Industrial locomotives

Name	No	Builder	Type	Built
Gothenburg	32	H/Clarke (680)	0-6-0T	1903
—	1	Barclay (1927)	0-4-0ST	1927
MR Mercury	1	Hibberd (3438)	4wDM	1950
Winfield	—	M/Rail (9009)	4wDM	1948
—	4002	H/Clarke (D1076)	6wDM	1959

Stock
44 BR Mk 1 coaches; 11 BR Mk 2 coaches, 1 GWR coach; 1 Bogie guard's coach; Cravens 50-ton steam crane RS1013/50 (1930), NER 5-ton hand crane DB915390 (1880) and Smiths 5-ton diesel crane (1939) plus over 80 goods vehicles

Owners
D335 and D345 the Class 40 Preservation Society
D99 and D5705 the Pioneer Diesel Group
6201 the 6201 Princess Elizabeth Locomotive Trust
65451 and 77172 The Class 504 Group
35009, 45407 and 76079 Riley & Sons (Railways)
D5054 the East Lancs Type 2 Group
47402 the Waterman Heritage Trust
50015 the Manchester Class 50 Group
Class 101 on loan from the National Railway Museum
D8233 the Class 15 Preservation Society
D5705 the Co-Bo Locomotive Group
55022 by Martin Walker

East Somerset Railway

Member: HRA

The ESR was created by David Shepherd and his friends in the early 1970s. Cranmore is still one of the few preserved railways offering only steam-hauled trains. The railway seeks to portray a country branch line, and offers a warm and personal welcome to all visitors who want to experience the sights and sounds of the steam era

Contact: Booking Office

Headquarters: East Somerset Railway, Cranmore, Shepton Mallet, Somerset BA4 4QP

OS reference: ST 664429

Telephone: Cranmore (01749) 880417

Fax: (01749) 880764

Internet address: *e-mail:* info@eastsomersetrailway.com *Web site:* www.eastsomersetrailway.com

Main station: Cranmore

Car park: Cranmore — free

Refreshment facilities: The Whistlestop Restaurant at Cranmore offers lunches, snacks, teas, etc. Group catering by arrangement. Picnic areas at Cranmore. Public and private Wine & Dine trains

Souvenir shop: Cranmore

On site facilities: Station shop. David Shepherd Gallery with railway and wildlife prints for sale. Children's play area. Engine shed and workshops open for viewing. Small railway museum

Depot: Engine shed and workshop at Cranmore West (0.25-mile from Cranmore)

Length of line: 2 miles

Locomotives

Name	No	Origin	Class	Type	Built
—	5637	GWR	5600	0-6-2T	1924
—*	B110	LBSCR	E1	0-6-0T	1877
—	30075	JZ	USA	0-6-0T	1950s

Industrial locomotives

Name	No	Builder	Type	Built
Lord Fisher	1398	Barclay (1398)	0-4-0ST	1915
—	705	Barclay (2047)	0-4-0ST	1937
Lady Nan*	1719	Barclay (1719)	0-4-0ST	1920
—	—	Sentinel (10199)	4wDH	1964
—	39	Sentinel (10204)	0-4-0DH	1965

*undergoing overhaul

Stock

Numerous ex-BR Mk 1 coaches; 25 assorted wagons, mostly LMS and SR

Owners

5637 the 5637 loco Group
30075 the Project 62 Group
D3032 on loan from Foster Yeoman
Sentinel (10204) Stratford Railway Society

Passenger trains: Cranmore to Mendip Vale via Cranmore West and Merryfield Lane. Return trip takes c35min. Ticket allows unlimited travel on normal operating days. All trains are steam-hauled

Period of public operation: Sundays in March; weekends and bank holidays in April, May; Wednesdays and weekends in June and July; Wednesdays, Thursdays and weekends in August; weekends in September and October; Sundays, plus 11th, in November. Please call for details and train times. Last admission 30min before closing time

Special events: Please contact for details

Facilities for disabled: All public areas and trains are accessible

Special Notes: Footplate experience courses available, both half day and full day. Please call for availability, prices and brochure. School groups, children's parties, private parties and Wine & Dine by arrangement — please call to discuss your requirements

Membership details: Please call for leaflet

Membership journal: *Cuttings* — 4 per year

Eastleigh Lakeside Steam Railway

Location: Lakeside Country Park, Eastleigh

Headquarters: Eastleigh Lakeside Steam Railway, Lakeside Country Park, Wide Lane, Eastleigh, Hants SO24 5PE

Contact: Clive Upton

Locomotives (10.25/7.25in gauge)

Name	No	Builder	Type	Built
Sandy River	7		2-4-2	1982
The Monach	1001	Bullock	4-6-2	1932
The Empress	1002	Bullock	4-6-2	1933
Rob Roy	70055	Pullen	4-6-2	1948
Sir Nigel Gresley	4498	Kirkland	4-6-2	1964

Above: No 39 is a Sentinel-built 0-4-0DH dating from 1965 and is seen here shunting at Cranmore. Since this photograph was taken corrosion of the shed roof has resulted in its removal. A serious amount of money is required for its reinstatement. *Alan Barnes*

Below: Whitehead, a 1908-built Peckett 0-4-0ST, and on loan from the Midland Railway — Butterley, is seen hauling a short train at Wirksworth on the Ecclesbourne Railway. *Alan Barnes*

Telephone: 023 8061 2020
Fax: 023 8061 2391
Internet address: *e-mail:*
clive@steamtrain.co.uk
Web site: www.steamtrain.co.uk
Car parking: On site
On site facilities: Station café open
daily except 25 December
Length of line: Over 1.25 mile,
7.25in and 10.25in gauges
Period of public operation:
Every weekend, daily July, August
and September and all school
holidays
Special events:
Day out with Thomas — 26 May-3
June, 8/9, 15/16 September, 26
December-2 January 2008;

Name	No	Builder	Type	Built
Sir Arthur Heywood	7	Williamson	2-6-2*	1990
Ernest Henry Upton	1908	G&S Engineering	4-4-2	1937
Eastleigh	D1994	Millard/Mattingley	B-B*	1994
William Baker	4789	Baker	4-4-2*	1947
Francis Henry Lloyd	3	Guest	4-8-4*	1959
Saint-Leonard	1A	Marshall	0-4-0-0-4-0*	2001
Sgt Murphy	—	Marshall	0-6-0T*	
Florence	92	ELR	0-6-0DH	1999
Eurostar	3221	Southampton Uni	Bo-BoBE	
Sanjo	—	Battle	0-4-0*	

*7.25in gauge, remainder 10.25in

Visiting Locomotives Weekends —
5-7 May, 6/7 October;
Double-headed Weekends — 14/15
July, 10/11 November;

Lakeside Fireworks Spectacular —
3 November (trains 18.00-17.30 and
after display; Santa Specials — 9.
15/16, 21-23 December

Steam Centre	# Ecclesbourne Valley Railway	Derbyshire

Member: HRA
Pasenger services commenced on
the Ecclesbourne Valley Railway
on 24 August 2004. The initial
length was just half-a-mile between
Wirksworth and Gorsey Bank level
crossing, but the plan is to reach
Duffield with a main line
connection in a few years. The
track is in situ but requires work to
bring it up to operational standard.
Meanwhile the section from
Wirksworth to Ravenstor, a further
half-mile, opened on 1 September
2005. This incorporates a grade of
1 in 30 and provides access to the
High Peak Trail. It is hoped the
Wirksworth to Idridgehay section
(3 miles) will reopen late summer
leaving a further five miles to be
restored before reaching Duffield
Managing Director:
Martin S. Miller
Headquarters: Wirksworth
Station, Coldwell Street,
Wirksworth, Derbyshire DE4 4FB
Telephone: 01629 823076
Fax: 01629 825922
Internet adresses: *e-mail:*
station@wyvernrail.co.uk
Web sites: www.wyvernrail.co.uk
www.evra.org.uk and
www.mytesttrack.com
Main station: Wirksworth
Other stations: Ravenstor,
Idridgehay (opening 2007), Shottle

Locomotive and multiple-units

Name	No	Origin	Class	Type	Built
—	03084	BR	03	0-6-0DM	1959
Margaret-Ann	D2158	BR	03	0-6-0DM	1960
—	31514	BR	31	A1A-A1A	1961
—	37075	BR	37	Co-Co	1962
—	51073	Gloucester	119	DMBC	1958
—	51360	P/Steel	117	DMBS	1959
—	54289	P/Steel	121	DTS	1959
—	56224	BR	108	DTC(L)	1959
—	55006	Gloucester	122	DMBS	1958
—	59496	P/Steel	117	TCL	1959
—	68500*	BR	489	GLV	1959
—	68506*	BR	489	GLV	1959
—	72501*	BR	491	FO	1973
—	72632*	BR	491	TSH	1973
—	72633*	BR	491	TSH	1973
—	72716*	BR	491	TS	1973
—	72717*	BR	491	TS	1973

*former Gatwick Express hauled-stock

Industrial locomotives

Name	No	Builder	Type	Built
Henry Ellison	—	Barclay (2217)	0-4-0ST	1947
Wee Yorkie	3	Barclay (2360)	0-4-0ST	1954
—	11520	R/Hornsby (319284)	0-4-0DM	1952
Sir Peter & Lady Hilton	—	R/Hornsby (402803)	0-4-0DE	1956
—	—	R/Hornsby (421037)	0-6-0DE	1958
—	—	R/Hornsby (421435)	0-6-0DE	1958
—	—	R/Hornsby (432479)	0-6-0DE	1958

Stock
1 BR Newspaper van (used as DMU support vehicle); 1 Taylor Hubbard
crane and runner wagon. Around 25 wagons for use in maintaining the line,
including examples of Grampus and Dogfish hopper wagons, plus 2

(opening 2008?), Duffield (opening 2009?)

OS references:
Wirksworth (SK 290541),
Ravenstor (SK 287548),
Gorsey Bank (SK 288533),
Idridgehay (SK 290489),
Shottle (SK 304469),
Hazelwood (SK 319449),
Duffield (North) (SK 337439)
Car parking: Wirksworth station
Access by public transport:
Bus –
Derby/Belper/Wirksworth/Matlock/
Bakewell
Location of refreshment facilities:
Wirksworth station
Souvenir shops & museum:
Wirksworth station
Length of line: Approx. 1 mile

Road/Rail vehicles. 5 Permaquip trolleys (3 people carriers, 1 tool carrier. 1 cliper), 3 Ultra Light Rail vehicles

Owners
37075 the 5C Locomotive Group
DMUs by Railcar Enterprises

(4 miles in 2007)
Opening times: Wirksworth station – daily (except Xmas day) 10.00-16.00
Public operation: Weekends March to December. Wednesdays May to September Wirksworth to Ravenstor. Wirksworth to Gorsey Bank on special event days
Facilities for the disabled:
Specially equipped toilets and fully accessible Museum Coach
Special facilities: Up to 40 covers

for meals in the splendid, air-conditioned, former 'Gatwick Express' first open coach. Trains can be run at anytime for the equivalent of 20 adult fares. 'Drive a diesel' experience days available.
Membership details: Ecclesbourne Valley Railway Association, 530 Kedleston Road, Derby DE22 2NG
Membership Journal:
Ecclesbourne Express – quarterly

Eden Valley Railway — Cumbria

Member: HRA
The mothballed Eden Valley Railway between Appleby and Warcop in Cumbria is one step closer to carrying passengers again. The EVR has plans to reopen the 6-mile railway which still connects with the famous Settle and Carlisle line at Appleby.
  Please contact or see web site for further details
Headquarters:
Eden Valley Railway Co and
Eden Valley Railway Trust,
1 Victoria Road, Barnard Castle, Co Durham DL12 8HW
Internet address:
e-mail: admin@evr.org.uk
Web site: www.evr.org.uk
Secretary: Gillian Boyd
Main station: Appleby
OS reference: NY 687208
Car park: Appleby
Access by public transport:
By bus: Stagecoach services from Penrith to Brough (stops at Warcop station (0870 6082608 for details); Carlisle to Eden Valley services (0870 6082608);
K. & B. Bainbridge services from Penrith to Appleby (01768 865446).
By rail: Appleby on the Settle-Carlisle line.
By road: M6 jct 40, A66 east to Warcop (23 miles); M6 jct 38, A685, B6260 to Appleby (20

Locomotives and multiple-units

Name	No	Origin	Class	Type	Built
—	68003	BR	419	MLV	1960
—	68005	BR	419	MLV	1960
—	60108†	BR	205	DMBS	1957
—	60658†	BR	205	DMBS	1957
—	60808†	BR	205	DTC	1957
—	31410*	BR	31	A1A-A1A	1960
—	20169*	BR	20	B0-B0	1966
—	37897	BR	37	C0-C0	1963
—	61798	BR	412	DMSO	1956
—	61799	BR	412	DMSO	1956
—	61804	BR	412	DMSO	1956
—	61805	BR	412	DMSO	1956
—	70229	BR	412	TSOL	1956
—	70539	BR	412	TSOL	1956
—	70354	BR	412	TBCK	1956
—	70607	BR	412	TBCK	1956

†unit 205009
*stored at Kirkby Stephen East station

Industrial locomotives

Name	No	Builder	Type	Built
—	21	Fowler (4220045)	0-4-0DH	1967
—	—	RSH (?????)	0-4-0DH	????

Stock
2 ex-BR Mk 1 coaches; 2 passenger-rated van; 1 rail-mounted 15-ton diesel cranes; selection of wagons for maintenance work

miles); A1 Scotch Corner, A66 west to Warcop (40 miles).
Refreshment facilities: Light refreshments available on open weekends, picnic area
Membership details: Membership

Secretary, EVR Trust, 60 Brisco Meadows, Upperby, Carlisle, Cumbria CA2 4NY

Elsecar Railway Preservation Group

Member: HRA

The Elsecar Railway runs between Elsecar Heritage Centre and the canal basin at Hemingfield, through a scenic conservation area alongside the Elsecar branch of the Dearne & Dove Canal

Location/headquarters: Elsecar Heritage Centre, Wath Road, Elsecar, Barnsley, South Yorkshire S74 8HJ

Telephone: (01226) 746746

Internet address: *Web site:* www.elsecarrailway.cjb.net

Main station: Elsecar

Length of line: 1-mile, 20min journey

Car park location: On site, free

Access by public transport: Main rail line Elsecar from Sheffield, Huddersfield, Leeds

Refreshment facilities: On site

Souvenir shops: On site

On site facilities: Refreshments, antiques centres, crafts and souvenir shop, toilets

Museum: Attractions include Educational Workshops, 'Living History Centre', Bottle Collection, Hot Metal Press, Newcomen Beam

Industrial locomotives

Name	No	Builder	Type	Built
Countess Fitzwilliam	544996	R/Hornsby (382808)	4wDM	1968
Earl Fitzwilliam	1917	Avonside (1917)	0-6-0ST	1923
Earl of Stafford	2895	YEC (2895)	0-6-0DH	1963
Mardy Monster	2150	Peckett (2150)	0-6-0ST	1954
—	10432	Drewry	0-4-0DH	1955
Louise	—	Hunslet (6950)	0-6-0DH	1967
—	—	V/Foundry	0-4-0DM	1945
—	—	NBL (27097	0-4-0DM	1953

Stock

4 ex-BR Mk 1 coaches, 1 Wickham trolley

Engine, working crafts people, various special events. Antiques centre open 7 days a week

Facilities for disabled: There are four disabled persons' toilets at different locations on the site. All buildings are fully wheelchair accessible at ground floor level

Public opening: Site open daily 10.00-17.00. Living History Centre open Tuesday to Sunday 10.30-16.30 (closed Monday except Bank Holidays). Please check for Christmas and New Year openings

The railway operates a public service on Sundays 12.00-16.00 all year, also Halloween and Christmas events, special event days and Bank Holidays

Special events: Include Thomas the Tank Engine, Vintage Weekend, Noddy Family Fun Event, Christmas Fair, Halloween Hauntings and Santa Specials on the railway

Special notes: Free admission to site except for some special events when a charge will be made. Charges apply to Living History Centre, railway and special events

---

Embsay & Bolton Abbey Steam Railway

Member: HRA, TT

Yorkshire's 'Friendly Line' operates from Embsay station built in 1888. The railway is very family-orientated with many events for children. The enthusiast is not forgotten, with one of the finest collections of ex-industrial tank engines in Britain. The railway is currently constructing a new museum and workshop complex, and the line's extension to Bolton Abbey opened in 1997. Bolton Abbey station has been built to the original Midland Railway style. An atmosphere of the rural branch line prevails, which is operated by ex-industrial locomotives

Operating Committee: Vacant

Business & Marketing Manager:

Locomotives and multiple-units

Name	No	Origin	Class	Type	Built
—	D2203	BR	04	0-6-0DM	1952
—	08700	BR	08	0-6-0DE	1960
—	08773	BR	08	0-6-0DE	1960
—	NCB 38 (D9513)	BR	14	0-6-0DH	1964
—	47004	BR	47	Co-Co	1963
—	31119	BR	31	A1A-A1A	1959
—	52005	BR	107	DMBS	1960
—	52012	BR	107	DMC	1960
—	52031	BR	107	DMCL	1960

Industrial locomotives

Name	No	Builder	Type	Built
Annie	9	Peckett (1159)	0-4-0ST	1908
Gladiator	8	H/Clarke (1450)	0-6-0ST	1922
Slough Estates No 5	—	H/Clarke (1709)	0-6-0ST	1939
Ann	—	Sentinel (7232)	4wVB	1927
Beatrice	7	Hunslet (2705)	0-6-0ST	1945

England

Stephen Walker. Tel: 01756 710614
(ext 3). Fax: 01756 710720
Internet address: *Web site:*
www.embsayboltonabbeyrailway.
org.uk
Location: Bolton Abbey Station,
Bolton Abbey, Skipton, Yorkshire
BD23 6AF
OS reference: SE 007533
Operating society/organisation:
Yorkshire Dales Railway Museum
Trust
Telephone: 01756 710614, 24hr
Talking Timetable 01756 795189
Car parks: Embsay and Bolton
Abbey
Access by public transport:
Pennine bus from Skipton, National
Park bus from Ilkley
On site facilities: Souvenir shop at
Bolton Abbey and Embsay —
transport and industrial
archaeological bookshop at Embsay
Catering facilities: Buffet and bar
on most trains. Buffet at both
Bolton Abbey and Embsay stations.
Special charters can be arranged,
meals for parties can be arranged on
normal service trains, subject to
advance booking, please write for
further details
Length of line: 4.5 miles
Public opening: Steam trains run
every Sunday throughout the year,
weekends from April to October,
Tuesdays in June, early July,
September and 1 June; 11/12, 18/19
July; 5/6 September; 26, 30
December. Daily from 13 July
(except 20 July), until the end of
August. Steam also operates
February and October half term
Wednesdays. DMU service 22/23,
25/26 October.
Additional services operated by
DMUs on Sundays in June, July,
August and September
Special events: Diesel Weekend —
24/25 March; Day out with Thomas
— 6-9 April; Ivor the Engine
Events — 5-7 May; Day out with
Thomas — 26-28 May; Scale Rail
Weekend — 21/22 July; Day out
with Thomas — 25-27 August;
1940s Weekend — 15/16
September; Harvest of Steam — 6/7

Name	No	Builder	Type	Built
Airedale	3	Hunslet (1440)	0-6-0ST	1923
York No 1	—	Yorkshire (2474)	0-4-0ST	1949
Illingworth	—	H/Clarke (1208)	0-6-0ST	1916
—	140	H/Clarke (1821)	0-6-0T	1948
Spitfire	S112	Hunslet (2414)	0-6-0ST	1942
Wheldale	S134	Hunslet (3168)	0-6-0ST	1944
Sir Robert Peel	8	Hunslet (3776)	0-6-0ST	1952
—	69	Hunslet (3785)	0-6-0ST	1953
Monkton No 1	—	Hunslet (3788)	0-6-0ST	1953
—	22	Barclay (2320)	0-4-0ST	1952
—	68005	RSH (7169)	0-6-0ST	1945
Thomas	4	RSH (7661)	0-4-0ST	1950
H. W. Robinson	—	Fowler (4100003)	0-4-0DM	1946
—	—	Fowler (4200003)	0-4-0DM	1948
—	MDE15	B/Drewry (2136)	4wDM	1938
—	887	R/Hornsby (394009)	4wDM	1955
—	—	Wickham (7610)	2w-2PMR	1957
—	—	R/Hornsby	4wDM	1957
—	—	R/Hornsby (394009)	4wDM	1955
Meaford	—	Barclay (440)	0-4-0DH	1958
—	36	H/Clarke (D1037)	0-6-0DM	1958

The following are 2ft gauge

—	—	Lister (9993)	4wPM	1938
—	—	Lister (10225)	4wPM	1938
—	—	R/Hornsby (175418)	4wDM	1936
—	—	R/Hornsby	4wDM	—
—	—	M/Rail (8979)	4wDM	1946
—	—	M/Rail (5213)	4wDM	1930
—	—	Simplex (60SD754)	4wDM	1980
—	—	Simplex (60SD755)	4wDM	1980

Stock
18 ex-BR Mk 1 coaches (SK, CK, 2xBCK, 5xTSO, 2xRMB, 1xBSO(T),
1xRBR and 1xSLS), 4 ex-LNER coaches; 2 SR parcels vans; Freight stock
and service vehicles, SR and GW brakes
Stephen Middleton collection of vintage coaches

Owners
Class 107 DMU vehicles the Class 107 Ltd
08773 the Newton Heath Group

Note
Items on display may vary

October; White Rose Vehicle Rally
— 7, 14 October; Santa Trains —
Sundays 18 November to 23
December, Saturdays 1 to 22
December; Mince Pie Specials —
26 December; New Year's Day
Specials — 1 January 2008
Special notes: Steam rides are on
the 4.5-mile line to the new station
and picnic area at Bolton Abbey.
Old Midland Railway buildings,
fine collection of industrial
locomotives
Membership details: Membership
Secretary at above address
Membership journal: *Dale Steam
YDR News* — 4 times/year

Epping-Ongar Railway

Member: HRA

A preserved section at the northern end of the former London Underground Central Line. The section between Ongar and North Weald opened in autumn 2004. 2005 wasthe first full season of the nearest heritage railway to London

Operating society/organisation: Epping Ongar Railway, Station House, High Street, Ongar, Essex CM5 9BN

Contact: Mark Dewell

Telephone: 01277 366616

Internet address: *Web site:* http://eorailway.co.uk

Main station: Ongar

Other station: North Weald

OS references: Ongar TL 551035; North Weald TL 49603)

Access by public transport: Use London Underground Central Line to Epping, then local bus service to Ongar or North Weald. Local buses also available from Harlow and Brentwood

On site facilities: Light refreshments only at Ongar

Length of line: 6 miles (4.5 miles operational)

Public opening: DMU service on Sundays 11-00-17.00

Special events: Please see web site

Locomotives

Name	No	Origin	Class	Type	Built
—	(1008)	Finnish*		4-6-2	1948
—	1060	Finnish*		2-8-2	1954
—	794	Finnish*		0-6-0T	1925
—	531	Finnish*	TK3	2-8-0	1919
—	1134	Finnish*		2-8-0	1946
—	51342	P/Steel	117	DMS	1959
—	51384	P/Steel	117	DMS	1959
—	L11	LT	—	—	1964

*1,524mm gauge, on static display

Industrial locomotives

Name	No	Builder	Type	Built
—	—*	Ruston (398616)	4wDM	1956
—	—	Ruston (512572)	4wDM	1965
Heather	D1995	Drewry (2566)	4wDM	1955

*for spares only

Stock

2 Finnish Railway wooden-bodied carriages (1,524mm gauge). Brake van, well wagon, Dogfish ballast hopper and box van

Owner

L11 Cravens Heritage Trains

Facilities for disabled: Level access to platforms. Ramp available for wheelchair access to guard's compartment

Membership details: Epping Ongar Railway Volunteer Society, c/o above address

Membership journal: *Mixed Traffic* — quarterly

Evesham Vale Light Railway

Member: BGLR

The Evesham Vale Light Railway takes you through the old apple orchards to a picnic and viewing area overlooking some of the most picturesque scenery in the Vale of Evesham. Steam locomotives are used on most days and it is possible to break your journey and walk to the river, returning on a later train. The railway is situated within Evesham Country Park, 1 mile to the north of the historic town of Evesham. Enjoy a day out and stroll around the 130 acre estate, including a mile and quarter of the River Avon. Visit the Ark Animal Sanctuary, browse in the relaxed atmosphere of the courtyard shops or try some of the freshly prepared lunches and snacks in the licensed Apple Barn restaurant

Location/headquarters: Evesham Vale Light Railway, Evesham Country Park, Twyford, Nr Evesham, Worcestershire WR11 4TP

Contact: Jim Shackell

Telephone: 01386 422282

Internet address: *e-mail:* enquiries@evlr.co.uk

Web site: www.evlr.co.uk

Main station: Twyford (adjacent to Evesham Country Park car park)

Other station: Evesham Vale (in the country park)

OS reference: SP 0446

On site facilities: Large car and coach park, licensed restaurant within park shopping complex. Small souvenir shop at Twyford station

Length of line: 1.25 miles, 15in gauge

Locomotive and carriage depots: Adjacent to Twyford station — viewing avaiable on request

Access by public transport: By train to Evesham main line station then bus — Stagecoach No 28 — from Evesham bus station, hourly

service will stop close to park entrance, then 15min walk to Twyford station
Public opening: Every weekend throughout the year plus Bank Holidays and main school holidays as follows: 31 March-15 April (Easter), 7 May, 26 May-3 June (half term), 21 July-2 September (summer), 20-28 October (half term), 22 December-6 January 2008 (excluding 25/26 December). Phone 24 hr information line 01386 422282 or visit web site (www.evlr.co.uk) to check dates and for special events. Trains run every half-hour from 10.30 to 17.00 (16.00 November to March)
Facilities for disabled: Wheelchair facilities on all trains

Locomotives

Name	No	Builder	Type	Built
Prince William	5751	G&S	4-6-2	1949
Sludge	—	Lister (41545)	4wDM	1955
Bessie	—	Eddy/Nowell	4wDM	2002
St Egwin	312	Exmoor Steam Rly	0-4-0T+T	2003
Dougal	3	Severn-Lamb	0-6-2T	1970
Scooter	—	Eddy/Nowell	4wPM	2004
R. H. Morse	712*	Morse	0-4-0	1950
John	103	Barnes	4-4-2	1921

*off-site for overhaul

Note: Engines can be viewed, by prior arrangement, on days when the railway is operating. No access when the railway is closed

Special facilities: Birthday parties can be held in railway picnic area. Group visits can be arranged on days when railway is not operating normally. Discounts available for advance bookings of groups 20+

Steam Centre	**Exbury Gardens Railway**	Hampshire

Member: BGLR, HRA
A comparatively new line with purpose-built locomotives and rolling stock around part of Exbury Gardens. Train fare is in addition to entrance fee
Location/headquarters: Exbury Gardens, Exbury, Southampton SO45 1AZ
Contact: Ian Wilson (railway foreman). Tel: 023 8089 2898
Telephone: 023 8089 1203
Internet address: *Web site:* www.exbury.co.uk
Access by public transport: Main line trains to Brockenhurst. New Forest Explorer bus calls into Gardens between 26 May and 2 September 2007. Visit: www.newforesttour.info
Car park: On site, free
On site facilities: Souvenir shop, with railway memorabilia (including prints and videos), refreshments and toilets adjacent to main car park
Length of line: 1.25 miles, 12.25in gauge
Public opening: 17 March to 4 November. Limited winter opening.
   Available for 2007 are driver

Industrial locomotives

Name	No	Builder	Type	Built
Rosemary	—	Exmoor (315)	0-6-2T	2001
Naomi	—	Exmoor (316)	0-6-2T	2002
	—	Exmoor	0-4-0DH	2001

Stock
8 coaches

experience courses and Railwayman's Packages for groups of 15 or more people (unlimited train rides, engine shed tour, guided walk around wood yard, footplate rides [limited numbers], plus two-course meal £25/head)
Special events: Spring Train — 18 March; Steam Railway Open Weekend — 24/25 March; Easter Bunny Trains — 7-9 April; Narrow Gauge in the Gardens — 16/17 June; 1940s Weekend — 7/8 July; Teddy on the Train — 4/5 August; Exbury Scarecrow Festival — 25-27 August; Steam in the Gardens — 6/7 October; Exbury Ghost Train — 23-28 October; Santa Steam Specials — 8/9, 15/16, December
Facilities for disabled: Yes, access to 4 coaches
Tickets:

High season (17 March to 10 June) entrance prices include a free voucher for a return to Exbury in October/November to see the autumn colours. Concessions available
   Season tickets are available for access to gardens only or gardens plus trains, additional on-site discounts are available to season ticket holders
Special facilities:
Engine shed licensed for civil weddings, capacity 100, and avaiable for private hire.
Railway available for private charter (minimum 'steamin-up' fee £100).
Footplate experience days avaiable — £199 for 1:1 course, 8 trips, 10 miles

Foxfield Steam Railway

Member: HRA

The railway was built in 1893 to carry coal from Foxfield Colliery to the North Staffordshire Railway at Blythe Bridge. Following closure of the colliery in 1965 the line was rescued for preservation. The Society is working towards rebuilding the railway a further 0.75 mile down the famous Foxfield Bank to the site of Foxfield Colliery as part of a half million pound lottery grant

Chairman: G. Walker

Headquarters: Foxfield Steam Railway, Blythe Bridge, Stoke-on-Trent

Postal address: P.O. Box 1967, Stoke-on-Trent ST4 8YT

Telephone: 01782 396210 or 01782 643507

Fax: 01782 396210

Internet address: *Web site:* www.foxfieldrailway.co.uk

Main station: Blythe Bridge

Industrial locomotives

Name	No	Builder	Type	Built
*Bellerophon**	—	Haydock Foundry (C)	0-6-0WT	1874
—	1827	B/Peacock (1827)	0-4-0ST	1879
—	6	R/Heath	0-4-0ST	1886
—	4101	Dübs (4101)	0-4-0CT	1901†
Henry Cort	—	Peckett (933)	0-4-0ST	1903††
Millom	—	Avonside (1563)	0-4-0ST	1908†
Moss Bay	—	K/Stuart (4167)	0-4-0ST	1920††
Cranford	—	Avonside (1919)	0-6-0ST	1924†
Helen	—	Simplex (2262)	4wDM	1924
Marston No 3	—	H/Leslie (3581)	0-6-0ST	1924†
—	—	K/Stuart (4388)	0-4-0ST	1926•
Lewisham	—	Bagnall (2221)	0-6-0ST	1927
Rom River	—	K/Stuart (4421)	6wDM	1929
Boots No 1	—	Barclay (1984)	0-4-0F	1930††
Ironbridge No 1	—	Peckett (1803)	0-4-0ST	1933††
Spondon No 2	—	E/Electric (1130)	4wBE	1939††
Roker	—	RSH (7006)	0-4-0CT	1940††
Hawarden	—	Bagnall (2623)	0-4-0ST	1940
—	WD820	B/Drewry (2157)	0-4-0DM	1942
(Hercules)	242915	R/Hornsby (242915)	4wDM	1946
—	11	Peckett (2081)	0-4-0ST	1947•
Whiston	—	Hunslet (3694)	0-6-0ST	1950
—	9535	Sentinel (9535)	4wVBGT	1952•

INDUSTRIAL RAILWAY SOCIETY

England

(Caverswall Road)
OS reference: SJ 957421
Car park: Blythe Bridge
Access by public transport: Main line railway Blythe Bridge (400yd). PMT bus service to Blythe Bridge
Refreshment facilities: Buffet and real ale bar at Blythe Bridge
Souvenir shop: Blythe Bridge
Passenger trains: Steam-hauled trains operate from Blythe Bridge (Caverswall Road) to Dilhorne Park and return
Family ticket: Available (2 adults + 2 children or 1 adult + 4 children)
Length of line: 3.5 miles. Current operation over 2.5 miles of line
Period of public operation: Steam trains operate Sundays and Bank Holiday Mondays Easter-end October inclusive between Blythe Bridge and Dilhorne Park.
Special events: 40th Anniversary Celebration Weekend — 5-7 May; Steam Gala — 28/29 July; Halloween and Santa Specials, weekends in December (both pre-booked events). Please contact for details
Facilities for disabled: Access to

Name	No	Builder	Type	Built
Florence No 2	—	Bagnall (3059)	0-6-0ST	1953†
Meaford No 2	—	RSH (7684)	0-6-0T	1951
Wimblebury	—	Hunslet (3839)	0-6-0ST	1956
(Gas-oil)	88DS	R/Hornsby (408496)	4wDM	1957†
Wolstanton No 3	—	Bagnall (3150)	0-6-0DM	1960
B. R. C. (Megan)	—	Thomas Hill (103C)	0-4-0DH	1957
Rachel	—	R/Hornsby (423637)	0-4-0DE	1958
(Roman)	165DS	R/Hornsby (424841)	0-4-0DE	1960
Ludstone	—	YEC (3207)	0-4-0DH	1961
Leys	—	Bagnall (2868)	0-6-0DE	1962
Meaford No 4	—	Barclay (486)	0-6-0DH	1964

†under overhaul
††static exhibit
•awaiting overhaul
*on loan for ten years

Stock
3 ex-BR Mk 1 CK coaches; 1 ex-BR Mk 2a TSO coach; 4 other coaches; 3 scenery vans (converted for other uses); 79 assorted wagons, 16-ton mineral wagons; 1 rail-mounted self-propelled diesel-electric crane

Owner
Bellerophon the Vintage Carriages Trust

majority of Caverswall Road station is on the level; disabled toilets. Advance notice essential for those wishing to travel on the train.

Induction loop
Membership journal: *Foxfield News* — quarterly

Timetable Service	Gartell Light Railway	Somerset

Owned and operated by three generations of the Gartell family, the Gartell Light Railway offers visitors the chance to travel by train along the route of the old Somerset & Dorset Joint Railway. A half-mile section of the line from Pinesway Junction to Park Lane runs along the old S&D trackbed, while work has started on an extension northwards from Pinesway Junction along the S&D formation towards Templecombe. A flyover has been constructed to carry the extension over the existing line to the terminus at Common Lane and tracklaying has begun. On most open days a three train service is operated, with departures every 15min and trains crossing at Pinesway Junction. The GLR is fully signalled using a variety of upper and lower quadrant, colour light and shunt signals controlled by two full size signalboxes. The GLR's first steam locomotive, a

Industrial locomotives
2ft gauge:

Name	No	Builder	Type	Built
Amanda	1	GLR	Bo-BoDH	2003
Andrew	2	R/Hornsby	4wDH	1964/5
Alison	5	A/Keef (10)	4wDH	1983
Mr G	6	N. Dorset Loco Wks	0-4-2T	1998

Rolling stock — coaches: 9 fully enclosed bogie coaches

Rolling stock — wagons: goods guard's van, tool van, open wagon, bogie PW gang/tool van, bogie hopper, bogie open, bogie well, bogie flat and bogie crane

locally built 0-4-2T, specially designed to cope with the steep gradients and sharp curves of the section from Common Lane up to Pinesway Junction, entered service in 1998.
Location/headquarters: Gartell Light Railway, Common Lane, Yenston, Nr Templecombe, Somerset BA8 0NB
Telephone: 01963 370752

Internet address: *Web site:* http://www.glr.co.uk
General Manager: John Gartell
Main station: Common Lane
Other stations: Pinesway Junction, Park Lane
Car park: Large free car park at Common Lane
OS reference: ST 718218
Access by public transport: 1.5 miles south-east of Templecombe

railway station
Refreshment facilities:
Refreshment room at Common
Lane serving a range of hot and
cold snacks and drinks. Lakeside
picnic area at Pinesway Junction
Visitor centre: Common Lane
Souvenir shop: Common Lane
Depot: Common Lane (not open to
public)
Length of line: 0.75-mile

Facilities for disabled: Two of the
three trains in service have
accommodation for a disabled
visitor in a wheelchair
Special facilities: Clean, well-
maintained independent caravan site
with running water close to railway.
The Pines function suite available
for outside hire, with entertainment
licence, licensed bar and seating for
200; ideal for weddings,

anniversaries, children's parties, etc.
Train rides can be arranged
Period of public operation:
9 April; 7, 28 May; 24 June;
29 July; 5, 12, 19, 26/27 August;
30 September, 28 October.
10.30-16.30
Special events: Santa Specials
(must be pre-booked) — 15/16
December

Timetable Service — Gloucestershire Warwickshire Railway — Glos

Member: HRA
Part of an ambitious project to link
Cheltenham with Stratford, much
has been done to re-create the
railway and buildings that made up
this cross-country route. The
railway is home to many owners of
private locomotives and rolling
stock, so from time to time the
items on display may vary. The
extension from Gotherington to
Cheltenham Racecourse opened in
April 2003.

2006 saw the centenary of the
opening of the line and the 25th
anniversary of the GWR Ltd
Location: Toddington station,
Toddington
OS reference: SO 050322
Operating society/organisation:
Gloucestershire Warwickshire
Steam Railway plc, The Station,
Toddington, Cheltenham, Glos
GL54 5DT
Telephone: Toddington (01242)
621405
Internet address:
e-mail: enquiries@gwsr.com
Web site: www.gwsr.com
Main station: Toddington
Other public stations:
Winchcombe, Cheltenham
Racecourse, Gotherington (request
halt, off-peak only)
Access by public transport:
Hourly service from Cheltenham to
Greet for Winchcombe station.
Local bus service Castleways will
answer timetable queries on
(01242) 602949. Regular
Stagecoach service to Cheltenham
station. Racecourse Park & Ride
(approx half mile to GWR station)
Car park: All stations
On site facilities: Sales, catering,

Locomotives and multiple-units

Name	No	Origin	Class	Type	Built
—	2807	GWR	2800	2-8-0	1905
—	4270	GWR	4200	2-8-0T	1919
Kinlet Hall	4936	GWR	6959	4-6-0	????
Raveningham Hall	6960*	GWR	6959	4-6-0	1944
Owsden Hall	6984	GWR	6959	4-6-0	1948
Foremarke Hall	7903	GWR	6959	4-6-0	1949
—	7069	LMS	—	0-6-0DE	1939
Peninsular & Oriental SNCo	35006	SR	MN	4-6-2	1941
—	8274	LMS	8F	2-8-0	1941
—	76077	BR	4MT	2-6-0	1956
Black Prince	92203	BR	9F	2-10-0	1959
—	03069	BR	03	0-6-0DM	1959
—	D2182	BR	03	0-6-0DM	1952
—	D9553	BR	14	0-6-0DH	1965
—	D8137	BR	20	Bo-Bo	1966
—	24081	BR	24	Bo-Bo	1960
—	26043	BR	26	Bo-Bo	1959
—	37215	BR	37	Co-Co	1964
Clydebridge	37324	BR	37	Co-Co	1962
Phaeton	45149	BR	45	1Co-Co1	1961
—	47105	BR	47	Co-Co	1963
Freightliner 1995	47376	BR	47	Co-Co	1965
—	56003	BR	56	Co-Co	1977
—	73129	BR	73	Bo-Bo	1966
—	51950	BR	108	DMBS	1960
—	52062	BR	108	DMC	1960

*off-site under repair

Industrial locomotives

Name	No	Builder	Type	Built
Wemyss Private Rly	15	Barclay (2138)	0-6-0ST	1945
—	19	Fowler (4240016)	0-6-0DH	1964
—	21	Fowler (4210130)	0-4-0DM	1957
John	—	Peckett (1976)	0-4-0ST	1939
King George	—	Hunslet (2409)	0-6-0ST	1942
—	1	Drewry/RSH (2573/7859)	0-6-0DM	1956
—	2	Drewry/RSH (2574/7860)	0-6-0DM	1956
—	—	Hunslet (5511)	0-6-0DM	1957

Stock
4 ex-GWR coaches; 59 ex-BR coaches; 4 ex-LMS coaches; Baguley/
Drewry inspection vehicle; 2 Wickham trolleys; plus over 150 wagons

70

England

Driver Experience Courses for both steam and diesel locomotives feature in a number of heritage railways attractions, being an unusual type of present. This Class 37 diesel locomotive provides the excitement at Winchcombe on the Gloucestershire Warwickshire Railway. *Alan Barnes*

narrow gauge rides, toilets, new children's play area

Length of line:
Standard gauge 10 miles
Narrow gauge 1 mile

Public opening: On non-operating mid weekdays the station is closed. Public services: weekends, Bank Holiday Mondays, between March and November, some summer weekdays

Special events: Spring Diesel Gala — 30 March to 1 April; Day out with Thomas —28/29 April; Summer Steam Gala — 31 May to 3 June; Summer Diesel Gala 15-17 June; Transport Nostalgia Days — 910 June, 8 July, 23 September; Steam Gala —15/16 September; Day out with Thomas — 29/30 September; Autumn Steam & Vintage Rally — 13/14 October; Autumn Diesel Gala— 3/4 November; Santa Specials — 1/2, 8/9, 15/16, 22-24 December; Xmas Diesel Day — 27 December

Special notes: The site is being developed as the headquarters of the railway between Cheltenham and Stratford. The GWR owns the railway land between Cheltenham and Broadway and operates over 10 miles from Toddington to Cheltenham Racecourse with an intermediate station at Winchcombe.

No public access to restoration area or sheds except on guided tours. Please ring for details.

Guest locomotives will be operating during the year with special guest *City of Truro* expected along with GWR 2-6-2T No 5542 and S160 No 5197.

Wine & Dine train 'Elegant Excursions' at www.excursions@freeserve.co.uk

(including 12 brake vans, 45-ton steam crane, 18-ton diesel crane)

Owners
2807 the Cotswold Steam Preservation Ltd (www.gwr2807.co.uk)
35006 the P&O Locomotive Society
8274 and 7069 the Churchill (8F) Locomotive Co
92203 David Shepherd
26043 and 45149 the Cotswold Mainline Diesel Group
D9553 Cotswold Diesel Preservation Group
37215 and 37324 the Growler Group
47105 and 47376 the Brush Type 4 Fund
D8137 the English Electric Type 1 Group

North Gloucestershire Railway
Industrial narrow gauge locomotives (2ft gauge)

Name	No	Builder	Type	Built
Isibutu	5	Bagnall (2820)	4-4-0T	1946
George B	—	Hunslet (680)	0-4-0ST	1898
Chaka	—	Hunslet (2075)	0-4-2T	1940
Justine	—	Jung (939)	0-4-0WT	1906
Brigadelok	—	Henschel (15968)	0-8-0T	1918
—	2	Lister (34523)	4wDM	1949
—	3	M/Rail (4565)	4wPM	1928
Spitfire	—	M/Rail (7053)	4wPM	1937
—	1	R/Hornsby (166010)	4wDM	1932
—	L5	R/Hornsby (181820)	4wDM	1936
—	—	R/Hornsby (354028)	4wDM	1953

Stock
3 coaches; 11 wagons

Round trip tickets give unlimited travel on day of purchase.

Family tickets available

Facilities for disabled: Visitors with impaired mobility welcomed, please inform staff in advance if possible. Wheelchairs can be accommodated in specially converted carriages. The platform at Racecourse is reached via a steep slope which may be difficult for some visitors. Disabled toilets and parking at Toddington and Cheltenham Racecourse stations

Special facilities: Steam and diesel experience courses. Hire of train (steam or diesel). hire of Directors' Saloon. Children's parties on-train or in Flag & Whistle tearooms.

Special trains to March and November race meetings at Cheltenham Racecourse. Contact Racing Tours 01386 834013 or www.racingtours.co.uk (advance booking essential)

Membership details: From above address

Membership journal: *The Cornishman* — quarterly

Timetable Service	**Great Central Railway**	Leicestershire

Member: HRA, TT

The original Great Central Railway's extension to London in 1899 was the last main line to be built in this country, most of which was closed in the 1960s. Steam-hauled services operate through attractive rolling Leicestershire countryside, crossing the picturesque Swithland reservoir. The railway's aim is to re-create the experience of British main line railway operation in the days of steam. The images of a main line are backed up by a double track line with long trains hauled by large locomotives

Headquarters: Great Central Railway plc, Loughborough Central Station, Great Central Road, Loughborough, Leicestershire LE11 1RW

Telephone: Loughborough (01509) 230726

Fax: 01509 239791

Internet address: *e-mail:* sales@gcrailway.co.uk

Web site: www.gcrailway.co.uk
Main stations: Loughborough Central, Leicester North
Other public stations: Quorn & Woodhouse, Rothley
OS reference: SK 543194
Car park: Quorn, Rothley
Access by public transport: Loughborough Midland station (0.75-mile). Add-on ticket from any National Rail station includes unlimited travel on day of visit. Arriva Fox County, Barton, Kinch, South Notts and Trent Buses serve Loughborough Baxtergate (0.5 mile). Arriva Fox County Nos 126/7 pass end of Great Central Road (A6 Leicester Road, 300yd)
Refreshment facilities: Licensed Griddle Car with hot and cold drinks on majority of trains and at Loughborough Central station. Light refreshment facilities available at all other stations. Luxurious First Class Restaurant Car, for which advance booking is obligatory, is provided on 13.15 train every Saturday and Sunday. Also provided on 19.30 train every Saturday and every Friday (June-September). Additional service may run at peak times. Private charter trains available, along with more details of all the above, on request
Souvenir shop: Loughborough
Museum: Loughborough
Depot: Loughborough
Length of line: 8 miles
Passenger trains: Loughborough-Leicester North
Period of public operation: Weekends and Bank Holidays throughout the year. Daily between 17 July and 30 August with additional services at times of peak demand
Special events: 1960s Gala — 23-25 March; Edwardian Evening at Rothley — 31 March; Diesel Gala — 28/29 April; MG Rally — 13 May; Day out with Thomas — 26-28 May; Quorn Swapmeet — 3 June; War Weekend 'Operation Brownsea' (Friday is schools day) — 15-17 June; Queen Victoria at Rothley — 1 July; Mail by Rail Gala — 28/29 July; Day out with Thomas — 24-27 August; Quorn Swapmeet — 2 September; Diesel Gala — 14-16 September; Beer Festival at Loughborough — 28/29 September; Steam Railway Gala — 13/14 October; Day out with Thomas — 20/21 October; Witches

Locomotives and multiple-units

Name	No	Origin	Class	Type	Built
—	4141	GWR	41xx	2-6-2T	1946
Witherslack Hall*	6990	GWR	'Hall'	4-6-0	1948
Sir Lamiel	30777	SR	N15	4-6-0	1925
Boscastle	34039	SR	WC	4-6-2	1946
Brocklebank Line Alderman	35025	SR	MN	4-6-2	1948
A. E. Draper	45305	LMS	5MT	4-6-0	1936
—	46521	LMS	2MT	2-6-0	1953
—	47406	LMS	3F	0-6-0T	1926
—	48305	LMS	8F	2-8-0	1943
—	63601	GCR	8K	2-8-0	1919
—	69523	GNR	N2	0-6-2T	1921
Oliver Cromwell	70013	BR	7MT	4-6-2	1951
—	73156	BR	5MT	4-6-0	1956
—	78019	BR	2MT	2-6-0	1954
—	D3101	BR	08	0-6-0DE	1955
§—	D4067	BR	10	0-6-0DE	1961
—	D8048	BR	20	Bo-Bo	1959
—	D8098	BR	20	Bo-Bo	1961
—	D5185	BR	25	Bo-Bo	1960
Harlech Castle	25265	BR	25	Bo-Bo	1963
—	26010	BR	26	Bo-Bo	1959
—	D5830	BR	31	A1A-A1A	1962
—	33116	BR	33	Bo-Bo	1960
—	37255	BR	37	Co-Co	1965
†—	D123	BR	45	1Co-Co1	1961
Sparrowhawk	D1705	BR	47	Co-Co	1965
Sir Herbert Walker	E6003	BR	73	Bo-Bo	1966
—	51427	BR	101	DMBS	1959
—	51616	BR	127	DMBS	1959
—	51622	BR	127	DMBS	1959
—	53193	BR	101	DMC	1959
—	53203	BR	101	DMBS	1957
—	53266	BR	101	DMC	1957
—	53321	BR	101	DMC	1958
—	59276	BR	120	TS	1958
—	62384	BR	421	MBSO	
—	76746	BR	421	DTCSO	
—	76817	BR	421	DTCSO	
—	70527	BR	411	TSOL	
—	W79976	AC Cars	—	Railbus	1958

*undergoing overhaul at Tyseley Locomotive Works
§ named *Alfred Thomas & Margaret Ethel Naylor*
† named *Leicestershire & Derbyshire Yeomanry*

Industrial locomotives

Name	No	Builder	Type	Built
(Arthur Wright)	D4279	Fowler (4210079)	0-4-0DE	1952
Duke of Edinburgh	28	A/Barclay (400)	0-4-0DM	1956

Owners
6990 the David Clarke Railway Trust
34099 the Boscastle Locomotive Syndicate
35025 the Brocklebank Line Association
45305 the 5305 Locomotive Association
46521, 73156 and 78019 Loughborough Standard Locomotives Group
47406, D3101, D4067 private
30777, 63601, 70013 and 33116 on loan from the National Railway Museum
69523 the Gresley Society
D5830, D8098 and D1705 the Type 1 Locomotive Co
E6003 the ED Locomotive Group

73

and Wizards Weekend — 27/28 October; Halloween Dining Train — 31 October; Bonfire Night — 5 November; Christmas Edwardian at Rothley — 8 December; Santa Specials — 24 November-24 December; Mince Pie Specials — 26-31 December; New Years Eve Dining Trains 31 December. For additional information phone 08708 308298

Facilities for disabled: Special carriage for wheelchair/disabled persons (advance notice required).

Class 101s Renaissance Railcars
37255 on loan from Fragonset Railways
D1705 the Type One Locomotive Co
26010 the Waverley Route Heritage Association

Wheelchair access good at Quorn and Rothley, can be arranged at Loughborough with advance notification. Boarding ramps at all stations

Membership & share details: Share enquiries: Company Secretary, Great Central Railway

plc
Membership: Membership Secretary, Main Line Steam Trust Ltd. Both c/o above address. Friends of Great Central Railway, Friends Co-ordinator c/o above address

---

Miniature Railway	Great Cockcrow Railway	Surrey

Emanating from the private Greywood Central Railway, built from 1946, the Great Cockcrow Railway opened in 1968 in the small village of Lyne near Chertsey. This is a 7.25in gauge system with a signalling system worked from four signalboxes.

Headquarters: Hardwick Lane, Lyne, Chertsey, Surrey

Contact: Jill Wright

Telephone:
Mon-Fri (01932) 255514;
Sun (01932) 565474

Internet address: e-mail:
jill.wright@ianallan.co.uk
Web site: www.cockcrow.co.uk

Main station: Hardwick Central

Car parking: On site

Access by public transport:
Chertsey railway station (1.25 miles); London Buslines 561, 586 Holloway Hill (half-mile)

On site facilities: Toilet, light refreshments, picnic area

Depots: Hardwick Central

Length of line: 1.75 miles, 7.25in gauge

Period of public operation:
Every Sunday Easter to October inclusive, 14.00-17.30

Journey time: About 15-20min

Facilities for disabled: Limited, but staff are happy to co-operate

Special note: Sponsored by Ian Allan Group. Send second class SAE for brochure to Terminal House, Shepperton, TW17 8AS. Fare £2.50 adult, £2 child. Gladesman £4 per person

Locomotives (7.25in gauge)

Name	No	Prototype	Builder	Type	Built
—	206	LNER K5	D. Simmonds	2-6-0	1956
—	837	SR S15	D. Curwen	4-6-0	1947
—	1239	NER R1	F. Baldwin	0-6-2T	1913
—	1249	NER T2	R. Sills	0-8-0	1986
—	1401	GWR 14xx	R. Sills	0-4-2T	1980
—	1442	NER C1	—	4-4-2	1989
Eureka	—	GCR	L. Shaw	4-6-2	1927
North Foreland	2422	LBCSR H2	J. Lester	4-4-2	1981
Sister Dora	5000	LMS 5P5F	A. Glaze	4-6-0	1989
—	5145	LMS 5P5F	—	4-6-0	1989
—	5241	LMS 5P5F	—	4-6-0	1989
The Glasgow Highlander	45157	LMS 5P5F	D. Grant	4-6-0	1996
Royal Scot	6100	LMS 6P	Barnet & Willoughby	4-6-0	1947
Royal Scot	6100	LMS 6P	J. Butt	4-6-0	1982
Scots Guardsman	6115	LMS 6P	P. Ormand	4-6-0	1989
—	8200	LMS 8F	P. Pownall	2-8-0	
—	8374	LMS 8F	Glaze, Hancock & York	2-8-0	1993
—	30541	SR Q	J. Butt	0-6-0	2000
—	30542	SR Q	J. Butt	0-6-0	2000
—	3151	GWR 31xx	K. Wilson	2-6-2T	1990
Winston Churchill	34051	SR BoB	N. Sleet	4-6-2	1995
General Steam Navigation	21C11	SR MN	N. Sleet & M. Lester	4-6-2	1993
Mercury	70020	BR 7MT	N. Sleet	4-6-2	1985
Lady of the Lake	70047	BR 7MT	J. Butt	4-6-2	1995
Grand Parade	2744	LNER A3	R. Warren	4-6-2	1990
Longmoor	73755	WD 8F	J. Liversedge	2-10-0	1951
A. B. Macleod	7028	BR Hymek	A. Glaze	B0-B0	1983
Faraday	11	BR 08	Jennings & Marden	0-6-0P	1958
—	40106	BR 40	N. Sleet	1Co-Co1	1992

74

Steam Centre — Great Whipsnade Railway — Bedfordshire

Member: HRA
Location: Whipsnade Wild Animal Park, Dunstable, Bedfordshire LU6 2LF
Telephone: (01582) 871332 (extension 2270)
Fax: (01582) 873748
Internet address: *e-mail:* whipsnade-operations@2sl.org
Railway Engineer: Kevin Edwins
Main station: Whipsnade Central
Length: 2 miles (2ft 6in gauge)
On site facilities: Car park (100yd), souvenir shop, refreshments (30yd)
Period of public operation: January — no trains; February — half term; March — weekends only; April to July — daily (steam at weekends); August daily steam

Locomotives

Name	No	Builder	Type	Built
Excelsior	2	K/Stuart (1049)	0-4-2T	1908
Superior	4	K/Stuart (4034)	0-6-2T	1920
Victor	—	Fowler (4160004)	0-6-0DM	1951
Hector	—	Fowler (4160005)	0-6-0DM	1951
Hercules	—*	23rd August Works (Bucharest)	0-6-0DH	1981
The Brick	—	Ruhrthaler	0-4-0DH	
—	3	B/Drewry	4wDH	1973

*Polish State Railways Class LYD2

Rolling stock: 10 carriages, 10 wagons

trains; September/October — daily (steam at weekends); November — school half term; December — no trains

Facilities for disabled: Carriage designed for wheelchairs

Museum — Haig Colliery Mining Museum — Cumbria

Member: HRA
Haig Colliery Mining Museum, Whitehaven, is an educational and informative museum under development based on local and social mining history. The Museum is situated in Cumbria's last deep coal mine that closed in March 1986. It houses the world's only Bever Dorling & Co Ltd winding engines, one of which is restored and operated daily
Location: Kells, half-mile south of Whitehaven, take the road to St Bees and follow brown tourist signs
OS reference: NX 967176
Operating society/organisation: The Haig Colliery Mining Museum Ltd, Solway Road, Kells, Whitehaven, Cumbria CA26 9BG
Charity number: 1050534
Telephone/Fax: 01946 599949 (general information)
Internet address:

Industrial locomotives

Name	No	Builder	Type	Built
Askham Hall	—	Avonside (1772)	0-4-0ST	1917
—	226	V/Foundry (5262)	0-4-0DM	
—	ND 3815	Hunslet (2389)	0-4-0DM	1941
—	244	Fowler (22971) rebuilt T/Hill (130C/1963)	0-4-0DH	1942

Rolling stock
Coles 10-ton diesel crane, 4 16-top open wagons, 2 flat bed wagons

e-mail: museum@haigpit.com
Web site: www.haigpit.com
Car park: On site
Access by public transport: By rail: Whitehaven is on the Barrow-Carlisle line
By bus: No 01 bus from bus station (opposite railway station) — 9min journey
On site facilities: Small gift shop, gardened area suitable for picnics. Toilets. Meet and Greet by museum guides. Locomotives viewable on request to the guides.
Public opening: Daily except Wednesdays (09.30-16.30). Free entry
Facilities for disabled: Parking area, toilets, wheelchair access to all areas

Hayling Seaside Railway

There are three stations on the line: Beachlands, the main station/storage/workshop building located seaward of the funfair; Eastoke Corner 1-mile to the east is the other end of the line; Hornby Halt (sponsored by Hornby the modelmakers) with passing loop is between

Headquarters: 20 Jasmond Road, Cosham, Portsmouth PO6 2SY
Managing Director: Bob Haddock
Telephone: 023 9237 2427
Internet address: www.easthaylinglight railway.co.uk
Main public station: Beachlands
Other public stations: Eastoke Corner, Hornby Halt
Car parks: Pay & display at all stations. Free parking during December, January and February
Access by public transport: Regular buses from Havant railway station
Refreshment facilities: At all stations
Journey time: Departures every 45 minutes. First train 11.00 from Beachlands

Locomotives

Name	No	Builder	Type	Built
Jack		Λ/Keef (23)	0-4-0DH s/o	1988
Alister	—	Ruston (201790)	4wDH	1940
Alan B	—	M/Rail (7199)	4wDM	1937
—	—	EHLR	0-4-0T	*
Edwin	—	R/Hornsby (1002-0967-5)	4wDH	1967

*under construction

Stock

2 4-wheel enclosed coaches built 1992/1997, 2 4-wheel balcony coaches built 1996, 1 enclosed bogie coach built 2004, 3 toastrack bogie coach built 2004/5/6. All built by East Hayling Light Railway in its own works

Length of line: 1 mile, 2ft gauge
Period of public operation: Every weekend and Wednesday (market day) all year round, plus school holidays. Daily 1 July to 2 September
Facilities for disabled: All platforms and coaches built to latest mobility standards
Special events: Please contact for full details; Pirates of Beachlands — May half term; Two train running, Santa Specials

Special notes: On display are the original BR station signs Hayling Island and Havant for Hayling
Special facilities: A train may be hired for birthday parties or other special occasions
Membership details: Terry Mercer 023 9271 7550
Membership journal: *The Hayling Billy* — quarterly

Hills Miniature Railway

Opened in 2000 the railway runs through the landscaped grounds of Hills Garden Centre
Location: Hills Garden Centre, London Road, Allostock, Knutsford, Cheshire WA16 9LU
Telephone: 01565 722567
Internet address: *Web site:* www.hills-miniature-railway.co.uk
Car parking: Space for 80 cars on site. One coach space available
Access by public transport: Holmes Chapel main line station is 4 miles away, as is the nearest bus station
Access by car: Exit M6 at jct 18 and follow A54 to Holmes Chapel. In Holmes Chapel turn left onto A50 London Road, follow for 5 miles. Hills garden Centre is on the left hand side
On site facilities: Souvenir shop, light refreshments
Length of line: 600yd, 1.25in gauge
Period of public operation: Weekends and Bank Holidays throughout the year. Trains operate 11.00-16.00. All trains weather permitting

Hollycombe Steam Collection

Member: HRA, TT

An extensive collection of working steam, including railways, traction engines, fairground rides, Bioscope, organs, the oldest Burrell Showman's engine *Emperor*, sawmill and engine from the paddle steamer *Caledonia*, set in woodlands and gardens

Location: Iron Hill, Hollycombe, near Liphook, Hants

OS reference: SU 852295

Operating society/organisation: Hollycombe Steam & Woodland Garden Society, Iron Hill, Midhurst Road, Liphook, Hants GU30 7LP

Telephone: Liphook (01428) 724900 (24hr answerphone)

Fax: (01428) 723682

Internet address: *Web site:* www.hollycombe.co.uk

Car park: On site

Access by public transport: Liphook main line station (1 mile)

Standard gauge industrial locomotives

—	V47*	Peckett (2012)	0-4-0ST	1941
Commander B	50	H/Leslie (2450)	0-4-0ST	1899
—	3	YEC (2679)	0-4-0DH	1962

Narrow gauge locomotives (2ft gauge)

Name	No	Builder	Type	Built
Pixie	—*	Bagnall (2090)	0-4-0ST	1919
Caledonia	70	Barclay (1995)	0-4-0WT	1931
Jerry M	38	Hunslet (638)	0-4-0ST	1895
—	16	R/Hornsby	4wDM	1941

*may arrive on site during 2007

On site facilities: Shop and refreshments, toilets, car park, *dogs allowed in car park only*

Length of lines: Standard gauge – quarter mile

2ft gauge 'Quarry Railway' – 1.5 miles

7.25in gauge – quarter mile

Public opening: All Easter weekend. Sundays and Bank

Holidays 8 April–7 October. Daily 29 July–27 August. 12.00–17.00.

Special events: Commercial Vehicle Gathering — 22 April; Railway Weekend — 2/3 June; Festival of Steam — 30 June / 1 July.

Please phone for details of other events

Ingrow Railway Centre Museum of Rail Travel

Member: HRA, TT, AIM, ABTEM

A fascinating collection of elderly railway carriages and small locomotives, interestingly presented. Sit in a fully restored, prize winning 1876-built Manchester, Sheffield & Lincolnshire Railway carriage or relive the dark days of wartime travel in one of the three Metropolitan Railway carriages. Listen to the 'Travellers' Tales' and view the collection of railway posters and other items. Video presentation. The carriages and locomotives have appeared in over 50 cinema and television productions including: *Housewife, 49* (2006), *Booze Cruise 3* (2005), *North & South* (2004), *Inside Out* (2003), *He Knew He Was Right* (2003), *The Forsyte Saga* (2002), *Calendar* (2003), *Hound of the Baskervilles* (2002), *No Man's Land* (2002),

Stock

Railway	BR or previous owner Number	Type	Date built	Seats	Weight	Length
MS&LR	176	4-wheel 1st/2nd/3rd/ luggage	1876	34	12T	28ft 0in
GNR	589	6-wheel 3rd brake	1888	40	14T	34ft 11in
MR	358	6-wheel 1st/3rd/ luggage	1886	32	15T	34ft 0in
Met	427	BS	1910	84	30T	54ft 0in
Met	465	S	1919	108	30T	54ft 0in
Met	509	F	1923	84	30T	54ft 0in
SR (SECR)	S3554S	BSK	1924	42	33T	65ft 3in
BR (SR)	S1469S	TSO	1951	64	32T	67ft 1in
GN	2856	Non vestibule composite, lav brake	1898	34	22T	45ft 0in

Industrial locomotives

Name	No	Builder	Type	Built
Bellerophon*	—	Haydock Foundry (C)	0-6-0WT	1874
Sir Berkeley†	—	M/Wardle (1210)	0-6-0ST	1891

Turner — The Man Who Painted Britain (2002), A for Acid (2001), The Hours (2001), The Way We Live Now (2001), The Cazalets (2000), Possession (2000), The Railway Children (1970 and 1968 versions)

Name	No	Builder	Type	Built
Lord Mayor	—	H/Clarke (402)	0-4-0ST	1893

*on loan to the Foxfield Railway for 10 years
†on 10 year loan to Middleton Railway

Location: Vintage Carriages Trust Museum, Ingrow Station Yard, Halifax Road, Keighley, West Yorkshire BD22 8NJ. On the A629 road
Operations Manager: Michael Cope, Hon Secretary, VCT
Operating society/organisation: Vintage Carriages Trust (a Registered Charity No 510776)
Telephone: Keighley (01535) 680425
Fax: (01535) 610796
Internet address: e-mail: admin@vintagecarriagestrust.org
Web site: www.ingrowrailwaycentre.co.uk
  Web site includes two databases: over 5,000 preserved carriages, with over 4,000 images; over 1,000 preserved wagons, with over 400 images.
Car Park: Yes. Also coach parking at Ingrow station
Access by public transport: Northern Rail through trains from Carlisle, Settle, Morecambe, Lancaster to Keighley (one mile). Fast and frequent Metro Train services from Bradford Forster

Square, Leeds, Shipley, and Skipton to Keighley. Then either KWVR train to Ingrow West (adjacent) or buses 500, 502, 663, 664, 665, 696, 697 and 720 from Keighley bus station.
Buses: First Calderline bus 502 from Hebden Bridge. Calderline bus 502 from Halifax (Sundays only). Keighley & District buses 696 and 697 from Bradford via Thornton and Denholme.
Tel: (0113) 245 7676 for bus and Metro Train information or log onto VCT web site for internet links to timetables and route map
On site facilities: Transport relics shop specialising in out of print magazines, lamps and hardware. Hot and cold drinks, ice cream and chocolate available. Toilets with full disabled access. A determined effort has been made to provide a museum which will interest the casual visitor who is not knowledgeable about railways
Public opening:
Daily 11.00-16.30, openings outside these times can be arranged for groups.

Closed 25 December
facilities for disabled: The museum building is level with easy access for wheelchair users. A stairlift has been provided to allow wheelchair users to view carriage interiors, and enter guards' brake areas, though naturally wheelchairs are too wide to enter individual passenger compartments. Toilets with full access for wheelchair users. Braille leaflet, guidebook and audio tape for loan during visit. Wheelchair available for loan.
  Winner of the 1998 Adapt Museum Award for best practice in access for disabled and older people. Runners up for the 1998 Yorkshire Electricity/Yorkshire & Humberside Museums Council Access Awards. Highly commended in the 1999 White Rose Tourist For All Awards
Special notes: Visitors are welcome to either browse in the shop or visit the museum
Membership details: Membership Secretary, c/o above address
Marketing names: Vintage Carriages Trust or VCT

Steam Centre — Irchester Narrow Gauge Railway Museum — Northants

Member: HRA
The aims of the controlling trust are to acquire and preserve narrow gauge railway locomotives, rolling stock and exhibits associated with Northamptonshire and the East Midlands, to display the collection for the benefit of the public and to restore exhibits to working order so they may be demonstrated in a proper manner
Location: Within Irchester Country Park, 2 miles south of Wellingborough
Operating society/organisation: The Irchester Narrow Gauge Railway Trust, 3 St Christopher's Close, Cranwell, Lincs NG34 8XB
On site facilities: Shop, museum, demonstration line, picnic area

Industrial locomotives

Name	No	Builder	Type	Built
—	85*	Peckett (1870	0-6-0ST	1934
—	86*	Peckett (1871)	0-6-0ST	1934
—	87*	Peckett (2029)	0-6-0ST	1942
Cambrai	—*	Corpet (493)	0-6-0T	1888
—	ND3645*	R/Hornsby (211679)	4wDM	1941
—	—†	R/Hornsby (281290)	0-6-0DM	1949
—	ED10*	R/Hornsby (411322)	4wDM	1958
—	—†	M/Rail (1363)	4wPM	1918
The Rock	—*	Hunslet (2419)	0-4-0DM	1941

* metre gauge
† 3ft gauge

Access by public transport: Main line Wellingborough (Midland Road) station, buses to Irchester and Little Irchester

Car Parks: Main park car parks
Toilets: Main park complex
Public opening: Every Sunday (summer 10.00-17.00, winter 10.00-

16.00), at other times by arrangement. Steam and demonstration weekends are held on last full weekend of the month — March-October

Facilities for disabled: Museum and site on level, staff available if required
Membership details: Membership Secretary, 3 St Christopher's Close,

Cranwell, Lincs NG34 8XB

Museum — Ironbridge Gorge Museums — Shropshire

The railway items form only a small part of the displays on two of the museum's main sites: Blists Hill Victorian Town and Coalbrookdale. The Blists Hill site offers an opportunity to see a number of industrial and other activities being operated in meticulously reconstructed period buildings. A working foundry is just one of the exciting exhibits. A full size working replica of Richard Trevithick's 1802 steam locomotive built by the Coalbrookdale Company can also be seen operating at certain times at the Blists Hill site. The Ironbridge Gorge was designated a World Heritage Site in 1987
Location: Ironbridge, Shropshire
OS reference: SJ 694033
Operating society/organisation: Ironbridge Gorge Museum Trust, Coach Road, Coalbrookdale,

Industrial locomotives

Name	No	Builder	Type	Built
—	—	Sentinel/Coalbrookdale (6185)	0-4-0VBT	1925
—	—	Sentinel/M/Wardle (6155)	0-4-0VBT	1925
—	5	Coalbrookdale	0-4-0ST	1865
—	—	A/Barclay	0-6-0ST	1896

All locomotives are at the Museum of Iron site.
Phone 01952 435900 for details

Telford, Shropshire TF8 7DQ
Telephone: Telford (01952) 433522
Fax: (01952) 435999
Internet address: *Web site:* www.ironbridge.org.uk
Car park: At the sites
Access by public transport: Various operators. Please telephone Telford Travel Link 01952 200005 or 0870 6082608 for further details
Catering facilities: Licensed Victorian pub, sweet shop and tea rooms at the Blists Hill site, serving drinks and mainly cold snacks. Tea, coffee and light refreshments at the Museum of Iron, Coalbrookdale and Coalport China Museum
Public opening: Main sites, including Museum of Iron and Blists Hill, daily (except Christmas Eve, Christmas Day and New Year's Day) 10.00-17.00
Special notes: Tickets for all the sites or just for single sites available. Call main phone number for special access details

Timetable Service — Isle of Wight Steam Railway — Isle of Wight

Member: HRA, TT
Separated from the mainland by the Solent, the line's isolation encouraged the maintenance and retention of Victorian locomotives and coaching stock which still operate on the line today. Its rural charm enhances its attraction for the island's holidaymakers during the summer season
Commercial Director: Jim Loe
General Manager: Peter Vail
Headquarters: Isle of Wight Steam Railway, Haven Street Station, Ryde, Isle of Wight PO33 4DS
Telephone: (01983) 882204
Internet addresses: *e-mail:*

Locomotives

Name	No	Origin	Class	Type	Built
Freshwater	W8 (32646)	LBSCR	A1X	0-6-0T	1876
Newport	W11 (32640)	LBSCR	A1X	0-6-0T	1878
Calbourne	W24	LSWR	O2	0-4-4T	1891
—	41313	LMS	2MT	2-6-2T	1952
—	D2554	BR	05	0-6-0DM	1956
—	D2059	BR	03	0-6-0DM	1959

Industrial and Army locomotives

Name	No	Builder	Type	Built
Invincible	37	H/Leslie (3135)	0-4-0ST	1915
Ajax	38	Barclay (1605)	0-6-0T	1918
Waggoner	192	Hunslet (3792)	0-6-0ST	1953
Royal Engineer	198	Hunslet (3798)	0-6-0ST	1953

Owners
Royal Engineer and *Waggoner* on loan from The Army Museum

79

England

ronlee@iwsteamrailway.co.uk
Web site:
www.iwsteamrailway.co.uk
Main station: Haven Street
OS reference: SZ 556898
Other public stations: Wootton,
Ashey and Smallbrook Junction
Car park: Haven Street
Access by public transport:
'Island Line' service from Ryde or
Shanklin to Smallbrook Jct
Refreshment facilities: Light
refreshments available (licensed)
Souvenir shop: Haven Street
Museum: Small exhibits museum
at Haven Street.
　　Carriage & Wagon workshop
open for viewing most days
Depot: Haven Street
Length of line: 5 miles
Passenger trains: Wootton-
Smallbrook Jct

Stock
1 IWR coach; 4 LBSCR coaches; 3 SECR coaches; 2 LCDR coaches;
5 IWR coaches (bodies only); 5 LCDR coaches (bodies only); 1 LBSCR
coach (body only); 1 crane; 1 Wickham trolley; 30 wagons; 6 parcels vans;
2 ex-LT hoppers; 1 ex-BR Lowmac; 1 LSWR Road van; 1 cattle van (on
loan from the National Railway Museum).
Non-passenger vehicles are not normally accessible for public viewing

Period of public operation: Daily
— June to mid-September. Selected
days — March to May and October
Special events: Real Ale Festival
— 5-7 May; diesel-hauled brake
van rides — 26 May; 1940s
Weekend — 30 June-1 July; Cuneo
Exhibition — 13-22 July; A Day
out with Thomas — 27-31 July;
Island Steam Show— 24-27
August; Morris Minor Rally — 2
September; Wine Tasting Festival
— 29/30 September; Wizard Week

— 22-28 October; Ghost Walks —
26/27 October; Santa Specials —
December (please contact for
details)
Facilities for disabled: Limited
facilities, but can be catered for
individually, or in groups (by prior
arrangement), toilets available
Membership details: Membership
Secretary at above address
Membership journal: *Island Rail
News* — quarterly

| Timetable Service | **Keighley & Worth Valley Railway** | West Yorkshire |

Member: HRA
1968 saw the reopening of the
Worth Valley branch following the
first sale of a standard gauge
railway to a preservation society.
Qualified volunteers have now
managed and operated the KWVR
every weekend, summer and winter
for three decades. The KWVR is
justifiably proud of having led the
British independent railway
movement in establishing the now
ubiquitous late 1950s/early 1960s
house style. Many have copied, but
few succeed so well as the Worth
Valley with totems, A5 handbills,
period posters, red uniform ties,
hanging baskets, gas lights and coal
fires. One of the most community-
orientated independent railways,
being the first to create a
'Resident's Railcard' discount fares
scheme
**Chairman, Joint Management
Committee:** Sam MacDougal
Headquarters: Haworth Station,
Keighley, West Yorkshire
BD22 8NJ
Telephone: Haworth (01535)
647777 24hr recorded timetable
and information service; Haworth
(01535) 645214 (other calls)
Internet address: *Web site:*

Locomotives and multiple-units

Name	No	Origin	Class	Type	Built
—	41241	LMS	2MT	2-6-2T	1949
—	43924	MR	4F	0-6-0	1920
—	45212*	LMS	5MT	4-6-0	1935
Bahamas	45596	LMS	'Jubilee'	4-6-0	1935
—	48431	LMS	8F	2-8-0	1944
—	47279	LMS	3F	0-6-0T	1925
—	1054	LNWR	—	0-6-2T	1888
City of Wells	34092	SR	WC	4-6-2	1949
—	80002	BR	4MT	2-6-4T	1952
—	75078	BR	4MT	4-6-0	1956
—	78022	BR	2MT	2-6-0	1953
—	30072	SR	USA	0-6-0T	1943
—	5775	GWR	5700	0-6-0PT	1929
—	957	L&Y	2F	0-6-0	1887
—	19*	L&Y	Pug	0-4-0ST	1910
—	51218	L&Y	Pug	0-4-0ST	1901
—	752	L&Y	—	0-6-0ST	1881
—	85	TVR	02	0-6-2T	1899
—	5820	USATC	S160	2-8-0	1945
—	90733	MoS	WD	2-8-0	1945
—	D226	BR	—	0-6-0DE	1956
—	D2511	BR	—	0-6-0DM	1961
—	D3336	BR	08	0-6-0DE	1954
—	D5209	BR	25/1	Bo-Bo	1963
—	D8031	BR	20	Bo-Bo	1960
—	50928	BR	108	DMBS	1959
—	51189	BR	101	DMBS	1958
—	51565	BR	108	DMC	1959
—	51803	BR	101	DMCL	1959
—	79962	W&M	—	Railbus	1958
—	79964	W&M	—	Railbus	1958

England

Above: Steam on the Isle of Wight as No 24 *Calbourne* heads a train of four-wheelers towards Wootton. No 24 is currently undergoing overhaul. *Phil Barnes*

Right: Former Lancashire & Yorkshire Railway No 957, in BR guise as No 52044, and BR Standard Class 4 No 76079, on loan from the East Lancs Railway pull out of Oakworth on the Keighley & Worth Valley Railway. *Alan Barnes*

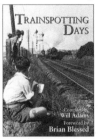
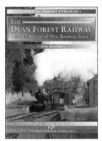

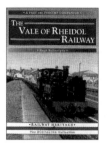
www.kwvr.co.uk
Main stations: Keighley, Ingrow West, Haworth, Oxenhope
Other public stations: Damems, Oakworth
OS reference: SE 034371
Car parks: Free at Keighley, Ingrow West, Oakworth and Oxenhope. Parking at Haworth (small charge, part refundable if travelling). Coaches at Ingrow West and Oxenhope only
Access by public transport: Fast and frequent electric Metro trains from Leeds, Bradford and Skipton to Keighley (joint station with KWVR). GNER direct services to Leeds and Keighley. Northern Trains through services from Glasgow, Carlisle, Morecambe, Lancaster to Keighley station. Northern Train services from Blackpool, Preston, Blackburn, Accrington, Burnley, Manchester to Hebden Bridge for connection via bus service 500 to Oxenhope (tel 01535 603284 for days of operation and timings)
Refreshment facilities: Buffet facilities at Oxenhope and Keighley (open when train service in

Industrial locomotives

Name	No	Builder	Type	Built
Hamburg	31	H/Clarke (679)	0-6-0T	1903
Nunlow	—	H/Clarke (1704)	0-6-0T	1938
Brussels	118	H/Clarke (1782)	0-6-0ST	1945
Tiny	—	Barclay (2258)	0-4-0ST	1949
Merlin	231	H/Clarke (D761)	0-6-0DM	1951
—	MDHB No 32	Hunslet (2699)	0-6-0DM	1944

*away on loan

Stock
30 coaches including examples of pre-Grouping types; BR Mk 1 stock including the oldest vehicle in existence, part of the prototype batch; 2 Pullman cars, NER and L&Y observation cars

Owners
19, 752 and 51218 the L&YRPS Trust
75078 and 78022 the Standard 4 Preservation Society
Bahamas, Nunlow, Tiny the Bahamas Locomotive Society
1054 the National Trust
52044 the Bowers 957 Trust
34092 the *City of Wells* Syndicate

operation). The only CAMRA-approved 'Real Ale' bar operates on most steam trains (March-October). Wine and Dine services by prior booking only — the 'White Rose Pullman' and 'West Riding Ltd'
Picnic areas: Keighley Station,

Haworth Locomotive Depot, Oxenhope Station
Viewing areas: Keighley (Garsdale) Turntable, Haworth Locomotive Depot
Souvenir shops: Keighley, Haworth and Oxenhope stations;

Ingrow Vintage Carriages Museum
Museums: Vintage Carriages Trust's carriage and locomotive museum at Ingrow Railway Centre. Open daily 11.00-16.30
Depots: Carriage and wagon — Oxenhope; Motive power/loco works — Haworth, 'Bahamas Locomotive Society' workshops and museum at Ingrow Railway Centre
Length of line: 4.75 miles
Passenger trains: Early morning local shoppers' services worked by diesel railbus/diesel multiple-unit, otherwise all steam-hauled
  Frequent bus service between Haworth station and Haworth village top on Sundays (May-September) and Bank Holidays
Period of public operation: Steam-hauled passenger services

every weekend and Bank Holiday throughout the year (in December diesel-hauled). Daily during July and August
Special events: Diesel Weekend 16/17 June; Day out with Thomas — 15/16 September; Steam Gala Weekends — 12-14 October; Beer & Music Festival — 26-28 October; Steam-hauled tours of the line — 19-21, 26-28 June; Vintage Trains Days — 3 June, 1 July, 5 August; Santa Specials — 1/2, 8/9, 15/16, 22/23 December; Mince Pie Specials 26 December-1 January 2008
Facilities for disabled: Level access to all stations.Wheelchair ramps available at all stations. Full disabled toilet facilities at Haworth station. Non-folding wheelchairs can be accommodated in guard's

compartments. Staff available to offer assistance and advice at all stations. Museum of Rail Travel at Ingrow offers easy access to wheelchair users (inc toilet facilities). Audio loop and Braille facilities available and attention given to those with special needs
Special notes: Accompanied children under 5 years of age free. Children 5-15 and senior citizens at discount rate. Family ticket available (2 adults + 3 children/senior citizen). Free entry to VCT Museum with rover tickets
Membership details: Membership Secretary c/o above address
Membership journal: *Push & Pull* — quarterly
Marketing name: Worth Valley

<table>
<tr><td>Timetable Service</td><td>Kent & East Sussex Railway</td><td>Kent</td></tr>
</table>

Kent & East Sussex Railway

Member: HRA, TT
The Kent & East Sussex Railway owes much of its charm to its origin as the world's first light railway. The tightly curved line with steep gradients is typical of those country railways that were developed on shoestring budgets to bring the 'iron horse' to sparsely populated areas. Services operate over 10.5 miles of line from the picturesque town of Tenterden to Bodiam.
  Pride of the line's coach fleet is the magnificently restored train of vintage carriages built between 1860 and 1901
Company Secretary: Nick Pallant
Headquarters: Kent & East Sussex Railway Co Ltd, Tenterden Town Station, Tenterden, Kent TN30 6HE
Telephone: Tenterden (01580) 762943 (24 hour talking timetable); Tenterden 087 060 060 74 (office)
Internet address: *Web site:* www.kesr.org.uk
Main station: Tenterden Town
Other public stations: Rolvenden, Wittersham Road, Northiam, Bodiam
Car parks: Tenterden, Northiam
OS reference: Tenterden TQ 882336,

Locomotives and multiple-units

Name	No	Origin	Class	Type	Built
Bodiam	3	LBSCR	A1X	0-6-0T	1872*
Knowle	2678	LBSCR	A1X	0-6-0T	1880*
—	753	SECR	P	0-6-0T	1909*
Wainwright	DS238	SR	USA	0-6-0T	1943
Maunsell	65	SR	USA	0-6-0T	1943
—	1638	GWR	1600	0-6-0PT	1951*
—	20	GWR	AEC	diesel railcar	1940
Norwegian	376	NSB	21c	2-6-0	1919
—	D2023	BR	03	0-6-0DM	1958◊
—	D2024	BR	03	0-6-0DM	1958*
—	08108	BR	08	0-6-0DE	1955*
Ashford	D6570	BR	33	Bo-Bo	1961*
—	51571	BR	108	DMC	1959*
—	53971	BR	108	DMBS	1959*

Industrial locomotives

Name	No	Builder	Type	Built
Marcia	12	Peckett (1631)	0-4-0T	1923
Charwelton	14	M/Wardle (1955)	0-6-0ST	1917
Holman F. Stephens	23	Hunslet (3791)	0-6-0ST	1952*
Rolvenden	24	Hunslet (3800)	0-6-0ST	1953*
Northiam	25	Hunslet (3797)	0-6-0ST	1953*
—	40	BTH	Bo-Bo	1932*

*in passenger traffic

Passenger stock in service
SECR family saloon; LNWR 6-wheel director's saloon; SECR 4-wheel full third; SR Maunsell CK; GER 6-wheel composite; District Railway 4-wheel full first; 2 SR Maunsell brake open 1st Class; SR Maunsell non-descript brake-open; BR Mk 1 RU and 5 other BR Mk 1 coaches; 1926 Pullman Parlour Cars *Barbara* and *Theodora*

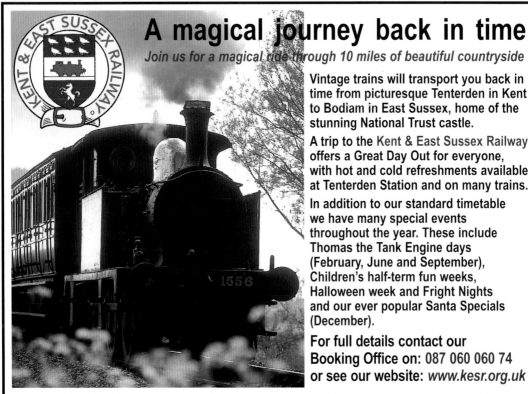

A magical journey back in time

Join us for a magical ride through 10 miles of beautiful countryside

Vintage trains will transport you back in time from picturesque Tenterden in Kent to Bodiam in East Sussex, home of the stunning National Trust castle.

A trip to the Kent & East Sussex Railway offers a Great Day Out for everyone, with hot and cold refreshments available at Tenterden Station and on many trains.

In addition to our standard timetable we have many special events throughout the year. These include Thomas the Tank Engine days (February, June and September), Children's half-term fun weeks, Halloween week and Fright Nights and our ever popular Santa Specials (December).

For full details contact our Booking Office on: 087 060 060 74 or see our website: *www.kesr.org.uk*

Northiam TQ 834266
Access by public transport:
Stagecoach No 400 from Ashford (Kent) main line station. Arriva No 12 Maidstone-Headcorn station-Tenterden & Rye.
Private hire: Wealden Cars
Refreshment facilities: Tenterden Town. Also on many trains. Lunch and afternoon teas on many trains (advance booking essential). Picnic areas at Tenterden, Wittersham Road, Northiam and Bodiam
Souvenir shop: Tenterden Town Station
Museum: Colonel Stephens Railway Museum at Tenterden Town
Depot: Rolvenden
Length of line: 10.5 miles
Passenger trains: Tenterden-Bodiam. All Bank Holidays and school holidays. Daily 24 July to 2 September. Most days ring for details, full service in August
Special events: All Fools Day — 1 April; Grandparents Weekend — 14/15 April; Country Music Weekend — 28/29 April; Colonel Stephens Weekend — 5-7 May; 40s Weekend — 19/20 May;

Stock
2 ex-SECR 'Birdcage' coaches; 2 ex-LSWR coaches; 1 GER observation car; 2 Pullman cars; 3 ex-SR Maunsell coaches; 3 steam cranes; large interesting collection of freight vehicles, totalling 51 vehicles

Evacuation Week — 22-24 May; Open Day — 28 May; Children's Fun Week — 29 May-1 June; Artist's Days — 6/7 May; Day out with Thomas* — 9/10, 16/17 June; Strawberry Express — 23/24 June; Victorian Experience — 26-28, 30 June, 1 July; Family/Railway History Day — 7 July; Tour de France — 8 July; 60s Transport Festival — 14/15 July; MG Car Rally — 28/29 July; Art Exhibition — 18/19 August; Open Day — 27 August; The Famous Hoppers Weekend* — 8/9 September; Pensioners' Treat (£7.50/seat) — 18-20 September; Day out with Thomas* — 22/23, 29/30 September; Tenterden Folk Festival — 6/7 October; Austin Counties Car Rally — 13/14 October; Half Term Fun Week — Halloween* — 22-26, 31 October; Autumn Walks — 3/4 November; Festive Programme* — 1/2, 7-9, 15/16,

21-24 December; Post Christmas Running — 27-31 December, 1 January 2008.
*tickets for reserved seats can be booked online
Facilities for disabled: A special coach for disabled people, 'Petros', is conveyed in many trains (telephone for confirmation of availability), reserved parking at Tenterden and Northiam.
Toilets with disabled access at Tenterden, Northiam and Bodiam, also in 'Petros'.
Plus induction loop at Tenterden
Special notes: The Wealden Pullman luxury dining car service operates on most Saturday evenings April to October and selected Fridays in the summer. Roast lunch served most Sundays. Advance booking is essential for these trains. Santa Special services operate on each Saturday and Sunday in December. Advance booking

recommended
Membership details: Membership Secretary, c/o above address

Membership journal: *The Tenterden Terrier* — 3 times/year

Steam Centre — Kew Bridge Steam Museum — London

The museum is housed in a magnificent 19th century Pumping Station and centres around the station's five world famous Cornish Beam Engines, three of which can be seen in steam on selected 'Cornish Engine Experience' weekends. Originally used to pump West London's water supply for more than a century, one of them, the 'Grand Junction 90', is the world's largest working beam engine. In surrounding buildings other large engines work at weekends, demonstrating more modern steam and diesel pumping machinery.

The Water For Life Gallery reveals the fascinating history of London's water supply from Roman toilet spoons to the massive 'high-tech' London ring main.

Many Victorian waterworks had their own railway. At Kew Bridge this is demonstrated by a short line, operated by the Hampshire Narrow Gauge Railway Trust. 1998 saw the return to steam of *Cloister* for the first time in 22 years

Location: 100yd from the north side of Kew Bridge, next to the tall Victorian tower

Operating group: Kew Bridge Engines Trust, Green Dragon Lane, Brentford, Middx TW8 0EN

Telephone: 020 8568 4757 (information line)

Internet address: *Web site:* www.kbsm.org

Car park: Free on site

Access by public transport: *Rail:* SouthWest Trains, Kew Bridge

Industrial locomotives

2ft gauge:

Name	No	Builder	Type	Built
Cloister	—	Hunslet (542)	0-4-0ST	1891
Alister	2	Lister (44052)	4wDM	1958

(from Waterloo via Clapham Junction) and North London Line to Gunnersbury; *Bus:* Nos 65, 237, 267, 391; *Tube:* Gunnersbury (District Line, then 237 or 267 bus), Kew Gardens (District Line, then 391 bus)

Length of line/gauge: About 140yd, 2ft gauge

Public opening:
Museum: Tuesdays to Sundays 11.00-17.00. Closed Mondays (except Bank Holidays), Good Friday and 22-26 December 2007. Railway: see below

Special events: Exhibition: 'Design for Living' (more wonderful gadgets from the past)— until 15 April; Stirling & Hot Air Engine Rally — 25 March; Kew Bridge Model Boat Show — 28*/29 April; Historic Fire Engine Rally — 20 May; Festival of Model Tramways — 21*/22 July; Waterworks at War - 1940s event — 25/26*/27 August; Model Steam Extravaganza — 6*/7 October; Live Steam Model Railway Show — 17*/18 November.

*The railway is scheduled to operate every Sunday March to November, plus Saturdays marked **

On site facilities:
Bookshop/toilets/car park. Refreshments available at weekends only

Facilities for disabled: Wheelchair access to 90% of ground floor areas via ramp and lift. Large print guide available and guide dogs welcome. Wheelchair loan service and wheelchair accessible toilet. Railway carriage can accommodate wheelchairs.

Special note: Groups of 10 or more can be given guided tours and a 10% discount on admission charges. Special steaming can be arranged and touch tours are available for partially sighted groups. All groups must be pre-booked.

Children under 13 must be accompanied by an adult.

Different admission rates apply to selected special events and tower tours. Please contact the museum for details

Special facilities: The museum can be hired for corporate or private events. Special steamings can be arranged. Please contact for brochure

Museum contact: Kew Bridge Engines Trust, c/o above address

Railway contact: HNGRT, 161 Bramley Crescent, Southampton, Hants SO1 9LG

Other attractions: Museum displays a selection of stationary steam engines and associated water supply displays

Museum — Kidderminster Railway Museum — Worcestershire

Established in an 1878 GWR warehouse, the museum houses an enormous collection of railway

relics, photographs and documents, with a number of 'hands-on' exhibits.

Contact address: Station Approach, Comberton Hill, Kidderminster, Worcestershire

DY10 1QX
General Manager: David Postle
Telephone: Kidderminster (01562) 825316
Internet address:
e-mail: krm@krm.org.uk
Web site: www.krm.org.uk
OS reference: SO 837763
Location: Adjacent to SVR station

Car park: SVR car park
Access by public transport: Kidderminster main line station, Midland Red bus service X92 to Kidderminster
Facilities for disabled: Ramp access for wheelchairs to ground level
Special events: Practical signalling

courses using Museum and SVR resources. Filmshows, model railway exhibitions, railway art exhibitions, postcard/photograph fairs,
On site facilities: Souvenirs, refreshments
Public opening: Open on SVR operating days

Timetable Service — Kirklees Light Railway — West Yorkshire

Member: HRA
Location/headquarters: Clayton West, A636 Wakefield-Denby Dale road
General Manager: Graham Hurd
Operating society/organisation: Kirklees Light Railway, Park Mill Way, Clayton West, Nr Huddersfield HD8 9XJ
Telephone: (01484) 865727
Internet address: *Web site:* www.kirkleeslightrailway.com
Location: Clayton West, the terminus of the railway, is situated midway between Wakefield, Barnsley, Holmfirth and Huddersfield, on the A636 Wakefield-Denby Dale Road
Main station: Clayton West
Other station: Cuckoos Nest, Skelmanthorpe, Shelley
Length of line: 4 miles, 15in gauge
Car park: Clayton West — free
Access by public transport: By bus: from Holmfirth No 484, from Leeds No 482 (484) from Wakefield No 484.
From Barnsley No 235, from Huddersfield Nos 235/240, from

Locomotives

Name	No	Builder	Type	Built
Fox	—	Taylor	2-6-2T	1987
Badger	—	Taylor	0-6-4T	1991
Tram Engine	7	Taylor	0-4-0	1995
Jay	—	Taylor	4wD	1992
Hawk	—	Taylor	0-4-4-0*	1998
Owl	—	Taylor	4w-4wT*	2000

*articulated

Rolling stock
2 rakes of six carriages (some heated in winter), 4-wheel tool van, 4-wheel ballast/stone wagon, heavy bogie flat car for rail carrying

Wakefield No 935. Ask driver for Park Mill Way, Clayton West.
By rail to Huddersfield, Wakefield or Denby Dale stations
Refreshment facilities: Clayton West, visitor centre and café
Souvenir shop: Clayton West
On site facilities: Toilets, swings, half-scale roundabouts, lake. HQ of Barnsley Society of Model Engineers
Facilities for disabled: Yes
Period of public operation: Winter— weekends & most school

holidays. Summer — daily from Spring Bank Holiday to end August
Special events: Easter Eggspress — 6-10 April; Day out with Thomas — 28/29 May, 23/24 June, 21/22 July, 31 August to 2 September; Halloween Ghost Train — 28/29 October; Santa Specials — weekends 25 November to 24 December
Special facilities: Footplate experience courses

Timetable Service — Lakeside & Haverthwaite Railway — Cumbria

Member: HRA, TT
Originally this Furness Railway branch line carried passengers and freight from Ulverston to Lakeside but now the only part remaining is the 3.5-mile section from Haverthwaite to the terminus at Lakeside where connections are made with the steamers which ply the 10-mile length of Windermere
General Manager: M. A. Maher

Headquarters: Lakeside & Haverthwaite Railway Co Ltd, Haverthwaite Station, Nr Ulverston, Cumbria LA12 8AL
Telephone: Newby Bridge (015395) 31594
Internet address: *Web site:* www.lakesiderailway.co.uk
Main station: Haverthwaite
Other public stations: Intermediate station at Newby

Bridge. Terminus at Lakeside
OS reference: SD 349843
Car parks: Haverthwaite, Lakeside
Access by public transport: Lakeside steamers on Windermere call at Lakeside. CMS bus to Haverthwaite
Refreshment facilities: Haverthwaite
Souvenir shop: Haverthwaite
On site facilities: Picnic area at

England

Haverthwaite. Disabled toilets
Depot: All rolling stock at
Haverthwaite
Length of line: 3.5 miles
Passenger trains: Steam-hauled
Haverthwaite-Lakeside
Period of public operation:
31 March to 28 October 2007
(inclusive)
Special events: Santa Specials
(advance booking essential) please
contact for details
Facilities for disabled: Access to
trains and restaurant
Special notes: Combined
railway/lake steamer tickets
available, from the station at
Haverthwaite and lake steamer
piers at Bowness and Ambleside.
Lake steamers are operated by
Windermere Lake Cruises Ltd
Membership journal: *The Iron
Horse* — quarterly

Locomotives and multiple-units

Name	No	Origin	Class	Type	Built
—	20	FR	A5	0-4-0	1863
—	42073	LMS	4MT	2-6-4T	1950
—	42085	LMS	4MT	2-6-4T	1951
—	17(AD601)	LMS	—	0-6-0DE	1945
—	5643	GWR	5600	0-6-2T	1925
—	8(D2117)	BR	03	0-6-0DM	1959
—	D2072	BR	03	0-6-0DM	1959
—	20214	BR	20	Bo-Bo	1967
—	D5301	BR	26	Bo-Bo	1958
—	52071	BRCW	110	DMBC	1961
—	52077	BRCW	110	DMBC	1961

Industrial locomotives

Name	No	Builder	Type	Built
Caliban*	1	Peckett (1925)	0-4-0ST	1937
Rachel	9	M/Rail (2098)	4wDM	1924
Repulse	11	Hunslet (3698)	0-6-0ST	1950
Princess	14	Bagnall (2682)	0-6-0ST	1942
—	10	Barclay (1245)	0-6-0T	1911
David	13	Barclay (2333)	0-4-0ST	1953
Cumbria	10	Hunslet (3794)	0-6-0ST	1953
Fluff	16	Hunslet/Fowler	0-4-0DM	1937
—	20	Jones crane	0-4-0DM	1952
Sir James	21	Barclay (1550)	0-6-0F	1917

*under restoration at Steamtown, Carnforth

Stock
10 ex-BR Mk 1 coaches; 1 ex-LNER BG; 1 ex-BR Mk 1 miniature buffet
coach, Royal saloon No 5 (built GER, Stratford 1898), North London
coach (c1890); selection of freight vehicles

Miniature Railway — Lakeside Miniature Railway — Lancashire

The longest continuously running
15in gauge railway in Great Britain,
running during both world wars.
The first train ran at 3pm on 25
May 1911. The line was extended
in 1948, now running between two
stations, Pleasureland and Marine
Parade.
Location: Marine Lake, Southport
Headquarters: 1 Wingates,
Penwortham, Preston, Lancs
PR1 9YN
Contact: Mr D. Clark
Telephone: 01772 745511
Internet address: *e-mail:*
jennifer.clark2@virgin.net
Web site:
www.lakesideminiaturerailway.co.uk
Car parking: In Ocean Piazza car
parks, opposite

Locomotives

Name	No	Builder	Type	Built
Duke of Edinburgh	—	Barlow	4-6-2+4-4DE	1947
Prince Charles	—	Barlow	4-6-2+4-4DE	1954
Golden Jubilee	—	Barlow	4-6w+4-4DE	1963
Princess Anne	—	S/Lamb	6w-6DH	1971
Jenny	—	A. Moss	2-6-2DH	2006

Rolling stock
3 sets of carriages each seating 72 passengers

On site facilities: Shop (selling ice
cream, soft drinks, and Thomas the
Tank Engine)
Length of line: 800yd, 15in gauge
Period of public operation:
Easter to end of October, and
during school holidays (weather
permitting). 11.00-16.30. Journey
time 5min (single) 14min (return)
Facilities for disabled: Wheelchair
access
Membership details: See web site
Fare: £15.0 (single, £2.00 (return)

| Steam Centre | Lappa Valley Railway | Cornwall |

Member: TT
Location/headquarters: Benny Halt, St Newlyn East, Nr Newquay, Cornwall TR8 5LX
Telephone: 01872 510317
Internet address: *web site:* www.lappavalley.co.uk
General Manager: Miss Amanda Booth
Main station: Benny Halt
Other station: East Wheal Rose, Newlyn Downs Halt
Car park: Benny Halt
Access by public transport: Bus service, Newquay to Truro and return. Western National and The Cornishman coaches to St Newlyn East. Signposted, half-mile walk from bus stop to railway. No direct bus service
Refreshment facilities: Café at East Wheal Rose serving hot and cold food, snacks, hot and cold drinks; licensed
Souvenir shop: East Wheal Rose and Benny Halt
On site facilities: 15in, 10.25in and 7.25in gauge railways. Canoes, paddle boats, crazy golf, pedal cars, electric motorbikes, children's play

Locomotives

Name	No	Builder	Type	Built
Muffin	2	Berwyn	0-6-0	1967
		rebuilt Tambling		1991
Zebedee	1	S/Lamb	0-6-4T	1974
		rebuilt Tambling		1990
Gladiator	3	Minirail	4w-4wDH	c1960
Pooh	4	Lister (20698)	4wDM	1942

(all 15in gauge)

Rolling stock
15in gauge — 10 passenger coaches
10.25in gauge — 4 passenger coaches, 2 wagons
7.25in gauge — 1 Mardyke APT set

area, brick path maze, listed engine house, walks and a video
Depot: Benny Halt
Facilities for disabled: Limited number of reserved parking bays. Toilets at East Wheal Rose and Benny Halt. All buildings are single storey with no steps. Level or gently sloping paths with even surfaces. Main steam train has compartments with doors that will accommodate wheelchairs (only the largest motorised wheelchairs are excluded), ramps and staff available

to assist. The smaller train at East Wheal Rose cannot take wheelchairs. Some other attractions are not suitable for wheelchair users (eg canoes, mine building, maze and country walks)
Public opening: Easter to end of October, usually daily but ring for early and late season opening days
Special notes: Entry by one all-in price, except for electric bikes.
Family tickets and reduced afternoon saver fares are available all days. Under 3s free

| Timetable Service | Launceston Steam Railway | Cornwall |

Member: HRA, TT
The railway runs through the beautiful Kensey Valley on a track gauge of 1ft 11.5in, following the trackbed of the old North Cornwall line. The locomotives formerly worked on the Dinorwic and Penrhyn railways in North Wales. Launceston station contains a museum of vintage cars and motorcycles and a collection of stationary steam engines which are demonstrated at work. There are catering, gift shop and bookshop facilities. At the far end of the line there are pleasant riverside walks and a shaded picnic area, adjacent to Newmills Farm Park (a popular separate attraction). The covered rolling stock ensures an enjoyable

Industrial locomotives

Name	No	Builder	Type	Built
Lilian	—	Hunslet (317)	0-4-0ST	1883
Velinheli	—	Hunslet (409)	0-4-0ST	1886
Covertcoat	—	Hunslet (679)	0-4-0ST	1898
Sybil	—	Bagnall (1760)	0-4-0ST	1906
Dorothea	—	Hunslet (763)	0-4-0ST	1901
—	—	M/Rail (5646)	4wDM	1933
—	—	M/Rail (9546)	4wDM	1950

Locomotive notes: All passenger trains are steam-hauled

Stock
1 electric inspection trolley; 4 bogie carriages (2 open, 2 closed), 1 diesel-electric railcar for maintenance staff
2 Post Office Railway 'Mail Train' units

visit whatever the weather. The station area was once the site of an Augustinian Priory some of which can be seen by visitors to the railway

Location: Newport Industrial Estate, Launceston, Cornwall
OS reference: SX 328850
Operating society/organisation: The Spice Settlement Trust Co Ltd, trading as the Launceston Steam Railway, Newport, Launceston PL15 8DA
Telephone: (01566) 775665
Stations: Launceston-Hunts Crossing-New Mills
Car park: Newport Industrial Estate, Launceston
Length of line: 2.5 miles

Gauge: 1ft 11.5in
Access by public transport: Main line Gunnislake 13 miles, Plymouth or Bodmin 25 miles then bus
On site facilities: Buffet, transport museum, workshop tours, gift and bookshop, all situated at Launceston
Period of public operation: Easter (6-13 April, Friday-Friday). Daily 27 May until 21 September EXCEPT Saturdays
Public opening: Trains run from 10.30-16.30. Departures about every 50min — 11.00, 11.50, 12.45, 14.00, 14.45, 15.35, 16.30. Day Rover Tickets, unlimited riding on date of issue of ticket
Family ticket: Available, 2 adults

and up to 4 children, £23. Adults £7.50, children £5
Free travel: Children under three years old
Senior citizens: Discounted tickets £6
Groups: Discounted tickets
Journey time: Return 35min
Facilities for disabled: Easy access to all areas except bookshop and motorcycle museum. No toilet facilities for disabled. However, public toilets are reasonably accessible
Special events: Double-headed trains on Wednesdays in August (whenever possible). Demonstration freight trains (contact for details)

Steam Centre — Lavender Line — East Sussex

Member: HRA

The Lavender Line is centred around a typical country station, which, somewhat untypically, is in the village it was built to serve. The image portrayed is of the transition steam-diesel era of the 1950s/1960s on the Southern Region of British Railways

Location: Isfield Station, Isfield, Nr Uckfield, East Sussex TN22 5XB. Isfield village is off the A26 between Lewes and Uckfield
OS reference: TQ 452171
Operating society/organisation: The Lavender Line Preservation Society
Telephone/Fax:
Information line: 0891 800645
Business/fax: 01825 750515 (24hr answerphone when not manned)
Internet address: *Web site:* www.lavender-line.co.uk
Car park: On site, free to patrons
Access by car: The village of Isfield lies just off the A26 between Lewes and Uckfield and is clearly signposted. From the Little Horstead rounabout on the A22 just outside Uckfield, take the A26 south towards Lewes and after about 1-mile take the small right hand turn marked Isfield. Follow the road until you see the railway on your right. From the A272 running between Uckfield and Haywards Heath, take the turn at Piltdown and follow the signs to the

Multiple-unit

Name	No	Origin	Class	Type	Built
—	69333	BR	422 / 4BIG	TRBS	1965
—*	60151	BR	205	DTC	1962
—*	60678	BR	205	DMBS	1962
—	60822	BR	205	DTC	1957
—*	60832	BR	205	DTC	1962

*unit 205033

Industrial locomotives

Name	No	Builder	Type	Built
Blackie	68012	Hunslet (3193)	0-6-0ST	1944
Austin No 1†	—	Kitson (5459)	0-6-0ST	1932
—	—	Sentinel (6515)	0-4-0VBT	1945
—	—	Barclay	0-4-0DM	1945
—	—	Vulcan	0-4-0DM	1945
—	15	Planet (3865)	4wDM	1965

*2ft gauge
†on hire from Llangollen Railway for 2007

Stock
A selection of BR Mk 1 vehicles including BCK, TSO and BG, as well as a selection of wagons

Lavender Line and Isfield. From Lewes take the A26 northwards towards Uckfield. After about 5 miles look for a turning on the left to Isfield, follow the road until you see the railway on your right
Access by public transport:
By bus: Service 29 run by Brighton & Hove Buses calls at Isfield and runs between Brighton and Tunbridge Wells. Tel: 01273 886200 or visit http://www.buses.co.uk

By rail: Main line stations at Lewes and Uckfield. On Sundays trains to Uckfield only operate on a much reduced frequency. Tel: 08457 484950
On site facilities: 'Cinders' buffet/restaurant, gift shop, goods shed museum, picnic area, access to signalbox. Children's parties arranged on operating days. Family area. Private functions, weddings and parties etc catered for
Length of line: 1 mile each out and

back trip, takes 15min

Public opening: Open Sundays all year, Bank Holidays, weekends in June, July and August.Wednesdays and Thursdays in August. Site open from 10.00-17.00, trains from 11.00
Please note that the Isfield site is normally open for viewing outside of operating dates
Facilities for disabled: Access to most facilities on site. Toilets with wheelchair access and baby changing facilities. Wheelchair access to most of site except signalbox and trains. A ramp is available for partially disabled access to the trains
Special events: Ivor the Engine — 2/3, 9/10 June, please ring for details. Santa Specials — 1/2, 8/9, 15/16, 18-23 December.
Ticket price is valid for unlimited rides on day of issue; however, on special event days entry prices, and conditions, may vary
Special facilities: Footplate courses, occasional wine and dine services. Please contact for details

Museum	Leeds Industrial Museum	Leeds

Location: The Leeds Industrial Museum, Armley Mills, Canal Road, Leeds LS12 2QF
OS reference: SE 275342
Operating society/organisation: Leeds City Council, Department of Learning & Leisure, The Town Hall, Headrow, Leeds LS1 2QF
Curator of Engineering: N. Dowlan
Telephone: (0113) 263 7861
Car park: Cark park adjacent to the Museum
Access by public transport: Nos 5A, 14, 66 and 67 from City Square, Leeds (outside the railway station)
Public opening: April-September: Tuesdays-Saturdays 10.00-17.00, Sundays 13.00-17.00. October-March: Tuesdays-Saturdays 10.00-17.00, Sundays 13.00-17.00. Closed Mondays (except Bank Holidays). NB: last admission 16.00 on all days
Special events: Plant in Steam — Tuesdays 24 July-11 September
On site facilities: Museum shop, refreshments (vending machines), picnic area
Special notes: Facilities for the disabled (toilets etc), lifts. Museum can be viewed by visitors in wheelchairs (most areas are accessible)
Details of locomotive and rolling stock: Locomotive collection includes steam, diesel, mines locomotives and a narrow gauge railway and engines

Industrial locomotives

Name	No	Builder	Type	Built
1ft 6in gauge				
Jack	—	Hunslet 684)	0-4-0WT	1898
Coffin	—*	G/Bat (1326)	0-4-0BE	1933
2ft gauge				
Barber	—	T/Green (441)	0-6-2ST	1908
Cheetal	—	Fowler (15991)	0-6-0WT	1923
Simplex	—	M/Rail (1369	4wPM	1918
Hudson Fordson	—	Hudson (36863)	4wDM	1928
Layer	—*	Fowler (21294)	4wDM	1936
Hudson Hunslet	—	Hunslet (2959)	4wDM	1944
Resin	—	Hunslet (2008)	0-4-0DM	1939
Nacob	—*	Hunslet (5340)	0-4-0DM	1957
Sharlston	—†	H/Clarke (1164)	0-4-0DM	1959
Demtox	—†*	Hunslet (6048)	0-4-0DM	1961
2ft 1in gauge				
Fricl	—*	Hunslet (4019)	0-4-0DM	1948
Pitpo	—*	Hunslet	0-4-0	1955
Calverton	—*	H/Clarke (1368)	0-4-0DM	1965
2ft 6in gauge				
Junin	—	H/Clarke (D557)	2-6-2DM	1930
Fimyn	—†	Hunslet (3411)	0-4-0DM	1947
2ft 8in gauge				
Ficol	—*	Hunslet (3200)	0-4-0DM	1945
2ft 11in gauge				
Lurch	—	H/Clarke (D571)	4wDM	1932
3ft gauge				
Lord Granby	—*	H/Clarke (633)	0-4-0ST	1902
Cement	—*	Fowler (20685)	2-4-0DM	1935
Lofti	—*	Hunslet (4057)	0-6-0DM	1953
3ft 6in gauge				
Pioneer	—	H/Clarke (D634)	0-6-0DM	1946
Festival of Britain	—*	H/Clarke (D733)	0-6-0DM	1951
Standard gauge				
Hodbarrow	—*	Hunslet (299)	0-4-0ST	1882
Aldwyth	—	M/Wardle (865)	0-6-0ST	1882
Capper	—	Fowler (22060)	0-4-0DM	1938

England

Name	No	Builder	Type	Built
Fort William	—*	Fowler (22893)	0-4-0DM	1940
Trecwn	—	Hunslet (2390)	0-4-0DM	1941
Elizabeth	—	H/Clarke (1888)	0-4-0ST	1958
Southam No 2	—*	H/Clarke (D625)	0-4-0DM	1942
Luton	—	G/Bat (1210)	0-4-0BE	1930
Smithy Wood	—*	G/Bat (2543)	0-4-0WE	1955

Notes

*not currently on public display

†on loan to Red Rose Steam Society/Astley Green Colliery Museum

Simplex is on loan to Moseley Industrial Railway Museum

Barber is on loan to the South Tynedale Railway Trust from February 2004

Timetable Service — Leighton Buzzard Railway — Bedfordshire

Member: HRA, TT

The LBR enables visitors to take a 70min journey into the vanished world of the English light railway. Sharp curves and steep gradients make the locomotives work hard and it is unique with its roadside running. The LBR possesses one of the largest collection of narrow gauge locomotives in Britain together with a varied selection of coaches and wagons — an important part of the national railway heritage. Many items are on permanent display, and some can be seen in action at special events

General Manager: J. Horsley

Headquarters: Leighton Buzzard Railway, Page's Park Station, Billington Road, Leighton Buzzard, Bedfordshire LU7 4TN

OS reference: Page's Park SP 928242

Telephone: (01525) 373888, 24hr answerphone with service and event details

Fax: (01525) 377814

Internet address: *e-mail:* info@buzzrail.co.uk

Web site: www.buzzrail.co.uk

Main station: Page's Park. The station is on the A4146 to the south of Leighton Buzzard, near its junction with the A505

Other public stations: Stonehenge Works

Car park: Page's Park, free

Access by public transport: Leighton Buzzard main line station, Silverlink County services from London (Euston), Watford, Hemel Hempstead, Milton Keynes and

Locomotives

Name	No	Builder	Type	Built
—	740	O&K (2343)	0-6-0T	1907
—	—	O&K (2544)	0-4-0WT	1907
Pedemoura	—	O&K (10808)	0-6-0WT	1924
—	778	Baldwin (44656)	4-6-0T	1917
—	—	Freudenstein (73)	0-4-0WT	1901
Sezela No 4	—	Avonside (1738)	0-4-0T	1915
Peter Pan	114	K/Stuart (4256)	0-4-0ST	1922
Chaloner	1	de Winton	0-4-0VBT	1877
Bluebell	1	Hibberd (2631)	4wDM	1938
Pixie	2	K/Stuart (4260)	0-4-0ST	1922
Rishra	3	Baguley (2007)	0-4-0T	1921
Doll	4	Barclay (1641)	0-6-0T	1919
Elf	5	O&K (12740)	0-6-0WT	1936
Falcon	7	O&K (8986)	4wDM	1938
—	8	Ruston (217999)	4wDM	1943
Madge	9	O&K (7600)	4wDM	1934
Haydn Taylor	10	M/Rail (7956)	4wDM	1945
P. C. Allen	11	O&K (5834)	0-4-0WT	1912
—	12	M/Rail (6012)	4wPM	1930
Arkle	13	M/Rail (7108)	4wDM	1937
—	14	Hunslet (3646)	4wDM	1946
—	15	Hibberd (2514)	4wDM	1941
—	16	Lister (11221)	4wDM	1939
Damredub	17	M/Rail (7036)	4wDM	1936
Feanor	18	M/Rail (11003)	4wDM	1956
—	19	M/Rail (11298)	4wDM	1965
—	20	M/Rail (60s317)	4wDM	1966
Festoon	21	M/Rail (4570)	4wPM	1929
—	22	under construction	4wDM	—
—	23	Ruston (164346)	4wDM	1932
—	25	M/Rail (7214)	4wDM	1938
—	24	M/Rail (11297)	4wDM	1965
Yimkin	26	Ruston (203026)	4wDM	1941
—	27	Ruston (408430)	4wDM	1957
RAF Stanbridge	28	Ruston (200516)	4wDM	1940
Creepy	29	Hunslet (6008)	4wDM	1963
—	30	M/Rail (8695)	4wDM	1941
—	31	Lister (4228)	4wPM	1931
—	32	Ruston (172892)	4wDM	1934
—	33	Hibberd (3582)	4wDM	1954
Red Rum	34	M/Rail (7105)	4wDM	1936

Northampton (Tel: 08457 484950).
Nearest bus stops at Morrisons
supermarket (5min walk) and
Leighton Buzzard town centre
(20 min walk). (Tel: 01234 228337
for details)
Refreshment facilities: Dobbers
buffet at Page's Park for hot & cold
snacks, drinks and ice creams.
Refreshments also at Stonehenge
Works
Souvenir shop: Page's Park and
Stonehenge Works
Depots: Page's Park and
Stonehenge Works
Length of line: 2.85 miles,
2ft gauge
Journey time: Single 25min, return
70min
Passenger trains: Page's Park-
Stonehenge Works
  Group discounts for pre-booked
parties of 10 or more people.
Packages such as Birthday Breaks,
Schools trains and Sunset Specials
available, plus train hire
Period of public operation:
Sundays 11 March-28 October,
11 November;
Mondays 9 April, 7, 28 May,
27 August;
Tuesdays 31 July, 7-21 August;
Wednesdays 4, 11 April, 30 May,
6-27 June, 4-25 July, 1-22 August,
24 October;
Friday 6 April;
Saturdays 7 April, 5, 26 May, 4-25
August, 8 September, 6 October.
Plus Christmas services in
December
Special events: Mothering Sunday
— 18 March; Easter Fun —
6-9 April; Teddy Bears' Holiday —
6 May; Father's Day — 17 June;
Vintage Vehicles Rally — 24 June;
Model Railways — 29 July; Family
Fun Day — 12 August; Steam Up

Name	No	Builder	Type	Built
Binky	35	Hunslet (6619)	0-4-0DM	1966
Caravan	36	M/Rail (7129)	4wDM	1938
—	37	Ruston (172901)	4wDM	1934
Harry Barnet	38	Lister (37170)	4wDM	1951
T. W. Lewis	39	Ruston (375316)	4wDM	1954
Trent	40	Ruston (283507)	4wDM	1949
Somme	41	Hunslet (2536)	4wDM	1941
Sarah	42	Ruston (223692)	4wDM	1944
—	43	M/Rail (10409)	4wDM	1954
—	44	M/Rail (7933)	4wDM	1941
—	45	M/Rail (21615)	4wDM	1957
—	46	Ruston (209430)	4wDM	1942
—	47	Hudson (38384)	4wDM	1930
MacNamara	48	Hunslet (4351)	4wDM	1952
—	49	Hibberd (2586)	4wDM	1941
—	50	Hibberd (1568)	4wPM	1927
Beaudesert	80	A/Keef (59R)	4wDM	1999
Peter Wood	81	Hunslet (9347)	4wDH	1994
—	3098	M/Rail (1369)	4wPM	1918
—	2182	M/Rail (461)	4wPM	1917
LOD 758009	—	M/Rail (8641)	4wDM	1941
LOD 758220	—	M/Rail (8745)	4wDM	1942
RTT/767182	—	Wickham (2522)	4wPMR	1938
WD 767139	—	Wickham (3282)	4wPMR	1943

Stock
10 coaches and a wide selection of wagons

A selection of locomotives and rolling stock is on public display at any one
time. Viewing of other stock is by prior arrangement

Weekend — 8/9 September; Steam
Glow — 6 October; Halloween
Haunting — 28 October; Armistice
Day — 11 November
Working Heritage Attractions:
Industry Trains — 8 April, 28 May,
17 June, 9 September
Sand Quarry — check web site for
details
Facilities for disabled: Priority
parking at Page's Park. Ramp
access to all facilities including
dedicated toilet at Page's Park.
Wheelchairs are conveyed in

specially adapted coaches. Advance
notice appreciated. Web site pages
and leaflets available in large print
on request
Membership details: The line is
operated by unpaid volunteers.
Membership secretary, c/o above
address
Membership journal: *Chaloner* —
quarterly
Marketing name: The Leighton
Buzzard Slow Train

Miniature Railway — Lightwater Valley Theme Park — North Yorkshire

Location: Lightwater Valley Theme
Park
Headquarters: North Stainley, Nr
Ripon, North Yorkshire
Contact: Operations &
Maintenance Dept: P. Walker
Telephone: 0870 458 0060,
0870 458 0040
(administration/party bookings)
Internet address:

Web site: www.lightwatervalley.net
Car parking: On site
Access by public transport: Main
line station Harrogate (12 miles)
and Thirsk (9 miles)
On site facilities: 125 acres of
country park featuring unique
white knuckle rides including
Europe's longest rollercoaster,
family attractions, go-karting.

Wide range of catering facilities
and themed shopping malls
Length of line: 15in gauge; 1 mile
long
Period of public operation:
Easter-October (daily in
June/July/August). Telephone for
details

England

Lincolnshire Wolds Railway

Members: HRA

The only standard gauge steam railway in Lincolnshire open to the public. The location is part of the original Great Northern Railway, which opened in 1848

Headquarters: The Railway Station, Ludborough, Grimsby, NE Lincs DN36 5SQ

Telephone: 01507 363881

Internet address: *Web site:* www.lincolnshirewoldsrailway. co.uk

Contacts: David Ambler / Frank Street

Main station: Ludborough

OS reference: TF 302986

Car park: Opposite station site

Access by public transport: No access by rail, very limited Grimsby-Louth bus service

Refreshment facilities: Light refreshments available in buffet car in bay platform on diesel and steam days

Souvenir shop: On site

Museum: On site

Depot: On site

Length of line: 1,600yd at present

Period of public operation: Site open for static viewing all weekends except Christmas. April to September 09.00-16.00, October to March 09.00-15.00. First train leaves at 11.00 on following dates

Special events: Steam dates for

Locomotives and multiple-units

Name	No	Origin	Class	Type	Built
—	D3167	BR	08	0-6-0DE	1955
—	97650	BR	—	0-6-0DE	1953
—	62887	BR	4CIG/ 421	MBS	1970

Industrial locomotives

Name	No	Builder	Type	Built
Lion	—	Peckett (1657)	0-4-0ST	1914
Fulstow	No 2	RSH (7849)	0-6-0ST	1955
M. F. P. No 1	—	Fowler (4210131)	0-4-0DM	1957
M. O. P. No 8	—	Fowler (4210145)	0-4-0DM	1958
Tioxide No 4	—	R/Hornsby (375713)	0-4-0DM	1954
Tioxide No 6	—	R/Hornsby (414303)	0-4-0DM	1957
Tioxide No 7	—	R/Hornsby (421418)	0-4-0DM	1958
—	—	Sentinel (10166)	0-6-0DH	1963
Colonel B	—	Hunslet (5308)	4wDH	1963

Stock

6 ex-BR Mk 2 coaches, various wagons

Owner

D3167 and 97650 on loan from Lincoln City Council

2007 are: 25 March, 8, 22 April; Vintage tractors — 6 May; 27 May; 3 June; Lincolnshire Louth Motor Club Day — 17 June; 8, 22 July; 13 August; 12, 26 August; 1940s Weekend 8/9 September; 23 September; 14, 28 October; 18 November; Santa Specials 9, 16 December

Facilities for disabled: Full facilities were available on site by

Easter 2006, a coach in process of adaptation for disabled use as another buffet car, access to rest of site and train is complete

Membership journal: *On the Line* — 3 times/year

Special note: Unlimited travel on the day

Locomotion — The NRM at Shildon

Member: HRA

Locomotion is an £11 million project, a joint venture between Sedgefield Borough Council and the National Railway Museum at York, the first branch of a national museum in the region. The development includes interactive displays within buildings which are of historical importance in terms of the town's railway heritage and a brand new high quality 6,000 sq ft

Locomotives and multiple-units

Name	No	Origin	Class	Type	Built
Sans Pareil		L&MR		0-4-0	1829
Cornwall	3020	LNWR	—	2-2-2	1847
—	563	LSWR	T3	4-4-0	1893
—	75S	W&CR	—	Bo electric	1898
—	68846	GNR	J52	0-6-0ST	1899
1		NER	BTH	Bo electric	1904
—	901	NER	T3	0-8-0	1919
—	2	NSR	New L	0-6-2T	1923
—	2500	LMS	4P	2-6-4T	1934
—	2700	LMS	5P4F	2-6-0	1934

England

centre, which houses up to 60 vehicles from the national collection.

Museum Manager: Dr George Muirhead

Location/address: Locomotion, Shildon, Co Durham DL4 1PQ

Telephone: 01388 777999

Telephone/Fax: 01388 771448

Internet addresses: *e-mail:* sjoyce@locomotion.uk.com

Web site: www.locomotion.uk.com

Car parking: Available on site, also disabled and coach parking

Access by public transport: Rail – 3min walk from Shildon station. Bus – local bus services (call Traveline on 0870 608 2608). Car – junction 58 A1M, take A68 and A6072 to Shildon and follow signs

On site facilities: Café, children's playground, picnic area, public art sculpture, shop

Length of line: 1 kilometre

Public opening: 10.00-17.00 every day from Easter to end of October. 10.00-16.00 Wednesday to Sunday from November to Easter. Closed 19 December-4 January

Special events: A full and exciting events programme, contact Locomotion for full details

Access for disabled: All buildings fully accessible. Call Locomotion in advance to book a wheelchair. Bio-bus accommodates disabled visitors to transport from one end of the site to the other.

Special facilities: There are three conference rooms, each holding from 10 to 65 people, catering and presentation equipment available. Space for 200 people for a sit down meal in the Collection building.

Special note: Steam train rides on summer Sundays and event days

Name	No	Origin	Class	Type	Built
—	10656	SR	2BIL	DMBSK	1937
—	12123	SR	2BIL	DTCK	1937
Deltic	—	E/Electric	-	Co-Co	1955
—	E5001	BR	71	Bo-Bo	1959
—	03090	BR	03	0-6-0DM	1960
Sans Pareil	—*	L&MR		0-4-0	1980

Industrial and Army locomotives

Name	No	Builder	Type	Built
Woolmer	—	Avonside (1572)	0-6-0ST	1910
Elidir	—**	Avonside (2071)	0-4-0T	1933
—	314	Hunslet (1215)	4-6-0T	1916
—	—	Simplex (4217)	4wPM	1925
Hexhamshire	15	A/Whitworth (D21)	0 4-0DE	1933
Merlin	—§	Peckett	0-4-0ST	1939
Hetton Loco	—	G. Stephenson	0-4-0	1851
King Fisal of Iraq	—	Hunslet (3183)	0-6-0ST	1944
—	1	Barclay (2373)	0-4-0F	1956
Rowntrees No 3	—	R/Hornsby (441934)	4wDM	1960
—	—	H/Clarke (D1345)	0-4-0DH	1970
Eustace Forth	—	R/Hornsby (7063)	0-6-0ST	1942
—	14†	H/Clarke (D1274)	0-6-0DM	1961
—	—	H/Clarke (D1345)	0-6-0DM	1967
MTR	9†	Hunslet (9227	B-BDH	1986

*replica of original Liverpool & Manchester Railway built for the 150th anniversary
§off-site for overhaul
†3ft gauge
**2ft gauge, on display until June 2007

Rolling stock powered units – gas turbine
1972　BR Advanced Passenger Train

Rolling stock powered units – electric
1983　BR APT prototype train

Rolling Stock Powered Units – Diesel
1937　SR Driving Motor Brake Third No S10656S
1937　SR Driving Trailer Composite No S12123S

Rolling stock – departmental
1850　GNR 4-wheel hand crane No 112
1891　NER snow plough No DE900566
1904　MR Officers' Saloon No 2234
1949　BR Matisa tamping machine No 74007
1957　BR Track recording trolley No DX 50002 Neptune

Rolling Stock — Passenger
1845　S&DR 1st/3rd Composite No 59
1850　SDR 3rd No 179
1872　NLR Directors' Saloon No 1032
1887　GWR 6-wheel tricomposite No 820
1905　LNWR Corridor 1st Brake 5154 (Royal Train)
1905　LNWR Corridor 1st Brake 5154 (support vehicle)
1908　ECJS Passenger Brake Van No 109
1927　Rhodesian Railways sleeping car
1928　LMS 3rd Sleeping Car No 14241
1962　BR Mk II 1st corridor No 21274

Rolling stock – freight and non passenger carrying

1826	Cramlington Colliery Chaldron Wagon
1870	S&DR Chaldron Wagon (replica)
1870	Seaham Harbour Colliery Chaldron Wagon
1889	Shell-Mex oil tank wagon No 512
1901	Shell/BP Tank Wagon No 3171
1907	NER 16-ton bogie stores van No 041273
1912	NER Sand wagon No DE14974
1920	GCR single bolster wagon
1920	GNR double bolster wagon
1926	GWR Fitted open wagon No 108246
1935	GWR Motor car van No 126438
1936	LMS Tube wagon No 499254
1940	WD Warflat No 161042
1940	LNER Tunnel Van No DE471818
1946	SNCF 16-ton mineral wagon No ADB192437
1946	LNER 20-ton hopper wagon No E270919
1950	BR 24-ton iron ore hopper wagon No B436275
1951	BR(SR) Show cattle wagon No S3733S
1952	BR 30-ton bogie bolster wagon No B943139
1953	Buxton Lime Quarries 23-ton bogie hopper wagon No 19154
1954	BR 27-ton iron ore Tippler No B383560
1954	National Benzole oil tank wagon No 2022
1955	BR china clay tip wagon No B743141
1957	BR Horse box No S96369
1959	BR Conflat No B737725
1960	BR Banana Van No B882593
1961	BR Presflo cement wagon No B873368
1964	Prototype HAA coal hopper wagon, No 350000
1965	BR Boiler Wagon Nos DB902805, DB902806, DB902807, DB902808
1970	Phillips Petroleum 100-ton GLW tank wagon No PP85209
1970	S&D Chaldron Wagon (replica), Shildon

Locomotive tender

SDR 'collier' class *Etherley*

Powered units

SR   2BIL unit, No 2090

Passenger stock

1850	SDR 3rd No 179
1908	ECJS Passenger brake van LNER No 396
1970	S&D chaldron wagon (replica)

Owners

H/Clarke (D1345) private
Hunslet (1215) the War Office Locomotive Society
R/Hornsby (441934) on loan from North Yorkshire Moors Railway

---

Museum	**London's Transport Museum**	London

Member: HRA, TT

The £20 million re-build and re-display project for London's Transport Museum in Covent Garden is fully underway. Over 400 objects have been moved to the Museum Depot in Acton since the Museum closed in September 2005.

The new, transformed, Museum will open in autumn 2007

The Museum's popular shop remains open throughout the

Museum's refurbishment at Unit 26 Covent Garden Piazza, it will reopen in its new Museum site in April 2007
Location: Covent Garden Piazza, London WC2E 7BB
OS reference: TQ 303809
Operating society/organisation: Transport for London
Telephone:
020 7565 7299 (24hr recorded)
020 7379 6344 (Administration, education service, group bookings, events and activities, corporate hospitality, mail order enquiries)
Fax: 020 7565 7250
Internet address:
E-mail:
resourcedesk@ltmuseum.co.uk
Web site: www.ltmuseum.co.uk
Access by public transport: Tube stations: Covent Garden, Holborn, Leicester Square
Main line station: Charing Cross. Buses to Strand or Aldwych
On site facilities: Photo and research library (by appointment only), Resource Centre, Lecture Theatre., shop, café, lift, toilets (inc disabled) and baby changing facilities
On site facilities closed until autumn 2007
Public opening: Closed until autumn 2007 .

Locomotives

Name	No	Origin	Class	Type	Built
—	23	Met Rly	A	4-4-0T	1866
John Hampden	5	Met Rly		Bo-Bo	1922
—	11152	LT	1938	DM	1938

Industrial locomotives

Origin	Builder	Type	Built
Wotton Tramway	A/Porter (807)	0-4-0TG	1872

Electric stock
4248 District Rly Q23 stock driving motor coach 1923
11182 LPTB 1938 stock driving motor coach
400 Met Rly bogie stock coach 1899
30 City & South London Rly 'Padded Cell' coach 1890
Great Northern Piccadilly & Brompton Railway 'Gate stock' car 1906 (section)

Stock
1 Met Rly milk van; 3 electric trams; 3 horse buses; 7 motorbuses; 1 trolleybus; 1 horse tram; 1 petrol-electric bus chassis

For group bookings please contact the Museum in advance, group rates are available for pre-booked parties
Facilities for disabled: A lift and ramps give access throughout the Museum. Facilities include a disabled toilet. Reduced admission for registered disabled visitors and person accompanying them
Membership details: Benefits of membership include free entry to the Depot open weekends (whilst the Museum in Covent Garden is undergoung refurbishment), discount on purchases made at Museum shops at Covent Garden and Acton, discounted rate on talks and events. These are just some of the benefits available. Details from the Friends of London's Transport Museum on 020 7565 7296

```
  _____     _____     _____
 /           \   /                         \   /           \
|   Museum    |-|     London's Transport    |-|   London    |
 _____/   |      Museum Depot        |   _____/
                 _____/
```

Member: HRA, TT
The Depot is a working museum store and treasure trove of over 370,000 objects. Attractions include rare road and rail vehicles, station models, signs, ticket machines, posters and original artwork
Contact: London's Transport Museum, 39 Wellington Street, London WC2E 7BB
Depot location:
118-120 Gunnersbury Lane, Acton, London W3 8BQ
Operating society/organisation: Transport for London
Telephone:
020 7565 7299 (24hr recorded information)
020 7379 6344 (Administration, education service, group bookings,

Locomotives and multiple-units

Name	No	Origin	Class	Type	Built
—	13	C&SLR	—		1890
—	ESL107	LT	—	Bo-Bo	1940
—	L35	LT	—	Bo-BoBE	1938
—	10012	LT	1938	DM	1938
—	012256	LT	1938	T	1939
—	12048	LT	1938	M	1939
—	11012	LT	1938	DM	1938
—	320	LT	Standard		1925-34
—	846	LT	Standard		1925-34
—	1789	LT	Standard		1925-34
—	3693	LT	Standard		1925-34
—	3328	LT	Standard		1925-34
—	4184	LT	Q	DM	1923
—	08063	LT	Q35	T	1935
—	4416	LT	Q38	DM	1938
—	4417	LT	Q38	DM	1938
—	22679	LT	R49	DM	1952
—	16	LT	Prototype	DM	1986
—	3530	LT	1972	DM	1972

England

events and archives, corporate hospitality, mail order enquiries)
Fax: 020 7565 7250
Internet address:
e-mail:
resourcedesk@ltmuseum.co.uk
Web site: www.ltmuseum.co.uk
Access by public transport: Bus (E3) or Underground to Acton Town station
Access by car: Parking on site is reserved for blue badge holders and must be requested in advance. Limited parking available in local area. Parking available for groups booking a private view
On site facilities: Museum shop (Depot open weekends only), lecture theatre, toilets
Public opening:
Pre-booked guided tours on the last Friday and Saturday of the month until the end of June 2007. Private views can be arranged for groups until the end of March 2007.
Open Weekends; Adults £6.95, Concessions £4.95, Friends (of LT Museum) and accompanied children under 16 free.
Guided tours: Adults £10.00, Concessions £8.50.
For group bookings, please contact

Name	No	Origin	Class	Type	Built
—	3763	LT	1983	DM	1983
—	—	MR*	—	TC	1887

*Metropolitan railway Jubilee coach body

Industrial locomotives

Origin	Builder	Type	Built
Wotton Tramway†	A/Porter (807)	0-4-0TG	1872

Rolling stock: freight
City & South London Railway ballast wagon, No 63 of 1921
Metropolitan Railway milk van of 1890

†on loan to Buckinghamshire Railway Museum

the Museum in advance on 020 7565 7265. Group rates available for pre-booked parties of 10 or more
Facilities for disabled: Disabled toilet, on the ground floor, ramps and wheelchair platforms to some areas and a lift to the first floor. Parking on site for blue badge holders must be booked in advance. The Museum offers a range of British Sign Language tours and talk, as well as object handling sessions. For further information, contact the Resource Desk on 020 7379 6344, minicom 020 7565

7310 or e-mail enquiry@ltmuseum.co.uk
Membership details: Details from the Friends of London's Transport Museum on 020 7565 7296. Benefits include free entry to the Depot Open Weekends (whilst the Museum in Covent Garden is undergoing refurbishment), discount on purchases made at London's Transport Museum shops in Covent Garden and Acton, discounted rate on talks and events. These are just some of the benefits available

---

Miniature Railway	**Longleat Railway**	Wiltshire

Contact: J. E. Hayton
Headquarters: Longleat Railway, Warminster, Wilts BA12 7NW
Telephone: 01985 845408
Internet address: *Web site:* www.longleat.co.uk
Car parking: On site
Access by public transport: Main line stations at Frome or Warminster
On site facilities: Too numerous to list, but include: grounds and gardens, safari park, historic house, Lord Bath's murals, safari boats, pets corner, etc
Souvenir shops: throughout the attraction
Length of line: 1.25 miles, 15in gauge
Opening times: House open all year (except Christmas Day). All

Locomotives

Name	No	Builder	Type	Built
Lenka	4	Longleat	4-4DHR	1984
Ceawlin	5	Longleat*	2-8-2DH	1989
John Hayton	6	Exmoor Steam Railway	0-6-2	2004
—	—†	Severn Lamb	4-4-0	1989
—	—†	Severn Lamb	4-4-0	1989

*rebuilt from Severn-Lamb 2-8-0DH dating from 1975
†ex Thorpe Park, Surrey, may arrive during 2007

Rolling stock
11 passenger coaches and 2 works wagons (additional works wagon under construction)

attractions open daily from mid-February to early November. Railway operates from March to November 10.00 (up to) 18.00 (might be earlier during off-peak season).

Please contact for opening times/dates of specific attractions.
Special events: Santa trains — end November and December (weekends)

Lynton & Barnstaple Railway

Member: HRA

The Lynton & Barnstaple Railway in North Devon is one of the world's most famous and picturesque narrow gauge lines. Passengers can now travel along part of the original route within the Exmoor National Park above the Heddon Valley near Parracombe. Awarded the HRA Annual Award for Small Groups 'for successfully re-creating the ambience of the legendary L&BR and for successfully running trains on the original trackbed at Woody Bay 69 years after the railway closed'

Location/headquarters: Lynton & Barnstaple Railway, Woody Bay Station, Martinhoe Cross, Parracombe, Devon EX31 4RA

Telephone: 01598 763487

Internet address: *Web site:* www.lynton-rail.co.uk

Contact: Tony Nicholson, 10 Castle Heights, Lynton, Devon EX35 6JD

Chairman L&BR Co: Mike Buse

Chairman L&BR Trust: Keith Vingoe

Locomotives

Name	No	Builder	Type	Built
Gertrude	—	A/Barclay 91578)	0-6-0T	1918
Pilton	—*	Drewry (2393)	0-6-0DM	1952
Heddon Hall	—	Hunslet (6660)	4wDH	1965
Holwell Castle	—†	Simplex	4wDM	1965
Titch	—	M/Rail (8729)	4wDM	1941

*under restoration off-site
†expected to leave during 2007
Two steam locomotives will also be available

Main station: Woody Bay
Other stations: Killington Lane, Chelfham
OS references:
Woody Bay SS 684464
Killington Lane SS 671458
Chelfham SS 610357
Car park: Woody Bay station only
Access by public transport: First Buses service 300 (Minehead-Ilfracombe), 309 and 310 (both Barnstaple-Lynton) all stop at Woody Bay station; the 310 largely follows the original route of the railway and also stops at Chelfham
Length of line: Currently 1 mile, 1ft 11.5in gauge

On site facilities: Light refreshments and souvenirs are available at Woody Bay station
Passenger services: most days between Easter and the end of October
Facilities for disabled: Toilets and access to trains and refreshments/shop
Membership details: Available from Woody Bay station
Membership journal: *Lynton & Barnstaple Railway Magazine* — three times a year

---

Mangapps Farm Railway Museum

Member: HRA

Mangapps re-creates the atmosphere of a rural light railway, featuring a large museum collection, strong in items of East Anglian interest, railway signalling and goods rolling stock. Other features include original station buildings from Mid-Suffolk Light, Great Eastern and Midland & Great Northern Railways

Superintendent of the Line: John Jolly

Commercial Manager: June Jolly

Location: Mangapps Farm Railway Museum, Southminster Road, Burnham-on-Crouch, Essex CM0 8QQ. (Entrance on B1021, 1 mile north of Burnham)

Locomotives and multiple-units

Name	No	Origin	Class	Type	Built
—	2018	BR	03	0-6-0DM	1958
—	03089	BR	03	0-6-0DM	1960
Lucie	03081	BR	03	0-6-0DM	1960
—	03399	BR	03	0-6-0DM	1961
—	D2325	BR	04	0-6-0DM	1961
—	51381	BR	117	DTS	1961
—	75033	BR	302	DTS	1958
—	75250	BR	302	DTS	1958
—	79963*	W&M	—	Railbus	1958
—	22624	LT	R38	DMS	1938
—	1030	LT	1959	DM	1959
—	2044	LT	1959	T	1959

*on loan from the Poppy Line

Industrial locomotives

Name	No	Builder	Type	Built
Minnie	—	F/Walker (358)	0-6-0ST	1878

England

Above: On loan from Bressingham Steam Experience, *Bronllwyd*, a 1883-built Hunslet 0-4-0ST, is seen in action on the Lynton & Barnstaple Railway.
Phil Barnes

Right: The Ivatt-designed 2-6-2Ts were introduced by the London, Midland & Scottish Railway. No 41312 was built by BR in 1952 and is seen at Medstead & Four Marks on the Mid-Hants Railway where it was restored. *Phil Barnes*

Telephone: (01621) 784898
Fax: (01621) 783833
Internet address: *Web site:*
www.mangapps.co.uk
Access by public transport:
Burnham station approx 1 mile
On site facilities: Station, car park,
souvenir shop, toilets, amenity and
picnic areas
Refreshment facilities: Teas and
light refreshments
Length of line: Three-quarter-mile
Public opening: Weekends & Bank
Holidays all year (except 25/26
December) and daily during
summer school holidays.
Closed 27 December-31 January.
Steam trains operate first Sunday
June to September, Bank Holiday
Sundays and Mondays and special
event days. Diesel trains run on all
other days

Name	No	Builder	Type	Built	
Brookfield	—	Bagnall (2613)	0-6-0PT	1940	
Empress	—	Bagnall (3061)	0-6-0ST	1954	
Toto	—	Barclay (1619)	0-4-0ST	1919	
—	8	Barclay (2157)	0-4-0ST	1943	
Hastings	—	Hunslet (469)	0-6-0ST	1888	
Elland	No 1	H/Clarke (D1153)	0-4-0DM	1959	
—	Army 226	Drewry (2180)	0-4-0DM	1945	
—	11104	Drewry (2252)	0-6-0DM	1948	
—	DS1169	R/Hornsby (207103)	4wDM	1941	
—		S/Henshaw (7502)	4wDM	1966	

Rolling stock
LNER Gresley and BR Mk1 coaching stock, extensive stock of goods
wagons

Opening times: Weekends (except
January), Bank Holidays (except
Christmas) daily during August
school holidays — 11.30-16.30

Special events: Santa Specials —
during December

Timetable Service

Mid-Hants Railway 'Watercress Line'

Hampshire

Member: HRA
Originally built as the Winchester
to Alton link, the Mid-Hants
Railway became known as the
Watercress Line through regularly
carrying this local produce to
London markets. Now restored, the
line runs from its main line
connection at Alton through rolling
countryside to its terminus at
Alresford. Large and powerful
locomotives work impressively
over the steeply inclined route,
known to railwaymen as 'the Alps'.
No 41312 entered service early
1999. No 34016 returned to service
in summer 2003. Nos 34016 and
73096 have seen considerable use
on the main line
Headquarters: Mid-Hants
Railway plc, Alresford Station,
Alresford, Hants SO24 9JG
Telephone: 01962 733810
Fax: 01962 735448
Talking timetable: 01962 734866
Internet address: *Web site:*
www.watercressline.co.uk
Main station: Alresford
Other public stations: Ropley,
Medstead & Four Marks, Alton
OS reference: Alresford SU
588325, Ropley SU 629324
Car park: Alresford, pay &

Locomotives

Name	No	Origin	Class	Type	Built
—	30499	LSWR	S15	4-6-0	1920
—	30506	LSWR	S15	4-6-0	1920
Harry A. Frith	E828	SR	S15	4-6-0	1923
—	31625	SR	U	2-6-0	1929
—	31806	SR	U	2-6-0	1926
—	31874	SR	N	2-6-0	1925
Bodmin	34016	SR	WC	4-6-2	1945
Swanage	34105	SR	WC	4-6-2	1950
Canadian Pacific	35005	SR	MN	4-6-2	1945
—	41312	LMS	2MT	2-6-2T	1952
—	45379	LMS	5MT	4-6-0	1937
Bittern	60019	LNER	A4	4-6-2	1937
—	73096	BR	5MT	4-6-0	1956
—	76017	BR	4MT	2-6-0	1954
—	92212	BR	9F	2-10-0	1959
—	D3358	BR	08	0-6-0DE	1957
—	12049	BR	11	0-6-0DE	1948
—	D5353	BR	27	Bo-Bo	1961
—	D6593	BR	33	Bo-Bo	1962
—	45132	BR	45	1Co-Co1	1961
—	51363	BR	117	DMBS	1959
—	51405	BR	117	DMS	1959
—	55003	BR	122	DMBS	1958
—	59505	BR	117	TC	1959
—	59510	BR	117	TCL	1959
—	59511	BR	117	TCL	1959
—†	60124	BR	205	DMBS	1957
—†	60824	BR	205	DTCL	1957

†unit No 205025

display (free Sundays & Bank Holidays). Alton station pay & display

Access by public transport:
SouthWest Train services — just over 1hr from London, Waterloo. Alternatively, travel to Winchester station and catch a bus from nearby City Road.
Bus services – operated by Stagecoach 0870 608 2608
Refreshment facilities: Buffet service on most trains; 'West Country' buffet, and new picnic area at Alresford; T. Junction picnic area at Ropley; tea/coffee available at Alton when information office open
Catering facilities: The 'Countryman Pullman' pre-booked Sunday lunch trains, Christmas specials, and some evening trains. The 'Watercress Belle' operates on certain Saturday evenings March-December. Early booking is essential, please telephone to confirm seat availability for both trains. Real Ale trains run selected Saturday evenings featuring beers from local breweries and light snacks to purchase

Industrial locomotives

Name	No	Builder	Type	Built
—	4	Fowler (22889)	0-4-0DM	1939
Thomas	1	Hunslet (3781)	0-6-0T	1954
Douglas	10	Hunslet (2890)	0-6-0	1943
—	62-521*	Djuro Djakovic	0-6-0T	1954

*based on 'USA' tank design

Stock
28 ex-BR Mk 1 coaches; 2 ex-BR Mk 2 coaches used for accommodation; 3 ex-BR Mk 1 Pullman Cars; 3 ex-SR coaches; 1 ex-LSWR coach; 1 ex-LMS coach; 3 steam cranes; numerous goods vehicles

Owners
30076 Project 62 Group

Souvenir shops: Alresford, Alton and Ropley
On site facilities: Picnic area, children's play area and viewing facilities at Ropley. Interpretative display in Alresford shop. Picnic area at Alresford
Depot: Ropley. Locomotive yard open on operating days 10.30-16.30
Length of line: 10 miles
Passenger trains: Phone Talking Timetable (01962 734866), or visit web site to confirm details. Bank Holidays and weekends January to

October; Tuesdays to Thursdays May to September (inc), school half term in February, October half term 'Wizard Week', Steam Galas, Day out with Thomas at Easter and August. Santa Specials in December (bookings commence October)
Journey time: Round trip 1hr 40min max
Special events: Steam Gala — 2-4 March; Day out with Thomas — 6-15 April; War on the Line — 23/24 June; 40th Aniversary of end of Southern Steam — 7/8 July; Bus

Rally — 15 July; Steam Gala — 21-23 September; Wizard Week — 20-28 October; Santa Specials — December
Facilities for disabled: Toilets at Ropley, the old good shed at Alresford station and Alton. Passengers in fixed wheelchairs can be carried in the brake compartment on most trains. Ramps are provided to ease entry to trains. Ask SouthWest Trains staff at Alton to cross foot crossing
Membership details: Membership Secretary, c/o above address

Timetable Service	Mid-Norfolk Railway	Norfolk

Member: HRA

A scheme to preserve part of the former Great Eastern line from Wymondham to Wells-next-the-Sea. The section from Wymondham to Dereham has been purchased and opened for passenger and freight traffic since May 1999. Clearance work is now completed on the Dereham-North Elmham section. The Mid-Norfolk Railway Preservation Trust also operates County School station as a tea room and visitor centre during the summer months

Headquarters: The Railway Station, Station Road, Dereham, Norfolk NR19 1DF

Locomotives and multiple-units

Name	No	Origin	Class	Type	Built
—	D8069	BR	20	Bo-Bo	1961
—	31235	BR	31	A1A-A1A	1960
Sister Dora	31530	BR	31	A1A-A1A	1961
—	31538	BR	31	A1A-A1A	1959
Aldeburgh Festival	47596	BR	47	Co-Co	1966
Ramillies	50019	BR	50	Co-Co	1968
Oystermouth	56040	BR	56	Co-Co	1978
—	51226	M/Cam	101	DMBS	1958
Matthew Smith	51434	M/Cam	101	MBS	1958
—	51499	M/Cam	101	DMBS	1959
—	51503	M/Cam	101	DMC	1959
—	55009	Gloucester	122	DMBS	1958
—	59117	M/Cam	101	TC	1958
—	56301*	Gloucester	100	DTC	1957
—	68004	BR	MLV / 419	DMVL	1959

*in use as static shop and tea room at County School station

MID-NORFOLK RAILWAY
Station Road, Dereham, NR19 1DF
01362 690633   www.mnr.org.uk
East Anglia's longest heritage railway

Main station: Dereham
Telephone: (01362) 690633
Talking timetable: (01362) 851723
(answerphone)
Fax: (01362) 698487
Internet address:
Web site: www.mnr.org.uk
e-mail: info@mnr.org.uk
Car park: At Dereham
Museum: Small relics museum at
Dereham
Souvenir shop: Dereham
Refreshment facilities: Railway
Buffet at Dereham (March-
December) and tea room at County
School station (summer only)
Access by public transport: Bus
from Norwich and King's Lynn.
'One' Anglia trains to Wymondham
Period of public operation:
Weekends and Bank Holidays
17 March to 28 October.
Wednesdays 9 May to 24 October.
Sundays 4 to 18 November
Special events: Diesel Gala —
16-18 March; Easter Specials —
8/9 April; Halloween Specials —
27 October; Santa Specials —
2, 8/9, 15/16, 22-24 December
Special facilitie: Operational main
line connection for charter, freight

Industrial locomotives

Name	No	Builder	Type	Built
—§	GET 2	Bagnall (8368)	0-4-0DM	1962
—§	GET 5	Drewry (2566)	0-4-0DM	1955
—§	GET 7	B/Drewry (3733)	4wDE	1977
—§	GET 8	R/Royce (10272)	0-6-0DM	1967
—§	GET 9	R/Hornsby (512842)	0-4-0DE	1965
—§	11103	Drewry (2583)	0-4-0DM	1956

§privately owned, stored at Hardingham and viewable from trains, no public access

Locomotive notes: D8069, 31235, 31538 and 50019, also various DMUs
are in service

Rolling stock: 1 BR Mk 1 coach, 9 BR Mk 2 coaches, BR Mk 2 TSO 5536
used as static bar coach, 10-ton rail-mounted crane, selection of freight
wagons, operational and stored at Hardingham

Owners
50019 and 68004 the Class 50 Locomotive Association
47596 the Stratford 47 Group
31235 the Colne Valley Enterprises Ltd
D8069 the Type One Association
GET the Great Eastern Traction group
56040 the Class 56 Group

trains, etc. Line used for training
purposes eg: low adhesion driving
techniques. Film location
Membership details: Membership

Secretary c/o Dereham Station
Membership journal: *The
Blastpipe* (four times a year)

Museum	**Mid-Suffolk Light Railway**	Suffolk

Member: HRA
The Mid-Suffolk Light Railway,
known affectionately as 'The
Middy', was a classic case of a
railway built late on in the great
railway age that never paid its way.
It effectively went broke before it
opened but still managed to struggle
on for 50 years. This example of
quirky English history is
remembered in Suffolk's only
railway museum
Location: Wetheringsett, Nr
Stowmarket, Suffolk IP14 5PW
OS reference: TM 129659
Operating organisation: Mid-
Suffolk Light Railway Company
Telephone: 01449 766899
Internet address: *Web site:*
www.mslr.org.uk
Car park: On site
Access by public transport: Some
local buses from Ipswich to Diss set
down and pick up on the A140
Ipswich-Norwich road near to the

Industrial locomotives

Name	No	Builder	Type	Built
Little Barford	—	Barclay	0-4-0ST	1939
—	1604	H/Clarke (1604)	0-6-0ST	1928
—	304470	R/Hornsby (304470)	0-4-0DM	1951

Rolling stock
GER 2-compartment brake third, GER 6-compartment brake third, GER
3-compartment first, 1 GER ventilated van, 1 GER non-ventilated van,
1 GER 5-plank wagon1 LMS van, 1 GWR van, private owner coal wagon
(rebuilt from BR open wagon), BR tube wagon, LNER brake van, NER
milk van body, 2 GER 5 compartment third bodies, GER ventilated van
body. GER steel outside frame ventilated van, GER horsebox body, conflat
(to provide underframe for horsebox), replica contractor open wagon

museum. Local buses from
Stowmarket to Wetheringsett.
Services tend to be infrequent and
the timetables are subject to change
at short notice. Details of services
can be obtained from Traveline
0870 608 2608 or
www.traveline.org.uk
On site facilities: Souvenir shop,

refreshments, railway walk (not
when trains are running),
railwayana and photographic
exhibition, toilets (including
disabled) and picnic area
Period of public opening: Usually
open on Sundays and Bank
Holidays from Easter to end
September, plus Wednesdays in

August (11.00-17.00)
Special events: Steam event days: Easter Sunday and Monday, early and late May Bank Holiday Sundays and Mondays. 17 June, 1, 15 July. 5, 12, 19 August. August Bank Holiday Sunday and Monday, 16, 30 September; Santa Specials — 2, 9, 16 December; Mince Pie Specials — 30 December

Special notes: Museum dedicated to Mid-Suffolk Light Railway. Original MSLR restored buildings and artefacts. Reproduction MSLR ticket on entry. *Railway World* award winner in 1994 and HRA award winner in 2002
Facilities for disabled: Most of the site is accessible for disabled users. A wheelchair is available on request

and there is wheelchair access to the demonstration passenger train. Toilets are accessible to wheelchair users
Membership details: Membership Secretary, Poachers Cottage, Church Hill, Stowmarket, Suffolk IP14 4SQ
Society journal: *Making Tracks —* quarterly MSLRS Newsletter

---

| Steam Centre | Middleton Railway | Leeds |

Member: HRA
This is a preserved section of 'the world's oldest working railway', authorised by the first railway Act of Parliament in 1758, and also the first standard gauge railway to be taken over by volunteers in 1960
Headquarters: Middleton Railway Trust Ltd, Moor Road, Hunslet, Leeds LS10 2JQ
Telephone: 0113 271 0320
Internet addresses: *e-mail:* info@middletonrailway.org.uk
Web site: www.middletonrailway.org.uk
Main station: Moor Road, Hunslet
OS reference: SE 302309
Car park: Moor Road (free)
Access by public transport: Nearest main line station, Leeds City. Bus service No 61 from Aire Street (next to Leeds City station) to Tunstall Road (then 150yd walk)
Directions by car: Next to M621, junction 5. There have been major road alterations around the Middleton Railway.
From the south: M621 northbound and exit at jct 5. Turn right at the top of the slip road and take the marked exit at the roundabout. The railway is 50yd on the right
From the west: M621 southbound and exit at jct 6. Turn left at the end of the slip road, and left at the next set of traffic lights into Moor Road. Bear right at the mini roundabout and railway is 150yd on the left
Souvenir shop: Moor Road
Museum: In preparation. Depot open weekends and Bank Holidays 10.00 to 16.30 in season
Length of line: 1.25 miles (extension pending)

Locomotives

Name	No	Origin	Class	Type	Built
—	1310	NER	Y7	0-4-0T	1891
—	68153	LNER	Y1	0-4-0VB	1933
—	385	DSB	HsII	0-4-0WT	1893
John Alcock	7051	LMS	—	0-6-0DM	1932
(Olive)	RDB998901	BR	—	4wDM	1950

Industrial locomotives

Name	No	Builder	Type	Built
John Blenkinsop	—	Peckett (2003)	0-4-0ST	1941
—	—	Peckett (2103)	0-4-0ST	1948
—	—	Bagnall (2702)	0-4-0ST	1943
Henry de Lacy II	—	H/Clarke (1309)	0-4-0ST	1917
Mirvale	—	H/Clarke (1882)	0-4-0ST	1955
Manchester Ship Canal No 67	—	H/Clarke (1329)	0-6-0T	1921
—	11	Hunslet (1453)	0-4-0ST	1925
Picton	—	Hunslet (1540)	2-6-2T	1927
—	1684	Hunslet (1684)	0-4-0T	1931
Brookes No 1	—	Hunslet (2387)	0-6-0T	1941
Windle	—	Borrows (53)	0-4-0WT	1909
Matthew Murray	—	M/Wardle (1601)	0-6-0ST	1903
Lucy	—	Cockerill	0-4-0VBT	1890
Sir Berkeley†	—	M/Wardle (1210)	0-6-0ST	1891
—	6	H/Leslie (3860)	0-4-0ST	1935
Carroll	—	H/Clarke (D631)	0-4-0DM	1946
Mary	—	H/Clarke (D577)	0-4-0DM	1932
—	DL15	H/Clarke (D1344)	0-4-0DM	1965
—	—	Hunslet (1786)	0-4-0DM	1935
—§	—	Hunslet (6273)	4wDH	1965
Flying Scotsman§§	—	Hunslet (8505)	4wDH	1981
—	—	Fowler (3900002)	0-4-0DM	1945
Conway	—	Kitson (5469)	0-6-0ST	1933
Austin No 1	—	Peckett (5003)	0-4-0DM	1961
—	—	Thomas Hill (138C)	0-4-0DH	1963
—*	D2999	Brush (91)/ Beyer Peacock (7856)	0-4-0DE	1958
—	—	G/Batley (420452)	4wDE	1979

*on loan from BSC Orb Works, Newport
†on 10 year loan from Vintage Carriages Trust, but may be away on hire at times
§3ft gauge
§§2ft 2in gauge

England

Period of public operation:
Weekends and Bank Holidays
31 March to 30 September
(except 14 April). Sundays only in
October and November (except
Halloween). Santa trains only on
pre-Christmas weekends in
December.
Diesel: Saturdays 13.00-16.40.
Steam: Sundays and Bank Holiday
Mondays from 11.00-16.00 and
most special events.
2007 prices: adult £4.50; child
£2.50; family (2 adults + 3
children) £12.00
Special events: Gala — 21/22
April; Bluebell Walk in conjunction
with Friends of Middleton Park —
6/7 May; Children's gala — 9/10
June; Model Railway in conjunction
with Leeds Model Railway Forum
— 7/8 July; Wednesdays in August
— diesel service at 13.00, 13.40,
14.20, 15.00; Gala — 22/23
September; Halloween — 27/28

Note: Nos 6, 11, 1310, 68153 and *Sir Berkeley* are under repair in the
workshops and may not be accessible to the public

Stock
2 CCTs converted for passenger use Nos 1867 and 2048; CCT as stores
van No 2073. Various goods vehicles; 5-ton Booth rail crane; 1 3-ton
Smith steam crane; 1 3-ton Isles steam crane; 7.5-ton steam crane

Owners
1310, 385 the Steam Power Trust
RDB998901 the EM2 Locomotive Society
Flying Scotsman and Hunslet 8505 on loan from National Mining Museum

October; Santa trains — 1/2, 8/9,
15/16, 22/23 December
Facilities for disabled: Good
access with additional assistance by
prior arrangement. Disabled toilets,
reserved car parking spaces
Special notes: Operating in every
year since 1758, the railway still
operates under its original Act of
Parliament. The first railway to
successfully use steam locomotives

commercially from 1812. Part of
South Leeds Heritage Trail,
highlighting former locomotive
works in the area, and other historic
places
Special facilities: Charter trains,
birthday parties on non-special
event running days; catering
facilities; training/conference room;
education facilities

Timetable Service	**Midland Railway — Butterley**	Derbyshire

Member: HRA, TT

The Midland Railway — Butterley
is a rapidly developing
Preservation Scheme with a
difference. The massive 57 acre
Museum site and 35 acre Country
Park enabled it to become 'More
than just a railway' as its publicity
says. The seven road Matthew
Kirtley Museum allows much of
the historic collection to be on
display and most of the
locomotives to be stored and
displayed under cover. A miniature
railway (3.5 and 5in gauge) and a
1-mile narrow gauge line (2ft
gauge) carries passengers through
the Country Park; Brittain Pit Farm
Park, with its wide variety of
livestock; and of course there is a
3.5-mile standard gauge line
complete with Midland signals,
three restored signalboxes,
Butterley station, the scenic
delights of Butterley Reservoir and
Golden Valley!

The Victorian Railwaymen's
Church, the demonstration
signalbox, and all the other many
attractions that make up the

Locomotives and multiple-units

Name	No	Origin	Class	Type	Built
Princess Margaret Rose	46203	LMS	8P	4-6-2	1935
Duchess of Sutherland	6233	LMS	8P	4-6-2	1938
—	44027	LMS	4F	0-6-0	1924
—	44932	LMS	5MT	4-6-0	1945
—	45491	LMS	5MT	4-6-0	1943
—	47564	LMS	3F	0-6-0T	1928
—	47327	LMS	3F	0-6-0T	1926
—	47357	LMS	3F	0-6-0T	1926
—	47445	LMS	3F	0-6-0T	1927
—	53809	SDJR	7F	2-8-0	1925
—	158A	MR	—	2-4-0	1866
—	73129	BR	5MT	4-6-0	1956
—	80080	BR	4MT	2-6-4T	1954
—	80098	BR	4MT	2-6-4T	1955
—	92214	BR	9F	2-10-0	1959
—	92219	BR	9F	2-10-0	1959
—	D2858	BR	02	0-4-0DM	1959
—	D2138	BR	03	0-6-0DM	1960
—	08590	BR	08	0-6-0DE	1959
—	12077	BR	11	0-6-0DE	1950
—	20001	BR	20	Bo-Bo	1957
—	20205	BR	20	Bo-Bo	1967
—	20227	BR	20	Bo-Bo	1968
—	D7671	BR	25	Bo-Bo	1967
Boudicea	31418	BR	31	A1A-A1A	1959
—	31421	BR	31	A1A-A1A	1959
—	33018	BR	33	Bo-Bo	1960
—	33201	BR	33	Bo-Bo	1962

Midland Railway — Butterley will be open throughout the year

Location: Midland Railway, Butterley Station, Nr Ripley, Derbyshire DE5 3QZ

OS reference: SK 403520

General Manager: John Hett

Operating society/organisation: Midland Railway Trust Ltd

Telephone: Ripley (01773) 747674, Visitor Information Line (01773) 570140.

Fax: (01773) 570271

Internet address:
e-mail: mrc@rapidial.co.uk
Web site: midlandrailwaycentre.co.uk

Car park: Butterley station on B6179 1 mile north of Ripley

On site facilities: Museum, award winning country park, Brittain Pit Farm Park, souvenir shops, miniature railway, narrow gauge railway, garden railway, model railways

Refreshment facilities: Butterley station buffet, Johnson Buffet (Swanwick), on-train bars and extensive 'Wine and Dine' trains, 'The Midlander' (details from above address).

'Midday Midlander' Sunday lunch trains will run on selected Sundays — these need to be booked in advance

Length of line: Standard gauge 3.5 miles, narrow gauge 0.8-mile

Public opening: In 2007 trains run every Saturday, Sunday and Bank Holiday EXCEPT 6, 13 January, 17, 24 March, 22, 29 September, 10 November

Trains will also run every day 10-18 February, 31 March-15 April, 26 May to 3 June, 21 July to 3 September, 20-28 October, 20-24 December

Golden Valley Light Railway: Trains will run every weekend and Bank Holiday April to October, EXCEPT 22, 29 September; and every day 6-8 April, 26 May-3 June, 21 July-3 September. Special steam days — check for details.

Butterley Park Miniature Railway: Trains will run Sundays and Bank Holidays Easter to September.

Journey time: Approximately 1hr

Special events: Day out with Thomas — 3/4, 10/11 March; Mother's Day Lunch Train — 18* March; Railway Experience Day— 24 March; Diesel Multiple Unit Gala — 31 March, 1 April; Easter

Name	No	Origin	Class	Type	Built
—	37190	BR	37	Co-Co	1964
Aureol	40012	BR	40	1Co-Co1	1959
Great Gable	D4	BR	44	1Co-Co1	1959
Royal Tank Regiment	45041	BR	45/1	1Co-Co1	1962
—	45133	BR	45/1	1Co-Co1	1961
—	46045	BR	46	1Co-Co1	1963
—	47401	BR	47	Co-Co	1963
—	D1516	BR	47	Co-Co	1963
Sir Edward Elgar	50007	BR	50	Co-Co	1967
Western Lady	D1048	BR	52	C-C	1962
Electra	27000	BR	EM2	Co+Co	1953
—	50015	BR	114	DMBS	1956
—	50019	BR	114	DMBS	1956
—	51073	BR	119	DMBC	1958
—	51188	BR	101	DMBS	1958
—	53170	BR	101	DMC(L)	1957
—	53253	BR	101	DMC(L)	1957
—	55513	BR	141	DMS	1983
—	55533	BR	141	DMS(L)	1983
—	55966	BR	127	DPU	1959
—	55976	BR	127	DPU	1956
—	56006	BR	114	DTC	1956
—	56015	BR	114	DMBSO	1956
—	56342	BR	101	DTC	1957
—	59575	M/Cam	111	TRBSL(L)	1957
—	59609	BR	127	TC	1959
—	79018	BR	—	MBS	1954
—	79612	BR	—	DTC	1954
—	29666	M/Cam	—	TC	1931
—	29670	M/Cam	—	TC	1931
Iris	M79900	BR	—	MBS	1956

Locomotive notes: In service 92214, 47327 (as *Thomas*), 6233, 53809, 80098, 73129, 46045, 08590, Class 114, *Iris* and 127 DMU, D4, 33201, 37190, 46045, 47401, 50007, D2138, 40012, 12077, 45133 and D7671. Under restoration: 44027, 45491, 44932, 47445, 80080. Awaiting repairs or stored: 46203, D1517, 92219. Boiler and frames only 47564. Static display: 158A, 27000. Expected to enter service in 2006: 53809

Industrial locomotives

Name	No	Builder	Type	Built
Gladys	—	Markham (109)	0-4-0ST	1894
Stanton	24	Barclay (1875)	0-4-0CT	1925
Whitehead	—	Peckett (1163)	0-4-0ST	1908
Victory	—	Peckett (1547)	0-4-0ST	1919
Lytham St Annes	—	Peckett (2111)	0-4-0ST	1949
Brown Bailey	4	N/Wilson (454)	0-4-0ST	1894
Castle Donnington	1	RSH (7817)	0-4-0ST	1954
Henry	—	RSH	0-4-0ST	19??
Neepsend		Sentinel (9370)	4wVBT	1947
Andy	2	Fowler (16038)	0-4-0DM	1923
—	RS9	M/Rail (2024)	0-4-0DM	1921
—	RS12	M/Rail (460)	0-4-0DM	1912
Boots	2	Barclay (2008)	0-4-0F	1935
Castle Donnington	2	Barclay (416)	0-4-0DM	1957
High Marnham	—	Barclay (441)	0-4-0DM	1949
Boots	—	R/Hornsby (384139)	0-4-0DE	1955
—	—	H/Clarke (D1152)	0-6-0DM	1959
Albert Fields	—	H/Clarke (D1114)	0-6-0DM	1958
Princess Elizabeth*	6201	H/Clarke (D611)	4-6-2DM	1938
Princess Margaret Rose*	6203	H/Clarke (D612)	4-6-2DM	1938

*21in gauge

England

Above: The Mid-Suffolk Light Railway recreates a classic case of a line built late on in the railway age that never paid its way. *Little Barford*, a Barclay 0-4-0ST dating from 1939 provides the action. *MSLR*

Below: This BR-built Standard Class 9F was one of the final main line steam locomotives to be built in the UK. Restored to service at the Midland Railway — Butterley, No 92214 is seen at Swanick. *Alan Barnes*

England

Eggstravaganza — 6-9 April; Easter Holiday Trains — 2-5, 10-13 April; Diesel Locomotive Gala — 21/22 April; Vintage Train Weekend — 5-7 May; 1940s Weekend — 12/13 May; Real Ale Train* — 12 May; Diesel and Steam Weekend — 19/20 May; Day out with Thomas — 26 May-3 June; Class 20 Diesel Locomotive Celebration — 9/10 June; Railway Modellers Weekend — 9/10 June; Diesel and Steam Weekend — 16/17 June; Father's Day Sunday Lunch — 17 June; Class 40 Diesel Locomotive Celebration — 23/24 June; Free for Disabled and half price for carers — 30 June, 1 July; Diesel and Steam Weekend — 7/8 July; Static Power Display — 8 July; Anything Goes Weekend — 21/22 July; Day out with Thomas — 4-12 August; Vintage Train Weekend — 17-19 August; Narrow Gauge and Garden Railway Galas— 18/19 August; Anniversary Week — 20-24 August; Anniversary Week — 25-27 August; Class 20 Diesel Locomotive Celebration — 8/9 September; 1940s Battle of Britain Weekend — 15/16 September; Real Ale Train* — 15 September; Railway Experience Day— 22 September; Diesel and Steam Day — 30 September; Day out with Thomas — 13/14 October; Wizards and Spooktacular Week 20-28 October; Fireworks Night — 27 October; Santa Specials — 17/18, 24/25 November, 1/2, 8/9, 13-16, 20-24 December; Day out with Thomas† — 27-29 December; Festive Trains — 30 December-1 January 2008. Winter Warmer Trains — 6, 13, 19, 20, 26, 28 January, 2/3, 9/10 February 2008. Half term Trains — 16-24 February 2008; Day out with Thomas† — 1/2, 8/9 March 2008
*These trains need to be booked in advance.
†events are provisional.
All Day out with Thomas are © Gullane (Thomas) Ltd 2007 and are licensed by Gullane (Thomas) Ltd a HIT Entertainment Company. Midday Midlander lunch trains run on selected dates – these need to be booked in advance
Facilities for disabled: Toilets, special coach, access to shop and cafeteria

Golden Valley Light Railway
2ft gauge unless otherwise shown

—	—	Deutz (10249)	4wDM	1932
Tubby	—	M/Rail (8667)	4wDM	1941
Pioneer	—	M/Rail (8739)	4wDM	1942
—	—	M/Rail (8756)	4wDM	1942
Campbell Brick Works	—	M/Rail (60S364)	4wDM	1968
—	—	Lister (3742)	4wDM	1931
—	—	M/Rail (11246)	4wDM	1963
—	2	O&K (7529)	0-4-0WT	1914
—	—	O&K (5215)	4wDM	1936
Wheal Jayne	19	BEV	4wBE	1985
—	—	Ruston (7002/0567/6)	4wDM	1966
Lyddia	—	Ruston (191646)	4wDM	1938
Berryhill	—	Ruston (222068)	4wDM	1943
Hucknall Colliery	3	Ruston (480678)	4wDM	1961
—	—	Hunslet (7178)	4wDH	1971
—	—*	Hunslet (8970)	4wDM	1979
—	—*	Hunslet (8972)	4wDM	1979
Calverton Colliery	22†	H/Clarke (1117)	0-6-0DM	1958
Natalie	—	H/Barclay (LD 9351)	0-4-0DM	1994
—	—	Lister (53726)	4wDM	1963
—	—	SMH (40SD529)	4wDM	1983
—	NG24	B/Drewry (3703)	4wBE	1974
Calverton No 7	7	Hunslet (8911)	4wDM	1980
Ellison	—	SMH (102T20)	4wDH	1979
Pearl 2	—	T. D. A. Civil (1)	0-4-2T	1997

*2ft 2in gauge, to be regauged to 2ft
†away on loan during 2007

Locomotive notes: In service: *High Marnham, Boots, Castle Donnington No 1, Castle Donnington No 2,* NG24, Ruston 222068, SMH (40SD529 & 102T20), *Calverton Colliery No 22,* Lister, Deutz 10249, *Albert Fields,* M/Rail 60S364, *Princess Margaret Rose.* Under restoration: *Andy,* O&K 7529, *Lytham St Annes, Castle Donnington No 1.* Awaiting repairs or stored on display: RS9, Hunslet 7178, M/Rails 5906/11246. Static display: *Gladys,* 4, *Boots No 2,* Sentinel 9370, *Welbeck Colliery, Victory,* RS12, *Stanton* No 24, *Brown Bailey* (as Oswald the talking engine)

Stock
Numerous carriages, wagons and cranes. Museum display includes MR Royal saloon, MR 4-wheeled coach, MR brake third, LD&ECR all third, BR horsebox, LMS travelling Post Office, L&YR family saloon, MR motor carvan, MR bogie brake third, restored freight vehicles, LMS 50-ton steam crane, and much more

Owners
158A, 44027 on loan from the National Railway Museum
47357, 47327, 47445, 47564, 73129 Derby City Council
46203, 6233, 46203, 80080, 80098 the Princess Royal Class Locomotive Trust
D4, 45041 and 46045 the Peak Locomotive Preservation Co Ltd
D7671 Derby Industrial Museum
33201 the Birmingham Railwaymen's Crompton Workgroup
Class 141 unit the Llangollen Railcar Group
51073 the Railcar Enterprises

Special facilities: The railway is licensed for weddings, civil partnership ceremonies, and baby naming ceremonies. There is a woodland burial ground in the country park adjacent to the railway. Trains can be chartered for special meals, educational visits or almost anything else. Footplate Experience and Railway Experience

England

courses are run. The large museum site is also used for exhibitions and displays. The railway also has an impressive track record in the restoration of diesel multiple-units

and coaches for other lines
Membership details: J. Hett, at above address
Membership journal: *The Wyvern* — quarterly

Marketing names: 'More than just a railway'; Golden Valley Light Railway (narrow gauge); Butterley Park Miniature Railway (miniature line)

Museum	Monkwearmouth Station Museum	Tyne & Wear

The Museum is one of Britain's finest neo-classical stations and was built in 1848 to commemorate the election of George Hudson as MP for Sunderland. Restored features include the booking office, unchanged since it was installed in 1866, waiting shelter on the west platform and siding area
Location: North Bridge Street, Sunderland SR5 1AP
Telephone: (0191) 567 7075
OS reference: NZ 396576
On site facilities: Car parking on

Rolling stock
NER brake van 1915, LNER CCT van 1939

museum forecourt, shop. Self-service refreshment dispenser
Access by public transport: 10min walk from Sunderland Central station. Served by several bus routes from Sunderland city centre, Newcastle and South Shields
Public opening: Daily 1 January-31 December (except New Year's Day, Christmas Day, Boxing Day

[please check for Good Friday and Easter Sunday opening times]).
Monday to Saturday 10.00-17.00.
Sunday 14.00-17.00. Free admission
Access for disabled: Ramped access, suitable for wheelchair users

Miniature Railway	Moors Valley Railway	Dorset

Location: Moors Valley Country Park, Horton Road, Ashley Heath, Nr Ringwood, Dorset BH24 2ET
General Manager:
Mr J. A. W. Haylock
Telephone: (01425) 471415
Internet address: *e-mail:*
shop@moorsvalleyrailway.co.uk
Web site: www.moorsvalley.co.uk
Car parking: On site
Access by public transport: Wilts & Dorset bus X34, from Bournemouth/Ringwood to Ashley Heath
On site facilities: Picnic areas, lakeside walks, adventure playground, railway shop and refreshments all set in the beautiful Moors Valley Country Park. Car park and toilets (including disabled)
Depots: Adjacent to main station
Length of line:7.25in gauge; 1 mile long
Period of public operation:
Weekends all year; daily all school holidays and Spring Bank Holiday to mid-September. Santa Specials

Locomotives — 7.25in gauge

Name	No	Builder	Type	Built
Horace	2	Haylock	0-4-2DH	1999
Talos	3	Marsh	0-4-2T	1978
Tinkerbell	4	Marsh	0-4-2T	1968
Snapper	5	Marsh/Haylock	4-6-0	1982
Medea	6	Narogauge Ltd	2-6-2T	1981
Aelfred	7	Narogauge Ltd	2-6-4T	1985
Jason	9	Narogauge Ltd	2-4-4T	1989
Offa	10	Narogauge Ltd	2-6-2	1991
Zeus	11	Narogauge Ltd	2-6-2	1991
Pioneer	12	Narogauge Ltd	4-6-2	1992
Horton	14	Narogauge Ltd	2-4-0	1991
William Rufus	15	Narogauge Ltd	2-4-0+0-4-2	1997
Robert Snooks	16	Mantlow	0-4-4T	1999
Hartfield	17	Colbourn	2-4-4T	1999
Thor	18	Jefford	4-6-2	2005
Athelstan	19	Couling	2-8-0	2006
Vixen	22	Narogauge Ltd	0-4-0+0-4-0DH	2005
Emmet*	20	Haylock	0-4-0T	2003

*2ft gauge

Rolling stock
36 passenger vehicles, selection of wagons

in December
Special events: Railway Open Day — 25 March; Tinkerbell Rally — 5/6 May; Grand Summer Gala — 9/10 June; American Weekend — 7/8 July; Hornby/Bachmann/LGB Weekend — 28/29 July; Tank Engine Day — 11 November; Santa Specials — 9, 16 December

Fare: Single and return journeys; day rovers; Midday Specials (Sundays only). Party rates available

Museum — Moseley Railway Trust — Staffordshire

Member: HRA
Chairman: Phil Robinson, 23 Chestnut Walk, Cheddleton, Staffs ST13 7BJ
Site address: Apedale Heritage Centre, Loomer Road, Chestreton, Newcastle-under-Lyme, Staffs ST5 7RR
Telephone: 0845 094 1953
Internet address: *Web site:* www.mrt.org.uk
Site includes: Apedale Heritage Centre, Country Park, car parking, refreshments, toilet. Open daily 10.30-16.00. Mine tours weekends and Bank Holidays

Railway and Museum under construction. No passenger trains during 2007. Please see railway press for details of first open days, but visitors welcome when volunteers on site
Length of line: Under construction, 2ft gauge
Membership details: Brian Bud, Eversley, 1 The Sidings, Whaley Bridge, High Peak SK23 7HE
Membership journal: *Moseley Matters* (quarterly)

Industrial locomotives (2ft gauge)

Name	No	Builder	Type	Built
Billet	1*	W/Rogers (C6717)	4wBE	1963
Cable Mill	2*	W/Rogers (C6716)	4wBE	1963
81A 186	3*	M/Rail (8878)	4wDM	1944
Stanhope	4**	K/Stuart (2395)	0-4-2ST	1917
—	5*	R/Hornsby (223667)	4wDM	1943
—	6*	M/Rail (9104)	4wPM	1942
—	7*	M/Rail (8663)	4wDM	1941
Electra	12*	Brook Victor (565)	4wBE	1970
—	13*	M/Rail (11142)	4wDM	1960
Knothole Worker	14*	M/Rail (22045)	4wDM	1959
Margaret	16	Hunslet (6056)	4wDH	1982
LCWW 81-03	18*	H/Hunslet (6299)	4wDM	1964
—	20	M/Rail (8748)	4wDMR	1942
—	21*	M/Rail (8669)	4wDM	1941
—	23*	Lister (52031)	4wDM	1960
Twusk	26*	H/Hunslet (6018)	4wDM	1961
Annie	27*	R/Hornsby (198297)	4wDM	1939
—	28*	Ruston (10/13)	4wDM	1944
Vanguard	29*	R/Hornsby (195846)	4wDM	1939
Friden	30*	R/Hornsby (237914)	4wDM	1946
—	31*	R/Hornsby (189972)	4wDM	1938
—	33*	M/Rail (7033)	4wPM	1936
—	34*	R/Hornsby (164350)	4wDM	1933
—	35*	Wickham (4131)	4wPMR	1947
Commercial	36	R/Hornsby (280865)	4wDM	1949
—	37*	R/Hornsby (260719)	4wDM	1948
Kenneth	38*	R/Hornsby (223749)	4wDM	1944
—	39	M/Rail (1111)	4wPM	1918
Sludge	40*	Simplex (40SD516)	4wDM	1979
—	41*	M/Rail (5821)	4wDM	1934
—	42	M/Rail (7710)	4wDM	1936
—	43	Simplex (104G063)	4wDM	1976
Chaumont	44*	Hudson (1002)	4wDM	1968
87008	45	R/Hornsby (179870)	4wDM	1936
—	47*	M/Rail (1369)	4wPM	1918
R12/ND6458	48*	R/Hornsby (235730)	4wDM	1943
—	49*	O/Koppel (4470)	4wPM	1930
—	50	Deutz (10050)	4wDM	1931
—	51*	Baguley (646)	0-4-0PM	1918
LAWR	52	Baguley (1965)	4wDM	1928
—	53	Hibberd (2306)	4wDM	1940
Yard No 54	54*	Hibberd (2196)	4wDM	1940
—	58	H/Clarke (D558)	4wDM	1938
—	59	O/Koppel (4588)	4wDM	1932
—	60*	M/Rail (6035)	4wPM	1937
—	61	M/Rail (1320)	4wBE	1918
—	64	R/Hornsby (256314)	4wDM	1949
—	66*	Pikrose (W/Rogers) (B0366V)	4wBE	1993

Name	No	Builder	Type	Built
—	67	W/Rogers (D6912)	4wBE	1964
Crystal	70*	W/Rogers (K7070)	4wBE	1970
—	71*	Clayton (5843)	4wBE	1971
Lady Anne	72	Clayton (B0922B)	4wBE	1975
—	74	O/Koppel (3444)	4wDM	1930
—	78*	M/Rail (5038)	4wDM	1930
—	80*	Lister (52610)	4wDM	
(87004)	82	M/Rail (2197)	4wPM	1923

*stored off site, due to arrive spring 2007
**in operation on West Lancs Railway

The Museum of Science and Industry in Manchester

Museum — **Manchester**

Member: HRA

Based in the buildings of the world's oldest surviving passenger railway station (dating from 1830), the Museum has colourful 'hands-on' galleries that amuse, amaze and entertain. Visitors can find out about our industrial past, and walk through a Victorian sewer complete with sounds and smells

Location: Liverpool Road, Castlefield, Manchester (off Deansgate near Granada TV)

OS reference: SJ 831987

Operating society/organisation: The Museum of Science and Industry in Manchester, Liverpool Road, Castlefield, Manchester M3 4FP

Telephone: (0161) 832 2244

Internet address: *e-mail:* marketing@msim.org.uk
Web site: http://www.msim.org.uk

Car parks: On site, plus parking in the area (Museum car park £5, subject to change)

Access by public transport: Manchester Victoria, Piccadilly, Oxford Road and Deansgate main line stations. GM bus 33. G-Mex Metrolink station

On site facilities: Oldest passenger railway station, listed buildings containing exhibitions about science, industry, aviation, space, water supply and sewage disposal, gas and electricity. Xperiment the 'hands-on' science centre and the 'Out of this world' space gallery. World's largest collection of working steam mill engines in the

Locomotives

Name	No	Origin	Class	Type	Built
Lion	57	L&MR	—	0-4-2	1838
Pender	3††	IoMR	—	2-4-0T	1873
Novelty	Replica of 1829 locomotive using some original parts				1986
—	3157†	PR	—	4-4-0	1911
—	2352§	SAR	GL	4-8-2+2-8-4	1929
Ariadne	1505 (27001)	BR	EM2 (77)	Co-Co	1954
Hector	26048	BR	EM1 (76)	Bo-Bo cab only	1952
Planet*	—		Replica—	2-2-0	1992

Industrial locomotives

Name	No	Builder	Type	Built
Lord Ashfield	—	Barclay (1964)	0-4-0ST	1929
—	258	E/Electric (1378)	4wBE	1944

*full scale model of 1830-built locomotive
††ex-Isle of Man Railways, 3ft gauge, sectioned (B/Peacock 1255)
†ex-Pakistan Railways, 5ft 6in gauge (V/Foundry 3064)
§ex-South African Railways, 3ft 6in gauge (B/Peacock 6693)

Rolling stock

BR Mk 2 SO E5241, 1966
Reproduction M&BR 1st class carriage c1840 using original fragments
2 full scale working models L&MR 2nd class carriages c1835
1914 L&YR ambulance carriage rebuilt 1923 as Medical Examination Car, LMS No 10825 (under restoration, assembled in 1917 from 1916 made modules)
B782903 4-wheeled covered goods van, BR (Wolverton), 1961
B783709 4-wheeled covered goods van, BR (Wolverton), 1962
3-plank loose coupled goods wagon, GCR (Chatham), c1890

Owners

Lion on loan from the National Museums, Liverpool
Novelty on loan from the National Railway Museum, York

Note:

Full scale (working) model — reproduction made to other than original specification
Replica — reproduction made by original company in original way
Reproduction — item made in original way by other than original company

Power Hall, demonstrated every afternoon. The Collections Centre has research facilities and access to reserve collections. Museum shop, restaurant, Learning and Conference Centres

Public opening: Daily except 24-26 December, including Saturdays and Sundays, 10.00-17.00. Entrance in Lower Byrom Street. Admission free to permanent galleries, although prices still apply for special exhibitions. Please ring for details. Groups can book a visit by calling (0161) 833 0027

Special notes: Good wheelchair access, toilets for the disabled, lecture and conference facilities

Museum — National Coal Mining Museum for England — West Yorkshire

Member: Registered Museum
Museum Director: Dr M. L. Faull
Address: National Coal Mining Museum for England, Caphouse Colliery, New Road, Overton, Wakefield, West Yorkshire WF4 4RH
Operating society/organisation: Natioanl Coal mining Museum for England Trust Ltd
Charity number: 517325
Telephone: 01924 848806
Fax: 01924 840694
Internet addresses:
e-mail: info@ncm.org.uk
Web site: www.ncm.org.uk
OS reference: SE 253164
Car park: Free - on site
Access by public transport:
Bus: No 232 from Huddersfield or Wakefield
Refreshment facilities: Licensed café providing hot and cold food
On site facilities: Souvenir shop
Running lines:
2ft gauge operated locomotive line providing a transport link between Caphouse Colliery and Hope Pit; 2ft 3in gauge rope-hauled demonstration 'paddy' line
Period of public operation: The museum is open daily 10.00-17.00 (except 24-26 December)
Special events: The museum has an extensive events programme. Planned for 2007 are: Brass Bands — 23 June; Miners' Gala — 22 July; Santa Underground — every weekend in December
Special facilities: Underground tours, conference centre, education facilities 'The Learning Curve'
Facilities for disabled: Toilets, full access to all galleries, audio loop, wheelchairs can be accommodated underground with prior booking

Standard gauge industrial locomotives

Name	No	Builder	Type	Built
Acton Hall No 3	—	Peckett (1567)	0-6-0ST	1920*
—	47	T/Hill (249V)	0-6-0DH	1978*
—	40	Hunslet (7307)	0-6-0DH	1973

Narrow gauge and underground locomotives
3ft gauge

Name	No	Builder	Type	Built
—	BEM403	Hunslet (3614)	0-4-0DMF	1948*

2ft 6in gauge

Name	No	Builder	Type	Built
Alicia	—	H/Clarke (DM746)	0-4-0DMF	1951*
—	—	R/Hornsby (480679)	4wDMF	1961*
Deborah	—	H/Clarke (DM1356)	0-4-0DMF	1965*
—	—	H/Clarke (DM1433)	0-6-0DMF	+
Kirsten	0592	GMT (0592)	4w-4wDMF	1981
Stephanie	0593	GMT (0593)	4w-4wDMF	1981*
Anna	—	GMT	4w-4wDMF	1984*
—	1	Clayton (3538)	4w-4wBEF	1989+

2ft 4in gauge

Name	No	Builder	Type	Built
—	—	Atlas (2463)	4wBEF	1945
—	—	R/Hornsby (375347)	4wDM	1954

2ft 3in gauge

Name	No	Builder	Type	Built
Caphouse Flyer	—	Hunslet (8832)	4wDEF	1978

2ft 2in gauge

Name	No	Builder	Type	Built
—	—	Hunslet (7530)	4wDF	1977*

2ft 1.5in gauge

Name	No	Builder	Type	Built
—	—	R/Hornsby (379659)	4wDM	1955*

2ft gauge

Name	No	Builder	Type	Built
Fryston No 2	—	H/Clarke (DM655)	0-4-0DMF	1949

*not currently on public display
+in use on Caphouse-Hope railway

Locomotives on loan
Standard gauge

Name	No	Builder	Type	Built
The Welshman	—	M/Wardle (1207)	0-6-0ST	1890
Airedale	—	Hunslet (1440)	0-6-0ST	1923
Antwerp	—	Hunslet (3180)	0-6-0ST	1944
Wheldale	—	Hunslet (3186)	0-6-0ST	1944
Progress	—	RSH (7298)	0-6-0ST	1946
—	9	YEC (2521)	0-6-0ST	1952
Monkton No 1	—	Hunslet (3788)	0-6-0ST	1953

Name	No	Builder	Type	Built
—	20	H/Clarke (D1152)	0-6-0DM	1958

3ft gauge

—	BEM402	Hunslet (8505)	0-4-0DMF	1981

2ft 3in gauge
Houghton Main

Flyer	—	Hunslet (7274)	4wDM	1973

2ft 2in gauge

Flying Scotsman	—	Hunslet (6273)	4wDM	1965

2ft gauge

—	—	R/Hornsby (441424)	4wDMF	1961

Carriages and wagons
The museum's collection contains several varieties of standard gauge coal trucks, various narrow gauge manriding cars, coal carrying cars and coal tubs. There are also two steam cranes

Owners
The Welshman and 9 the Chesterfield Locomotive Action Group, Barrow Hill Roundhouse
Airedale, Wheldale, Monkton No 1 the Embsay & Bolton Abbey Steam Railway
Antwerp the North Yorkshire Moors Railway
Progress the Tanfield Railway
20 the Midland Railway Centre, Butterley
BEM402 and *Flying Scotsman* the Middleton Railway
Houghton Main Flyer the Corris Railway
R/Hornsby (441424) the Chasewater Railway

Museum — National Railway Museum — North Yorkshire

Member: HRA, TT, MLSOG
Location: National Railway Museum, Leeman Road, York YO26 4XJ
OS reference: SE 594519
Operating society/organisation: Part of the National Museum of Science and Industry
Telephone: 0870 421 4001
Internet addresses: *e-mail:* nrm@nmsi.ac.uk
Web site: www.nrm.org.uk
Car park: Available on site, charge applies. Coach parking is available — pre-booking required
Access by public transport: The museum is within a few minutes' walking distance of the railway station and city centre. No 2 Green Line park & ride bus operates to the door. A road-train operates between the museum and the city centre (seasonal)

On site facilities: Museum shop, restaurant and toilets (all with baby changing facilities). Also model railway, miniature railway, train rides (seasonal), outdoor play areas, children's interactive learning centre, conference centre. Model railway and reference library closed until late 2007
Public opening: Daily 10.00-18.00. Closed 24-26 December. Admission is free for all. The museum reserves the right to charge for special events
Facilities for disabled: Most areas of the museum are accessible. Wheelchairs may be borrowed at the entrances. Disabled parking is available at the museum's City entrance
Special notes: The museum opened 1975 and has welcomed over 20 million visitors. It has received

numerous awards including the prestigious 'European Museum of the Year' award in 2001.
As the world's largest railway museum, it offers the visitor three extensive exhibition halls. The Great Hall, the Station Hall and The Works house the world's premier collection of railway related material.
In the Great Hall there is an impressive array of locomotives around the turntable (demonstrated daily). Icons such as *Mallard* and the Japanese Bullet Train (the only one on display outside Japan) can also be found in the hall, along with the story of British Rail and a display dedicated to the movement of Mail by Rail.
A new exhibition in The Works is dedicated to the story of the most famous locomotive in the world,

Flying Scotsman, which was saved for the nation in 2004. Once the current major overhaul of the locomotive is complete (late 2007/early 2008) it will spend time either on main line operations as one of the museum's working fleet, or in the new exhibition. Work in the museum's workshop on *Flying Scotsman* and other rolling stock can be viewed from the balcony galleries in The Works. Exhibitions on railway works and controlling the network can also be found on the balcony galleries, as can a live link to York's IECC signalbox and an external viewing area overlooking the mouth of York station. The Warehouse, also in The Works, is the museum's open store and is an Aladdin's cave of railway treasures.

The Station Hall illustrates the concept of travel by train — for passengers and freight. Several trains are drawn up at platforms and range from superb Royal carriages to humble freight wagons. Access is possible to some footplates and carriages opened on request by Explainers. A range of talks and tours is also offered, and staff are on hand to guide younger visitors in the Interactive Learning Centre, accessible via the South Yard.

New to the museum is the Norwich Union Yorkshire Wheel, a 60 metre observation wheel offering spectacular panoramic views of York's historic city centre (including many railway features) and the countryside beyond (charges apply).

As a venue for conferences, corporate events, private parties and weddings the museum acts as a spectacular backdrop. The civil ceremony licence has been extended to cover weddings on the Norwich Union Yorkshire Wheel. For more information call 01904 686227.

For details of the museum's support group contact The Secretary, Friends of the National Railway Museum, c/o the above address. For information on becoming a museum volunteer call 01904 685737 and speak to the Volunteering Manager.

The museum is currently developing an existing £3m library and archive centre. Due to extensive building work, the reference library (which includes photographic and drawing collections) is closed until late 2007. In the interim, library staff will continue to answer simple enquiries by post and e-mail (nrm.researchcentre@nmsi.ac.uk_

The tables which follow indicate the whereabouts (display, on loan, in store) of the National Railway Collection. It must be emphasised that the appearance of any particular item on public display cannot be guaranteed. To confirm the exact location of a specific item, enquirers should contact the museum before visiting

Locomotives — Steam

Name	No	Origin	Builder	Class	Type	Built
Agenoria	—	Shutt End Colliery	Foster/Raistrick	—	0-4-0	1829
Coppernob	3	FR	Bury, Curtis & Kennedy	—	0-4-0	1846
Pet	—	LNWR	Crewe	—	0-4-0ST	1865
Aerolite	66	NER	Gateshead	X1(LNER)	2-2-4T	1869
—	1	GNR	Doncaster	—	4-2-2	1870
Bauxite	2	Hebburn Works	B/Hawthorn	—	0-4-0ST	1874
—	1275	NER	Gateshead	—	0-6-0	1874
Boxhill	82	LBSCR	Brighton	A1	0-6-0T	1880
Gladstone	—	LBSCR	Brighton	—	0-4-2	1882
Wren	—	LYR	B/Peacock	—	0-4-0ST	1887
—	1008	LYR	Horwich	—	2-4-2T	1889
Hardwicke	790	LNWR	Crewe	—	2-4-0	1892
—	1621	NER	Gateshead	M	4-4-0	1893
—	993	RR	Sharp Stewart	7A	4-8-0	1896
—	245	LSWR	Nine Elms	M7	0-4-4T	1897
—	673	MR	Derby	—	4-2-2	1899
—	737	SECR	Ashford	D	4-4-0	1901
—	1000	MR	Derby	4	4-4-0	1902
—	87	GER	Stratford	J69	0-6-0T	1904
—	1217	GER	Stratford	J17	0-6-0	1905
—	2818	GWR	Swindon	2800	2-8-0	1905
Lode Star	4003	GWR	Swindon	'Star'	4-6-0	1907
Flying Scotsman	4472	LNER	Doncaster	A3	4-6-2	1923
Cheltenham	925	SR	Eastleigh	V/Schools	4-4-0	1934
Rocket (replica)	—		R. Stephenson	—	0-2-2	1934
—	5000	LMS	Crewe	5MT	4-6-0	1935
—	607	Chinese Govt Rlys	Vulcan	KF7	4-8-4	1935
Green Arrow	4771	LNER	Doncaster	V2	2-6-2	1936

114

Name	No	Origin	Builder	Class	Type	Built
Mallard	4468	LNER	Doncaster	A4	4-6-2	1938
Eustace Forth	15	—	RSH (7063)	—	0-4-0ST	1942
—	C1	SR	Brighton	Q1	0-6-0	1942
Winston Churchill	34051	SR	Brighton	BB	4-6-2	1946
Ellerman Lines	35029	BR(SR)	Sectioned	MN	4-6-2	1949
Frank Galbraith	5	Tees-Side Bridge & Engineering Co	Sentinel	—	4wTG	1957
Evening Star	92220	BR	Swindon	9F	2-10-0	1960
Rocket (replica)	—	—	Loco Enterprises	—	0-2-2	1979
Iron Duke (broad gauge replica)	—	GWR	RESCO	—	4-2-2	1985

Locomotives — Electric

Name	No	Origin	Builder	Class	Type	Built
—	1	NSR	Bolton & Sons	—	0-4-0WE	1917
—	809	GPO	Green Bat	—	2w-2E	1931
—	26020	BR	Gorton/Metrovick	76	Bo-Bo Electric	1951
—	RA.36	TML	Hunslet	—	4wBE/WE	1990
Royal Scot	87001	BR	Crewe	87	B0-B0	1973

Locomotives — Diesel

Name	No	Origin	Builder	Class	Type	Built
Rorkes Drift	—	WD	Drewry	_	0-4-0DM	1934
—	—	Yorkshire Water Authority	R/Hornsby (187105)	—	4wDM	1937
—	08911	BR	Horwich	08	0-6-0 DE	1962
—	D8000	BR	E/Electric	20	Bo-Bo	1957
—	5500	BR	Brush	31	A1A-A1A	1957
—	03090	BR	—	03	0-6-0DM	1960
—	D2860	BR	YEC	02	0-4-0 DH	1960
King's Own Yorkshire Light Infantry	D9000	BR	E/Electric	55	Co-Co	1961
Western Fusilier	D1023	BR	Swindon	52	C-C	1963
—*	41001	BR	Crewe	41	Bo-Bo	1972
Prince William	47798	BR	Crewe	47	Co-Co	1965

*stored at MoD Kineton

Rolling Stock Powered Units — Electric

1916   LNWR Motor Open Third Brake No 28249
1925   SR Motor Third Brake No S8143S
1937   SR Motor Third Open Brake No S11179S
1941†   LMS Class 502 BMS No 28361
1941†   LMS Class 502 DTC No 29896
1975   Birmingham Airport Maglev passenger car
1976   Series 'O' Shinkasen No 2214
  BR Class 423/4VEP DT No 76875
  BR Class 414/2HAP MBS No 61275
  BR Class 414/2HAP DTC No 75395

Rolling Stock Powered Units — Diesel

1959   BR DMU Class 108 Nos 51562 & 51922

Rolling Stock — Departmental

1890   GNR Locomotive Tender No 1002
1899   GWR Hand Crane No 537
1906   NER Dynamometer Car No 902502
1907   NER Steam Breakdown Crane No CME 13
1907   Match Truck No DE942114
1926   LNER Match Truck No DE320952
1931/2   LNER Petrol-driven platelayers' trolley No 960209
1936   GWR Ballast Wagon No 80659

1938   LMS Mobile test unit No 1, No 45053
1955   GEC 12.5-ton Coles Crane
1969   BR Plasser Tamping & Liner No 73010
1989   Molhouser side discharge muck car ASDR 3105 (Channel Tunnel)

Rolling Stock — Passenger

1834   B&WR 1st & 2nd composite
1834   B&WR 2nd class
1834   B&WR 3rd class
1842   L&BR Queen Adelaide's Saloon
1850   NER Brake End (body only)
1851   ECR 1st class No 1
1860   Cornwall Rly broad gauge coach (body only)
1861   NBR Port Carlisle branch 'dandy car'
1869   LNWR Queen Victoria's Saloon
1885   MR 6-wheel composite brake No 901
1885   WCJS 8-wheel TPO No 186
1887   GNR Brake Van No 848
1897   Lynton & Barnstaple Rly brake composite No 6992
1898   ECJS 3rd class No 12
1899   Privately owned Duke of Sutherland's Saloon No 57A
1900   LNWR (ex-WCJS) Dining Car LMS 76

1902	LNWR King Edward's Saloon No 800
1902	LNWR Queen Alexandra's Saloon No 801
1903	LSWR Tricomposite brake No 3598
1908†	ECJS Royal Saloon No 395
1913	Pullman Car Co 1st class parlour car *Topaz*
1914	MR Dining car No 3463
1930	L&MR 1st *Huskinson* (replica)
1930	L&MR 1st *Traveller* (replica)
1930	L&MR 2nd (replica)
1930	L&MR 2nd (replica)
1936	CIWL Night Ferry sleeping car No 3792
1937	LNER Buffet Car No 9135
1937	LMS corridor 3rd class brake No 5987,
1938	GJR TPO (replica)
1941	LMS Royal Saloon 799 (armoured car)
1945	GWR Royal Saloon No 9007
1955	BR Lavatory composite No E43046
1960	Pullman Car Co 1st class Parlour car No 326 *Emerald*
1962	BR Mk II 2nd brake corridor No 35468
1969	BR Mk IIb 2nd open No 5455

Rolling Stock — Freight & Non Passenger Carrying

1815	Little Eaton (Derby Canal) Gangroad Wagon
1815	Peak Forest Canal Tramway Wagon No 174
1816	Grantham Canal Tramway Truck
1828	Dandy Cart
1840	Stratford & Moreton Tramway Wagon
1894	LSWR Brake van No 99

1908	LNWR Open carriage truck No 11275
1912	GNR 8-ton van No E432764
1917	GCR Box Van
1917	LNWR Box Van
1920	LSWR Lowmac, No DE563024, NYMR
1924	LMSR Van
1931	GWR Fruit Van No 112884
1931	Stanton Iron Works 12-ton wagon
1933	LMSR 20-ton Goods Brake Van No 295987
1935	SR Bogie goods brake van No 56297
1935	PLM Train Ferry Van No 475014
1936	LMSR 3 plank open wagon No 472867
1937	GWR Siphon bogie milk van No 2775
1937	LMSR Milk Tank Wagon No 44057
1937	2 x Yorkshire Water Authority side-tipper wagons
1944	LMS Lowmac No M700728
1944	GWR 13-ton open wagon No DW143698
1949	BR Bogie bolster D No B941000
1950	BR 20-ton Weltrol No B900805
1951	ICI Liquid chlorine tank wagon No 47484
1951	BR 8-ton cattle wagon No B893343
1962	BR Speedfreight container No BA 4324B
1966	Milk Marketing Board 6-wheel tank No 42801
1970	BR 2,000gal Road/Rail Milk Tank No ADM707111
1989	TML side-tipping muck cart No R T239

†stored at MoD Kineton

Items on Loan from the NRM
Locomotives

Original type/No/Name	Location	Builder	Built
Wylam Colliery	Science Mus	—	1813
Hetton Colliery 0-4-0	Locomotion	G. Stephenson	1822
SDR 0-4-0 *Locomotion*	Darlington	R. Stephenson & Co	1825
L&MR 0-2-2 *Rocket*	Science Mus	R. Stephenson & Co	1829
L&MR 0-2-2 *Novelty*	Museum of Science & Technology (Manchester)	Braithwaite & Ericsson	1829
SDR 0-6-0 No 24 *Derwent*	Darlington Nth Rd Mus	A. Kitching	1845
GJR 2-2-2 *Columbine*	Science Mus	Crewe	1845
Wantage Tramway 0-4-0WT No 5 *Shannon*	Didcot Rly Ctr	G. England	1857
LNWR 0-4-0ST 1439	East Lancs	Crewe	1865
MR 2-4-0 No 158A	Midland Rly Ctr	Derby	1866
South Devon Rly 0-4-0WT *Tiny*	South Devon Rly	Sara	1868
LSWR 2-4-0WT No 30587	Bodmin	B/Peacock	1874
NER 2-4-0 No 910	Darlington Nth Rd Mus*	Gateshead	1875
NER 2-4-0 No 1463	Darlington Nth Rd Mus	Gateshead	1885
C&SL No 1	LT Museum	B/Peacock	1890
S&MR 0-4-2WT *Gazelle*	Col Stephens Rly Mus	Dodman	1893
GER 2-4-0 No 490	Bressingham	Stratford	1894
GWR 0-6-0 No 2516	Steam	Swindon	1897
TVR 0-6-2T No 28	Dean Forest	TVR	1897
GNR No 990 *Henry Oakley*	Bressingham	Doncaster	1899
LSWR 4-4-0 No 120	Bluebell Rly	Nine Elms	1899
LT&SR 4-4-2T No 80 *Thundersley*	Bressingham	R. Stephenson	1909
GCR 2-8-0 No 102	Great Central	Gorton	1911
WD No 1377 (2ft Gauge)	LBR	Simplex	1918
GCR 506 *Butler Henderson*	Barrow Hill	Gorton	1920
NSR No 2	Locomotion	Stoke	1922
GWR 4-6-0 No 4073 *Caerphilly Castle*	Steam	Swindon	1923
LMS 0-6-0 No 4027	Midland Rly Ctr	Derby	1924

England

Original type/No/Name	Location	Builder	Built
GWR 2-2-2 *North Star* (replica)	Steam	R. Stephenson	1925
SR 4-6-0 No 777 *Sir Lamiel*	GCR	N/British	1925
SR 4-6-0 No 850 *Lord Nelson*	Eastleigh Works†	Eastleigh	1926
GWR No 6000 *King George V*	Steam	Swindon	1927
GWR 0-6-0PT No 9400	Steam	Swindon	1947
BR 4-6-2 No 70013 *Oliver Cromwell*	Great Central	Crewe	1951
BR 1Co-Co1No D200	NYMR	E/Electric	1958
BR Bo-Bo No E3036	Barrow Hill	N/British	1960

†private site
*expected to return to NRM

Powered Units

NER	electric parcels van No 3267, G. Stephenson Mus	
GWR	diesel railcar No 4, Steam	
BR	Class 101 vehicle Nos 51192/54352 East Lancs	

Departmental Stock

1932	LMS Ballast plough brake van No 197266, Embsay
1949	BR(LMS) Dynamometer car No 3, No 45049, Barrow Hill

Passenger Stock

1846	SDR 1st & 2nd composite No 31, Beamish
1850	NER 4-wheel coach body, Darlington
1910	GCR Open 3rd class No 666, Nottingham
1925	GWR 3rd class dining car No 9653, Severn Valley Rly
1925	LMS 3rd class vestibule No 7828 *(on loan to LMS Carriage Association)*
1934	GWR Buffet Car No 9631, Steam,
1936	LNER 3rd Open, No 13254, NYMR
1941	LMS Royal saloon No 798, Glasgow Museum of Transport
1960	Pullman Car Co 1st class Kitchen car No 311

	Eagle, Bluebell
1985	GWR 3rd (broad gauge replica), Didcot

Freight & Non Passenger Carrying Stock

1850	South Hetton Colliery Chaldron Wagon No 1155, D Bahn Museum, Nuremberg
1898	CR well trolley bogie crocodile, Bo'ness
1902	NER 20-ton wooden hopper wagon No 4551, Tyne & Wear
1909	GWR Girder Wagon Set (Pollen E) Nos DW84997, 84998, 84999, 85000, Didcot
1912	LBSCR Open wagon No 27884, Yeovil
1912	LSWR Gunpowder van No KDS61209, Yeovil
1914	GWR Shunters' truck No W94988, Steam
1922	LBSCR cattle truck No 7116, Isle of Wight Steam Rly
1928	ICI Nitric acid tank wagon No 14, Yeovil
1941	LNER 20-ton brake van, No 246710, NYMR
1948	BR(SR) 12-ton shock absorbing wagon No 14036, NYMR
1950	BR 12-wheel well wagon, No KDB901601, East Lancs
1955	BR 16-ton mineral wagon No B227009, Middleton
1959	BR Fish van No B87905, Hull

Museum — National Waterways Museum — Glos

The museum completed a Lottery update of the galleries and site in 2001

Location: Gloucester Docks — signposted 'Historic Docks'
OS Reference: SO 826183
Operating society/organisation: National Waterways Museum, The Waterways Trust, Llanthony Warehouse, Gloucester Docks, Gloucester GL1 2EH
Tel: (01452) 318200
Fax: (01452) 318202
Internet address: *e-mail:* bookingsnwm@thewaterwaytrust.org

Web site: www.nwm.org.uk
Car parks: Pay & display outside museum. Free coach parking
Access by public transport: Main line Gloucester station, 1 mile
On site facilities: Tea room, souvenir and specialist bookshop (canal-related with some railway literature). School room/children's holiday activities. Working demonstrations vary. Tug driving and blacksmith courses. Trip boats and other museums in docks
Facilities for disabled: Full facilities, lifts, ramps, toilets. All indoor displays, quaysides and tea room accessible. Floating exhibits not accessible
Public opening: Daily, 10.00-17.00, except 25 December. Admission charged. Last admissions 16.00
Special events: Preservation, modellers' & craft events; leisure learning courses (send for further information)
Membership details: 'Friends' support organisation. Membership Secretary, c/o Museum address, Volunteers active in restoration/fundraising. Winter Meetings programme

Membership journal: *Llanthony Log* — quarterly

Industrial locomotives

Name	No	Builder	Type	Built
—	1	A/Barclay (2126)	0-4-0F	1942

Ex-Gloucester Corporation, Castle Meads Power Station, Gloucester Docks. Now on static display

Rolling stock

William Balmforth of Rodley crane, c1880. Small collection of GW, Midland, LMS and BR vans with local connections. Sharpness Docks open wagons and Gloucester-built flat wagon, Manchester Ship Canal (ex-GWR) Toad brake van

---

Timetable Service — Nene Valley Railway — Cambs

Member: HRA, TT

This unique railway's collection includes locomotives and coaches from 10 countries and two continents. It is a regular location for TV and film makers — from films like *Goldeneye* with Pierce Brosnan as 007 to ITV's *London's Burning*. The railway and the pleasant Cambridgeshire countryside have doubled for locations as diverse as Russia and Spain

General Manager: Cris Rees

Headquarters: Nene Valley Railway, Wansford Station, Stibbington, Peterborough, Cambs PE8 6LR

Telephone: Stamford (01780) 784444; Talking Timetable (01780) 784404

Main station: Wansford

Other public stations: Orton Mere, Ferry Meadows, Peterborough NVR (15min walk from city centre)

OS reference: TL 903979

Car park: Wansford, Orton Mere, Ferry Meadows, Peterborough NVR

Access by public transport: Buses from Peterborough to Orton Mere and Ferry Meadows

Refreshment facilities: Wansford, bar coach on most trains

Souvenir shops: Wansford

Exhibition: Wansford

Depot: Wansford

Locomotives

Name	No	Origin	Class	Type	Built
Mayflower	1306	LNER	B1	4-6-0	1948
City of Peterborough	73050	BR	5MT	4-6-0	1954
—	D9504	BR	14	0-6-0DH	1964
—	D9516	BR	14	0-6-0DH	1964
—	D9523	BR	14	0-6-0DH	1964
—*	14029*	BR	14	0-6-0DH	1964
—†	31271	BR	31	A1A-A1A	1961
Atlantic Conveyor	D306	BR	40	1Co-Co1	1960
British Fuels	56057	BR	56	Co-Co	1978
—	64.305-6	DB	64	2-6-2T	1936
—	7173	DB	52	2-10-0	1943
—	656	DSB	F	0-6-0T	1949
—	101	SJ	B	4-6-0	1944
—	1178	SJ	S	2-6-2T	1914
—	3.628	Nord	3500	4-6-0	1911
—	5485	PKP	Typ	0-8-0T	19xx
—	51401	BR	117	DMS	1959
—	51347	BR	117	DMBS	1959
—	59508	BR	117	TCL	1959

*on hire to Channel Tunnel Rail Link
†on loan from Midland Railway

Industrial locomotives

Name	No	Builder	Type	Built
—	—	Avonside (1945)	0-6-0ST	1926
Toby	—	Cockerill (1626)	0-4-0VBT	1890
Yvonne	—	Cockerill (2945)	0-4-0VBT	1920
Muriel	—	E/Electric (1123)	0-4-0DH	1966
Rhos	—	H/Clarke (1308)	0-6-0ST	1918
Derek Crouch	—	H/Clarke (1539)	0-6-0ST	1924
Thomas	—	H/Clarke (1800)	0-6-0T	1947
Jacks Green	—	Hunslet (1953)	0-6-0ST	1939
—	75006	Hunslet (2855)	0-6-0ST	1943
—	—	R/Hornsby (294268)	4wDM	1951
Doncaster	—	YEC (2654)	0-4-0DE	1957
—	11	Rebuilt Hill	4wD	1963
Stanton No 50	—	YEC (2670)	0-6-0DE	1958

England

Built by British Railways in 1954 Class 5 No 73050 was one of the first locomotives to arrive on the Nene Valley Railway, where it gained the name *City of Peterborough*. *Alan Barnes*

Length of line: 7.5 miles

Passenger trains: Yarwell Junction-Wansford-Ferry Meadows-Orton Mere-Peterborough NV

Period of public operation: Sundays from mid-February; weekends from Easter to end of October; Wednesdays from May, plus other midweek services in summer. Santa Specials at end of November and throughout December (telephone for details)

Special events: Take place throughout the year including Thomas Weekend, Gala Weekend, Steamin' Blues and Vintage Rail/Mail Weekend (telephone for details). The shop, café, bookshop, model railway and exhibition are open on operating days and the locomotive yard is open all year for viewing. NVR is also the home of *Thomas* the children's favourite engine.

Facilities for disabled: Ramp access to all stations and shops. Full toilets in Wansford station, souvenir shop. Disabled persons and helpers are eligible for concessionary fares. Passengers can be assisted on and off trains

Membership details: Bill Foreman, c/o above address

Membership journal: *Nene Steam* — 3 times/year

Marketing name: Britain's International Steam Railway

Name	No	Builder	Type	Built
Barabel	—	R/Royce (10202)	0-4-0DH	1967
—	DL83	R/Royce (10271)	0-6-0DH	1967

Stock

15 BR Mk 1 coaches; Wagons Lits sleeping car, Italian-built; Wagons Lits dining car, Belgian-built; 6 coaches from Denmark; 1 coach from France; 4 coaches from Belgium; 1 steam rail crane; SR Travelling Post Office; TPO coach M30272M; 20 12-ton Vanfits plus items of freight stock

England

North Bay Railway

This 20in gauge railway opened in 1931 and is almost a mile long, with all the features of a main line railway including a tunnel, bridges, signals stations and gradient boards reproduced to scale. The steam outline locomotives are based on Sir Nigel Gresley's Class A1 design for the LNER.

Location: Northstead Manor Gardens, Scarborough

Headquarters: Peasholme Park Station, Northstead Manor Gardens, Scarborough

Telephone: General enquiries: 01723 383636

Internet address: *e-mail:* office.cclr@btconnect.com

Main public station: Peasholme Park

Other public stations: Scalby Mills

Car parks: Nearby pay & display

Access by public transport: The railway is within walking distance of the main line stations and local bus services

Refreshment facilities: Within the gardens

Length of line: 0.875 mile, 1ft 8in gauge

Period of public operation: 7 April until end October, then weekends and school holidays at other times

Locomotives

Name	No	Builder	Type	Built
Neptune	1931	H/Clarke (D565)	4-6-2DH s/o	1931
Robin Hood	—	H/Clarke (D570)	4-6-4DH S/O	1932
Triton	1932	H/Clarke (D573)	4-6-2DH s/o	1932
Poseidon	—	H/Clarke (D582)	4-6-2DH S/O	1933

Stock

10 bogie coaches, 4 x toastrack coaches

North Ings Farm Museum

The museum contains agricultural equipment, tractors and railway items

Contact: Tim Hall or Malcolm Phillips (joint owners)

Headquarters: North Ings Farm Museum, Fen Road, Dorrington, Lincoln LN4 3QB

Telephone: 01526 833100

Internet address: *e-mail:* info@northingsfarmmuseum.co.uk

Web site: www.northingsfarmmuseum.co.uk

Car parks: At the museum entrance

Access by public transport: Nearest main line station Ruskington, 3 miles

Refreshment facilities: Only available by prior arrangement

Length of line: 600yd, 2ft gauge

Period of public operation: Open first Sunday, April to October. 10.00-17.00

Facilities for disabled: Toilet, wheelchairs can be accommodated on the train. Part of the museum is not easily accessible for wheelchairs

Locomotives

Name	No	Builder	Type	Built
Swift	—	Marshall	0-4-0VBT	1970
—	—	R/Hornsby (200744)	4wDM	1940
—	—	R/Hornsby (371937)	4wDM	1956
—	—	R/Hornsby (375701)†	4wDM	1954
—	—	R/Hornsby (421433)	4wDM	1959
—	—	M/Rail (7403)	4wDM	1939
—	—	M/Rail (7493)	4wDM	1940
—	—	O&K	4wDM	1932
—	—	Lister Railtrack*	4wDM	—
—	—	H/Hunslet (77120)	4wDM	1969

†dismantled
*constructed from spare parts

Owners

M/Rail (7403) and R/Hornsby (200744) on loan from Narrow Gauge Railway Museum Trust

Museum — North Woolwich Old Station Museum — London

This attractive Victorian terminus building overlooks the Thames. Railway artefacts, documents, drawings, etc, are well displayed in glass cases or on the walls, the stock being stabled in the platform area. Convenient for City Airport and connections for the Docklands Light Railway.

During 2007 the Museum will be starting a three year revamp that includes the absorption of the closed line to Silvertown and later to Custom House, and the establishment of RailSchool, a railway industry vocational training facility aimed at 14-19 year olds. In connection with this, additional locomotives and rolling stock are expected to arrive in the first half of 2007 and a programme of events will start in September 2007. Updates are available via the web site www.londonrail.org

Locomotives

Name	No	Origin	Class	Type	Built
—	229	GER	209	0-4-0ST	1876

Industrial locomotives

Name	No	Builder		Type	Built
—	—	Hibberd (3294)		4wDM	1948

Stock
1 ex-LNER coach; 2 compartment sections of LTSR coach; NLR Luggage Van; 1 ex-Royal Arsenal Ammunition Van (18in gauge)

Location: North Woolwich Old Station Museum, Pier Road, North Woolwich, London E16 2JJ
OS reference: TQ 433798
Organisation: London Rail Heritage Centre
Telephone: 020 8407 9998
Internet address: *Web site:* www.londonrail.org
Car park: Only in adjoining streets
Public transport:

Buses: 101 and 473
Facilities: Museum shop
Public opening: Open weekends January-November 13.00-17.00. Daily during Newham children's school holidays only 13.00-17.00
Admission: Free
Facilities for disabled: Access to all displays, indoors and out

---

Timetable Service — North Yorkshire Moors Railway — North Yorkshire

Member: HRA, TT
This 18-mile line runs through the picturesque North York Moors National Park and is host to an extensive collection of main line locomotives.
General Manager: Philip Benham
Headquarters: Pickering Station, Pickering, North Yorkshire YO18 7AJ
Telephone: Pickering (01751) 472508 for passenger enquiries, charter and diner bookings
Internet address: *e-mail:* admin@nymrpickering.fsnet.co.uk
Web site: www.northyorkshiremoorsrailway.com
Main station: Pickering
Other public stations: Grosmont, Goathland, Levisham
OS reference: Pickering NZ 797842, Levisham NZ 818909, Goathland NZ 836013, Grosmont NZ 828053

Locomotives and multiple-units

Name	No	Origin	Class	Type	Built
George Stephenson	44767§	LMS	5MT	4-6-0	1947
Eric Treacy	45428*	LMS	5MT	4-6-0	1937
—	53809††	S&DJR	7F	2-8-0	1925
—	2392	NER	P3	0-6-0	1923
—	63395*	NER	T2	0-8-0	1918
Sir Nigel Gresley	60007	LNER	A4	4-6-2	1937
Lord of the Isles	62005	LNER	K1	2-6-0	1949
—	69023	LNER	J72	0-6-0T	1951
—	3814*	GWR	2884	2-8-0	1940
—	6619	GWR	5600	0-6-2T	1928
—	825	SR	S15	4-6-0	1927
—	30830††	SR	S15	4-6-0	1927
Repton	30926	SR	V	4-4-0	1934
Hartland	34101	SR	WC	4-6-2	1950
—	75029	BR	4MT	4-6-0	1954
—	80135	BR	4MT	2-6-4T	1956
Dame Vera Lynn	3672††	MoS	WD	2-10-0	1943
—	2253††	USATC	S160	2-8-0	1943
—	D2207	BR	04	0-6-0DM	1953
—	08556	BR	08	0-6-0DE	1959
—	4018	BR	08	0-6-0DE	1961
Helen Turner	D5032†	BR	24	Bo-Bo	1959
—	D5061	BR	24	Bo-Bo	1960

Car parks: Grosmont, Goathland, Levisham, Pickering

Access by public transport: Arriva Northern rail service to Grosmont from Whitby and Middlesbrough. Bus services Leeds-York-Malton-Pickering-Goathland-Whitby; Helmsley-Pickering-Scarborough

Refreshment facilities: Available on most trains and at Grosmont, Goathland and Pickering. Tea bar at Levisham most weekends

Souvenir shops: Pickering, Goathland, Grosmont and Grosmont MPD

Locomotive Depot: Grosmont

Length of line: 18 miles

Passenger trains: Steam-hauled services Grosmont-Pickering. Pullman evening dining service and 'Moorlander' Sunday lunch service run regularly. Saloons are also available for special occasions (eg wedding parties, conferences, etc) *Note:* NYMR trains operate to/from Whitby throughout the year. Ring for details

Special events: Diesel Gala —20-22 April; LNER Festival — 28/29 April, 4-7 May; 60s Weekend —

Name	No	Origin	Class	Type	Built
Sybilla	D7628	BR	25	Bo-Bo	1965
Lion	50027	BR	50	Co-Co	1968
—	51511	BR	101	DMC	1959
—	53204	BR	101	DMBS	1957
—	59539	BR	101	TSL	1958
—	60110†	BR	205	DMBS	1957
—	60810†	BR	205	DTS	1957

†unit 205205
*undergoing major overhaul at Grosmont
§undergoing major overhaul off-site
††awaiting overhaul

Industrial locomotives

Name	No	Builder	Type	Built
—	29	Kitson (4263)	0-6-2T	1904
—	5††	R/Stephenson (3377)	0-6-2T	1909
Antwerp	—††	Hunslet (3180)	0-6-0ST	1944
Neil D. Barker	12139	E/Electric (1553)	0-6-0DE	1948
—	16	Drewry	0-4-0DM	1941
—	2	R/Hornsby (421419)	4wDM	1958
—	3*	R/Hornsby (441934)	4wDM	1960
Ron Rothwell	1	Vanguard (129V)	0-4-0DM	1963
—	2	Vanguard (131V)	0-4-0DM	1963

*on loan to Middleton Railway
††awaiting overhaul

Stock

5 pre-Grouping, 12 pre-Nationalisation, 32 x BR Mk 1, 4 x Pullman, 5 other BR coaches, 2 x Camping Coach, 1 x BR Mk 3 sleeper, 11 x brake vans, 4 x diesel cranes, 2 x 45-ton steam cranes, 88 other vehicles

16/17 June; Vintage Vehicle Weekend — 14/15 July; Music on the Moors — 26/27 August; Day out with Thomas — 8/9 September; Steam Gala — 28-30 September; Wartime Weekend — 12-14 October; Autumn Wizard Weekend — 27/28 October; Bonfire Special — 3 November
Period of public operation: Daily 17 March-4 November, Santa Specials and other Xmas and New Year services in December/January
Facilities for disabled: The NYMR welcomes disabled visitors and special attention will gladly be provided if advance notice is given
Special notes: Operates through North York Moors National Park and to Whitby town

Owners
825 and 30830 the Essex Locomotive Society
62005, 63395 and 69023 the North Eastern Locomotive Preservation Group
60007 Sir Nigel Gresley Locomotive Preservation Trust
Antwerp the National Mining Museum
5 and 29 Lambton Locomotives Trust
D5032 T. J. Thomson & Co
D5061 the Class 24 Society
50027 the Class 50 Support Group
3814, 6619, 34101 and 44767 private
53809 the 13809 Preservation Group
75029 the North Yorkshire Moors Historical Railway Trust

Steam Centre	Northampton & Lamport Railway	Northants

Member: HRA
Part of the Northampton to Market Harborough branch originally opened in 1859 and finally closing in 1981. That year a group was formed with the intention of re-opening the branch. Trains restarted in 1995 with 0.75 mile of running line and sidings. When completed to Lamport the line will be 6 miles long
Headquarters: Pitsford & Brampton Station, Pitsford Road, Chapel Brampton, Northampton NN6 8BA
Location: About 5 miles north of Northampton, Pitsford Road off A5199 (formerly A50) or A508
Chairman: Dr Colin Wilson
Operating company: Northampton Steam Railway Ltd
Telephone: 01604 820327 Sundays and weekday afternoons, recorded announcements other times
Internet address: *Web site:* www.nlr.org.uk
Access by public transport: None
On site facilities: NLR souvenir shop, buffet coach, toilets, second-hand bookshop
Length of line: 1.3 miles, extension to bridge 14 now open
Public opening: Every Sunday and Bank Holiday Monday from 6 March to 28 October. Santa

Locomotives and multiple-units

Name	No	Origin	Class	Type	Built
—	3862	GWR	2884	2-8-0	1942
—	27056	BR	27	Bo-Bo	1962
—	31289	BR	31	A1A-A1A	1961
—	33008	BR*	33	Bo-Bo	1960
The Royal Artilleryman	45118	BR	45	1Co-Co1	1962
—	47205	BR	47	Co-Co	1965
—	56098	BR	56	Co-Co	1981
—	97651	BR	97	0-6-0DE	1959
—	51359	BR	117	DMBS	1959
—	51400	BR	117	DMS	1959
—	55001	BR	122	DMBS	1958

*expected to arrive following restoration
27056 on loan to Great Central Railway

Industrial locomotives

Name	No	Builder	Type	Built
Colwyn	45	Kitson (5470)	0-6-0ST	1933
Westminster	1378	Peckett (1378)	0-6-0ST	1914
	2104	Peckett (2104)	0-4-0ST	1948
Vanguard	5374	Chrzanow (5374)	0-6-0T	1959
Bunty	146C	Fowler (4210018)/ rebuilt T/Hill	0-4-0DH	1950 1964
—	21	Fowler (4210094)	0-4-0DH	1955
—	1	R/Hornsby (275886)	4wDM	1949
Sir Gyles Isham	764	R/Hornsby (319286)	0-4-0DM	1953

Stock
Coaches: 2 x BR Mk 1 TSO; 1 x BR Mk 1 BSO; 1 x BR Mk 1 CK; 1 x BR Mk 1 RBR; 1 x Mk 2 TSO; 1 x Mk 2 BSO (trolley buffet); 1 x BR Mk 1 NAV; 2 x BR NJV; 2 x SR PMV; 1 x GWR full brake; 1 x LMS CCT
Wagons: A number of various types

Specials every Saturday and Sunday from 3-23 December. Plus some Saturdays during special events **Special events:** Easter Egg Specials — 7-9 April; Day out with Thomas — 5-7 May; Teddy Bears' Holiday — 22-28 May; Classic & Sports Car Show — 3 June; Day out with Thomas — 25-27 August; Railway at War Weekend — 22/23 September; Day out with Thomas — 13/14 October; Diesel Gala —

21/22 October; Santa Specials — weekends 2-23 December (pre-booking essential); Mince Pie Specials — 30 December/1 January 2008 **Membership details:** Membership

Secretary, Pitsford & Brampton Station, Pitsford Road, Chapel Brampton, Northampton NN6 8BA **Membership journal:** *Premier Line* — 4 times a year

Steam Centre — Northamptonshire Ironstone Railway Trust — Northants

The museum is a working display as well as a collection of historic memorabilia. Many of the items that are currently being renovated are housed in a shed that accommodates the museum display
 Initial opening will be alternate weekends with special events, along with Santa Specials in December. Please see railway press or contact for updates
Location: Hunsbury Hill Industrial Museum, Hunsbury Hill Country Park, Hunsbury Hill Road, Camp Hill, Northampton
OS reference: SP 735584
Operating organisation: Northamptonshire Ironstone Railway Trust Ltd
Telephone: 01604 702031
Contact: W. Nile, 14 Lyncrest Avenue, Dunston, Northampton (Tel: 01604 757481)
Access by public transport: Northampton Transport bus routes, 24, 25 to Camp Hill from Greyfriars bus station
On site facilities: Light refreshments, shop, toilets. Children's play areas and picnic areas
Length of line: 2.25 miles with yard, engine shed and workshops, 2 stations and level crossing
Public opening: Please contact for details
Times of opening: Please contact for details
Facilities for the disabled: Passenger coach can accommodate wheelchairs
Special notes: Museum to the Ironstone Industry of Northamptonshire, the museum

Multiple-units

Name	No	Origin	Class	Type	Built
—	13004	SR	4DD	DMBS	1949
—	56285	BR	121	DTS	1960
—	70284	BR	4CEP / 411	TS	1956
—	70296	BR	4CEP / 411	TS	1956
—	69304	BR	4BIG / 422	TSRB	1965
—	14352†	BR	415 / 4EPB	DMS	1954
—	15396†	BR	415 / 4EPB	TS	1954
—	14351†	BR	415 / 4EPB	DMS	1954

†unit No 415176

Industrial locomotives

Name	No	Builder	Type	Built
Vigilant†	—	Hunslet (287)	0-4-0ST	1882
Belvedere◊	—	Sentinel (9365)	0-4-0TG	1946
Musketeer◊	—	Sentinel (9369)	0-4-0TG	1946
Hylton	—	Planet (3967)	0-4-0DH	1961
Charles Wake	—	Fowler (422001)	0-4-0DH	1965
Lois	—	Fowler (422033)	0-4-0DH	1965
Muffin	46	R/Hornsby (242868)	4wDM	1946
—	16	Hunslet (2087)	0-4-0DM	1940
AMOCO	56	R/Hornsby	0-4-0DM	1956
Shire Lodge	53	R/Hornsby	0-4-0DM	1954
Sir Alfred Wood	46	R/Hornsby (319214)	0-6-0DM	1953
—	5	R/Hornsby (338489)	0-4-0DM	1956
—*	87	Peckett (1871)	0-6-0ST	1934
Northampton†	1	Bagnall (2565)	0-4-0ST	1934
*Cherwell***	—	Bagnall (2654)	0-6-0ST	1942
—	—	Grafton	Steam crane	1934

* metre gauge on loan to Irchester Country Park
◊ static display
† being rebuilt
**3ft gauge

England

houses photographs, documents and other items connected with the ironstone industry. The railway is laid on the old trackbed of the quarry system and partly on a new formation with remains of the quarry face and cuttings available for exploration
Membership details: Mr R. Coleman, c/o above address

| Steam Centre | Nottingham Transport Heritage Centre | Notts |

Member: HRA

Along with access to nearly 10 miles of the ex-Great Central Railway main line in Nottinghamshire, the Centre is host to a road and rail transport heritage vehicle collection. Ambitious plans are afoot to reconnect its section of main line railway to the existing Great Central Railway based at Loughborough. This will provide visitors with the unique experience of travelling on one of the longest heritage railways in the UK in a realistic re-creation of main line travel of the 1950s and 1960s

Location: On the A60 just south of Ruddington, 3 miles south of Nottingham city centre, off A52, 7 miles north of Loughborough. Signposted

Operating society/organisation: Great Central (Nottingham) Ltd, Nottingham Heritage Centre, Mere Way, Ruddington, Nottingham NG11 6NX

Telephone: (0115) 940 5705

Fax: (0115) 940 5905

Internet address:
Web site: www.nthc.co.uk

Access by public transport: Buses from city centre and Broad Marsh (tel: [0115] 924 0000), via Nottingham Midland station

On site facilities: Car park, shop and café, picnic area and country park walks. 700m-long passenger-carrying miniature railway. Extensive bus museum

Length of line: 7 mile steam train ride

Facilities for disabled: Accessible, and access to toilets

Public opening: Sundays & Bank Holidays Easter to early October, plus Spooky Ghost Trains, Bonfire Night and Santa Specials. Open 10.45-17.00 (first trains around 11.30)

Special events: 3rd Model Railway Event — 19/20 August. For other

Locomotives and multiple-units

Name	No	Origin	Class	Type	Built
—	D4115*	BR	08	0-6-0DE	1962
—	13180	BR	08	0-6-0DE	1955
—	D7629	BR	25	Bo-Bo	1965
—	D8048	BR	20	Bo-Bo	1959
—	D9520†	BR	14	0-6-0DH	1964
—	47765	BR	47	Co-Co	1964
—	56097	BR	56	Co-Co	1981
—	51138	BR	116	DMBS	1958
—	51151	BR	116	DMS	1958
—	53645	BR	108	DMBS	1958
—	53926	BR	108	DMBS	1959
—	59389	BR	108	TS	1958
—	2138	USATC	S160	2-8-0	—

Gatwick Express units 8301/10, 9108
*expected to depart soon
†off site for further restoration at Nene Valley Railway

Industrial locomotives

Name	No	Builder	Type	Built
Victor	2996	Bagnall (2996)	0-6-0ST	1951
—	54	H/Clarke (1682)	0-6-0ST	1937
—	56	RSH (7667)	0-6-0ST	1950
—	63	RSH (7761)	0-6-0ST	1954
Rhiwnant	—	M/Wardle (1317)	0-6-0ST	1895
Dolobran	—	M/Wardle (1762)	0-6-0ST	1910
Abernant	—	M/Wardle (2009)	0-6-0ST	1921
Toby	—	R/Hornsby (235513)	4wDM	1945
—	2 / D2971	R/Hornsby (313394)	0-4-0DM	1954
(Quag)	(1)	R/Hornsby (371971)	0-4-0DM	1954
Staythorpe	D2959	R/Hornsby (449754)	0-4-0DE	1961
Churchill	423	R/Hornsby (459518)	0-4-0DM	1961
—	8	R/Hornsby (494436)	0-4-0DE	1965
—	15100	M/Rail (1930)	4wPM	1919
—	—	M/Rail (2028)	0-4-0DM	1932

Rolling stock: 1 BR Mk 1 FO, 1 BR Mk 2 BSO, 1 BR Mk 2 BFK, 1 BR (ex-WR) cinema coach, 5 ex-Gatwick express coaches, GCR coach (body) CBL No 1663 (oldest surviving GCR coach, built 1903), 4 Barnum coaches, suburban coach, 2 MS&LR 6-wheel coaches, 1 'Internation' concert coach (used as display area and will not run), 1 LNER 45-ton steam breakdown crane, 1 SR GUV, various goods wagons

Owners

Class 108 and 116 DMUs the Nottingham (GC) DMU Group
56097 and 423 the 56097 Locomotive Group
M/Rails 1930, 2028, R/Hornsbys 371971, 449754 the Simplex 2028 Association
R/Hornsby (313394) the Cheshire Locomotive Preservation Group

126 **England**

events please contact for details
Membership details: Great Central Northern Development Association, c/o above address
Society journal: Quarterly

Attraction — Old Kiln Light Railway — Surrey

The Old Kiln Light Railway is located in the grounds of the Rural Life Museum which houses the largest countryside collection in the south of England. and bank holidays only
Location: Rural Life Centre, Reeds Road, Tilford, Farnham, Surrey GU10 2DL
Telephone: (01252) 795571 (museum)
Internet address: *Web site:* www.rural-life.org.uk
On site facilities: Fre parking, picnic areas, shop, cafe
Access by road:
The museum is 3 miles south of Farnham, just off the A287 and midway between Frensham and Tilford villages
Length of line: Half mile, under extension, 2ft gauge
Public opening: Late March to October, 10.00-17.00, Wednesday to Sunday and bank holidays. Winter opening 11.00-16.00

Industrial locomotives (2ft gauge)

Name	No	Builder	Type	Built
Pamela	—	Hunslet (920)	0-4-0ST	1922
Elouise	—	O&K (9998)	0-4-0ST	1-06
—	—	M/Rail (5297)	4wPM	1931
—	—	M/Rail (6035)	4wPM	1937
—	—	M/Rail (5713)	4wDM	1936
—	—	M/Rail (8887)	4wDM	1944
—	—	M/Rail (8981)	4wDM	1946
—	—	Ruston (392117)	4wDM	1956
—	—	Wickham (3031)	4wDM	1941
—	—	Wickham (3287)	2w-2PMR	1943

Stock
Glyn Valley replica coach, Baguley open coach, RNAD van, brake van

Wednesdays and Sundays only. The railway operates on Sundays and bank holidays only
Special events (transport related): Steam Toy Rally — 7 April; Model Railway Exhibition — 5 May; Village at War — 13 May; Bus & Coach Rally — 27 may; Rustic

Sunday — 29 July; Citroen & Renault Car Rally — 12 August; Classic Vehicle Gathering — 16 September; Steam & Vintage Weekend — 30 September
Disabled facilities: Good access to all areas

Steam Centre — Oswestry Railway Centre (Cambrian Railways Society) — Shropshire

Member: HRA
The Gobowen to Blodwell line is some 8.25 miles long and is currently in an operational 'mothballed' state. The society is negotiating with Network Rail to lease this former Cambrian branch line with a view to restoring a heritage railway service between Gobowen and Llanyblodwell and eventually Llanymynech. The society now operates on four separate sites.
   July 2004 saw the purchase of the

Industrial locomotives

Name	No	Builder	Type	Built
—	1	H/Clarke (D843)	0-4-0DM	1954
—	—	H/Clarke (D893)	0-4-0DM	1953
Adam	1	Peckett (1430)	0-4-0ST	1916
—	3	Hunslet (D3526)	0-6-0DM	1954
Oliver Velton	6	Peckett (2131)	0-4-0ST	1951
—	8	Barclay (885)	0-6-0ST	1900
—	322	Planet (3541)	4wDM	1952
Norma	3770	Hunslet (3770)	0-6-0ST	1952
—*	—	Hibberd (3057)	4wDM	1946
—	—	Planet (3716)	0-4-0DM	1955
Telemon	—	Drewry/Vulcan (2568)	0-4-0DM	1955

*mobile compressor

England

former Cambrian Institute on Gobowen Road; now open as a social club (19.00-23.00) seven days a week and is available for functions and events.

The Oswestry Railway Centre, Oswald Road, was awarded Phase II status recognition, the Museum being of national importance.

The Society-owned Grain Transfer Warehouse at Weston, on the outskirts of Oswestry, is now home to the Denbigh and Mold Junction Railway.

August 2004 saw the purchase of the 1.5-mile former Nant Mawr branch line and the start of a two year project to restore this to operational status

Location: Oswestry station yard, Oswald Road, Oswestry, Shropshire SY11 1RE

OS reference: SJ 294297

Operating society/organisation: Cambrian Railways Society Ltd, Oswald Road, Oswestry, Shropshire SY11 1RE

Stock
1 GWR auto-trailer; 1 GWR brake van; 1 LMS brake van; 2 tank wagons; 1 open wagon, 1 box van, 1 tank wagon (No 5), 2 tank wagon 4-wheel chassis (tanks removed) ex-Machynlleth Refuelling Depot, 4-wheel van, 12-ton box van, ex-S&M 10-ton box van.

Owners
Telemon the Cambrian Diesel Group

Telephone: (01691) 671749
Internet address: *Web site:* www.cambrianrailwayssociety.co.uk
Car park: In Society's depot
Access by public transport:
By rail — Gobowen station is 2.5 miles north.
By bus — 2min walk from Oswestry bus station.
Please note that there is no Gobowen-Oswestry bus service on Sundays
Length of line: 400yd, opened 7 December 1996, the Light Railway Order having been granted
Public opening: Oswestry Transport Museum is open:

Monday-Saturday 09.00-16.00. Sunday 11.00-16.00.
Please contact to confirm when trains are expected to operate.
On site facilities: Refreshment room — the 'Whistle Stop' (open on special days in former Llansantffraid signalbox) and picnic area
Special notes: Railwayana and artefacts. Peckett 2131 and Hunslet 3770 are on display inside the building. Group discount available. Also known as Oswestry Transport Museum

---

| Timetable Service | Paignton & Dartmouth Steam Railway | Devon |

Member: HRA

The Paignton & Dartmouth Steam Railway is the holiday line with steam trains running for seven miles in Great Western tradition along the spectacular Torbay coast to Churston and through the wooded slopes bordering the Dart estuary to Kingswear. The scenery is superb, with seascapes right across Lyme Bay to Portland Bill on clear days. Approaching Kingswear is the beautiful River Dart, with its fascinating craft, and on the far side, the 'olde worlde' town of Dartmouth and Britannia Royal Naval College, Butterwalk, Bayard's Cove and Dartmouth Castle

Director & General Manager: J. B. S. Cogar

Headquarters: Paignton Queen's Park station, Paignton, Devon
Telephone: Paignton (01803) 555872
Main station: Paignton Queen's Park
Other public stations: Goodrington, Churston, Kingswear (for Dartmouth)

Locomotives and multiple-units

Name	No	Origin	Class	Type	Built
Warrior	4555	GWR	4500	2-6-2T	1924
Trojan	4588	GWR	4575	2-6-2T	1927
Goliath	5239	GWR	5205	2-8-0T	1924
Ajax	6435	GWR	6400	0-6-0PT	1937
Lydham Manor	7827	GWR	7800	4-6-0	1951
Braveheart	75014	BR	4MT	4-6-0	1951
Ardent	D2192	BR	03	0-6-0DM	1962
Volunteer	D3014	BR	08	0-6-0DE	1954
Hercules	D7535	BR	25	Bo-Bo	1965
—	59003*	BR	116	TS	1957
—	59004*	BR	116	TS	1957
—	59488*	P/Steel	117	TCL	1959
—	59494*	P/Steel	117	TCL	1959
—	59503*	P/Steel	117	TCL	1959
—	59507*	P/Steel	117	TCL	1959
—	59513*	P/Steel	117	TCL	1959
—	59517*	P/Steel	117	TCL	1959

*converted to locomotive-hauled vehicles

Stock
15 ex-BR Mk 1 coaches; 1 Pullman observation coach; 2 auto-coaches

OS reference: SX 889606
Car parks: Paignton municipal car park, Goodrington, Dartmouth (ferry to Kingswear)
Access by public transport: Adjacent to both Paignton main line

station and bus station
Refreshment facilities: Paignton and Kingswear
Depot: Churston
Length of line: 7 miles
Passenger trains: Paignton-

128

Kingswear, views of Torbay and Dart estuary, 495yd tunnel
Period of public operation: Easter to October and Santa Specials in December
Facilities for disabled: Limited, special ramp to take wheelchairs onto trains. Disabled toilets at

Paignton
Special events: Santa Specials — please see timetable and press for details. Combined river excursions available
Special facilities: Private charters, details on request
Special note: The railway also

operates excursion vessels on the River Dart. Combined river excursions available, Boat trains and Round Robin tickets. Round Robin — single journey to Kingswear, 1hr 30min boat cruise to Totnes and bus back to Paignton

---

Timetable Service	Peak Rail plc	Derbyshire

Member: HRA

In 1968 the railway between Matlock and Buxton, through the Peak National Park was closed and lifted. This was once part of the Midland Railway's route between Manchester Central and London. In 1975 efforts were started to reopen the line. Services between Matlock and Darley Dale commenced in 1991

Location: *Registered Office:* Matlock Station, Matlock, Derbyshire DE4 3NA

OS reference: Matlock SK 060738

Operating society/organisation: Peak Rail plc, Matlock Station, Matlock, Derbyshire DE4 3NA

Telephone: (01629) 580381

Internet address: *Web site:* www.peakrail.co.uk

Car parks: Matlock station, Darley Dale, Rowsley South station

Length of line: 4 miles — Matlock Riverside-Rowsley South. A 2ft gauge railway is now operational at Rowsley

On site facilities: Shop at Matlock. Shops and buffets at Darley Dale and Rowsley South. Picnic area and riverside walk

Public opening: Sundays throughout the year, Saturdays April to October. Midweek during summer. Timetable varies

Facilities for disabled: Darley Dale and Rowsley. Matlock Riverside unsuitable for disabled passengers. Specially adapted carriage is fully accessible to wheelchair users (not available on DMU services)

Period of public operation: Not advised, see timetable supplement

Special events: Please contact for details

Locomotives and multiple-units

Name	No	Origin	Class	Type	Built
—	48624	LMS	8F	2-8-0	1943
—	D2953	BR	01	0-4-0DM	1956
—	D2854	BR	02	0-4-0DH	1960
—	D2866	BR	02	0-4-0DH	1961
—	03027	BR	03	0-6-0DM	1958
—	03099	BR	03	0-6-0DM	1960
—	D2139	BR	03	0-6-0DM	1960
—	D2199	BR	03	0-6-0DM	1961
—	D2229	BR	04	0-6-0DM	1955
Alfie	D2272	BR	04	0-6-0DM	1960
—	D2284	BR	04	0-6-0DM	1960
Dorothy	D2337	BR	04	0-6-0DM	1961
—	D2587	BR	05	0-6-0DM	1959
—	07013	BR	07	0-6-0DE	1961
Geoff L. Wright	D3023*	BR	08	0-6-0DE	1953
—	12061	BR	11	0-6-0DE	1949
—	D9502	BR	14	0-6-0DH	1964
—	D9525	BR	14	0-6-0DH	1964
—	31270	BR	31	A1A-A1A	1961
—	37151	BR	37	Co-Co	1963
Penyghent	D8	BR	44	1Co-Co1	1959
Renown	50029	BR	50	Co-Co	1968
Repulse	50030	BR	50	Co-Co	1968
—	97654	BR	—	0-6-0DM	1959
—	50627	BR	108	DMBS	1958
—	51566	BR	108	DMSL	1959
—	51567	BR	108	DMSL	1959
—	51933	BR	108	DMBS	1960
—	53933	BR	108	DMBS	1959
—	54484	BR	108	DTC	1960
—	54504	BR	108	DTC	1960
—	59387	BR	108	TS	1958
—	51973 (977806)	BR	108	DMBS	1958

*on loan to Bluebell Railway

Industrial locomotives

Name	No	Builder	Type	Built
The Duke	2746	Bagnall (2746)	0-6-0ST	1944
—	64	Brush (803)	0-6-0DE	1978
Royal Pioneer	150	RSH (7136)	0-6-0ST	1944
Zebedee	—	RSH (7597)	0-6-0ST	1949
Vulcan	—	V/Foundry (3272)	0-4-0ST	1918
—	—	T/Hill	0-6-0DH	
Lucky	48	T/Hill	0-6-0DH	
Claire	—	H/Clarke (D1389)	0-4-0DM	1967

England

Name	No	Builder	Type	Built
Castlefield	—	H/Clarke (D1388)	0-6-0DH	1970
—	20	R/Hornsby (432479)	0-4-0DM	1959
Rotherham	—	YEC (2480)	0-4-0DM	
Bigga	—	Fowler (4200019)	0-4-0DM	1947
—	—	Drewry (2552)	0-6-0DM	1953

Rolling stock — coaches: 2 BR Mk 1 RMB, 1 BR Mk 1 SLF, 3 BR Mk 1 TSO, 2 BR Mk 1 SO, 3 BR Mk 1 SK, 1 BR Mk 1 BSK, 2 BR Mk 1 BG, 1 BR Mk 1 GUV, 1 BR Mk 2 SO, 1 BR Mk 2 BSO, 1 BR Mk 2 BFK, 1 LMS TK, 2 LMS BCK, 1BTK, 1 Bullion coach, 3 parcels vans

Rolling stock — wagons: 1 5 plank, 1 LMS 5 plank, 3 match wagons, 1 LNER flat wagon, 1 LMS 5 plank tube, 1 LMS 2 plank tube, 1 BR Grampus 20-ton ballast, 1 LNER flat, 1 LMR water bowser, 1 Plasser & Theurer tamper, 2 LMS fish vans, 2 Austrian ferry wagons, 1 SR parcels van, 1 Shell tank wagon, 1 Esso tank wagon, 2 tank wagons, 2 LNER 2 plank dropsides, 3 BR 12-ton box vans, 1 12-ton van (wooden underframe), 2 BR Pallet vans, 1 Charles Roberts covered van, 1 LNER crane, 2 LMS brake vans, 1 BR brake van, 1 MR brake van, 1 BR Sturgeon rail wagon, 1 BR Lowmac, 1 BR Welltrol, 1 BR Salmon, 2 BR Dogfish ballast hoppers

Owners
50029 and 50030 The Renown Repulse Restoration Group
D8 the North Notts Loco Group
Vulcan the Vulcan Loco Trust
7597 Peak Rail and Peak Railway Association
D2199 and D3023 the Heritage Shunters Trust
12061 on loan to the Heritage Shunters Trust

Derbyshire Dales Narrow Gauge Railway
Industrial narrow gauge locomotives (2ft gauge)

Name	No	Builder	Type	Built
—	—	M/Rail (22070)	4wDM	1960
—	—	R/Hornsby (264252)	4wDM	1952
—	85049*	R/Hornsby (393325)	4wDM	1956
—	85051*	R/Hornsby (404976)	4wDM	1956
—	—	R/Hornsby (487963)	4wDM	1963

*plant numbers carried by former British Railways locomotives

Miniature Railway	**Perrygrove Railway**	Glos

Member: Britain's Great Little Railways (corporate member of HRA)
Headquarters: Perrygrove Railway, Coleford, Gloucestershire GL16 8QB
Contact: Michael Crofts
Telephone/Fax: 01594 834991
Internet address:
Web site: www.perrygrove.co.uk
OS reference: SO 579094
Main station: Perrygrove
Other public stations: Rookwood, Heywood, Oakiron

Locomotives (15in gauge)

Name	No	Builder	Type	Built
Spirit of Adventure	—	ESR (295)	0-6-0T	1995
Ursula	—*		0-6-0T	
—	—†		0-4-0+0-4-0	1990
Workhorse	—	Simplex (1064)	0-4-0DM	1963
Jubilee	—	Hunslet (9337)	0-4-0DH	1994

*based on Heywood locomotive of 1916
†Tasmanian K1 Garratt, may not be on site for all of 2007

Stock
Various carriages and assorted wagons including original Victorian vehicles built by Sir Arthur Heywood

England

Above: The workhorse of a number of heritage lines is the Hunslet-designed 0-6-0ST, these were produced in quantity during World War 2, subsequently being adopted as a standard design for the National Coal Board and War Department. This example was built by Robert Stephenson & Hawthornes in 1944.
As WD No 150 *Royal Pioneer* it is seen at Rowsley South on Peak Rail.
Phil Barnes

Car park: Parking at Perrygrove for 60 cars plus 2 coach bays
Access by public transport:
Network Rail: Lydney (7 miles). Dean Forest Railway: Parkend (3 miles). Bus routes from: Cinderford — Duke Travel 732; Gloucester — Stagecoach 31;
Lydney — Duke Travel 721; Monmouth — Duke Travel 722; Ross on Wye — Duke Travel 35; Ruardean — Duke Travel 738. Enquiries: 01452 425610
Refreshment facilities: Light refreshments in Perrygrove station café

Souvenir shops: Small shop at Perrygrove
Museum: Heywood Collection of minimum gauge railways on display at Perrygrove
Depot: All sheds are at Perrygrove. Tours are encouraged under supervision when staff are available
Length of line: 0.75 miles, 15in (381mm) gauge
Period of public operation: Six days per week in local school holidays (closed Fridays) plus many other weekends
Special events: Christmas trains operate, advance booking essential.

The railway has an informal enthusiasts' day to coincide with the annual open day at Alan Keef Ltd, light railway engineers. Usually first or second weekend in September
Facilities for disabled: All disabilities catered for. About 75% of the site is accessible to wheelchairs, although some of the woodland paths are rough. There is space for a wheelchair on the train
Membership details: No formal society but volunteers welcome
Membership journal: Diary pages on web site

Steam Centre — Plym Valley Railway — Devon

Member: HRA
A scheme dedicated to the restoration of services over the former GWR Marsh Mills-Plym Bridge line, a distance of 1.5 miles

Location: 5 miles from centre of Plymouth, Devon, north of A38. From Marsh Mills roundabout, take B3416 to Plympton, follow signs
Internet address: *Web site:*

www.plymrail.co.uk
OS reference: SX 517564
Operating society/organisation: Plym Valley Railway Co Ltd, Marsh Mills Station, Coypool Road,

Marsh Mills, Plymouth, Devon PL7
4NW

Access by public transport: Buses
from Plymouth, Nos 20, 20A, 21,
22A, 51 stop close to site
On site facilities: Shop and
refreshments at Marsh Mills,
Coypool (Sundays only)
Public opening: Sundays from
10.00, and other selected days.
Trains are scheduled to operate: 8
April; 13 May; 10, 17 June; 8, 22
July; 12, 26 August; 9, 23
September; 14 October, 11
November, 9, 16, 23 December.
13.00-16.00 at half hourly intervals
Length of line: Half-mile currently
in use for passenger rides
Special events: Hot Cross Bus
Specials — 8 April; Father's Dzay
— 17 June; Mince Pie Specials —
9, 16, 23 December
Special notes: Visitors are advised
that, at the moment, the railway and
two locomotives are still under
restoration. 2 working locomotives
and DMU. The line was extended

Locomotives and multiple-units

Name	No	Origin	Class	Type	Built
—	75079	BR	4MT	4-6-0	1956
—	13002	BR	08	0-6-0DE	1953
William Cookworthy	37207	BR	37	Co-Co	1963
—	51365	BR	117	DMBS	1960
—	51407	BR	117	DMS	1960

Industrial locomotives

Name	No	Builder	Type	Built
Byfield No 2	—	Bagnall (2655)	0-6-0ST	1941
Albert	—	Barclay (2248)	0-4-0ST	1948
—	3	H/Leslie (3597)	0-4-0ST	1926
—	—	T/Hill (125V)	4wDH	1963
—	—	Hibberd (3281)	4wDM	1948

Rolling stock: 3 x BR Mk 1 coaches, 1 LBSCR compartment coach (body
only), 2 x BR GUVs, 3 x brake vans, various wagons. Self-propelled Smith
& Rodley diesel crane of 1956

beyond the first bridge in 2003.
Train rides behind the 13002 on
some Sundays (normally 2nd in the
month)
Membership details: Tina Newton,
Plym Valley Railway, Marsh Mills

Station, Coypool Road, Marsh
Mills, Plymouth, Devon PL7 4NW
Membership journal: Plym Valley
Railway News — 3/year
Marketing name: The Woodland
Line

Timetable Service — The Poppy Line (North Norfolk Railway) — Norfolk

Member: HRA, TT
Part of the former Midland & Great
Northern Joint Railway, other
elements of the LNER have crept
in in the guise of the 'B12' and a
Gresley buffet car. GER 'J15' is
now in service. Guest locomotives
can be viewed at various times
throughout the year. The line runs
through beautiful coast, wood and
heathland scenery with a nature
trail running along its side between
Weybourne and Kelling Heath
Managing Director: Hugh Harkett
Headquarters: North Norfolk
Railway plc, Sheringham Station,
Sheringham, Norfolk NR26 8RA
Telephone: Sheringham (01263)
820800
Fax: (01263) 820801
Internet address: Web site:
www.nnr.co.uk
Main station: Sheringham
Other public stations: Weybourne,

Locomotives and multiple-units

Name	No	Origin	Class	Type	Built
—	65462	GER	J15	0-6-0	1912
A. J. Hill	69621	GER	N7	0-6-2T	1924
—	65033†	NER	J21	0-6-0	1889
—	61572	LNER	B12	4-6-0	1928
—	68088	LNER	Y7	0-4-0T	1923
92 Squadron	34081	SR	BB	4-6-2	1948
—	90775	MoS	WD	2-10-0	1943
—	D2280	BR	04	0-6-0DM	1960
Camulodunum	D3940	BR	08	0-6-0DE	1960
—	D3935	BR	08	0-6-0DE	1961
—	12131	BR	11	0-6-0DE	1952
—	D5207	BR	25	Bo-Bo	1962
—	5580	BR	31	A1A-A1A	1960
—	31207	BR	31	A1A-A1A	1960
Mirage	D6732	BR	37	Co-Co	1962
—	47367	BR	47	Co-Co	1965
—	51228	M/Cam	101	DTSL	1958
—	54062	M/Cam	101	DMBS	1957
—	79960	W&M	—	Railbus	1958
—	79963*	W&M	—	Railbus	1958
—	LEV1	BR/Leyland	—	Railbus	1978

Guest locomotives for 2007 include No 34081 92 Squadron

132

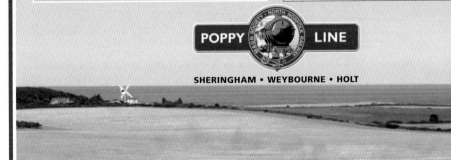

Kelling Halt, Holt
OS reference: Sheringham TG 156430, Weybourne TG 118419
Car parks: Sheringham (public), Weybourne, Holt
Access by public transport: By train to Sheringham station ('one' railway)
Refreshment facilities: Sheringham, Weybourne, Holt
Souvenir shops: Sheringham, Weybourne, Holt
Depot: Weybourne
Length of line: 5.25 miles
Passenger trains: Steeply graded (1 in 80), Sheringham-Weybourne-Holt
Period of public operation: Most days from 1 April to end October. Weekends in November and December plus Christmas week
Special events: Diesel Weekend — 9/10 June; Railway Children's Charity Cheese & Wine Special — 29 June (evening); Living History Day — 1 July; Vintage Transport Day — 8 July; 6th Poppy Line Beer Festival — 13-15 July; Shareholders' Day — 18 August; Grand Steam Gala —31 August, 1/2 September; The Great '40s Weekend — 15/16 September; Santa Specials — 1/2, 8/9, 15/16, 20-24 December; Mince Pie Specials — 26 December-2 January; Winter Steam Gala — 29-31 December

*on loan to Mangapps Farm Railway
†on long term loan from Beamish

Industrial locomotives

Name	No	Builder	Type	Built
Ring Haw	—	Hunslet (1982)	0-6-0ST	1940
Wissington*	—	H/Clarke (1700)	0-6-0ST	1938
—	—	Bagnall (2370)	0-6-0F	1929

*under restoration

Stock
3 ex-LNER coaches, GNR quad set (not yet available for public viewing), 7 ex-BR coaches, 3 coach King's Cross suburban set; Gresley buffet, Wisbech & Upwell Tramway coach, 2 CCT wagons, small number of wagons and Southern Railway PMV

Owners
65462, 61572, 31207 and 90775 the Midland & Great Northern Railway Society
69621 East Anglian Railway Museum
34081 the Battle of Britain Locomotive Society
5580 A1A Locomotives
47367 The Stratford Class 47 Group
LEV1 on loan from National Railway Museum

Special facilities: Weybourne station is licensed for weddings. Special dining trains can be booked for corporate and party entertaining. Online booking available on www.nnr.co.uk
William Mariott Museum: This new museum is now open in a replica M&GN goods shed at Holt station. Artefacts and ephemera commemorating the man who built the railway and ran it for almost 40 years. Open on operating days

Facilities for disabled: All stations have level access. Wheelchair access to most trains, and to gift shop and buffet at Sheringham. Disabled parking at Holt station
Membership details: Midland & Great Northern Joint Railway Society, Mr D. Bicknell, 55 Monmouth Close, Ipswich, Suffolk IP2 8RS
Tel: 01473 604402
Membership journal: *Joint Line* — quarterly

Steam Centre — The Railway Age, Crewe — Cheshire

Location: Crewe Heritage Centre, Vernon Way, Crewe
OS reference: SJ 709552
Operating society/organisation: Crewe Heritage Trust Ltd
Telephone: (01270) 212130
Internet address: *Web site:* www.therailwayage.co.uk
Car park: On site, town centre, Forge Street, Oak Street,
Access by public transport: Main line Crewe
Refreshment facilities: Adjacent Safeway superstore
On site facilities: Gift shop, picnic area, children's corner, weekend

Locomotives and multiple-units

Name	No	Origin	Class	Type	Built
—	485	LNWR	G2	0-8-0	1921
—	5224§	GWR	4200	2-8-0T	1924
—	6638	GWR	5600	0-6-2T	1928
—	D2073	BR	03	0-6-0DM	1959
—	31442	BR	31	A1A-A1A	1960
—	D120†	BR	45	1Co-Co1	1961
Ixion	D172†	BR	46	1Co-Co1	1962
—	D1842	BR	47	Co-Co	1965
Robert Burns	87035	BR	87	Bo-Bo	1974
—	18000	BR	—	A1A-A1A	1949
—	55032*	P/Steel	121	DMBS	1960

†on site occasionally, but usually kept at private locations
*may not be on site for all of 2007
§on loan to West Somerset Railway

England

train rides, standard gauge and miniature railway, exhibition hall, main line viewing area, 3 working signalboxes with 'hands-on' visitor operation

Public opening: Daily 10.00-16.00 (last admission 15.00). Family tickets available. Please contact for details of events

Facilities for disabled: Toilets

Membership details: Heritage Centre Supporters Association, c/o above address

Notes: Steam locomotives passed for use over main line tracks are stabled between duties from time to time

Industrial locomotives

Name	No	Builder	Type	Built
Robert	—	H/Clarke (1752)	0-6-0T	1943

Rolling stock

APT vehicle Nos 48103, 48106, 48404, 48602, 48603, 48606, 49002; 1 BR Mk 1 BSK; various ex-BR coaches and passenger brake vans from time to time for repairs

Owners

485 the National Railway Museum

Museum	**Railworld**	Cambs

Member: HRA

Railworld is a 'Sustainable Transport Centre' and a '21st Century Rail Showcase'. It has a superb model railway, hands-on exhibits to delight children and film shows. In addition it has a museum which is mainly about Peterborough's railway history. There are also 'Age of Steam' exhibits and a database of over 7,000 names of local railworkers since the 1840s (50p extra access charge)

Location: Situated alongside the Town station of the Nene Valley Railway. Walk — 15min walk from train and bus stations, Stagecoach route 1 (every 10min). By car — turn off A1139 at jct 5, signs to City Centre, at first roundabout (large) follow brown and white 'Lttle Puffer' signs to Oundle Road into Council's long stay car park, drive through to Railworld. The Railworld car park is free to visitors. By bike — situated on the 'Green Wheel' cycle route. By boat — alongside river quay

OS reference: TL 189981

Operating society/organisation: Railworld, Oundle Road, Peterborough, Cambridgeshire PE2 9NR

Charity number: 291515

Locomotives

Name	No	Origin	Class	Type	Built
—	996	DSB	4MT	4-6-2	1950

Industrial locomotives

Name	No	Builder	Type	Built
—	804	Alco (77778)	Bo-Bo	1949
Nutty*	5	Sentinel (7701)	4wVBT	1929
—†	740	O&K (2343)	0-6-0T	1907

*2ft 6in gauge (off-site at present)
† 2ft gauge and on loan to Leighton Buzzard Railway until August 2007 remainder standard

Other stock: Britain's RTV 31 Hovertrain vehicle, Presflo 2-axle flyash wagon (No B874076 of 12965) and a 2-axle 8,650gal tank wagon (No 55223 of 1966). Birmingham International Airport Maglev car No 01 of 1984 supplied by Metro-Cammell, operational 1984-1995 — the world's first train without wheels in commercial service

Contact: Rev Richard Paten

Telephone: 01733 344240

Fax: 01733 319362

Internet address: *e-mail:* railword@aol.com

Web site: www.railworld.net

On site facilities: Buffet and small shop, open weekends March to October. Picnic area. Model railway

Public opening: Daily March-October 11.00-16.00. Also Monday to Fridays November-March 11.00-16.00

Special events: National Science Week — 11-20 March;

'Environment Week' (Integrated Transport) — 11-19 June

Access for disabled: Reasonable wheelchair access

Admission charge: Adult £5, Child £2.50, Concessions £4, Family £13 (2A+4C)

Membership details: John Crane, 21 St Margarets Road, Peterborough PE2 9EA

Membership journal: *Friends of Railworld* — biannually

Special notes: Railworld is a no smoking site

Ravenglass & Eskdale Railway

Member: HRA

From the coast through two of Lakeland's loveliest valleys to the foot of England's highest mountain, small steam engines haul trains in the heart of the national park

General Manager: Trevor Stockton

Headquarters: Ravenglass & Eskdale Railway, Ravenglass, Cumbria CA18 1SW

Telephone: (01229) 717171

Fax: (01229) 717011

Internet address: *e-mail:* rer@netcomuk.co.uk

Web site: www.ravenglass-railway.co.uk

Main station: Ravenglass

Other public stations: Muncaster Mill, Irton Road, The Green, Beckfoot, Eskdale (Dalegarth)

OS reference: SD 086964

Car parks: All stations

Access by public transport: Main line services to Ravenglass; bus service from Whitehaven

Refreshment facilities: Ravenglass, Dalegarth. Bar meals at 'Ratty Arms'

Picnic areas: At both termini

Souvenir shops: Ravenglass, Dalegarth

Museum: Ravenglass

Length of line: 7 miles, 15in gauge

Passenger trains: Steam- or diesel-hauled narrow gauge trains

Locomotives

Name	No	Builder	Type	Built
River Irt	—	Heywood	0-8-2	1894
River Esk	—	Davey Paxman (21104)	2-8-2	1923
River Mite	—	Clarkson (4669)	2-8-2	1966
Northern Rock	—	R&ER	2-6-2	1976
Bonnie Dundee	—	K/Stuart (720)*	0-4-2	1901
Shelagh of Eskdale	—	R&ER/Severn-Lamb	4-6-4D	1969
				rebuilt 1998
Quarryman	—	Muir-Hill (2)	0-4-0P/Paraffin	1928
Perkins	—	Muir Hill (NG39A)	0-4-4DM	1929
Lady Wakefield	—	R&ER	B-B	1980
Synolda	—	Bassett-Lowke	4-4-2	1912
—	—	Greenbat (2782)	0-4-0BE	1957
Cyril	—	Lister	0-4-0DM	1987
Douglas Ferreira	—	TMA Engineering	Bo-Bo	2005

*rebuilt to 15in gauge 1981

Ravenglass-Dalegarth

Period of public operation: Daily late March-early November. Limited winter service November-March

Family ticket: All day travel at reduced price

Facilities for disabled: Special coaches for wheelchair passengers. Advance notice preferred. Wheelchair access to toilets, café and museum at Ravenglass; toilets, shop and café at Eskdale (Dalegarth)

Special notes: At Ravenglass the R&ER has two camping coaches and the company also operates the

'Ratty Arms' public house formed by conversion of the former BR station buildings. During the high summer, mid-July through August, five steam locomotives are normally in use Monday-Thursday

Membership details: Mr N. Dickinson, 3 Clifton Terrace, Ravenglass, Cumbria CA18 1SE

Membership journal: *The R&ER Magazine* — quarterly

Marketing names: 'la'al Ratty' — Cumbrian dialect for little narrow track, now a watervole stationmaster!

Ribble Steam Railway

Member: HRA

Preston Docks have had a railway infrastructure since 1850, and when the final tar trains ran in 1995, it looked like that tenancy had come to an end. However, Steamport Southport began negotiations with Preston Borough Council, and during 1999, the group formerly based at the old engine shed in Southport moved to their new home on the dockside at Preston.

Due to the main line traversing the swing bridge in the Marina, the

Locomotives and multiple-units

Name	No	Origin	Class	Type	Built
—	46441	LMS	2MT	2-6-0	1950
—	1097	LYR	—	0-4-0ST	1910
—	D2148	BR	03	0-6-0DM	1960
—	03189	BR	03	0-6-0DM	1961
—	D9539	BR	14	0-6-0DH	1965
—	601	NSR	—	0-6-0DE	1956
—	625	NSR	—	0-6-0DE	1956

Industrial locomotives

Name	No	Builder	Type	Built
—	272	G/Ritchie (272)	0-4-0T	1894
Daphne	—	Peckett (737)	0-4-0ST	1899

timetable will be dictated by the tide — the only preserved steam line to have such a feature.

Heritage passenger and modern freight operations blend together as restored diesel locomotives handle bulk bitumen trains on behalf of Total Bitumen. This traffic has switched from road transport since the railway reopened

Location: Off Chain Caulway, Riversway, Preston Docks, Preston, Lancs

OS reference: SD 504295

Operating society/organisation: Steamport Southport Ltd, 3 Lincoln Drive, Old Road, Liverpool L10 3LJ

Telephone: 01772 72882

Internet address: *e-mail:* enquiries@ribblesteam.org.uk

Web site: www.ribblesteam.org.uk

Car park: On site

Main station: Chain Caul Road

Other station: Strand Road

Access by public transport:
By train — to Preston (www.nationalrail.co.uk).
By bus — Preston Bus 27, 127 Preston to Larches; Stagecoach 75 Preston to Poulton.
Buses stop on Peddars Way between McDonalds and roundabout on Navigation Way.
By road — follow the signs for Riversway Docklands

On site facilities: Buffet, museum and workshop.

Car paring: On site

Length of lines: 1.5 miles (under restoration)

Public opening: Weekends and bank holidays 31 March to 30 September, plus 7, 14, 21, 28 October.
Open from 10.30. Trains hourly 11.00-16.00.
Return trip c40min
Unlimited travel on day of admission

Special events: Please see web site for details

Name	No	Builder	Type	Built
The King	—	Borrows (48)	0-4-0WT	1906
Lucy	—	Avonside (1568)	0-6-0ST	1909
Efficient	—	Barclay (1598)	0-4-0ST	1918
MDHB No 26	—	Avonside (1810)	0-6-0ST	1918
—	1883	Avonside (1883)	0-6-0ST	1922
Alexander	—	Barclay (1865)	0-4-0ST	1926
Heysham No.2	—	Barclay (1950)	0-4-0F	1928
Derbyshire	—	Barclay (1969)	0-4-0ST	1929
Gasbag	—	Sentinel (8024)	4wVBT	1929
Hornet	—	Peckett (1935)	0-4-0ST	1937
Linda	—	H/Leslie (3931)	0-6-0ST	1938
Kinsley	—	Hunslet (1954)	0-6-0ST	1939
North Western Gas Board	—	Peckett (1999)	0-4-0ST	1941
Walkden	—	Hunslet (3155)	0-6-0ST	1944
St Monans	—	Sentinel (9373)	4wVBT	1947
Agecroft No.2	—	RSH (7485)	0-4-0ST	1948
No. 6	—	Barclay (2261)	0-4-0ST	1949
Respite	—	Hunslet.(3696)	0-6-0ST	1950
Shropshire	—	Hunslet (3793)	0-6-0ST	1953
Glasshoughton No.4	—	Hunslet (3855)	0-6-0ST	1954
Hotto	—	Howard (965)		1930
Mighty Atom	—	H/Clarke (D628)	0-4-0DM	1943
Sparky	—	H/Clarke (D629)	0-4-0DM	1945
Persil	—	Fowler (4160001)	0-4-0DM	1950
Margaret	—	H/Clarke (D1031)	0-4-0DM	1956
BICC	—	NBL (27653)	0-4-0DH	1957
D2595	—	Hunslet (7179)	0-6-0DM	1959
D2870	—	YEC (2667)	0-4-0DH	1960
Mardale	—	YEC (2748)	0-6-0DE	1959
Simon	—	Sentinel (10020)	4wDH	1959
Energy	DH23	Sentinel (10165)	4wDH	1965
Stanlow	—	T/Hill (160V)	0-4-0DH	1966
Enterprise	—	Sentinel (10282)	4wDH	1968
Progress	—	Sentinel (10283)	4wDH	1968
'YellowBat'	—	E/Electric (EE788)	4wBE	1930
Greenbat	—	G/Batley (2000)	4wBE	1945

Rolling stock

Owners
625 and 653 Middlepeak Railways

Membership details:
RSR Memberships, 4 Powell Drive, Billinge WN5 7RX
Membership journal: *The Ribble Pilot* — 3 copies a year
Special note: The railway is not open or accessible at any other times than those advertised. Access will be refused outside these times

Romney, Hythe & Dymchurch Railway

Member: HRA

This line was built in 1926/27 as a one-third size miniature main line, and is by far the longest and most fully equipped 15in gauge railway in the world. It carries not only daytrippers and holidaymakers but also children to and from the local school at New Romney.

Headquarters: Romney, Hythe & Dymchurch Railway, New Romney Station, Kent TN28 8PL

Telephone: (01797) 362353/363256

Fax: 01797 363591

Internet addresses: *e-mail:* info@rhdr.org.uk
Web site: http://www.rhdr.org.uk

OS reference: TR 074249

Main station: New Romney

Other public stations: Hythe, Dymchurch, St Marys Bay, Romney Sands, Dungeness

Car parks: Hythe, Dymchurch, New Romney, Dungeness

Access by public transport: Folkestone Central station (South Eastern Trains) and then bus to Hythe (4 miles) or Rye station (Southern) and then bus to New Romney (8 miles)

Refreshment facilities: Cafeterias at New Romney and Dungeness, picnic areas at Dymchurch, New Romney and Dungeness. Also licensed observation coach on certain trains

Souvenir shops: Hythe and New Romney (plus Dymchurch and Dungeness in main season)

Model Railway Exhibition: New Romney, with displays of old, and not so old, toys; plus two large operating model railways. Open all operating days and selected other days

Depot: New Romney

Length of line: 13.5 miles, 15in gauge

Passenger trains: Train frequency depends on the time of year: maximum frequency is 40 minutes, more frequent on certain special event days

Period of public operation: Trains

Locomotives

Name	No	Builder	Type	Built
Green Goddess	1	Davey Paxman	4-6-2	1925
Northern Chief	2	Davey Paxman	4-6-2	1925
Southern Maid	3	Davey Paxman	4-6-2	1926
The Bug	4	Krauss (8378)	0-4-0TT	1926
Hercules	5	Davey Paxman	4-8-2	1926
Samson	6	Davey Paxman	4-8-2	1926
Typhoon	7	Davey Paxman	4-6-2	1926
Hurricane	8	Davey Paxman	4-6-2	1926
Winston Churchill	9	YEC (2294)	4-6-2	1931
Doctor Syn	10	YEC (2295)	4-6-2	1931
Black Prince	11	Krupp (1664)	4-6-2	1937
John Southland	12	TMA Birmingham	Bo-Bo	1983
Captain Howey	14	TMA Birmingham	Bo-Bo	1989
—	PW1	M/Rail (7059)	4wDM	1938
—	PW2	RH&DR	4wPM	1965
Redgauntlet	PW3	Jacot/RH&DR	4wPM	1963
Trembly*	—	Lister (37658)	4wDM	1952

*on loan fitted with a *Toby* body for Thomas the Tank events

Stock

40 saloon bogie coaches; 12 open bogie coaches; 5 luggage/brake saloons; 1 parlour car; 1 mess coach; 40 assorted wagons

run daily from 1 April to 1 October. Also weekends and school holidays in February, March and October. Out of season the school train departs New Romney at 15.00 with limited public accommodation (Monday-Friday, term times only)

Special events: Mother's Day — 18 March; The Big Day Out Family Event with Kent Tourism — 31 March; Basil the Bug's Family Fun Day — 21 April; Festival of Seaside Railways — 12/13 May; Father's Day — 17 June; Dungeness Fisherman — 23 June; Romney Marsh Breakfast Wildlife Safari — 2 July; Laurel and Hardy Day — 8 July; 80th Anniversary Celebration Weekend — 14/15 July; RNLI Dungeness Lifeboat Station Open Day — 21 August; Day out with Thomas — 1/2 September (special fares apply); Dungeness Fisherman — 15 September; Double-header Day — 6 October; Basil the Bug's Family Fun Day — 20 October; Halloween Celebrations — 25-28 October; Mince Pie Specials — 29-31

December, 1 January 2008. Santa Specials in December (pre-booking essential).

Special notes: Senior citizen concessions any day except Bank Holidays and advertised special events. Family tickets available. Parties can be catered for at New Romney and Dungeness cafés and Jazz trains. Evening dining train service on selected summer Saturdays

Special facilities: Special trains can be run at most times by prior arrangement.

Facilities for disabled: Ramps and level crossings at all stations for easy access. Special wheelchair coach available on any train by prior arrangement. Stair lift between café and Model Railway Exhibition. Disabled toilets at Hythe, Dymchurch, New Romney and Dungeness

Membership details: RH&DR Association, 26 Norman Close, Battle, East Sussex TN33 0BD

Membership journal: *The Marshlander* — quarterly

Rother Valley Railway

Diesel Centre — Rother Valley Railway — **East Sussex**

Member: HRA

The original section of what was to become known as the Kent & East Sussex Railway was thought to be lost to preservation for ever following decisions of Transport Minister, Barbara Castle, in the late 1960s. However, more enlightened attitudes in recent years mean that work is now in hand to reinstate the missing link between Robertsbridge and the K&ESR at Bodiam

Location/headquarters:
Robertsbridge Station, Robertsbridge, East Sussex TN32 5DG
Telephone: 01580 881833
Internet addresses: *Web site:* www.rvr.org.uk
Operating society/organisation: Rother Valley Railway Ltd, 3-4 Bower Terrace, Maidstone, Kent ME16 8RY, and the Rother Valley Railway Supporters Association, 375 New Hythe Lane, Larkfield, Aylesford, Kent ME20 6RY
OS reference: TQ 734235
Access by public transport: SouthEastern Trains on Charing Cross and Tunbridge Wells to Hastings service call at

Industrial locomotives

Name	No	Builder	Type	Built
Titan	43	Vulcan/Drewry	0-4-0DM	1955
—	7	Sentinel	0-4-0DH	1959
—	D77	Vulcan/Drewry	0-4-0DM	1947
—	97701	Matisa	0-4-0DE	1975

Rolling stock

Ex-SR brake van, ex-SR Maunsell brake third, ex-SR Maunsell open third, ex-SR corridor Comp (converted to General Manager's saloon), ex-BR Mk 1 TSO, ex-SR GBL, BY, and PMV vans, Trout hopper wagon, 2 tank wagons, open wagon, Lowmac, Permaquip Panex track machine and a Thos Smith 5-ton rail crane

Robertsbridge station. Arriva bus services 4 and 5 on Maidstone-Hastings service call at High Street, Robertsbridge
Car parks: Robertsbridge station and Station Road, Robertsbridge
On site facilities: Visitor centre housed in former VSOE lounge with souvenir shop and buffet. Rolling stock under restoration, picnic area
Facilities for disabled: Access to the visitor centre, buffet, shop and all public areas
Length of line: Standard gauge — c400yd at present. When restored, length to Bodiam will be 3.5 miles,

with end-on connection to K&ESR
Public opening: Every Sunday and Bank Holiday (except Christmas and Boxing Day). 09.00-17.00 (dusk if earlier)
Special events: Annual model railway exhibition. Subject to Ministry approval, brake van rides will commence this year
Membership secretary: Peter Coombs, 375 New Hythe Lane, Larkfield, Aylesford, Kent ME20 6RY. (Tel: 01622 717491)
Society journal: *The Phoenix —* quarterly

Royal Victoria Railway

Miniature Railway — Royal Victoria Railway — **Hampshire**

Location: Royal Victoria Country Park
Headquarters: Royal Victoria Railway, Royal Victoria Country Park, Netley, Southampton SO31 5GA
Contact: Peter Bowers
Telephone: 023 8045 6246
Internet address: *Web site:* www.royalvictoriarailway.co.uk
Main station: Netley
Car parking: On site £1.20
Access by public transport:
By rail: SouthWest Trains to Netley, follow signs to Royal Victoria Country Park.
By road: Exit M27 at jct 8 and follow brown tourist signs to Royal

Locomotives

Name	No	Builder	Type	Built
Maurice the Major	1	P. Bowers	Bo-Bo	1995
Basil the Brigadier*†	2	Kitson	2-6-0-0-6-2	1935
Trevithick	3	R. Marsh	0-6-2	1976
Isambard Kingdom Brunel	4	D. Curwen	2-6-0	1977
Peter the Private	5	Narrowgauge	2-4-4	1984
Western Independence	D1000	D. Curwen	Co-Co	1964
Western Thunderer	1011	D. Curwen	Co-Co	1964
Royal Scot*§	6100	B/Lowke	4-6-0	1938
Royal Scot*†	6100	E. Dove	4-6-0	c1950

*historic locomotive
†off site under overhaul
§on site awaiting restoration

Rolling stock
2 Triang Pullman coaches, 4 Triang toastrack coaches, 2 4-car articulated units (2 covered, 2 open carriages), various goods vehicles

Victoria Country Park, approx 3 miles
On site facilities: Small souvenir shop. Museum on site for Royal Victoria Hospital
Depots: At main station, engine and carriage sheds and turntable, possibly largest for 10.25in gauge railway
Length of line: 1 mile, 10.25in gauge
Period of public operation: All local school holidays except

Note: If wishing to view the historic locomotives please contact before making journey

3 days before Xmas and closed Christmas Day. Weekends all year
Special events: Please check web site
Facilities for disabled: Most areas accessible

Timetable Service — Rudyard Lake Railway — Staffordshire

Member HRA, Britain's Great Little Railways.

The railway is the third on this site and provides a 3 mile scenic return trip alongside the lake that gave Rudyard Kipling his name. Trains are normally steam hauled and a two train service operates on busy days. The fleet of goods wagons is extensive and impressive and so goods trains also often feature. A further one mile extension is being planned

Contacts: Mike & Eileen Hanson, Directors
Headquarters: Rudyard Station, Rudyard, Nr Leek, Staffordshire ST13 8RS
Telephone: 01995 672280
Fax: 01995 672280
Internet address:
e-mail: info@rlsr.org
Web site: www.rlsr.org
Main station: Rudyard
OS reference SJ 955579
Other stations: The Dam (SJ 953584), Hunthouse Wood (SJ 946598)
Car parking: On site, free at Rudyard
Access by public transport; Nearest mainline rail at Stoke on Trent, Macclesfield, Congleton. Bus services to Leek
Souvenier shop: On trains

Locomotives

Name	No	Builder	Type	Built
Modred	2	T. Stanhope	4w	1969
Rudyard Lady	5	L. Smith	4-4w	1989
Waverley		D. Curwen	4-4-2	1952
Excalibur	6	Exmoor SR (293)	2-4-2T	1993
Merlin	7	Exmoor SR (296)	2-4-2T	1998
Pendragon	9	Exmoor SR (297)	2-4-2T	1994
King Arthur	8	Exmoor SR (324)	0-6-2T	2005

Rolling Stock
10 coaches
1 4w vans, 3 4w open, 1 4w crane, 1 4w brake van, 3 bogie ballast

Owner
Waverley — the Waverley Group

Special Notes
Driver training courses run throughout the year

Refreshment facilities: Café at Dam Head, alight at Dam station
Length of Line: 1.5 miles, 10.25 inch gauge
Operation: Every Sunday & Bank Holiday 11 March to 28 October 2007, 11.00-16.20; Every Saturday 5 May to 30 September, 11.00-16.00. All school holidays — every Tuesday, Wednesday and Thursday February to October
Special Events:

Easter Egg Specials — 6-11 April; Lollipop Specials — 5-7, 26-28 May, 25-27 August; Steam Gala — 22/23 September; Halloween Special — 28 October; Santa Specials — 9, 16 December
Disabled Facilities: Access to all stations but wheelchairs not allowed on trains. Disabled toilets at the Dam Head.
Membership details: Eileen Hanson at above address or via e-mail

Ruislip Lido Railway

Member: HRA

The 12in gauge line is operated by enthusiast volunteers as an attraction within Ruislip Lido, a country park which is maintained by the London Borough of Hillingdon

Location: Ruislip Lido, Reservoir Road, Ruislip, Middlesex

Operating society/organisation: Ruislip Lido Railway Society Ltd, Secretary, Mr E. Ferrand, RLR, Suite 123, Rye House, 113 High Street, Ruislip, Middx HA4 8JN

Telephone: 020 8866 9654

Car park: Available at Lido

Access by public transport: Ruislip Underground station (Metropolitan and Piccadilly lines) then by bus H13 or 331 nearby (daily). Lido is off the A4180 road

Refreshment facilities: New family pub/restaurant (Brewers Fayre) on site. Picnic areas also available

Length of line: 1.25-mile single journey, 2.5 miles return including new extension now open which

Locomotives

Name	No	Builder	Type	Built
Robert	3	Severn-Lamb	B-2 DH	1973
Lady of the Lakes	5	Ravenglass & Eskdale Railway	B-B DM	1985
Mad Bess	6	RLRS	2-4-0ST+T	1998
Graham Alexander	7	Severn-Lamb	B-B DM	1990
Bayhurst	8	Severn-Lamb	B-B DM	2003
John Rennie	9	Severn-Lamb	B-B DM	2005

Locomotive notes: All locomotives are normally available for service. Limited steam-hauled service

Stock

6 open coaches; 9 closed coaches; miscellaneous service stock

terminates near the main entrance to car park

Public opening: The line is open at weekends from 10 February to 18 November. Daily throughout July and August, also daily during Hillingdon school holidays. Sunday Santa Specials on 2, 9, 16, 23 December

24-hour recorded train information service (01895) 622595. Full service leaflet on request to 01923 250646. Party bookings 01895 632020

Journey time: Single 20min, return 40min

Facilities for disabled: Wheelchair passengers can travel on all trains

Membership details: Membership Secretary, M. Stretton, RLR, Suite 123, Rye House, 113 High Street, Ruislip, Middx HA4 8JN

Membership journal: *Woody Bay News* — 3 issues per year

Rutland Railway Museum

Member: HRA

This museum is dedicated to portraying the ironstone quarrying history of the Midlands and has a wide range of authentic locomotives and rolling stock. Indeed, its collection of quarry freight rolling stock is probably the most comprehensive in the country and regular demonstrations are a feature of the 'open days'.

Location: Cottesmore Iron Ore Mines Siding, Ashwell Road, Cottesmore, near Oakham, Rutland — museum situated midway between villages of Cottesmore and Ashwell, approximately 4 miles north of Oakham (locally signposted)

OS reference: SK 886137

Industrial locomotives

Name	No	Builder	Type	Built
Stamford	—	Avonside (1972)	0-4-0ST	1927
Dora	—	Avonside (1973)	0-4-0ST	1927
Cranford No 2	—	Bagnall (2668)	0-6-0ST	1942
Firefly	—	Barclay (776)	0-4-0ST	1896
BSC No 2	—	Barclay (1931)	0-4-0ST	1927
Drake	—	Barclay (2086)	0-4-0ST	1940
Sir Thomas Royden	—	Barclay (2088)	0-4-0ST	1940
Uppingham	—	Peckett (1257)	0-4-0ST	1912
Elizabeth	—	Peckett (1759)	0-4-0ST	1928
Singapore	—	H/Leslie (3865)	0-4-0ST	1936
—	24	Hunslet (2411)	0-6-0ST	1941
Coal Products No 6	—	Hunslet (2868)/ (Rebuilt Hunslet 3883)	0-6-0ST	1943 1963
—	65	Hunslet (3889)	0-6-0ST	1964
—	8	Peckett (2110)	0-4-0ST	1950
—	7	Sentinel (9376)	4wVBT	1947
—	—	Barclay (352)	0-4-0DM	1941
—	1	Barclay (415)	0-4-0DH	1957
—	20-90-01	Barclay (499)	0-4-0DH	1965

Secretary: Simon Layfield 07798
641105
Operating society/organisation:
Rutland Railway Museum,
Cottesmore Iron Ore Mines Siding,
Ashwell Road, Cottesmore, Nr
Oakham, Rutland LE15 7BX
Telephone: Oakham (01572)
813203
Car park: Free car park on site
Access by public transport:
Nearest main line station, Oakham.
Bus service, Paul James,
Nottingham-Melton Mowbray-
Ashwell-Oakham,
Corby/Peterborough-Oakham-
Ashwell (service 19).
On site facilities: Train rides, open
air quarry feature, demonstration
freight trains, toilets, museum,
picnic sites, demonstration line with
lineside walk and viewing areas,
static displays of quarrying
equipment, large operational wagon
collection, steam and diesel
locomotives.
Museum shop and refreshments
available on open days
Length of line: Three-quarter-mile
Passenger trains: Regular service
operates on open days
Public opening: Open Sundays,
Easter to end of September (11.00-
17.00) and Thursdays (working
days, after noon.
   (Leaflets available, SAE please).
   School and private parties by
special arrangement
Special events: Easter Weekend —
8/9 April; Steam Freight Gala —
6/7 May; Children's Weekend —
27/28 May; Driver for a Fiver — 17
June; Quarry Railway Heritage Day
— 1 July; Vintage Vehicle Day —
15 July; Summer Steam Day — 29
July; Quarry Railway Heritage Day

Name	No	Builder	Type	Built
—	4	Fowler (4240012)	0-6-0DH	1961
—	—	Fowler (4240015)	0-6-0DH	1962
Phoenix	—	Hibberd (3887)	4wDM	1958
—	3	N/British (27656)	0-4-0DH	1957
Betty	8411/04	R/Royce (10201)	0-4-0DH	1964
—	—	R/Hornsby (305302)	4wDM	1951
—	—	R/Hornsby (306092)	4wDM	1950
—	110	R/Hornsby (411319)	4wDM	1958
—	3	R/Hornsby (421436)	0-4-0DE	1958
—	20-90-02	R/Hornsby (504565)	0-4-0DH	1965
—	—	R/Hornsby (544997)	0-4-0DE	1969
—	CEGB 24	T/Hill (188c)	4wDH	1967
		(Rebuild of Sentinel 9597/1955)		
—	—	YEC (2641)	0-6-0DE	1957
—	20	YEC (2688)	0-6-0DE	1959
—	No 28	YEC (2791)	0-6-0DE	1962
—	1382	YEC (2872)	0-6-0DE	1962

Locomotive notes: In service *Singapore, 7*

Stock
1 coach; 4 brake vans; 14 covered goods vans; 57 wagons (includes rakes
of wagons as used in local ironstone and industrial railways); 3 rail cranes

Owners
110 the National Army Museum

— 12 August; Model Railway and
Model Engineering Day — 26/27
August; Shire Horse Shunting Day
— 9 September; Autumn Ruston
Gala — 6/7 October; Santa Special
Event — 9, 16, 23 December
Special facilities: Driver
Experience Days (pre-bookings
only) on 11, 21 April; 13, 16 June;
14, 25 July;
Facilities for disabled: Site
relatively flat. Members willing to
assist
Special notes: The open-air
museum houses an extensive
collection of industrial locomotives
and rolling stock typifying past

activity in local ironstone quarries,
nationwide mines and factories. A
demonstration line approximately
three quarters of a mile long has
been relaid on the former MR
Cottesmore mineral branch
(originally built to tap local
ironstone quarries), on which
restored locomotives and stock are
run
   Free admission at weekends for
general viewing, charges on Steam
and Diesel Open Days (11.00-
17.00). Special rates for Santa
Specials
Membership details: Membership
Secretary, c/o above address

Railway Centre — S&D Mendip Main Line Project (Midsomer Norton South Station) — Somerset

Member: HRA
The S&D Mendip Main Line
Project has secured a foothold on
the northern part of the S&D where
previous preservation attempts
failed. The S&DRHT has the

central object of preserving the
route and infrastructure wherever
the opportunities arise, whether for
heritage or conventional railways
or, more simply, for public
recreation and conservation. In

practice, energies are being
concentrated at Midsomer Norton,
with the aim of extending the
running line southwards up the
notorious 1 in 53 grade to
Chilcompton, and potentially

142

northwards down to Radstock. The Trust is leasing former trackbed with the aim of securing a total run of nearly one mile within 3-5 years. Midsomer Norton station has become one of the few significant visitor attractions in this former coal-mining community, with the S&D legend attracting national and international attention

Main station: Midsomer Norton South

OS Reference: ST 664537

Officers: Chairman: John Baxter; Secretary: Peter Russell; Finance Director: Steve Sainsbury; Membership Secretary: Tim Deacon; Vice-President: Richard Stevens,

Headquarters: Somerset & Dorset Railway Heritage Trust, Midsomer Norton Station, Silver Street, Midsomer Norton, BA3 2EY

Telephone: 01761 411221

Internet address:
e-mail: info@sdjr.co.uk
Web site: www.sdjr.co.uk
and
http://somersetanddorset.blogspot.com

Car park: Limited parking on site. 200-place free car parking — 300yd towards town centre (OS ref: ST 666542). Somervale School (300yd west, weekends) and Norton Hill School (100yd east, Saturday and Sunday pm only)

Access by public transport: Nearest rail stations Bath Spa (13 miles), Frome (13 miles), Trowbridge (15 miles). Bus (First) 173, 174, 176 and 178 drop off at Norton Hill School or Town Hall weekdays; 173, 778, 969, 984 on Sundays; 184 connects with Frome station.

Industrial locomotives

Name	No	Builder	Type	Built
David James Cook	—	E/Electric (D1120)	0-6-0DE	1966
—	—	Sentinel (????)	0-4-0DE	1927

Ex-BR locomotives to be hired in for future main events

Rolling stock:
Coaches — Mk 1 brake, BR Mk 3 buffet car, Mk 1 TSO and Mk 1 Pullman (both expected 2007)
Wagons — 2 ex-MoD box vans, LSWR box van, 4 brake vans (2 LMS, 1 SR, (GWR), milk tanker, Dogfish, Dace, Sturgeon, Lafarge cement internal box van, Kilmersdon Colliery coal wagon

Updated information on www.firstgroup.com

On site facilities: Sales/information area in main station building during opening times; toilets. Static buffet coach in sidings (light refreshments and meals). Museum building for static exhibits under development during 2007. Reconstructed signalbox being re-equipped during 2007. Goods shed workshop open for guided viewing

Length of line: Fifth of mile running line through station, plus sidings in goods yard. Extension under-way over further fifth of mile. Planned southward extension for approx two-thirds mile towards Chilcompton Tunnels

Opening times: Site and buildings open Sundays and Mondays 10.00-17.00 throughout the year. Shop and buffet may extend to other days during 2007. Only site open for viewing at other times. Train operations — phone to check; steam train times announced in press and on the web

Special events: Please see railway/local press and web site. Expected dates in 2007:

Midsummer at Midsomer — 14/15 July; Santa event — 8/9 December

Disabled access: Wheelchairs can access station forecourt, down platform, main building (via platform) and up platform via barrow crossing. Parking for disabled in station forecourt; phone to ensure space is reserved. Buffet coach, picnic area and museum accessed by gently ramped path

Membership details: Tim Deacon, 38 Bay Crescent, Swanage, Dorset BH19 1RB

Rates for 2006-07: Ordinary Adult (16+) £12, Junior or Senior Citizen £8; Senior Citizen Family £14; Family/Household £16; Corporate £20;

Life membership: (single member) £180; Family/Corporate £250; retired spouses/partners £150; retired single £100.

Visitor / membership leaflets available on request or at station

Membership journal: *The S&D Telegraph* — 3 times per annum (free to members). Current and back numbers £2.95 each (£2.50 before No 27), subject to availability

Museum	Science Museum	London

Built on land acquired with the profits from the Great Exhibition of 1851, the Science Museum was one of the first to include industrial archaeology. The railway exhibits are drawn from the collection based at the National Railway Museum. They form part of a major gallery, 'Making the Modern World', which opened in June 2000

Locomotive

Name	No	Origin	Class	Type	Built
Rocket	—	Liverpool & Manchester Railway	—	0-2-2	1829
Columbine	—	Grand Junction Railway	—	2-2-2	1845
Puffing Billy	—	Wylam Colliery	—	0-4-0	1814

Locomotive note: Restored to static display condition

on the site of the former Land Transport gallery
Location: South Kensington
OS reference: TQ 268793
Operating society/organisation: Science Museum, Exhibition Road, South Kensington, London SW7 2DD
Telephone: 020 7942 4000
Internet address: *Web site:* www.sciencemuseum.org.uk

Access by public transport: South Kensington Underground station
Catering facilities: Cafés on ground floor, hot meals, tea, coffee, sandwiches, etc. Picnic area in basement
On site facilities: Bookshop, toilets on most floors
Public opening: Daily 10.00-18.00. Closed 24-26 December
Special events: All organised by

the National Railway Museum, York, which is part of the Science Museum. Telephone (01904) 621261 for details
Facilities for disabled: Toilets on most floors, ramp and lifts to all floors. Parties should contact before arrival if extra assistance is required
Special notes: Static exhibits only in 'Making the Modern World'

Timetable Service — Seaton & District Electric Tramway — Devon

Member: HRA, South West Tourism
A unique 2ft 9in gauge electric tramway, operating on the trackbed of the former Southern Railway branch line between Seaton and Seaton Junction in east Devon. Trams operate between Seaton, Colyford and Colyton. Panoramic views of the beautiful Axe Valley and estuary together with a host of wading birds and other wildlife
Location: Harbour Road Car Park, Seaton; Swan Hill Road, Colyford (next to White Hart Inn); Station Road, Kingsdon, Colyton
OS reference: SY 252904
Operating society/organisation: Modern Electric Tramways Ltd t/a Seaton Tramway, Car Depot, Harbour Road, Seaton, Devon EX12 2NQ
Telephone: 01297 20375
Fax: 01297 625626
Internet address:
e-mail: info@tram.co.uk
Web site: www.tram.co.uk
Access by public transport: Nearest railway station: Axminster. Buses: Axe Valley Mini Travel service 885 from Axminster, service 899 from Lyme Regis and Sidmouth. First Southern National service X53 from Weymouth and Exeter, service 20 from Taunton and Honiton. Bus enquiries 0870 608 2608 or www.devon.gov.uk/devonbus
On site facilities: Gift shops at Seaton and Colyton. Restaurant, ice cream parlour and picnic area at Colyton
Length of line: 3 miles, 2ft 9in gauge
Period of public operation and

Trams

No	Prototype based on	Type	Built
2	London Metropolitan Tramways	A	1964
4	Blackpool	'Boat'	1961
6	Bournemouth (later Llandudno & Colwyn Bay)	'open-top'	1954
7	Bournemouth (later Llandudno & Colwyn Bay)	'open-top'	1954
8	†—	—	1968
9	Blackburn/Plymouth	double-deck	2004
10	Blackburn/Plymouth	double-deck	2005
11	Blackburn/Plymouth	double-deck	2006
12	London Metropolitan Tramways	'Feltham'	1966
14*	London Metropolitan Tramways	A	1904
16*	Bournemouth		1921
17	Manx Electric Tramway	'toastrack'	1988
19*	Exeter Corporation	—	1906

†a larger version of the ex-Bournemouth design of cars 6 and 7
*rebuilds of actual prototypes
9, 10, 11 are based on elements of designs from Plymouth and Blackburn

departure times (2007):
Daily 10-25 February, 10.00-16.00.
Saturdays & Sundays 3-25 March, 10.00-16.00.
Daily 31 March-20 July, 10.00-17.00.
Daily 21 July- 3 September, 10.00-20.40.
Daily 4 September-4 November, 10.00-16.00.
Saturday & Sunday 10 November-24 December, 10.00-16.00.
Halloween Tram of Terror — 31 October. Santa Specials — 16, 22-24 December, enquire for details.
Private hire all year round for groups of 20+
Special events: Vintage Vehicle Rally — 9 June; Gala Day — 10 June; Seaton Carnival Late Night Service — 1 September;

Colyton Carnival Late Night Service — 8 September; End of Season Gala — 27/28 October
Fares for 2007: Seaton to Colyton return fares — Adult £7.95, OAP £7.15, Child £5.55. Single fares and rover tickets also available. Family ticket (2+2) £24.00. Discounts for loyalty cardholders, families and parties of 12 or more
Facilities for disabled: Tramcar No 17 carries up to 12 wheelchairs. Please note that it has open sides and is therefore exposed to the weather. It is sometimes possible to accommodate individuals at short notice, but groups should book in advance. Larger trams accommodate 1-2 wheelchairs and depart on the hour. Please phone for times. Disabled toilets at Seaton and Colyton

144

Special notes: Tram driving lessons available through the season except 21 July-2 September. Bird watching trips available January to May and September to December. Enquire for details. Service operated by open-top double-deck bogie cars (enclosed saloon cars during inclement weather)

| | Timetable Service | | Severn Valley Railway | | Worcestershire | |

Member: HRA, TT

The railway hosts more main line engines than any other preserved line in the country, enjoying the back-up of a large volunteer and professional workforce and extensive engineering workshops and equipment. Railway travel like it used to be

General Manager: Vacant

Headquarters: Severn Valley Railway Co Ltd, Railway Station, Bewdley, Worcs DY12 1BG

Telephone: Bewdley (01299) 403816; 24hr timetable — (01299) 401001

Internet address: *Web site:* http://www.svr.co.uk

Main stations: Bridgnorth, Bewdley, Kidderminster Town

Locomotives and multiple-units

Name	No	Origin	Class	Type	Built
Gordon	AD600	LMR	WD	2-10-0	1943
—	43106	LMS	4MT	2-6-0	1951
—	46443	LMS	2MT	2-6-0	1950
RAF Biggin Hill	45110	LMS	5MT	4-6-0	1935
—	47383	LMS	3F	0-6-0T	1926
—	48773	LMS	8F	2-8-0	1940
—	42968	LMS	5P4F	2-6-0	1933
—	813	GWR	—	0-6-0ST	1901
—	2857	GWR	2800	2-8-0	1918
—	5164	GWR	5101	2-6-2T	1930
—	4150	GWR	5101	2-6-2T	1947
—	5764	GWR	5700	0-6-0PT	1929
—	7714	GWR	5700	0-6-0PT	1930
—	4566	GWR	4500	2-6-2T	1924
Bradley Manor	7802	GWR	'Manor'	4-6-0	1939
Erlestoke Manor	7812	GWR	'Manor'	4-6-0	1939
Hinton Manor	7819	GWR	'Manor'	4-6-0	1939
*Hagley Hall**	4930	GWR	'Hall'	4-6-0	1929

Other public stations: Arley, Highley, Hampton Loade, Northwood Halt, Country Park Halt

OS reference: Bridgnorth SO 715926, Bewdley SO 793753

Car parks: At all main stations

Access by public transport: First Bus service 192 to Kidderminster and Bewdley and 125 & 297 to Bridgnorth. Rail service to Kidderminster (main line) with immediate connections to SVR station. Through tickets available from all manned main line stations

Refreshment facilities: At most stations, but not on all operating days and on most trains. Fully licensed bars at Bridgnorth and Kidderminster Town

Souvenir shops: Bridgnorth, Kidderminster Town

Depots: Bridgnorth (locomotives), Bewdley and Kidderminster (stock)

Model railways: At Kidderminster and Hampton Loade

Length of line: 16.5 miles

Passenger trains: Steam-hauled trains running frequently from Kidderminster Town to Bewdley and Bridgnorth. Diesel-hauled service on limited occasions as advertised

Period of public operation: Every weekend, Santa Steam Specials weekends in December. Daily service 5 May to 30 September, plus February, Easter and October local school holidays. Open for limited viewing at other times

Special events: Day out with Thomas — 12/13, 19/20 May; 1940s Weekends — 23/24 June, 30 June, 1 July; Severn Valley in Bloom — 28/29 July; Day out with Thomas — 1/2, 8/9 September; Autumn Steam Gala — 21/23 September; Diesel Gala — 11-13 October; Classic Vehicle Day — 14 October; Santa Steam Specials — 1/2, 8/9, 15/16, 22/23 December. Festive Season service — 26 December-1 January 2008

Facilities for disabled: Facilities available, special vehicle available to carry wheelchairs by prior arrangement. Disabled people's toilets and ramp access to refreshment facilities at Kidderminster and Bridgnorth. Enlarged versions of all leaflets are available for the visually impaired from staffed booking offices

Name	No	Origin	Class	Type	Built
Taw Valley	34027	SR	WC	4-6-2	1946
—	1501	GWR	1500	0-6-0PT	1949
—**	7325	GWR	4300	2-6-0	1932
—	75069	BR	4MT	4-6-0	1955
—	80079	BR	4MT	2-6-4T	1954
Greyhound	D821	BR	42	B-B	1960
Western Ranger	D1013	BR	52	C-C	1962
Western Courier	D1062	BR	52	C-C	1963
—	D3022	BR	08	0-6-0DE	1952
—	08133	BR	08	0-6-0DE	1955
—	D3586	BR	08	0-6-0DE	1953
—	D3937	BR	08	0-6-0DE	1960
—	12099	LMS	11	0-6-0DE	1952
—	D5410	BR	27	Bo-Bo	1962
—	D7029	BR	35	B-B	1963
—	37906	BR	67	Co-Co	1963
Hood	D431	BR	50	Co-Co	1968
Ark Royal	50035	BR	50	Co-Co	1968
Exeter	D444	BR	50	Co-Co	1968
Defiance	D449	BR	50	Co-Co	1967
—§	E6005	BR	73	Bo-Bo	1962
—§	E6006	BR	73	Bo-Bo	1962
—	51935	BR	108	DMBS	1960
—	51941	BR	108	DMBS	1960
—	52064	BR	108	DMC	1960
—	56208	BR	108	DTCL	1958
—	59250	BR	108	TBS	1958

*on display at the McArthur Glen complex, Swindon, to return during 2007
**on display at Steam: Museum of the Great Western Railway, Swindon, to return during 2007
§on loan from the Dean Forest Diesel Association

Industrial locomotives

Name	No	Builder	Type	Built
Warwickshire	—	M/Wardle (2047)	0-6-0ST	1926
The Lady Armaghdale	—	Hunslet (686)	0-6-0T	1898
—	—	Ruston (319290)	0-4-0DM	1953
—	—	R/Hornsby (414304)	0-4-0DM	1957
—	—	R/Hornsby (408297)	0-4-0DM	1957

Stock
27 ex-GWR coaches; 13 ex-LMS coaches; 24 ex-BR Mk 1 coaches; 9 ex-LNER coaches; numerous examples of ex-GWR, LMS and other freight vehicles and two 30-ton steam cranes

Owners
813 the GWR 813 Fund
1501 the 15xx Fund
2857 the 2857 Fund
42968 the Stanier Mogul Fund
4150 the 4150 Locomotive Fund
4566 the 4566 Fund
5164 the 51xx Fund
5764, 7714 the Pannier Tank Fund
34027 is privately owned
7325 the Great Western (SVR) Association
7802 and 7812 the Erlestoke Manor Fund
7819 the Severn Valley Rolling Stock Trust
43106 the Ivatt 4 Fund
46443 the SVR 46443 Fund
47383 the Manchester Rail Travel Society
48773 the Stanier 8F Locomotive Society
D431, 50035, D444 and D449 Class 50 Alliance Ltd

England

Special notes: A number of special enthusiasts' weekends and special events are held when extra trains are operated. In addition, supplementary trains with diesel haulage are run as advertised. Severn Valley Limited' and 'Severn Valley Venturer' Restaurant Car service operates on Sundays, some Wednesdays and as required on other occasions. Advance booking required. Charter trains with or without dining facilities can be arranged
Membership details: Mrs Kate Kirk, c/o above address

D7029 the Diesel Traction Group
75069 the 75069 Fund
80079 the Passenger Tank Fund
AD600 the Royal Corps of Transport Museum Trustees
D821 and D7029 the Diesel Traction Group
D1013 and D1062 the Western Locomotive Association
D3022 the Class 08 Society
D5410 Sandwell Metropolitan Council
4930 and 45110 the SVR(H) plc

Membership journal: *Severn Valley Railway News* — quarterly
Share details: Mrs W. Broadhurst, c/o above address

| Museum | The Silk Mill — Derby's Museum of Industry and History | Derbyshire |

Member: TT
As would be expected of a railway town, the museum has an extensive collection of railway material including locomotives and rolling stock (most on display at the Midland Railway Centre). The railway gallery tells the stories of railway industries in Derby, especially as they relate to the Midland Railway and its successors. Replica Midland Railway signalbox and model railway (under construction). The story is brought up to date by the Railway Research Gallery which looks at the role of the

Railway Technical Centre and includes a replica of an InterCity 225 driving cab. The museum is now also home to the Midland Railway Study Centre. Appointments can be made on (01322) 255308 or through www.midlandrailwaystudycentre.org.uk
Location: Silk Mill Lane, off Full Street, Derby DE1 3AF
Operating society/organisation: Derby City Council
Telephone: (01332) 255308
Fax: (01332) 255108
Car park: Local car parks around city

Access by public transport: Bus station quarter mile, railway station three-quarter mile
On site facilities: Shop, baby changing facilities
Opening times: Admission free. Mondays 11.00-17.00, Tuesdays to Saturdays 10.00-17.00, Bank Holidays 13.00-16.00 Sundays 13.00-16.00
Facilities for disabled: Parking by arrangement. Level access to building, lifts and ramps to all gallery areas, toilets, sign language and subtitles in Rolls-Royce gallery

---

| Timetable service | Sittingbourne & Kemsley Light Railway | Kent |

Member: HRA
The Sittingbourne & Kemsley Light Railway is part of the 2ft 6in gauge railway built to convey paper and other materials between mills at Sittingbourne and Kemsley and the dock at Ridham on the banks of the Swale. The first section of the line opened in 1877 with horse-drawn haulage, while steam haulage was introduced in 1906. Two of the engines then in use remain on the line today. The

Locomotives

Name	No	Builder	Type	Built
Alpha	—	Bagnall (2472)	0-6-2T	1932
Triumph	—	Bagnall (2511)	0-6-2T	1934
Superb	—	Bagnall (2624)	0-6-2T	1940
Unique	—	Bagnall (2216)	2-4-0F	1924
Premier	—	K/Stuart (886)	0-4-2ST	1905
Leader	—	K/Stuart (926)	0-4-2ST	1905
Melior	—	K/Stuart (4219)	0-4-2ST	1924
Edward Lloyd	—	R/Hornsby (435403)	4wDM	1961
Victor	—	Hunslet (4182)	4wDM	1953
Barton Hall	—	Hunslet (6651)	4wDM	1965

railway now operates on the old paper mills trackbed as a tourist attraction. Passenger trains are normally steam-hauled and are formed of a varied selection of open and covered coaches. For the first half mile of the journey the narrow gauge railway twists and turns through Milton Regis on a unique early which was one of the first reinforced concrete viaducts.

2006 marked the start of the second centenary of steam operation

Operations Director: Noel Young
Registered Charity: 1057079
Headquarters: Sittingbourne & Kemsley Light Railway Ltd, PO Box 300, Sittingbourne, Kent ME10 2DZ
Telephone: 0871 222 1568 (general enquiries & talking timetable) or 0871 222 1569 (advance bookings — evenings)
Internet address:
e-mail: info@sklr.net
Web site: www.sklr.net
Main station: Sittingbourne Viaduct
Other public stations: Milton Regis Halt, Kemsley Down
Car park: Sittingbourne Viaduct (opposite McDonalds and Homebase)
Party, credit card & advance bookings and Footplate Experience courses: Tony Nokes, 111 Hillary Road, Penenden Heath, Maidstone, Kent ME14 2JX. Tel: 01622 755313
Access by public transport: Sittingbourne Viaduct — Sittingbourne (South Eastern) station; Milton Regis Halt — Mill Way, Sittingbourne (access from ASDA car park); (Kemsley Down

Industrial standard gauge locomotives

Name	No	Builder	Type	Built
Bear	—	Peckett (614)	0-4-0ST	1896
—	1	Barclay (1876)	0-4-0F	1925

Locomotive notes: In service: *Triumph, Melior, Victor, Edward Lloyd, Barton Hall.* Under repair: *Superb, Leader* (expected back in service during 2007/8)
Static display: *Premier, Alpha, Unique* and standard gauge exhibits

Stock
10 bogie coaches (including 4 ex-Chattenden & Upnor Railway); 2 open coaches; 39 various wagons

access by rail or on foot from Saxon Shore Way only)
Access by road: M2, A249 then A2 to Sittingbourne (follow brown tourist signs)
OS reference:
Sittingbourne TQ 905642, Milton Regis Halt TQ 909648 Kemsley Down TQ 920661
On site facilities at Kemsley Down: Refreshment facilities; Souvenir shop; small exhibits museum; museum walk; wildlife garden; children's play/picnic area; model and miniature railways
Depot: Kemsley Down (access by rail or on foot from Saxon Shore Way only)
Length of line: 2 miles, 2ft 6in gauge
Passenger trains: Hourly from 11.00, or 13.00 to 16.00 (refer to timetable: www.sklr.net or 0871 222 1568
Journey time: 15min each way
Period of public operation: April to end September. Sundays and Bank Holidays. Wednesday during most school holidays during season
Special events: Extended openings and timetables for special events including: StoryTime (Jack the

Station Cat and Edward Bear) — 6/7 May; Father's Day — 17 June; Steam and Beer Festival — 7/8 July (Festival fares apply); Model Railway Day — 12 August; Gala Weekend — 29/30 September; Santa Specials — 1/2, 8/9, 15/16, 22/23, 26 December
Special notes: There is no public access to Kemsley Down other than by the railway or on foot from Saxon Shore Way on operating dates. When the line is closed all stock is stored within security compounds within the paper mill premises. Family fares and senior citizens tickets available. Special rates for parties.
Disabled facilities: Limited access by prior arrangement until full facilities are completed. Tel: 01795 599511 for details
Special facilities: Footplate experience courses, special trains and children's parties available. Movie filming opportunities
Membership details: John Sparrow, 20 Park Road, Sheerness, Kent ME12 1UY
Marketing name: Sittingbourne's Steam Railway

Museum — Snibston Discovery Park — Leicestershire

Members: TT
Location: Snibston Discovery Park, Ashby Road, Coalville, Leicestershire LE67 3LN
Telephone: (01530) 278444
Fax: (01530) 813301
Operating group: Leicestershire County Council, Commercial & Support Services, Community

Services Dept.
Tel: 01530 278444
Internet address: *e-mail:* snibston@leics.gov.uk
Web site: www.snibston.com
Museum contact: Mr N. Pell, Assistant Keeper, Transport & Mining (museum collection enquiries). Tel: 01530 278452

Public opening: April-September — daily 10.00-17.00. October-March — Monday to Friday 10.00-15.00, weekends (10.00-17.00)
Car & coach parking: On site, free
Access by public transport: Arriva Fox from Loughborough and Nottingham (route 99); X1 and X2

from Leicester (217 and 218 on Sundays); Hinckley (route 159); routes 118 and 254 also run from Leicester. Connections at Ashby with Burton upon Trent. Further information, tel: 0870 608 2608

On site facilities: Shop, toilets, car park, café. Conference facilities. Family tickets, picnic areas, science play area, Sheepy Magna wheelwrights workshop. Special event days, nature reserve, golf driving range, colliery building tours

Disabled facilities: Fully available on site apart from small section of colliery tour. Access to passenger trains

Railways on site: Approx two thirds of a mile of standard gauge track with passenger trains on selected days. Please telephone for further information.

Narrow gauge railway about 80yd in length (non operational).

Volunteers to help maintain and run the railway are welcome to join our 'Friends of Coaltracks' support group; please contact Mr N. Pell at above address if interested

Multiple-unit

Name	No	Origin	Class	Type	Built
—	70576	BR	4CEP/411	TBC	1956

Industrial locomotives (standard gauge)

Name	No	Builder	Type	Built
Mars II†	—	RSH (7493)	0-4-0ST	1948
—	2§	Barclay (1815)	0-4-0F	1924
—*	—§	Brush (314)	0-4-0ST	1906
Claire	—	H/Clarke (D1388)	0-6-0DH	1970
Cadley Hill No 1†	—	Hunslet (3851)	0-6-0ST	1962
Pitt the Colliery Engine	16	Hunslet (6289)	0-6-0DM	1966
—	—	R/Hornsby (393304)	4wDM	1955

§on display in museum galleries

Industrial locomotives (2ft 6in gauge)

		Builder	Type	Built
—	—	E/Electric (2416)	4wBE	1957
—	—	H/Clarke (DM1812)	0-6-0DM	1960
—	63/000/449	Hunslet (8973)	4wDH	1979

Locomotive notes: 2007 locomotives for passenger trains will be Hunslet 6289, *Pitt the Colliery Engine* and Hudswell Clarke (1388) *Claire*
†locomotive is stored, but may be brought out for display on special events
*originally Powlesland & Mason No 6 taken over by GWR in 1924 and numbered 921
Plus 2ft 6in gauge English Electric battery-operated electric man-riding locomotives — ex-NCB

Rolling stock: 1920 Midland Railway brake van, other goods vehicles

---

Museum — Somerset & Dorset Railway Trust — Somerset

Member: HRA
Situated at Washford on the West Somerset Railway, the Trust Museum houses Somerset & Dorset memorabilia and artefacts to stir memories of cross-country travel in the era of steam. The sidings and restoration shed give the visitor a chance to see locomotives, wagons and carriages close up. Midford signalbox display

Headquarters: Washford Station, Minehead Road, Washford, Somerset TA21 0PP

Telephone: 01984 640869

Internet address: *Web site:* http://www.sdrt.org

Car park: Small car park by main road

Access by public transport: West Somerset Railway trains on operating days, March to end October. Nearest main line station:

Locomotive

Name	No	Origin	Class	Type	Built
—	88	S&DJR	7F	2-8-0	1925

Industrial locomotives

Name	No	Builder	Type	Built
Isabel	—	H/Leslie (3437)	0-6-0ST	1919
Kilmersdon	—	Peckett (1788)	0-4-0ST	1929

Stock
3 Somerset & Dorset 6-wheeled coaches undergoing restoration. Large wagon collection. Display of narrow gauge equipment from Sedgemoor peat railways

Taunton. First Bus service 28 (Taunton-Minehead) passes the station

On site facilities: Souvenir counter at the station. No refreshments on station but adjacent inn offers food and children are welcome

Public opening: 10.30-16.30 throughout June, July, August and September, plus Bank Holiday weekends and Gala Days

Membership details: Ian Briggs, S&DJR Trust, 24 Preston Close, Stanton-under-Bardon, Markfield, Leics LE67 9TX

Membership journal: *Pines Express* (4 issues/year, plus 2 newsletters/year)

South Devon Railway

Member: HRA, TT

A typical West Country branch line meandering up the Dart Valley to Buckfastleigh which is home to the railway's workshops, a butterfly and otter farm and several other attractions. The line is accessible from Totnes (main line) via a footbridge (4min walk).

General Manager: R. Elliott

Headquarters: South Devon Railway, Buckfastleigh Station, Buckfastleigh, Devon TQ11 0DZ

Telephone: 0845 345 1470

Internet addresses: *e-mail:* southdevonrailway.org
Web site: www.southdevonrailway.org

Main station: Buckfastleigh

Other public stations: Staverton, Totnes (Littlehempston)

OS reference:
Buckfastleigh SX 747663, Staverton SX 785638

Car park: Buckfastleigh (free), Staverton (free). Totnes — use main line pay & display or council car parks

Access by public transport: Bus, X38/9 Exeter-Plymouth; 88 Newton Abbot-Buckfastleigh; X80 Plymouth-Torquay. Main line trains to Totnes

Refreshment facilities: Buckfastleigh, Totnes (café at Totnes Rare Breeds Centre adjacent to and only accessible via SDR station)

Souvenir shop: On the train and Buckfastleigh station

Museum: Buckfastleigh

Depot: Buckfastleigh

Vintage bus: Operates to Buckfast Abbey and Buckfastleigh town most days (free service)

Miniature railway: Operates most Sundays and gala days at Buckfastleigh (7.25in gauge, half mile)

Model railway: Extensive 00 gauge model railway at Buckfastleigh. Admission included in train fare

Length of line: 7 miles

Passenger trains: Buckfastleigh-Totnes alongside the River Dart

Period of public operation: Daily April to October

Locomotives and multiple-units

Name	No	Origin	Class	Type	Built
—	1420	GWR	1400	0-4-2T	1933
—	1369	GWR	1366	0-6-0PT	1934
—	3205	GWR	2251	0-6-0	1946
—	3803	GWR	2884	2-8-0	1939
Dumbleton Hall	4920	GWR	'Hall'	4-6-0	1929
—	5526	GWR	4500	2-6-2T	1929
—	5786	GWR	5700	0-6-0PT	1930
—	D2246	BR	04	0-6-0DM	1956
—	D3666	BR	09	0-6-0DE	1959
—	8110	BR	20	Bo-Bo	1962
—	20118	BR	20	Bo-Bo	1962
—	25901	BR	25	Bo-Bo	1966
—	33002	BR	33	Bo-Bo	1960
Loch Trieg	37037	BR	37	Co-Co	1962
Superb	50002	BR	50	Co-Co	1967
—	51592	BR	127	DMBS	1959
—	51604	BR	127	DMBS	1959
—	55000	BR	121	DMBS	1959
—	59659	BR	115	TS	1960
—	59719	BR	115	TCL	1960
—	59740	BR	115	TS	1960

Broad gauge — 7ft 0.25in

Name	No	Origin	Class	Type	Built
Tiny	—	SDR	—	0-4-0VBT	1868

Industrial locomotives

Name	No	Builder	Type	Built
Ashley	1	Peckett (2031)	0-4-0ST	1942
Lady Angela	1690	Peckett (1690)	0-4-0ST	1926
Sapper	WD132	Hunslet (3163)	0-6-0ST	1943
Glendower	—	Hunslet (3810)	0-6-0ST	1954
Carnarvon	47	Kitson (5474)	0-6-0ST	1935
—	—	Fowler (421014)	0-4-0DM	1958
Errol Lonsdale	68011	Hunslet (3796)	0-6-0ST	1953

4ft 6in gauge

Name	No	Builder	Type	Built
Lee Moor No 2	—	Peckett (784)	0-4-0ST	1899

Stock

13 ex-BR Mk 1 coaches; 12 ex-GWR coaches; 3 ex-GWR auto trailers; 25 wagons. Lee Moor Tramway china clay wagon (4ft 6in gauge)

Owners

Tiny, 7ft 0.25in gauge, part of the National Collection
Glendower is privately owned
5526 the 5526 Ltd
D2246 and 50002 the Devon Diesel Society
D8110, 20118, 25901 and 33002 the South Devon Diesel Traction Group
5786 the Worcester Locomotive Society
Errol Lonsdale, Sapper, 3803 and 4920 the South Devon Railway Trust
1369 and 1420 the South Devon Railway Association

Facilities for disabled: Good

Membership details: South Devon Railway Association, c/o above address

Membership journal: *Bulliver* — quarterly

England

South Tynedale Railway

Member: HRA

A narrow gauge line passing through the attractive scenery of the South Tyne valley, in the North Pennine area of outstanding natural beauty

Location: Approximately 0.75-mile north of Alston town centre, on A686 Hexham road

OS reference: NY 717467

Operating society: South Tynedale Railway Preservation Society, The Railway Station, Alston, Cumbria CA9 3JB

Telephone: Alston (01434) 382828 (timetable information); (01434) 381696 (other enquiries)

Internet address: *Web site:* www.strps.org.uk

Car park: Alston station

Access by public transport: Bus services vary seasonally. Routes include Haltwhistle-Alston, Carlisle-Alston and Newcastle-Hexham-Alston-Penrith. Please check with local Tourist Information Centres or, for public transport information in Cumbria, phone 0870 608 2608

On site facilities: Book and souvenir shop, picnic area, toilets (including disabled persons), parking, lineside footpath

Catering facilities: Most weekend trains serve coffee, tea, soft drinks and snacks. (Tea room at Alston is not operated by Society.) Confectionery, ice cream and soft drinks on sale in the railway shop at Alston

Length of line: 2.25 miles, 2ft gauge from Alston to Kirkhaugh

Public opening: Trains will run: 31 March; 1-15, 21/22, 28/29 April; 5-7, 12/13, 19/20, 26-31 May; 1-3, 5, 7, 9/10, 12, 14, 16/17, 19, 21, 23/24, 26, 28, 30 June; 1, 3, 5, 7/8, 10, 12, 14-31 July; daily in August; 1/2, 4, 6, 8/9, 11, 13, 15/16, 18, 20, 22/23, 25, 27, 29/30 September; 6/7, 13/14, 20/21, 23, 25, 27/28 October; 8/9, 15/16, 21-23 December

Locomotives

Name	No	Builder	Type	Built
Barber	—	T/Green (441)	0-6-2ST	1908
Naworth	4	H/Clarke (DM819)	0-6-0DM	1952
Thomas Edmondson	6	Henschel (16047)	0-4-0T	1918
—	9	Hunslet (4109)	0-4-0DM	1952
Naklo	10	Chrzanow (3459)	0-6-0WTT	1957
Green Dragon	—	Fowler (13355)	0-4-2T	1914
Cumbria	11	Hunslet (6646)	0-4-0DM	1967
—	13	Hunslet (5222)	0-4-0DM	1958
Helen Kathryn	14	Henschel (28035)	0-4-0T	1948
—	—	Hunslet (4110)	0-4-0DM	1952
—	—	H/Clarke (DM1167)	0-6-0DM	1960
—	15	H/Clarke (DM1366)	0-6-0DM	1965
—	—	EE/Baguley (2519/3500)	4wBE	1958
—	17	B/Drewry (3704)	4wBE	1973
		rebuilt A/Barclay (6526)		1987
Carlisle	16	Hunslet (1859)	0-4-2T	1937
Permanent Way	DB965062			
Trolley		Wickham (7597)	4wDM	1957

Owners

4, 6, 9, 10 & 16 the South Tynedale Railway Preservation Society
11, 13, 14, 15, DM4110, DM1167, 2519/3500, DB965082 and Baguley/Drewry are privately owned

Stock

5 bogie coaches; 1 brake vans; 3 bogie open wagons; 8 4-wheel open wagons; 1 4-wheel box van; 3 4-wheel flat wagons; 1 4-wheel fuel tank wagon; 2 bogie well wagons, 4 4-wheel skip wagons; 5 bogie flat wagons; 6 bogie hopper wagons; 1 4-wheel hopper wagon; 1 4-wheel weedkiller wagon; 1 bogie compressor wagon; 2 4-wheel chassis

Owner

Barber is on loan from Leeds Industrial Museum

Steam haulage scheduled for: 6-9 April; 5-7, 26-28 May; 2/3, 9/10, 16/17, 23/24, 30 June; 1, 7/8, 14/15, 21/22, 28-31 July, daily in August; 1/2, 8/9, 15/16, 22/23 September; 27/28 October; 8/9, 15/16, 21-23 December

Special events: Teddy Bears' Picnic — 23/24 June; Gala Weekend — 22/23 September; Halloween Specials — 27/28 October; Santa Specials — 8/9, 15/16, 21-23 December

Facilities for disabled: A carriage with access for wheelchair users is available. Advance booking is recommended: tel: 01434 381696. Wheelchair accessible toilet at Alston

Special notes: The line has been constructed on the trackbed of the former BR Haltwhistle-Alston branch

Membership details: Membership Secretary, c/o above address

Membership journal: *Tynedalesman* — quarterly

Marketing name: England's Highest Narrow Gauge Railway

Southall Railway Centre

Due to circumstances the GWRPG were forced to end their activities within the former steam/DMU depot in 1997 and adopt new activities. With the vacation of part of the former depot by *Flying Scotsman* (now on display at the National Railway Museum) the Group were able to move into the former Wheel Drop Shop and anciliary building including open areas and sidings.

The Group now has to make the site suitable for public access which may take some time. Throughout 2006 much progress has been made in regard to and in preparation for being open to the public. To this extent 2006 has seen the Centre opened in a limited way to the local public who have shown much interest in the new activities. The programme for 2007 is still in formation and it is intended to include both steam and diesel passenger carrying operation on principal weekends; followers of the activities both old and new will be made welcome

Operating society/organisation: GWR Preservation Group Ltd, 16 Grange Close, Heston, Middx TW5 0HW

Contact: Bob Gorringe, Chairman

Tel: 020 8574 1529

Fax: 020 8571 6538

Internet address: *Web site:*

Locomotives

Name	No	Origin	Class	Type	Built
—	2885*	GWR	2885	2-8-0	1938
—	4110†	GWR	4100	2-6-2T	1936
—	9682§	GWR	5700	0-6-0PT	1949

*cosmetically restored and on display at Moor Street station, Birmingham
†under restoration at Tyseley Locomotive Works
§on hire to Chinnor & Princes Risborough Railway

Industrial locomotives

Name	No	Builder	Type	Built
William Murdoch	—	Peckett (2100)	0-4-0ST	1949
Birkenhead	—	RSH (7386)	0-4-0ST	1948
—	1	AEC	0-4-0	1939
—	AD251	R/Hornsby (390772)	0-4-0DM	1956
—	AD911	B/Drewry	4wDM	—

Rolling stock

BR Mk 1 TSO, BR Mk 1 BSK, BR box van, LMS brake van, BP tank wagon, BR generator van, BR stores van, BR parcels van, LNER CCT, GWR Rectank, GWR Gane A, GWR 'Mink' tool van, GWR Toad brake van

Owners

William Murdoch the GWRPG are custodians for Portsmouth City Museum

www.gwrpg.co.uk

Location: Southall, former steam/DMU depot

Car parking: Currently on site

Access by public transport: Southall station, access via Park Avenue or Armstrong Way

On site facilities: Light refreshments and shop are scheduled

Period of public opening: Weekends once opening date fixed

Membership details: Andrew Hunter c/o above address

Membership journal: *Southall Semaphore* — quarterly

Spa Valley Railway

Member: HRA

This railway originally formed part of a system of cross-country lines in East Sussex running through the Wealden countryside

Location: The main station at Tunbridge Wells West is located in the western end of the town close to the A26 road and the popular 'Pantiles' area

OS reference: Tunbridge Wells West station TQ 577384

Locomotives and multiple-units

Name	No	Origin	Class	Type	Built
Sutton	32650*	LBSCR	A1X	0-6-0T	1876
—	47493	LMS	3F	0-6-0T	1927
—	68077*	LNER	J94	0-6-0ST	1947
—	09004	BR	09	0-6-0DE	1959
Colonel Tomline	D3489	BR	10	0-6-0DE	1958
—	15224	BR	12	0-6-0DE	1949
R J Mitchell	33063	BR	33/0	Bo-Bo	1962
Sealion	33065*	BR	33/0	Bo-Bo	1962
—	E6047	BR	73	Bo-Bo	1966
—	51669†	BR	115	DMBS	1960

England

Above: No 3205 enters the passing loop at Staverton on the South Devon Railway at the head of a demonstration goods train, this type of re-enactment is becoming more popular with some heritage lines now scheduling regular runs. *Alan Barnes*

Right: Diesel Gala Day on the Spa Valley Railway as two Class 33s, Nos 33069 and 33063, leave Birchden to the delight of the passengers. *Phil Barnes*

England

General Manager: Stephen Woolven

Operating society/organisation: Tunbridge Wells & Eridge RPS, Tunbridge Wells West Station, Nevill Terrace, Tunbridge Wells, Kent TN2 5QY

Telephone: 01892 537715

Internet address: *Web site:* www.spavalleyrailway.co.uk

Car parking: Tunbridge Wells West — several car parks nearby in town centre. Note: Sainsbury's car park, adjacent to station, is limited to 2 hours for their customers only. High Rocks — large free car park. There is *no* parking at Groombridge

Access by public transport: National Rail services to Tunbridge Wells, then 15min walk, or short bus ride. Nearest bus stop served by many local bus services is at Sainsbury's, Tunbridge Wells, then approx 100yd walk

Refreshment facilities: Static buffet car at Tunbridge Wells West. Also bar car *Kate* on some trains

Souvenir shop: Tunbridge Wells West (within engine shed)

Depot: Tunbridge Wells West shed is an original LBSCR design dating from 1891 and consists of four roads which house various items of rolling stock and motive power

Length of line: 4 miles Tunbridge Wells-Birchden Jct. Plus future extension planned Birchden Jct to Eridge, 1 mile

Passenger trains: Regular services Tunbridge Wells West-Groombridge; special services Groombridge-Birchenden

Period of public operation: Weekends and Bank Holidays from 5 April to 28 October plus some weekdays in April, July and August. Santa Specials in December.

Name	No	Origin	Class	Type	Built
—	51849	BR	115	DMBS	1960
—	54408	BR	101	DTS(L)	1958
—	60142*	BR	207	DMBS	1962
—	60616§	BR	207	TC	1962
—	60916*	BR	207	DTS	1962

*undergoing overhaul
†converted to locomotive hauled stock
§undergoing restoration off-site, expected to arrive during 2007

Industrial locomotives

Name	No	Builder	Type	Built
Samson*	57	RSH (7668)	0-6-0T	1950
North Downs*	13	RSH (7846)	0-6-0T	1955
Princess Margaret	—	Barclay (376)	0-4-0DM	1947
Lady Ingrid	—	Barclay (2315)	0-4-0ST	1951
Southerham	—	Drewry/Vulcan (2591)	0-4-0DM	1959
Topham*	—	Bagnall (2193)	0-6-0ST	1922
Fonmon	—	Peckett (1636)	0-6-0ST	1924
Spartan*	—	Chrzanow (3135)	0-6-0T	1954
Hotspur*	—	Chrzanow (2944)	0-6-0T	1952

*undergoing overhaul

Stock
5 BR Mk 1 coaches; 1 BR Mk 2 coaches; buffet car from Class 420 EMU; 2 ex-London Transport T stock coaches; 1 LCDR coach body; 4 brake vans, 3 cranes; various freight wagons

Owners
Sutton by the London Borough of Sutton
33063 and 33065 the South East Locomotive Group

Special events: Easter Specials — 8/9 April; Day out with Thomas — 21/22, 28/29 April; Diesel Day — 5 May; Morris Day — 7 May; Father's Day — 17 June; Children's Weekend — 30 June/1 July; Wings Wheels & Steam — 22 July; Diesel Gala — 3-5 August; Teddy Bears' Picnic — 18/19 August; Bus Day — 2 September; Main Line Gala — 15/16 September; Day out with Thomas — 6/7, 13/24 October; Santa Specials — 1-24 December

Facilities for disabled: Separate disabled persons' toilet at Tunbridge Wells West station. Level or ramp access to all station platforms. Ramps available for wheelchair access to trains

Special facilities: A private train can be hired for the day. Please contact address above for details

Membership details: c/o Tunbridge Wells West Station

Membership journal: *Spa Valley Starter* and *Eridge Express*

STEAM — Museum of the Great Western Railway

Museum   Wiltshire

Member: HRA
STEAM — Museum of the Great Western Railway tells the remarkable story of the men and women who built, operated and travelled on the Great Western Railway. Situated on the old Swindon Railway Works site, the museum is housed in a 72,000sq ft Victorian machine shop. As well as locomotives, carriages and wagons the story is told by imaginative displays and plenty of 'hands-on' exhibits — build a bridge and shunt the wagons! Have a go at putting a locomotive together and take a ride on the train-driving simulator

Keeper: Felicity Ball

Location: Kemble Drive, Swindon, Wiltshire SN2 2TA
OS reference: tba
Operating society/organisation: Swindon Borough Council
Telephone: Swindon (01793) 466646
Internet address: *Web site:* www.swindon.gov.uk/steam
Car park: Shared with the Great Western Designer Outlet Centre
Access by public transport: Swindon main line station 1 mile (20min walk)
On site facilities: Shop
Facilities for disabled: Fully accessible
Period of public opening: Daily 10.00-17.00. Closed Christmas Day, Boxing Day and New Year's Day
Membership details: The Friends of Swindon Railway Museum, c/o STEAM
Membership journal: *North Star* — quarterly

Locomotives

Name	No	Origin	Class	Type	Built
—	2516	GWR	2301	0-6-0	1897
—	4248	GWR	4200	2-8-0T	1916
Caerphilly Castle	4073	GWR	'Castle'	4-6-0	1923
King George V	6000	GWR	'King'	4-6-0	1927
—	9400	GWR	9400	0-6-0PT	1947
*North Star**	—	GWR	—	2-2-2	1837
—	4	GWR	Diesel railcar	Bo-Bo	1934
Hagley Hall†	4930	GWR	'Hall'	4-6-0	1929
—	7325	GWR	4300	2-6-0	1932
Glorious	50033	BR	50	Co-Co	1968

*broad gauge (7ft 0.25in) replica
†on display in McArthur Glen's 'Designer Outlet' shopping centre located in the old works

Owners

4930 and 7325 on loan from Severn Valley Railway, to return during 2007
All other locomotives are part of the National Railway Museum Collection

---

Stephenson Railway Museum & North Tyneside Railway

Steam Centre

Tyne & Wear

Member: HRA
A display in buildings which began life as the Tyne & Wear Metro Test Centre now features locomotives and exhibitions which illustrate railway development from waggonways to the present day
Location: Middle Engine Lane, West Chirton
OS reference: NZ 396576
Internet address: *NTSRA web site:* ntsra.org.uk
Operating society/organisation: The Stephenson Railway Museum and the North Tyneside Railway are managed as a partnership between North Tyneside Council, Tyne & Wear Museums and the North Tyneside Railway Association (NTSRA). Each can be contacted c/o Stephenson Railway Museum, Middle Engine Lane, West Chirton, North Shields, Tyne & Wear NE29 8DX
Car park: On site, free
Length of line: North Tyneside Railway, 2 miles, Stephenson

Locomotive and multiple-unit

Name	No	Origin	Class	Type	Built
—	D2078	BR	03	0-6-0DM	1959
—	3267	NER	—	DMLV	1904

Industrial locomotives

Name	No	Builder	Type	Built
Billy	—	Killingworth or RS & Co (1)	0-4-0	c1826
—	A No 5	Kitson (2509)	0-6-0PT	1883
Ashington No 5 / Jackie Milburn	5	Peckett (1970)	0-6-0ST	1939
Ted Garrett, JP, DL, MP	1	RSH (7683)	0-6-0T	1951
—	E4	Siemens-Schuckert (457)	Bo-BoWE	1909
Thomas Burt MP 1837-1902	401	Bagnall (2994)	0-6-0ST	1950
—	10	Consett Iron Co	0-6-0DM	1958

Stock

1 LNER Gresley BFK; 3 BR Mk 1 non-gangwayed coaches, 2 BR Mk 2 coaches, 1 LNER Gresley BGP

Owner

NER van National Railway Museum

Railway Museum to Percy Main Village
Access by public transport: Bus services 300 from Newcastle (Haymarket bus station); 337/339 from Wallsend (Metro station interchange). Ring 0870 608 2608 for times and fares. Tyne & Wear Metro to Percy Main (then short walk to NTR station) when North Tyneside Railway is in operation
Public opening: May to

September: Museum — daily (except Fridays), admission free; railway — Sundays and Bank Holiday Mondays, also Saturdays during local school holidays. Closed October to April. Write, phone (0191 200 7146) or visit the NTSRA web site for details, including early/late season variations and special events
Special notes: Stephenson Railway Museum and North Tyneside

Railway share facilities in buildings. North Tyneside Steam Railway Association operates and maintains exhibits from the Museum Collection
Facilities for disabled: Access for wheelchairs to Museum building at Middle Engine Lane. Access to stations; also wheelchair ramp onto train

Timetable Service — Swanage Railway — 'The Purbeck Line' — Dorset

Member: HRA

Overlooked by the historic ruins of Corfe Castle, this railway is slowly extending towards Wareham and a connection to the main line network

Location: Swanage station
Operations Manager: Mike Stanghaft
Passenger Services Manager: David Green
Operating society/organisation: Swanage Railway Co Ltd, Station House, Swanage, Dorset BH19 1HB
Telephone: Swanage (01929) 425800. Talking Timetable — (01929) 425800
Fax: (01929) 426680
Internet addresses: *e-mail:* info@swanage-railway.co.uk
Web site: www.swanagerailway.co.uk
Other public stations: Herston Halt, Harman's Cross, Corfe Castle and Norden
OS reference: SZ 026789
Car park: Norden park & ride signposted off A351 Wareham-Swanage road on the approach to Corfe Castle. Limited parking available at Swanage station
Access by public transport: Regular bus services operated by Wilts & Dorset from Bournemouth, Poole and Wareham to Swanage and Norden park & ride
On site facilities: Souvenir shop at Swanage. Buffet car on most trains. Picnic areas at Swanage, Harman's Cross and Norden. Exhibition and cinema coach at Corfe. 5in gauge railway at Swanage on some

Locomotives and multiple-units

Name	No	Origin	Class	Type	Built
—	6695	GWR	5600	0-6-2T	1928
—	30053*	LSWR	M7	0-4-4T	1905
Sidmouth	34010	SR	WC	4-6-2	1945
Eddystone	34028†	SR	WC	4-6-2	1946
Manston	34070	SR	BB	4-6-2	1947
257 Squadron	34072	SR	BB	4-6-2	1948
—	80078	BR	4MT	2-6-4T	1954
—	80104	BR	4MT	2-6-4T	1955
—	08436	BR	08	0-6-0DE	1957
—	D3591	BR	08	0-6-0DE	1958
—	20188	BR	20	Bo-Bo	1967
Stan Symes	D6515	BR	33	Bo-Bo	1960
—	33034	BR	33	Bo-Bo	1960
Vampire	33108	BR	33	Bo-Bo	1960
—	51341*	P/Steel	117	DMBS	1959
—	51346	P/Steel	117	DMBS	1959
—	51353*	P/Steel	117	DMBS	1959
—	51356*	P/Steel	117	DMBS	1959
—	51388	P/Steel	117	DMS	1959
—	51392*	P/Steel	117	DMS	1959
—	51395*	P/Steel	117	DMS	1959
—	51398*	P/Steel	117	DMS	1959
—	59486*	P/Steel	117	TCL	1960
—	59492*	P/Steel	117	TCL	1960
—	59516	P/Steel	117	TCL	1960
—	59521*	P/Steel	117	TCL	1960

*undergoing overhaul off-site
†on loan to Bluebell Railway

Industrial locomotives

Name	No	Builder	Type	Built
May	2	Fowler (4210132)	0-4-0DM	1957
Beryl	—	Planet (2054)	4wPM	1937
Progress	—	Peckett (1611)	0-4-0ST	1923
Secondus*	—	Bellis & Seekings	0-6-0WT	1874
Snapper†	—	R/Hornsby (283871)	4wDM	1950

*2ft 8in gauge, on display in Corfe Castle goods shed
†2ft gauge, stored nearby for use on Purbeck Mineral & Mining Museum project

weekends. Travel Agency at Swanage station
Length of line: 6 miles, Swanage-Herston Halt-Harman's Cross-Corfe Castle-Norden
Public opening: Swanage station open every day except Christmas Day. Trains operate weekends all year round from 3 March to 25 November. Daily from 1 April until 28 October. Also 26 December 2007 to 1 January 2008
Special events: Branchline Weekend — 31 March/1 April; Easter Specials — 6-9 April; Swanage Railway Beer Festival — 11-13 May; 40th Anniversary of the end of Southern Steam — 7-9 July; Swanage Regatta & Carnival — 28 July and 4 August; Steam Gala & Vintage Transport Rally — 7-9 September; Day out with Thomas — 20-28 October; 1960s Weekend — 24/25 November; Santa Specials — 1/2, 8/9, 15/16, 22-24 December.

Locomotive notes: 30053, 80078 and 80104 will be away periodically on short-term loan

Stock
3 ex-LSWR coach bodies; 4 ex-SR vans; 9 ex-SR coaches; 17 ex-BR Mk 1 coaches; 1 ex-BR Mk 1 Pullman; 15 various types of wagons; 1 ex-BR Mk 3 Sleeping coach; 1 ex-SR 15-ton diesel-electric crane; 1 ex-BR Corridor 2nd converted to disabled persons' coach. Brake vans from SR, LMS, LSWR including 3 'Queen Marys', GWR

Owners
6695 the Great Western Railway Preservation Group
34010, 34028, 34070, 34072, 80078 and 80104 the Southern Locomotives Ltd
30053 the Drummond Locomotive Society
D6515 and 33034 the 71A Locomotive Group
33108 the Class 33/1 Preservation Co Ltd

See press for details of local special events
Facilities for disabled: Access to shop and toilets; disabled facilities on most trains
Membership details: Sue Payne, c/o Southern Steam Trust at above

address
Membership journal: *Swanage Railway News* — quarterly
Marketing name: The Purbeck Line

| Steam Centre | Swindon & Cricklade Railway | Wiltshire |

Member: HRA, TT
This is the only preserved section of the former Midland & South Western Junction Railway, the society having had to re-lay track and associated works. There is the station and the engine shed complex at Hayes Knoll
Location: Tadpole Lane, Blunsdon (approximately midway between Blunsdon St Andrew and Purton)
Chairman: J. Larkin
Operating society/organisation: Swindon & Cricklade Railway, Blunsdon Station, Blunsdon, Swindon, Wiltshire SN25 2DA
Telephone: 01793 771615
Internet address: *Web site:* www.swindon-cricklade-railway.org
Station: Blunsdon
OS reference: SU 110897
Length of line: 1 mile
Car park: Tadpole Lane, Blunsdon
Refreshment facilities: Blunsdon station in former Norwegian State Railways coach. Buffet car at Hayes Knoll on open days. Picnic area
Toilet: Blunsdon station amenities

Locomotives and multiple-units

Name	No	Origin	Class	Type	Built
Foremarke Hall†	7903	GWR	'Hall'	4-6-0	1949
—	4277	GWR	4200	2-8-0T	1920
—*	5637	GWR	5600	0-6-2T	1924
—	2022	BR	03	0-6-0DM	1958
—	D2152	BR	03	0-6-0DM	1960
—	13261	BR	08	0-6-0DE	1956
Sir Herbert Walker	E6003	BR	73	Bo-Bo	1962
—	51074	GRCW	119	DMBC	1959
—	51104	GRCW	119	DMS	1958
—	59514	P/Steel	117	TCL	1959
—	60127	BR	207	DMBS	1962
—	60901	BR	207	DTS	1962

*on loan to East Somerset Railway
†on loan to Gloucestershire Warwickshire Railway

Industrial locomotives

Name	No	Builder	Type	Built
Swordfish	—	Barclay (2138)	0-6-0ST	1941
Salmon	—	Barclay (2139)	0-6-0ST	1942
—	—	Barclay (2352)	0-4-0ST	1954
Richard Trevithick	—	Barclay (2354)	0-4-0ST	1954
Woodbine	—	Fowler (21442)	0-4-0DM	1936
—	—	Fowler (4210137)	0-4-0DM	1958
—	—	Fowler (4220031)	0-4-0DH	1964
—*	70	H/Clarke (1464)	0-6-0T	1921
Slough Estates No 3	—	H/Clarke (1544)	0-6-0ST	1924
—	—	H/Clarke (1857)	0-6-0T	1952
Isabel	—	H/Leslie (3437)	0-6-0ST	1919

157

England

building

Souvenir shop: Blunsdon station. Various sales stands on Open Days around station area. Museum

Depot: Hayes Knoll

Public opening: Site open: 10.00-16.00 Saturdays, Sundays and Bank Holidays throughout the year and Wednesdays in local school holidays.

Passenger trains: A steam train planned to operate from 11.00-16.00 every Sunday from Easter to 14 October and on the dates listed below unless stated otherwise. A train service will also operate from 11.00-16.00 every Saturday and Sunday when special events are not planned and on Wednesdays during local school holidays

Special events:
Special Diesel Weekend — 17/18 March; Easter Egg Specials (diesel) — 6/7 April; Easter Egg Specials (steam) — 8/9 April; Real Ale Weekend — 5-7 May; Murder Mystery Evening* — 19 May; Children's Treasure Hunt — 27/28 May; Teddy Bears' Balloon Race — 24 June; Model Railway Weekend — 7/8 July; 70th Anniversary of closure of Blunsdon station — 21/22 July; Murder Mystery Evening* — 21 July; Vintage Transport Weekend — 11/12 August (10.30-17.00); Tubby the

Talking Engine — 25-27 August; Wartime Weekend — 8/9 September (10.30-17.00); Halloween Ghost Train — 26 October (18.30-20.45) 27 October (18.00-20.45);
Santa Specials — 24/25 November, 8 (and 18.00-20.00)/9, 15/16, 22/23 December.
*Ticket only events

Service operate:
School holidays (diesel), Wednesdays 11.00-16.00 — 4, 11 April, 30 May, 1, 8, 15, 22, 29 August, 24 October;
Saturday service (diesel), 11.00-16.00 — Saturdays throughout the year;
Sunday service (steam),

Name	No	Builder	Type	Built
Gunby	—	Hunslet (2413)	0-6-0ST	1941

*on loan to Avon Valley Railway

Stock
10 BR Mk 1 coaches; 3 GWR coaches; Selection of goods rolling stock; Wickham railcar. Self-propelled Plasser & Theurer track machine (98504 of 1985)

Owners
7903 the Foremarke Hall Locomotive Group
5637 the 5637 Locomotive Group
Slough Estates the Slough & Windsor Railway Society
51074, 51104 and 59514 the Gloucester Railcar Trust
E6003 the Electro-Diesel Group

11.00-16.00 — Sundays from 15 April to 14 October;
Sunday service (diesel), 11.00-16.00 — Sundays to 1 April, 21 October to 18 November

Facilities for disabled: Access to trains, locomotive shed, shop, toilets and refreshments

Special facilities: Licensed for civil/wedding ceremonies. Suitable for up to 60 guests. Trains can be hired for special events

Membership details: Membership Secretary, c/o above address

Membership journal: S&CR magazine, quarterly

Timetable Service	**Tanfield Railway**	County Durham

Member: HRA

The oldest railway in the world, featuring 1725 route, 1725 Causey embankment, 1727 Causey arch, 1766 Gibraltar bridge and 1854 Marley Hill engine shed. Also collection of local engines, Victorian carriages and vintage workshop

Location: Off the A6076 Sunniside to Stanley road

OS reference: NZ 207573

Operating society/organisation:
The Tanfield Railway, Marley Hill Engine Shed, Sunniside, Gateshead NE16 5ET

Telephone: (0191) 388 7545

Internet address: *Web site:* www.tanfield-railway.co.uk

Main stations: Andrews House, Sunniside, Causey, East Tanfield

Locomotive

Name	No	Origin	Class	Type	Built
—	M2*	TGR	M	4-6-2	1951

*3ft 6in gauge, Tasmanian Government Railways (RSH 7630)

Industrial locomotives

Name	No	Builder	Type	Built
—	9	AEG (1565)	4w-4wE	1913
Gamma	—	Bagnall (2779)	0-6-0ST	1945
—	—	Baguley (3565)	2w-2DHR	1962
Horden	—	Barclay (1015)	0-6-0ST	1904
—	6	Barclay (1193)	0-4-2ST	1910
—	17	Barclay (1338)	0-6-0T	1913
—	32	Barclay (1659)	0-4-0ST	1920
Beryl	—	S/Crossley (7697)	0-6-0DM	1953
—	3	E. Borrows (37)	0-4-0WT	1898
—	6	Fowler (4240010)	0-6-0DH	1960
Enterprise	—	R&W Hawthorn (2009)	0-4-0ST	1884
Cyclops	112	H/Leslie (2711)	0-4-0ST	1907
—	2*	H/Leslie (2859)	0-4-0ST	1911

England

Car park: Marley Hill, Causey picnic area, East Tanfield

Access by public transport: X30 (weekdays) stops outside main entrance; 705, 706, 770 Sundays to Sunniside only, near to Sunniside station

Catering facilities: Light refreshments available on operating days

On site facilities: Shop and toilets

Length of line: 3 miles

Public opening: Trains run every Sunday and Bank Holiday Monday from January to November. Also Wednesdays and Thursdays in summer. Santa trains in December before Christmas. Marley Hill engine shed open daily for viewing

Special events: Mother's Day — 18 March; Group Organisers Day — 25 March; Easter Eggstravaganza — 6-9 April; Teddy Bear Day — 22 April; Spring Bank Holiday — 27/28 May; Father's Day — 17 June; Children's Day — 24 June; Railway Treasure Hunt — 8 July; Steam and Cream — 22 July; Branch Line Day — 29 July; Teddy Bear Day — 12 August; Victorian Bank Holiday Weekend — 26/27 August; Gala Weekend — 15/16 September; Children's Day — 30 September; Coal Train Day — 14 October; Halloween — 29 October

Family tickets: Available

Facilities for disabled: Access to East Tanfield and Andrews House stations and Marley Hill engine shed. Toilets at Causey car park and Andrews House station

Membership details: Miss E. Martin, 33 Stocksfield Avenue, Fenham, Newcastle upon Tyne NE5 2DX

Membership journal: *Tanfield Railway News* — 4 times/year

Special notes: Families can alight at Causey station for 2 miles of walks through the picturesque Causey Woods; picnic facilities and toilet available in car park

Name	No	Builder	Type	Built
Stagshaw	—	H/Leslie (3513)	0-6-0ST	1923
—	3	H/Leslie (3575)	0-6-0ST	1923
—	13	H/Leslie (3732)	0-4-0ST	1928
—	3	H/Leslie (3746)	0-6-0F	1929
Renishaw Ironworks No 6	—	H/Clarke (1366)	0-6-0ST	1919
Irwell	—	H/Clarke (1672)	0-4-0ST	1937
—	38	H/Clarke (1823)	0-6-0T	1949
—	501	Hunslet (6612)	0-6-0DH	1965
—	—	Planet (3716)	0-4-0DM	1955
—	4	Sentinel (9559)	0-4-0T	1953
Twizell†	3	Stephenson (2730)	0-6-0T	1891
—	L2	R/Hornsby (312989)	0-4-0DE	1952
—	35	R/Hornsby (418600)	0-4-0DE	1958
—	158	RSH (6980)	0-4-0DM	1940
Hendon	—	RSH (7007)	0-4-0CT	1940
—	62	RSH (7035)	0-6-0ST	1940
—	3	RSH (7078)	4w-4wE	1940
—	49	RSH (7098)	0-6-0ST	1943
Progress	—	RSH (7298)	0-6-0ST	1946
Cochrane	—	RSH (7409)	0-4-0ST	1948
Bromborough No 2	—	RSH (7746)	0-6-0DM	1954
—	44	RSH (7760)	0-6-0ST	1953
—	38	RSH (7763)	0-6-0ST	1954
—	21	RSH (7796)	0-4-0ST	1954
—	47	RSH (7800)	0-6-0ST	1954
—	1	RSH (7901)	0-4-0DM	1958
—	16	RSH (7944)	0-6-0ST	1957
FGF	—	Barclay (D592)	0-4-0DH	1969
—	—	Barclay (D615)	0-4-0DH	1977
—	2	A/Whitworth (D22)	0-4-0DE	1933

*on loan to Locomotion
†on long-term loan from Beamish

2ft gauge

Escucha	11	B/Hawthorn (748)	0-4-0ST	1883
—	—	Clayton (133141)	4wBE	1984
—	—	Hunslet (7332)	4wDM	1973
—	—	L/Blackstone (53162)	4wDM	1962
—	—	L/Blackstone (54781)	4wDM	1962
—	—	R/Hornsby (323587)	4wDM	1952
—	—	R/Hornsby (244487)	4wDM	1946
—	25	RSH (8201)	4wBE	1960
—	—	W/Rogers	4wBE	—

Stock

19 4-wheel carriages; 3 6-wheel carriages; 1 6-wheel van; 14 hopper wagons; 9 contractors bogies; 3 brake vans; 3 steam cranes; 8 covered wagons; 4 open wagons; 4 black wagons; 3 flat wagons

Telford Horsehay Steam Trust

Member: HRA

Telford Steam Railway is based at Horsehay & Dawley station and goods yard in Telford on the Great Western branch from Wellington to Craven Arms via Ironbridge. The site at Horsehay has a longer history, being at the site of one of the Coalbrookdale companies' first blast furnaces. The line saw its last passenger train in 1962 but the route from Lightmoor to Horsehay was kept open for freight traffic until 1979. The TSR acquired the former goods yard at Horsehay & Dawley in 1983. The railway is now extending northwards to Lawley Common, and southwards to Doseley. Excavation of Lawley Common cutting is continuing

Location: Horsehay, Telford, Shropshire

OS reference: SJ 675073

Operating society/organisation: Telford Horsehay Steam Trust, The Old Loco Shed, Horsehay, Telford, Shropshire TF4 2LT

Sales line: 07765 858348

Internet address: *Web site:* www.telfordsteamrailway.co.uk

On site facilities: Extensive model railway display, tea room, picnic area, children's play equipment, narrow gauge steam tramway, miniature railway operated by Phoenix Model Engineers (separate charge); ticket gives unlimited travel (except miniature railway)

Public opening: Every Sunday and Bank Holiday from Easter until last Sunday in September including

Locomotives and diesel multiple-units

Name	No	Origin	Class	Type	Built
—	5619	GWR	5600	0-6-2T	1925
—	08395	BR	08	0-6-0DE	1958
—	50531	BRCW	104	DMC	1957
—	50479	BRCW	104	DMBS	1957
—	50556	BRCW	104	DMC	1957
—	59228	BRCW	104	TBSL	1958
—	RB004	Leyland		Railbus	1984

Industrial locomotives

Name	No	Builder	Type	Built
Ironbridge No 3	—	Peckett (1990)	0-4-0ST	1940
Beatty	—	H/Leslie (3240)	0-4-0ST	1917
—	MP1	Barclay (1944)	0-4-0F	1944
Tom	27414	N/British (27414)	0-4-0DH	1954
—	D2959	R/Hornsby (382824)	4wDM	1955
Folly	—	R/Hornsby (183062)	4wDM	1937
—	—	R/Hornsby (525947)	0-4-0DH	1968
Joanna	—	T/Hill (177C)	0-4-0DM	1967
		rebuild of Sentinel (9401) 0-4-0ST of 1950		
—	—	YEC (2630)	0-6-0DE	1956
—	—	YEC (2687)	0-4-0DE	1968
Thomas	—*	Kierstead	4wVBT	1979

*2ft gauge

Stock

2 ex-BR Mk 1 coaches; 1 ex-BR Mk 3 sleeper; 1 ex-GWR auto-trailer; 1 ex-GWR Toad brake van; 1 ex-GWR 3-ton hand crane; 1 Wickham trolley; Permaquip PW transporter vehicle No 68800; various wagons

Bank Holidays 11.00-16.30. Last Sunday in month steam-hauled and also steam on Bank Holidays and all Sundays in August, but steam tram every Sunday. Also pre-Christmas weekends in December when Thomas the Tank pays a visit

Facilities for disabled: Limited, see below, or Accessibility on web site.

Mk 1 coaches are not really suitable for wheelchair access, DMUs when in service on diesel days have ramped brake van access. Small chairs can be accommodated in GWR brake van, platforms have easy access and shop, although steep ramp at Horsehay & Dawley. Tea room and model railway have level access

---

Tiverton Museum of Mid Devon Life

The Museum, dominated by No 1442, affectionately known as the 'Tivvy Bumper', houses a large collection of railway relics

Location: Tiverton, Devon

OS reference: SS 955124

Operating society/organisation: Tiverton & Mid Devon Museum Trust, Beck's Square, Tiverton,

Locomotives

Name	No	Origin	Class	Type	Built
(Tivvy Bumper)	1442	GWR	1400	0-4-2T	1935

Devon EX16 6PJ

Telephone: (01884) 256295

Car park: Short term in Beck's Square, long term in multi-storey

Access by public transport: Rail to Tiverton Parkway, then by bus, or bus from Exeter

On site facilities: Museum, shop

and toilets
Public opening:
February to Christmas:
Monday to Friday — 10.30-16.30;

Saturdays — 10.00-13.00;
closed Sundays
Special notes: Disabled access to
view locomotive. The transport

gallery re-opened in April 2006
following re-display

Steam Centre — Tyseley Locomotive Works — Birmingham

Member: HRA
Location: 670 Warwick Road
(A41), Tyseley, Birmingham
B11 2HL
OS reference: SP 105841
Operating organisation: Tyseley
Locomotive Works Ltd
Supporting society: Vintage Trains
Society
Telephone: (0121) 708 4960
Fax: (0121) 708 4963
Internet address: *Web site:*
www.vintagetrains.co.uk/brm.htm
Car park: Site
Access by public transport: Travel
West Midlands route No 37 from
city centre. Main line rail service
to Tyseley station (Central Trains
and Chiltern Railways)
On site facilities: The Museum is
on the site of a former GWR/BR
steam shed and has been equipped
with specialised railway
engineering machinery. It carries
out many contract repairs to steam
locomotives and rolling stock.
Souvenir shop, passenger
demonstration line and station
Refreshment facilities: Available
in visitor centre
Length of line: Third of a mile
Public opening: Weekends and
Bank Holidays only 10.00-16.00.
Special events: 'Shakespeare
Express' runs from July to
September 2007 from Birmingham
Snow Hill to Stratford-upon-Avon
twice daily
Special notes: Tyseley is a centre
for 'Steam on the Main Line'
railtours over a large area of the
national rail network
Membership details: Membership
is available to the public, providing
free entry to site events and four
copies of *Steam in Trust* magazine
Facilities for disabled: Disabled
access to 'Shakespeare Express'
available, but must be notified in
advance
Note: All attractions and facilities
are advertised subject to availability

Locomotives

Name	No	Origin	Class	Type	Built
Kinlet Hall	4936	GWR	'Hall'	4-6-0	1929
Pitchford Hall	4953	GWR	'Hall'	4-6-0	1929
Rood Ashton Hall	4965	GWR	'Hall'	4-6-0	1929
Nunney Castle	5029	GWR	'Castle	4-6-0	1934
Earl of Mount Edgcumbe	5043	GWR	'Castle	4-6-0	1936
Defiant†	5080	GWR	'Castle'	4-6-0	1939
Clun Castle	7029	GWR	'Castle'	4-6-0	1950
—	4110	GWR	5101	2-6-2T	1937
—	4121	GWR	5101	2-6-2T	1937
—	7752	GWR	5700	0-6-0PT	1930
—	7760	GWR	5700	0-6-0PT	1930
—	9600	GWR	5700	0-6-0PT	1945
Kolhapur§	5593	LMS	'Jubilee'	4-6-0	1934
Duchess of Hamilton	46229	LMS	'Duchess'	4-6-2	1939
—	670	LNWR*	Bloomer	2-2-2	1986
—	13029	BR	08	0-6-0DE	1953
—	20059	BR	20	Bo-Bo	1961
—	20177	BR	20	Bo-Bo	1966
—	31422	BR	31	A1A-A1A	1962
—	37264	BR	37	Co-Co	1965
Royal Oak	50017	BR	55	Co-Co	1968
Rodney	50021	BR	55	Co-Co	1968
Les Ross	86259	BR	86	Bo-Bo	1965

*replica built at Tyseley Locomotive Works
†on loan to Buckinghamshire Railway Centre
§on loan to Barrow Hill Roundhouse

Industrial locomotives

Name	No	Builder	Type	Built
Cadbury No 1	—	Avonside (1977)	0-4-0T	1925
—	1	Peckett (2004)	0-4-0ST	1942
—	—	Baguley (800)	0-4-0PE	1920

Note: Not all locomotives are on site, and some are undergoing restoration.
Contract restoration work includes Nos (GWR) 5029, (LMS) 46229 (for
streamlining), and GWR steam railmotor and industrial RSH 7289/1945;
locomotives away on loan include 5593 and *Henry* (Barrow Hill), 5080
(Buckinghamshire).

Stock
22 BR Mk 2 coaches, 3 BR Mk 1 coaches, 3 BR Mk 1 Pullman Cars,
goods and departmental vehicles, steam and diesel cranes

161

Volks Electric Railway

East Sussex

Member: HRA

In 1883 Magnus Volk opened an electric powered railway along the seafront at Brighton. It was the first 'proper' electric railway in Britain. Today it holds the deserved position of being the oldest remaining operating electric railway in the world

Manager: Stuart Strong

Headquarters: Quality of Life & Green Spaces, Brighton & Hove City Council, Kings House, Grand Avenue, Hove BN3 2LS

Office/Works: 285 Madeira Drive, Brighton BN2 1EN

Telephone:
01273 292718 (railway)

Internet address: *Web site:* www.brighton-hove.gov.uk or the Volks Electric Railway Association website: www.volkselectricrailway.co.uk

Motor cars

Nos	Type	Seats	Body	Built
3, 4	Semi-opens	40	—	1892
5	Winter car		—	1930
6, 7, 8	Semi-opens	40	—	1901
9	Open	40	—	1910
10	Open	40	—	1926

Main stations: Aquarium, Black Rock (5min walk from Marina)

Other public stations: Peter Pan's Playground

Car parks: Along the Promenade and city centre car parks

Access by public transport:
Main line trains to Brighton
Bus services: No 7 from station to Marina (every 7min) then short walk to Black Rock station; Nos 12 and 13 from Churchill Square, Nos 14 and 27 from main line station (also 77 on Sundays and weekdays during local school holidays)

Depot: Peter Pan's Playground

Length of line: Approx 1 mile, 2ft 8.5in gauge

Period of public operations:
Weekdays (11.00-17.00)
Weekends (11.00-18.00)

Facilities for disabled: Disabled toilets in Black Rock station building and 50yd from Aquarium. Disabled access to stations and trains

---

Waltham Abbey Royal Gunpowder Mills

Essex

The Royal Gunpowder Mills at Waltham Abbey are set in 175 acres of natural and peaceful parkland. It boasts 21 buildings of major historical importance

Main visitor entrance: Royal Gunpowder Mills, Beaulieu Drive, Waltham Abbey, Essex EN9 1JY

Postal address: Royal Gunpowder Mills, Powdermill Lane, Waltham Abbey, Essex EN9 1BN

Telephone: 01992 707370

Fax: 01992 707372

Internet address: *e-mail:* info@royalgunpowdermills.com

Web site: www.royalgunpowdermills.com

Car parking: Free on site

Cycle parking: Cycle shed is available to secure bicycles and motor bikes

Access by car: Just off jct 26 on M25, follow A121 towards Waltham Abbey, cross traffic lights into Beaulieu Drive

Industrial locomotives

Name	No	Builder	Type	Built
—	—*	Clayton (B3482A)	0-4-0BE	1988
—	—*	Hunslet (8828)	0-4-0BE	1988
—	—*	G/Batley (3825)	4wBE	1964
—	—†	G/Batley (6099)	2w-2DE	1964
—	—§	Avonside (1748)	0-4-0T	1916
—	—§	R/Hornsby (235624)	4wDM	1945
Carnegie	—§	Hunsley (4524)	0-4-0+0-4-0DM	1954
Woolwich	—§	Avonside (1748)	0-4-0T	1916

*2ft 6in gauge
†3ft 0in gauge
§1ft 6 in gauge

Rolling stock
Selection of wagons of the above gauges

Access by public transport:
By rail: trains from London Liverpool Street and Tottenham Hale Underground station to Waltham Cross, then 25min walk or short bus ride.

Railway enquiry line:
08457 484950
Transport for London enquiries:
020 7222 1234
By bus: 5min walk from Waltham Abbey town centre, served by

routes 21, 212, 231, 240, 250, 505 and 517. Enquiries: 0870 6082608
On site facilities: Toilets, café, baby changing. Bench-style seats and picnic tables around the site
Length of line: 2ft 6in gauge under construction
Period of public operation: Weekends and bank holidays 28 April to 7 October. Wednesdays during school summer holidays. 11.00-17.00, last entry 15.30. It is suggested that 3-4 hours are allowed for the visit
Special facilities: Guided group visits available on Tuesdays and Wednesdays by appointment, minimum group size applies. Lecture Theatre and Saltpetre House available for meetings

Facilities for disabled: A Land Train can accommodate wheelchairs (please check availability on arrival). Only guide and assistant dogs will be allowed on site, and must remain harnessed during visit
Special note: Wear comfortable walking shoes and allow 3-4 hours for a leisurely visit

Museum	Weardale Railway	Co Durham

Member: HRA

The line was originally built by the Stockton & Darlington Railway in 1847 to transport limestone to the ironworks of Teesside, and by 1895 had been extended to its final terminus of Wearhead. Although the passenger service was withdrawn in 1953, the line was retained for freight use transporting bulk cement from the Blue Circle works at Eastgate. This use also ceased in 1993, so the line was mothballed and threatened with lifting. 1993 saw the formation of the Weardale Railway with services re-commencing in 2004. Financial difficulties towards the end of 2004 saw the railway service suspended. A new company was formed in 2006 and passenger services re-commenced from August 2006

Administrative Manager: Trevor Hewitt
Headquarters: Weardale Railways Ltd, Stanhope Station, Station Road, Stanhope, Bishop Auckland, Co Durham DL13 2YS
Telephone: 0845 600 1348
Internet addresses: *e-mail:* info@weardale-railway.org.uk
Web site: www.weardale-railway.org.uk
Main stations: Wolsingham and Stanhope
Other public stations: Frosterley

Locomotives and multiple-units

Name	No	Origin	Class	Type	Built
—	20107	BR	20	Bo-Bo	1961
—	37003	BR	37	Co-Co	1960
—	37175	BR	37	Co-Co	1963
—	37275	BR	37	Co-Co	1965
—	37414	BR	37	Co-Co	1965
—	55503	BR	141	DMS	1984
—	55510	BR	141	DMS	1984
—	55523	BR	141	DMSL	1984
—	55530	BR	141	DMSL	1984

Industrial locomotives

Name	No	Builder	Type	Built
—	3809	Hunslet (3809)	0-6-0ST	1953
—	7412	RSH	0-6-0ST	1948
—	7765	RSH (7765)	0-6-0T	1954

Car park: Limited parking at each station
Access by public transport: Buses from Bishop Auckland and Crook daily. Main line station at Bishop Auckland
Refreshment facilities: Stanhope (the Signal Box Café) in station building with light refreshments
Souvenir shop: Stanhope (in station building)
Depot: Wolsingham (no public access)
Length of line: Present length in 5.5 miles, Wolsingham to Stanhope. 18.5 miles when fully opened, Bishop Auckland to Eastgate

Period of public operation: A mixture of weekends and daily service throughout the year. For full details telephone or access web site as above
Special events: Several planned — Mother's Day, Father's Day, Commercial Vehicle Rally, Military Vehicle Trust Rally, Transport Festival, Halloween Special and Santa Specials
Membership details: Mr Frank Holmes, Membership Secretary, Weardale Railway Trust, at above address. Tel: 01388 526262
Membership journal: *Between the Lines* — quarterly

Wells & Walsingham Light Railway

Timetable Service — **Norfolk**

Member: HRA, TT

One man's railway, the life and love of retired naval commander, Roy Francis, this delightful line which is totally uncommercialised runs along the old Wells branch to Walsingham where the old station has been transformed into a Russian Orthodox Church by the addition of an onion-shaped dome to its roof. A must if you find yourself nearby

Location: On A149, Stiffkey Road, Wells next the Sea, Norfolk

General Manager: Lt-Cdr R. W. Francis

Operating organisation: Wells & Walsingham Light Railway, Wells next the Sea, Norfolk NR23 1RB

Enquiries: 01328 711630

Car park: Yes

Access by public transport: Eastern Counties buses

On site facilities: Souvenir shop, toilets and tea shop

Length of line: 4 miles, 10.25in gauge

Public opening: Daily Good Friday to the end of October

Special notes: Journey may be commenced at either end. Believed to be the world's longest 10.25in gauge line. Built on the old Wells & Fakenham Railway trackbed. Old Swainsthorpe signalbox on site at Wells. Motive power is provided by a Garratt and a tram locomotive.

Life passes in the form of a gilt edged enamel medallion now available, please enquire for details

Facilities for disabled: Disabled can be seated in normal carriages and wheelchairs carried in luggage van. Occupied wheelchairs cannot be carried due to limitations of track gauge

Membership details: Membership Secretary, Wells & Walsingham Light Railway Support Group, c/o above address

Membership journal: Newsletter — quarterly

Wensleydale Railway

Timetable Service — **North Yorkshire**

Member: HRA

The Wensleydale Railway Association was formed in 1990 with a view to restoring the route from Northallerton to Garsdale. In 2000 agreement was reached to transfer the remaining 22 miles of line from Northallerton to Redmire to Wensleydale Railway plc. In 2003 services started between Leeming Bar and Leyburn, extending in 2004 to Redmire (17 miles). Medium term plans are to extend eastwards to Northallerton and in the west from Redmire and then on towards Aysgarth. The ultimate aim is to restore the entire route from Northallerton to Garsdale

Contact address:
Wensleydale Railway plc, Leeming Bar Station, Leases Road, Leeming Bar, Northallerton DL7 9AR

Ticketline: 08454 505474

Fax: 01677 776240

Internet addresses: *e-mail:* admin@wensleydalerailway.com

Web site: www.wensleydalerailway.com

Main stations: Leeming Bar and Leyburn

Locomotives and multiple-units

Name	No	Origin	Class	Type	Built
Western Waggoner	03114	BR	03	0-6-0DM	1961
—	31166	BR	31	A1A-A1A	1960
—	31188	BR	31	A1A-A1A	1960
—	51210	BR	101	DMBS	1958
—	51247	BR	101	DMBS	1958
—	53746	BR	101	DMC	1957
—	59500	BR	117	TSL	1959
—	59509	BR	117	TSL	1959
—	51813	BRCW	110	DMBC	1961
—	51842	BRCW	110	DMCL	1961
—	59701	BRCW	110	TSL	1961

Industrial locomotives

Name	No	Builder	Type	Built
Wensley	—	R/Hornsby (476141)	4wDM	1963

Owners

Class 31s Colne Valley Diesels
Class 101 and 117 Wensleydale Railway plc
Class 110 Allan Schofield
R/Hornsby the Wensleydale Railway Association
03144 the UK Government

Other stations: Bedale, Finghall and Redmire

Car Parking: On site

Access by public transport: Yes

Refreshment facilities: Leeming Bar and Leyburn

Souvenir shops: Leeming Bar and Leyburn

Depots: Leeming Bar

Length of line: 22 miles;

164

(18 additional miles to rebuild)
Passenger trains: See above
Period of public operation:
Daily Easter to autumn, and winter
weekends. Also Santa Special.
Phone ticketline for current
brochure 08454 505474 or see web
site
Special events: Day out with
Thomas — 9/10 June, 20/21
October

Facilities for disabled:
Ramp to facilitate access to trains.
All platforms are wheelchair
friendly. No disabled toilets
Membership details:
Wensleydale Railway Association:
c/o above address
Membership journal:
Relay – 3 per year.
Special notes: Very helpful tourist
information centre at Leyburn – tel

01969 623069 – will deal with a
wide range of enquiries including
Wensleydale Railway matters

West Lancashire Light Railway

Member: HRA
The WLLR is located in the village
of Hesketh Bank, midway between
Preston and Southport. Built by
enthusiasts in 1967 in an endeavour
to conserve some of the mainly
industrial equipment that was fast
disappearing. The railway serves as
a working museum for a variety of
historic locomotives and other
railway equipment from industrial
sites from Britain and overseas
Location: Alty's Brickworks,
Station Road, Hesketh Bank, Nr
Preston, Lancashire PR4 6SP
OS reference: SD 448229
Operating society/organisation:
The West Lancashire Light Railway
Association, Secretary, 8 Croft
Avenue, Orrell, Wigan, Lancs WN5
8TW
Telephone: (01772) 815881
Railway (24hr) or (01695) 622654
Secretary (evenings)
Internet address:
e-mail: sec@westlancs.org
Web site: www.westlancs.org
Car parks: On site
Access by public transport: Main
line rail to Preston or Southport.
Bus route — service 2, between
Preston and Southport
On site facilities: Gift shop, light
refreshments, picnic tables, 2ft
gauge line
Public opening: Steam trains
commence 1 April and then operate
every Sunday to 28 October.
Opening times 12.30-17.30

Industrial locomotives

Name	No	Builder	Type	Built
Clwyd	1	R/Hornsby (264251)	4wDM	1951
Tawd	2	R/Hornsby (222074)	4wDM	1943
Irish Mail	3	Hunslet (823)	0-4-0ST	1903
Bradfield	4	Hibberd (1777)	4wPM	1931
—	5	R/Hornsby (200478)	4wDM	1940
—	7	M/Rail (8992)	4wDM	1946
Pathfinder	8	H/Hunslet (4480)	4wDM	1953
Joffre	9	K/Stuart (2405)	0-6-0T	1915
—	10	Hibberd (2555)	4wDM	1946
—	11	M/Rail (5906)	4wDM	1934
—	16	R/Hornsby (202036)	4wDM	1941
—	19	Lister (10805)	4wPM	1939
—	20	Baguley (3002)	4wPM	1937
—	21	H/Hunslet (1963)	4wDM	1939
—	25	R/Hornsby (297054)	4wDM	1950
—	26	M/Rail (11223)	4wDM	1963
Mill Reef	27	M/Rail (7371)	4wDM	1939
—	30	M/Rail (11258)	4wDM	1964
Montalban	34	O&K (6641)	0-4-0WT	1913
Utrillas	35	O&K (2378)	0-4-0WT	1907
—	36	R/Hornsby (339105)	4wDM	1953
—	38	Hudswell (D750)	0-4-0DM	1949
—	39	Hibberd (3916)	4wDM	1959
—	40	R/Hornsby (381705)	4wDM	1959
—	41	Lister (29890)	4wPM	1946
—	43	Greenbat (1840)	4wBE	1942
Welsh Pony	44	Wingrove (640)	4wWE	1926
—	45	Chrzanow (3506)	0-6-0T+WT	1957
Stanhope	46	K/Stuart (2395)	0-4-2ST	1917
—	47	Henschel (14676)	0-8-0T	1917
—	48	Fowler (15513)	0-4-2T	1920

Stock
Toastrack coach built 1986 by WLLR
Semi-open coach built 1993 by WLLR
Brake van built 1987 by WLLR
Large collection of goods rolling stock

West Somerset Railway

Special events: Friendly Engines Day — 1 April; Easter — Good Friday (6 April) Easter Sunday and Monday (8/9 April); Teddy Bears' Day — 13 May; Gala Weekend — 11/12 August, Autumn Gala — 7 October; Santa Specials — 16, 22/23 December. A Children-in-Need will also be held on a date to be confirmed

Membership details: The Hon Secretary, WLLR, Station Road, Hesketh Bank, Nr Preston, Lancashire PR4 6SP

Member: HRA, TT

Running for 20 miles, the WSR is Britain's longest standard gauge heritage line and superbly captures the secondary main line atmosphere of the great age of steam. There are many points of railway interest. Williton signalbox is the only working example built by the Bristol & Exeter Railway and Blue Anchor box still controls a traditionally operated level crossing. Destinations served include the historic port of Watchet and medieval Dunster with its castle

General Manager: Paul Conibeare

Headquarters: West Somerset Railway, The Railway Station, Minehead, Somerset TA24 5BG

Telephone:
Minehead (01643) 704996

Internet address: *e-mail:*
info@west-somerset-railway.co.uk
Web site:
www.west-somerset-railway.co.uk
WAP-phone:
www.wapdrive.com/wsrwap/

Main station: Minehead

Other public stations: Dunster, Blue Anchor, Washford, Watchet, Williton, Doniford Halt, Stogumber, Crowcombe, Bishops Lydeard

OS reference: Minehead SS 975463, Williton ST 085416, Bishops Lydeard ST 164290

Car parks: Free parking at Bishops Lydeard, Crowcombe Heathfield, Stogumber, Williton and Dunster. Pay & display at Minehead and Watchet. No parking at Doniford Halt

Access by public transport:

Locomotives and multiple-units

Name	No	Origin	Class	Type	Built
—	88	S&DJR	7F	2-8-0	1925
—	3850	GWR	2884	2-8-0	1942
—	4160	GWR	5101	2-6-2T	1948
—	4561	GWR	4500	2-6-2T	1924
—	9351	GWR	9351	2-6-0	2004
—	5542†	GWR	4575	2-6-2T	1928
—	6412	GWR	6400	0-6-0PT	1934
Dinmore Manor	7820	GWR	'Manor'	4-6-0	1950
Odney Manor	7828	GWR	'Manor'	4-6-0	1950
Braunton	34046	SR	WC	4-6-2	1946
—	80136	BR	4MT	2-6-4T	1956
—	D2119	BR	03	0-6-0DM	1959
—	D2133	BR	03	0-6-0DM	1959
—	D2271	BR	04	0-6-0DM	1952
—	D3462	BR	08	0-6-0DE	1957
—	D9526	BR	14	0-6-0DH	1964
—	25173	BR	25	Bo-Bo	1963
—	D6566	BR	33	Bo-Bo	1961
—	*33057	BR	33	Bo-Bo	1961
—	D7017	BR	35	B-B	1962
—	D7018	BR	35	B-B	1962
Western Campaigner	D1010	BR	52	C-C	1962
—	51663	BR	115	DMBS	1960
—	51852	BR	115	DMBS	1960
—	51859	BR	115	DMBS	1960
—	51880	BR	115	DMBS	1960
—	51887	BR	115	DMBS	1960
—	59506	BR	117	TC	1960
—	59678	BR	115	TC	1960

Note: 9351 rebuilt from '5151' class 2-6-2T No 5193
*for spares reclamation
†on South Devon Railway during 2007

Industrial locomotives

Name	No	Builder	Type	Built
Isabel	—	H/Leslie (3437)	0-6-0ST	1919
Kilmersdon	—	Peckett (1788)	0-4-0ST	1929
—	24	Ruston (210479)	4wDM	1941
—	—	Ruston (183062)	4wDM	1937
—	16	Sentinel (10175)	0-6-0DH	1964

166

Nearest main line station, Taunton. Dedicated bus link to WSR, plus First Bus services 28 and 28A
Refreshment facilities: Minehead, Bishops Lydeard (limited opening). Dining trains from Bishops Lydeard (01823 433856). Please contact for dates, reservations essential.
Buffet car on most steam trains
Souvenir shops: Large shops at Bishops Lydeard (01823 432125) and Minehead (01643 700387). Sales counters at other stations except Doniford Halt. 'Readers Halt' second-hand stall at Minehead
Museum: Somerset & Dorset Railway Museum Trust, Washford (contact 01984 640869 for opening times). GWR Museum at Blue Anchor (open Sundays and Bank Holidays during main WSR operating season plus Gala events). Gauge Museum at Bishops Lydeard (open daily). Diesel Heritage Visitor Centre open Saturdays May-September, plus during Gala events
Depots: Bishops Lydeard, Williton, Washford, Minehead
Length of line: 20 miles

Stock
23 ex-BR Mk 1 coaches; 2 ex-BR Restaurant cars; 1 ex-BR Sleeping car; 3 ex-S&DJR 6-wheel coaches, 7 ex-GWR camping coaches; 1 ex-GWR Sleeping coach; 1 ex-GWR 5-ton hand crane; more than 40 freight vehicles.
*a return of some of these ex-GWR Toplight coaches to form a working vintage train is being planned by the West Somerset Steam Railway Trust. Details from Williton Station, Somerset TA4 4RQ

Owners
88, *Isabel, Kilmersdon* the Somerset & Dorset Museum Trust
D1010, D7017, D7018 and D9526 the Diesel and Electric Preservation Group
D2119, D3462 and D7523 Dr John F. Kennedy
5542 the 5542 Ltd
3850 and 7820 the Dinmore Manor Locomotive Ltd
4160 the 4160 Ltd
7828, 9351 and D2271 the WSR plc

Passenger trains: Steam and diesel trains to Bishops Lydeard

Period of public operation: 3/4, 10/11, 17/18, 20-25, 27-29, 31, March; daily April (EXCEPT 16, 20, 23, 27); daily May (EXCEPT 4, 11, 14, 18, 21); daily in June, July, August and September; daily October (EXCEPT 8, 12, 15, 19); 1 November; 27 December-2 January 2008

Main special events: Spring Steam Gala — 17/18, 22-25 March (advance booking strongly recommended); Mixed Traffic Gala — 15-17 June (advance booking recommended); Days out with Thomas — 7/8 July; Steam Fayre & Vintage Rally at Bishops Lydeard — 4/5 August; Toy Trains and Collectors' Fair — 5 August; CAMRA Real Ale Festival at Minehead — 15/16 September (advance booking recommended); Autumn Steam Gala — 4-7 October

(advance booking strongly recommended); Somerset in Autumn — 27/28 October (advance booking recommended); Santa Specials — 1/2, 8/9, 15/16, 22-24 December (advance booking essential); Dunster by Candlelight — 7/8 December (advance booking essential) ; Carol Trains — 17/18 December (advance booking essential) ; Winter Steam Festival — 29 December

Other special events: Cream Tea Specials — Friday afternoons 25 May to 28 September (except 15 June); Fish & Chip Specials — 5 May, 9 June, 29 September ; Walking Week — 13-20 May; Jazz on a late Spring Evening — 26 May; A Midsummer Nights Murder — 23 June; Swing Night — 28 July; Murder Mystery Train — 8 September; Cream, Steam and Carnage — 14 October; Halloween Murder Mystery — 27 October.

Advance booking essential for most of the above. Ring 01643 704996 or see web site for avaiability

Facilities for disabled: Trains have limited accommodation for passengers in wheelchairs. There is level or ramped access to all stations except Doniford, and RADAR key access toilets at Bishops Lydeard and Minehead. Advance booking essential for groups

Special facilities: Conference room in Gauge Museum at Bishops Lydeard (details 01643 433856); Steam footplate experience courses (01643 700398)

Membership details: West Somerset Railway Association, The Railway Station, Bishops Lydeard, Taunton TA4 3BX. Tel: 01823 433856

Membership journal: *WSR Journal* — quarterly

| Museum | Winchcombe Railway Museum | Glos |

One mile from Winchcombe station on the Gloucestershire Warwickshire railway, the diverse collection includes signalling equipment, lineside fixtures, horse-drawn road vehicles, tickets, lamps, etc. Indoor and outdoor displays set in half an acre of traditional Victorian Cotswold garden. Visitors are encouraged to touch and operate exhibits

Location: 23 Gloucester Street, Winchcombe, Gloucestershire

OS reference: SP 023283

Operating society/organisation: Winchcombe Railway Museum Association, 23 Gloucester Street, Winchcombe, Gloucestershire

Telephone: Winchcombe (01242) 609305

Car park: On street at entrance

Access by public transport: Bus service from Cheltenham operated by Castleways Ltd

On site facilities: Relics and souvenir shop

Public opening: Easter to end October 2007. Wednesdays, Thursdays, Fridays, weekends and Bank Holiday Mondays — 13.30-17.00; daily throughout August, 13.30-17.00

Facilities for disabled: Access to all parts except toilets

Special notes: Many visitor-operated exhibits, picnic area, pet animals

Steam Centre — Windmill Farm Railway — Lancashire

The line was set up in 1997 by Austin Moss as a place to store and operate the historic engines and rolling stock he had collected. Of particular interest is the collection of ex-Fairbourne Railway locomotives and rolling stock; these include *Katie* and *Whippet Quick*.

Location: Situated within the grounds of Windmill Animal Farm
Headquarters: Windmill Animal Farm, Red Cat Lane, Burscough, L40 1UQ
Contact: Austin Moss
Telephone: Farm 01704 892282; Austin Moss 07971 221343;
Internet address: *Web site:* www.windmillfarmrailway.co.uk
Main station: At Farm
Other station: Lakeview, 1/2 mile away
Car parking: On site
Access by public transport: None
On site facilities: Farm café, shop
Depots: At farm site
Length of line: 1/2 mile each way (1 mile return) 15in gauge
Period of public operation: 14 February to Christmas 10.00-17.00. Weekends March to

Industrial locomotives

Name	No	Builder	Type	Built
Blue Pacific	4	Guinness	4-6-0VB	1935
Whippet Quick	–	Lister	4w-4DM	1935
Gwril	–	Lister	4wPM	1943
Princess Anne	—	Barlow	4-6w-2DE	1948
Duke of Edinburgh	—	Barlow	4-6-2	1950
Prince Charles	—	Barlow	4-6-2	1950
Katie	—	Guest	2-4-2	1953
Siân	—	Guest	2-4-2	1963
Connie	–	Severn-Lamb	2-8-0DH	1974
Neptune / (St Nicholas)	–	Severn-Lamb	2-8-0GH	1978
–	14	Walker	2w-2PM	1985
City Of London Jubilee	2870	Volante	4-6-0DH	1987
'The Bar Stool'	—	Moss	2w-2PM	1989
St Christopher	—	Exmoor	2-6-2T	2001

December. Daily Easter to end of September plus school holidays. Santa weekends in December, Daily June to September plus school holidays
Trains every 1/2 hour from 11.00 until 16.30
Special events: None planned but see web site
Facilities for disabled:

Accessibility for wheelchairs around farm facilities etc, prior warning on railway
Membership details: No membership as such, just volunteer. Contact Austin Moss for details
Fare: £1.00 adults, 75p children plus farm entry fee.

Timetable Service — Wirral Transport Museum — Merseyside

The museum and tramway are owned by Wirral Borough Council and run by employees assisted by volunteers. The tramway licence is also held by the council as are two Hong Kong-built 4-wheel trams. The museum houses several locally rebuilt trams owned by the Merseyside Tramway Preservation Society which are used in turn with the Hong Kong trams. The museum also contains numerous local buses, cars, lorries, motorbikes, etc, and a 1930s garage scene.

Location/Headquarters: Wirral Transport Museum, 1 Taylor Street, Birkenhead, Wirral CH45 8NX
Telephone: 0151 647 2128
Fax: As above, but must ring first
Internet address: *e-mail:*

Trams

No	Trucks	Builder	Date
69		Homg Komg	1992
70		Homg Komg	1992

birkenheadtram@tiscali.co.uk
Web site: www.wirraltransportmuseum.org
Car parking: Pay & display at Woodside Ferry, limited free parking in local roads
Access by public transport: Merseyrail stations at Hamilton Square (0.25 miles from Woodside Ferry) and Conway Park (0.5 miles from museum) with services from Liverpool Lime Street and Chester. Bus stations at Woodside Ferry (25 metres) and Birkenhead town centre

(half mile)
On site facilities: Model shop (limited opening) in museum, along with Merseyside Tramway Preservation Society (open Sundays when trams are operating). Gift shop at Woodside Ferry Terminal
Depots: Wirral Transport Museum/depot across Old Colonial pub car park
Length of line: 0.7 mile (c1km) of standard gauge. Woodside Ferry Terminal via Pacific Road to Old Colonial tramstop

Refreshments:
None on site, but several pubs and cafés around Chester Street and Hamilton Square.
Period of public operation:
Most weekends, Wednesday to Sunday during school holidays, all bank holidays.
Half hour service operates from both ends —13.00-17.00

Special events: Annual Bus & Tram Show — 1st Sunday in October; Merseyside Model Railway Show — last weekend in October
Special facilities: Tram rides and tours for school parties, midweek and weekends (ring Ernie Ruffler 0151 666 4000)
Facilities for disabled: Access to

both levels in museum. Audio visual display for those unable to travel on the trams. No toilet facilities in museum, but places with toilets close to tramway

Railway Centre | Yeovil Railway Centre | Somerset

Member: HRA

The Yeovil Railway Centre is operated by the South West Main Line Steam Co and is adjacent to the former London & South Western Railway main line at Yeovil Junction. It features the original British Railways turntable

Location: Adjacent to the main line at Yeovil Junction on the London (Waterloo)-Salisbury-Exeter line

Chaiman: Richard Abbott

Contact address: South Western Main Line Steam Co (Yeovil Railway Centre), Yeovil Junction Station, Stoford, Nr Yeovil, Somerset BA22 9UU

Telephone: 01935 410420

Fax: 01935 478373

Internet address: *Web site:* www.yeovilrailway.free servers.com

Car park: On site. Follow signs to Yeovil Junction from Yeovil town centre or from A35 Dorchester-Yeovil road

Access by public transport: SouthWest Trains to Yeovil Junction or bus from Yeovil Bus station

On site facilities: Exhibition of relics and photographs in the newly acquired transfer shed (dating from 1864) and shop. Light refreshments

Locomotive

Name	No	Origin	Class	Type	Built
Fearless	50050	BR	50	Co-Co	1967

Industrial locomotive

Name	No	Builder	Type	Built
Pectin	—	Peckett (1579)	0-4-0ST	1921
—	—	Fowler (22900)	0-4-0DM	1941
Cockney Rebel	—	Fowler (4000007)	0-4-0DM	1947
Yeo	DS1174	R/Hornsby (458959)	4wDM	1961

Locomotive notes: Main line locomotives occasionally present for servicing during railtours

Rolling stock: Selection of freight wagons

when brake van rides are operating

Length of line: 500 metres

Opening times: Shop open Sunday mornings throughout the year (except Christmas/New Year). Train Days run from April to September (see web site or telephone for dates and times). Brake van rides, shunting and turntable demonstrations feature. Also open on days when main line steam is being serviced (telephone or see web site for details), for Santa Specials in December and special events

Special facilities: Transfer shed

available for wedding receptions, parties, shows, etc (train hire can be arranged)

Disabled access: To site, but no wheelchair access (at present) to brake van rides

Membership details: Quentin McConnell, High Croft, Yeovil Junction, Stoford, Somerset BA22 9UU

Membership journal: *The Turntable*, quarterly

England

Scotland

The Alford Valley Railway operates from the restored station yard which once marked the terminus of the branch line linking the villages of upper Donside with Kintore Junction, thence to Aberdeen

Location: On A944, 25 miles west of Aberdeen, adjacent to Grampian Transport Museum

Headquarters: Alford Valley Railway Co Ltd, Alford Station, Alford, Aberdeenshire

Internet adress: *Web site:* www.alford.org.uk/avr.htm

Main station: Alford

Car park: On site

Length of line: 3km, 2ft gauge

Museum: Grampian Transport Museum adjacent

Depot: Alford station

Period of public operation: Railway operates: April, May and September — weekends only (13.00-17.00); June — Monday to Friday (10.30-14.30), Saturdays and Sundays (13.30-16.30); July and August — daily 13.00-17.00. Trains run every half hour during these times. Seasonal tickets available. Alford Heritage Centre is open daily (10.00-17.00)

Special events: Easter Fayre, Santa Specials — please contact for details

Membership details: Membership Secretary, AVR Association, Creagmwor, Main Street, Alford, Aberdeenshire AB33 8AD

Industrial locomotives

Name	No	Builder	Type	Built
Hamewith	—	Lister (3198)	4wDM	c1930
—	—	A/Keef (63)	4wDM	2001
—	—	M/Rail (22129)	4wDM	1962
—	—	M/Rail (2221)	4wDM	1964
James Gordon	—	Keef (63)	0-4-0T (SO)	2001
Aberdeen Corporation Gas Works	3*	A/Barclay (1889)	0-4-0ST	1926

*standard gauge

Rolling stock

Two 24-seat coaches, 50-seat coach, 24-seat ex-Aberdeen tramcar, various wagons

Member: HRA

Part of a wide-ranging heritage centre containing a museum of Scotland's shale oil industry with award winning children's exhibits, working watermill, farmsteading with traditional livestock. indoor play areas, countryside walks and farmhouse kitchen tea room.

Operating society/organisation: Almond Valley Heritage Centre, Millfield, Livingston Village, West Lothian EH54 7AR

OS reference: NT 034667

Telephone: 01506 414957

Fax: 01506 497771

Industrial locomotives

Name	No	Builder	Type	Built
05/576	—	Barclay (557)	4wDH	1970
Oil Company No 2	—	Baldwin (20587)	4wWE	1902
—	20	Brook Victor (612)	4wBE	1972
—	38	Brook Victor (698)	4wBE	1972
—	42	Brook Victor (700)	4wBE	1972
—	—	Brook Victor (1143)	4wBE	1972
3585	13	Greenwood (1698)	4wBE	1940
ND3059	Yard No B10	Hunslet (2270)	0-4-0DM	1940
—	7330	Hunslet (7330)	4wDM	1973
—	—	Simplex (40SPF522)	4wDM	1981
—	—	B/Drewry (3752)	4wDM	1980

Note

Barclay 557 and Hunslet 2270 operate passenger services

Bo'ness & Kinneil Railway

West Lothian

Internet address: *e-mail:* info@almondvalley.co.uk
Web site: www.almondvalley.co.uk
Access by public transport: Main line trains to Livingston North (1 mile)
On site facilities: Children's exhibits, indoor play areas, tea room

Public opening: Daily (except 25/26 December, 1/2 January) 10.00-17.00.
Trains operate weekends from March-September, daily July and August and certain public holidays
Length of line: 500m 2ft 6in gauge

line from Livingston Mill to Almondhaugh stations, with plans to extend
Facilities for disabled: Full disabled access to site, but not to coaches

Member: HRA, TT, Registered Museum
Historic railway buildings, including the station and train shed, have been relocated from sites all over Scotland. In two purpose-built exhibition halls, the Scottish Railway Exhibition tells the story of the development of the railways in Scotland, and their impact on the people. The rich geology of the area, with its 300 million year old fossils, is explained during a conducted tour of the caverns of the former Birkhill Fireclay Mine
Operating society/location: Scottish Railway Preservation Society, Bo'ness Station, Union Street, Bo'ness, West Lothian, EH51 9AQ
Access by public transport: Nearest ScotRail station — Linlithgow. Bus services from Linlithgow, Falkirk, Stirling
OS reference: NT 003817
Telephone: Train services & Events 01506 825855
Talking timetable: 01506 822298
Fax: 01506 828766
Internet address: *e-mail:* enquiries@srps.org.uk
Web site: www.srps.org.uk
Main station: Bo'ness
Other station: Birkhill
Car parks: At Bo'ness and Birkhill (free)
Refreshment facilities: Extensive (unlicensed) buffet at Bo'ness. Picnic tables at both stations
Souvenir shop: Bo'ness
Depot: Bo'ness
Length of line: 3.5 miles
Period of public operation: Weekends 31 March to 30 October, Tuesdays 5 June to 26 June, daily 30 June to 26 August (Mondays in

Locomotives

Name	No	Origin	Class	Type	Built
—	419	CR	439	0-4-4T	1908
Morayshire	246	LNER	D49	4-4-0	1928
Glen Douglas	256	NBR	D34	4-4-0	1913
—	42	NBR	Y9	0-4-0ST	1887
Maude	673	NBR	J36	0-6-0	1891
—	80105	BR	4MT	2-6-4T	1955
—	D2774	BR	—	0-4-0DH	1960
—	08443 (D3558)	BR	08	0-6-0DE	1958
—	D8020	BR	20	Bo-Bo	1959
—	25235 (D7585)	BR	25	Bo-Bo	1965
—	25309 (D7659)	BR	25	Bo-Bo	1966
—	26004 (D5303)	BR	26	B0-Bo	1958
—	26024 (D5323)	BR	26	Bo-Bo	1959
—	27001 (D5347)	BR	27	Bo-Bo	1961
—	D5351	BR	27	Bo-Bo	1961
—	37025	BR	37	Co-Co	1961
—	47643	BR	47	Co-Co	1968
—	51017*	BR	126	DMS	1959
—	51043	BR	126	DMS	1959
—	59404	BR	126	TC	1959
—	79443	BR	126	TRBF	1956

*at Midland Railway — Butterley for restoration

Industrial locomotives

Name	No	Builder	Type	Built
Clydesmill	3	Barclay (1937)	0-4-0ST	1928
—	3	Barclay (2046)	0-4-0ST	1937
—	24	Barclay (2335)	0-6-0T	1953
Texaco	—†	Fowler (4210140)	0-4-0DM	1958
(Lord King)	—	H/Leslie (3640)	0-4-0ST	1926
—	19	Hunslet (3818)	0-6-0ST	1954
DS3	—	R/Hornsby (275883)	4wDM	1949
DS4	P6687	R/Hornsby (312984)	0-4-0DE	1951
(Ranald)	—	Sentinel (9627)	4wVBT	1957
—	970214	Wickham (6050)	2w-2PMR	c1951
—	—	Matisa (48626)	—	—
—	5	Hunslet (3837)	0-6-0ST	1955
—	(7)	Bagnall (2777)	0-6-0ST	1945
Borrowstounness	—*	Barclay (840)	0-4-0T	1899
—	—*	M/Rail (110U082)	4wDH	1970
—	—	Wickham (10482)	2w-2PMR	1970
—	(17)	Hunslet (2880)	0-6-0ST	1943
—	970213	Wickham (6049)	2w-2PMR	c1951
—	17†	Barclay (2296)	0-4-0ST	1952

172

July diesel-hauled)

Special events: Easter Egg Specials — 6-9 April; Diesel Gala — 28/29 April; Day out with Thomas — 19-21 May; Transport Through The Ages — 17 June; Day out with Thomas — 10-12 August; Diesel Gala — 29/30 September; Day out with Thomas — 15/16 October; Steam 'n' Scream — 28/29 October; Santa Specials — 1/2, 8/9, 15/16, 22/23 December; Black Bun Specials — 30/31 December

Special facilities: Private trains can be hired. Available for weddings

Facilities for disabled: Disabled access to platform and a specially adapted carriage for wheelchair users. Toilets at Bo'ness station. No facilities for wheelchairs at Birkhill Fireclay Mine

Special notes: Two large museum buildings: Fireclay Mine at Birkhill (both open same days as trains operate, except December)

Name	No	Builder	Type	Built
Lady Victoria	3	Barclay (1458)	0-6-0ST	1916
The Wemyss Coal Co Ltd	20	Barclay (2068)	0-6-0T	1939
—	(6)	Barclay (2127)	0-4-0CT	1942
No 1	—	Barclay (343)	0-6-0DM	1941
City of Aberdeen	—**	B/Hawthorn (912)	0-4-0ST	1887
F82 (Fairfield)	—	E/Electric (1131) (244)	4wBE	1940
Kelton Fell	13	Neilson (2203)	0-4-0ST	1876
Lord Roberts	1§	N/Reid (5710)	0-6-0T	1902
(Tiger)	—	N/British (27415)	0-4-0DH	1954
Kilbagie	DS2	R/Hornsby (262998)	4wDM	1949
—	—	R/Hornsby (321733)	4wDM	1952
DS6	(1)	R/Hornsby (421439)	0-4-0DE	1958
St Mirren	(3)	R/Hornsby (423658)	0-4-0DE	1958
—	D88/003	R/Hornsby (506500)	4wDM	1965
(Denis)	—	Sentinel (9631)	4wVBT	1958
—	—	Arrols (Glasgow)	2w-2DM	c1966

*3ft 0in gauge
**on loan to Tanfield Railway
†at present off site at Scottish Vintage Bus Museum, Lathalmond, Fife
§official licensed 'Thomas' replica locomotive

Stock
A large selection of coaching stock, many built by Scottish pre-Grouping companies, ex-BR Class 126 DMU, and an appropriate collection of early freight vehicles

Owners
80105 and (Denis) the Locomotive Owners Group (Scotland)
246 and 24 the Museum of Scotland
256 the Glasgow Museum of Transport
27001 the Class 27 Preservation Group
26004 and 26024 the 6LDA Group
37025 the Scottish Class 37 Group

Timetable Service	Caledonian Railway (Brechin)	Angus

Member: HRA

This Scottish country steam railway is a classic branch line starting at the Strathmore line junction station of Bridge of Dun, last stomping ground of the Gresley 'A4' Pacific locomotives, and climbs some steep gradients through scenic farmland with assorted wildlife and flora. The summit is reached at the Edzell & Forfar junction just short of Brechin station, itself one of the most impressive of Britain's preserved railways.

The National Trust for Scotland property House of Dun, built by William Adam in 1730, is approximately 1 mile from Bridge

Locomotives

Name	No	Origin	Class	Type	Built
Brechin City	D3059	BR	08	0-6-0DE	1954
*—	12052	BR	11	0-6-0DE	1949
*—	12093	BR	11	0-6-0DE	1951
—	25072	BR	25	Bo-Bo	1963
—	25083	BR	25	Bo-Bo	1963
—	D5314	BR	26	Bo-Bo	1959
—	26035	BR	26	Bo-Bo	1959
—	27024	BR	27	Bo-Bo	1962
Loch Joy	37097	BR	37	Co-Co	1962

*on loan from Scottish Industrial Railway Centre

Industrial locomotives

Name	No	Builder	Type	Built
—†	—	Barclay (1863)	0-4-0ST	1926
Harlaxton†	—	Barclay (2107)	0-6-0T	1941
BAC No 1	—	Peckett (1376)	0-4-0ST	1915
Menelaus	—	Peckett (1889)	0-6-0ST	1935

of Dun station, which is also close to the Montrose Basin, a tidal wildlife centre. Brechin itself has many attractions including the cathedral and round tower and the new Pictavia centre.

The railway is run entirely by volunteer members of the Brechin Railway Preservation Society

Headquarters: Caledonian Railway (Brechin) Ltd, The Station, 2 Park Road, Brechin, Angus DD9 7AF

Telephone: 01356 622992 (or 07740 363958)

Internet address: *e-mail:* calrail@engineer.com
Web site: www.caledonianrailway.co.uk

Main stations: Brechin and Bridge of Dun

OS reference: NO 603603

Car park: Brechin, Bridge of Dun

Access by car: Via A90 Dundee/Aberdeen to Brechin bypass. Brown tourist signs to stations. Free parking

Access by public transport: By ScotRail, GNER and Virgin services to Montrose (5 miles). By bus from Montrose, Strathtay Scottish — Dundee (01382) 228054/227201

Refreshment facilities: Light refreshments at Brechin on operating days

Picnic area: Bridge of Dun

Souvenir shop: Brechin

Museum: Brechin

Length of line: 4 miles 22 chains

Depot: Brechin

Passenger trains: Industrial steam and heritage diesel-hauled trains between Brechin and Bridge of Dun

Period of public operation: Trains run every Sunday 5 May to 15 September plus other dates as shown below. Brechin station is open daily for static viewing Tuesday-Friday 11.00-16.00, Bridge of Dun site open daily all week

Special events: Easter Specials — 7/8 April; Sulzerfest Diesel Gala — 5-7 May; Father's Day — 17 June; Day out with Thomas — 7/8, 14/15 July; A Murder on the Brechin

Name	No	Builder	Type	Built
FC Tingey†	—	Peckett (2084)	0-6-0ST	1948
—	5	Peckett (2153)	0-6-0ST	1954
Diana	1	Hunslet (2879)	0-6-0ST	1943
—	6	Bagnall (2749)	0-6-0ST	1944
—	16	Bagnall (2759)	0-6-0ST	1944
—	—	Hibberd (5198)	4wDM	1955
—	144-6	R/Hornsby (421700)	4wDM	1959
Dewar Highlander†	—	R/Hornsby (458957)	4wDM	1961

†expected to be operational during 2005, others in store/under restoration

Coaching Stock
In service 6 x BR Mk 1, 3 x BR Mk 2s
Stored 4 x BR Mk 1s, plus 1 x BR Mk 1 in use as volunteer accommodation
BR Mk 3a restaurant car in use as a buffet

Engineer's Stock
c50 wagons including: 1 ex-BR diesel-electric 12-ton crane, 2 Dogfish, 1 Mermaid, 4 warflats, 3 rectanks, 1 Ferry van, 2 Lowmacs, 2 minfit, 1 21-ton minfit, 2 LNER vans, 2 LMS vans, 2 demountable tank wagons, 1 ex-BR bolster

Departmental Stock
1 CR origin electrification coach, 1 ex-BR BCK, various vans

Owners
No 1 and *Menelaus* the Angus Railway Steam Engineers
D5314 the Class Twenty Six Preservation Group
D3059, 26035 and 27024 the Caledonian Diesel Group

In addition to the above, the following is under restoration adjacent to Bridge of Dun station

Locomotives

Name	No	Origin	Class	Type	Built
—	46464	LMS	2MT	2-6-0	1950

Express — (evenings) 21 July, 4 August, 18 August; Day out with Thomas — 25/26 August; Santa Specials — 10, 16/17, 23/24 December

Facilities for disabled: Ramp access to both stations. Vehicular access to Brechin platforms by prior arrangement. Coach converted to take wheelchairs and attendants, prior notice required for access and car parking

Family tickets: Available

Disclaimer: The Caledonian Railway (Brechin) Ltd reserves the right to amend, cancel or add to these events. And whilst every effort will be made to maintain the above services, the company does not guarantee that trains will depart or arrive at the time stated and reserves the right to suspend or alter any train without notice and will not accept any liability for loss, inconvenience or delay thereby caused

Membership details: M. Jackson, c/o above address

Membership journal: Quarterly

Marketing name: The Friendly Line

Museum — Glasgow Museum of Transport — Glasgow

Member: HRA, TT

A new Museum of Transport on the Clyde is under development by Glasgow Museums in collaboration with other Council departments and Glasgow Harbour Ltd. This landmark museum will create a more accessible and environmentally stable home for Glasgow's significant Transport and Technology collections and for the first time allow proper interpretation of Glasgow's important maritime history through the museum site, the *Glenlee* tall ship and unique ship model collection

The railway collection represents one of the best efforts by a municipal authority to preserve a representative collection of items appropriate to the 'locomotive builders of the Empire'

Access by public transport: Strathclyde PTE Underground. Kelvinhall: Strathclyde Buses 6, 6A, 8, 8A, 9, 9A, 16, 42, 42A, 57, 57A, 62, 62A, 62B, 64; Kelvin Scottish Buses 5, 5A; Clydeside Scottish Buses 17

Operating society/organisation:

Locomotives

Name	No	Origin	Class	Type	Built
—	123	CR	123	4-2-2	1886
—	9	G&SWR	5	0-6-0T	1917
—	103	HR	—	4-6-0	1894
Gordon Highlander	49	GNSR	F	4-4-0	1920

Industrial locomotives

Name	No	Builder	Type	Built
—	1	Barclay (1571)	0-6-0F	1917
—	—	Chaplin (2368)	0-4-0TG	1888
—	—	BEV (583)	B	1927

Stock

Glasgow District Subway car 39T; Glasgow Corporation Underground cars 1 and 4; LMS King George VI's saloon 498 of 1941

Glasgow City Council, Dept of Cultural & Leisure Services
Location: Museum of Transport, Kelvin Hall, 1 Bunhouse Road, Glasgow G3 8DP
Telephone: (0141) 287 2623 or (0141) 287 2721
Fax: (0141) 287 2692
Internet address: *Web site:* www.glasgowmuseums.com
Car park: Opposite Museum entrance
On site facilities: Toilets, cafeteria, shop and public telephone, cloaking facility
Public opening: Monday-Thursday 10.00-17.00; Friday and Sunday 11.00-17.00. Closed 1/2 January and 25/26 December only. Please check before travelling
Facilities for disabled: Both single-sex and uni-sex disabled facilities now available. A passenger lift to allow disabled access at the front entrance is now in operation

Timetable Service — Keith & Dufftown Railway — Banffshire

Member: HRA

The Keith & Dufftown Railway is an 11 mile line linking the World's Malt Whisky Capital, Dufftown, to the market town of Keith. Re-opened to Keith in 2001, the line passes through some of Scotland's most picturesque scenery. The line links the two towns famous round the world for names such as Chivas Regal and Glenfiddich

Operating society/organisation: Keith & Dufftown Railway Association, Dufftown Station, Dufftown, Banffshire AB55 4BA
Contact: Maureen H. Webster (Chairman)
Telephone: (01340) 821181
Internet address: *e-mail:*

Locomotives and multiple-units

Name	No	Origin	Class	Type	Built
—	73119	BR	73	Bo-Bo	1966
—	51568	BR	108	DMC(L)	1959
—	56491	BR	108	DTC(L)	1959
—	53628	BR	108	DMBS	1958
—	52053	BR	108	DMC(L)	1960
—	55500*	BR	140	DMS	1981
—	55501*	BR	140	DMS	1981
—	Car 87§	M/Cam	5BEL	TPS	1932
—	Car 91§	M/Cam	5BEL	DMPBS	1932

§ex-'Brighton Belle' Pullman cars, converted to locomotive-hauled
*unit No 140001

Industrial locomotives

Name	No	Builder	Type	Built
Spirit o' Fife	—	E/Electric (D1193)	0-6-0DH	1967
Wee Mac	—	Clayton	4wDH	1979

175

Scotland

kdra@dial.pipex.com
or
info@keith-dufftown.org.uk
Web site:
www.keith-dufftown.org.uk
Main station: Dufftown
Other public stations: Drummuir (access by rail only), Keith Town (not the ScotRail station)
Length of line: 11 miles, with 42 bridges and the twin span 60ft high Fiddich Viaduct
Car park: Dufftown, Keith
Access by public transport: ScotRail station at Keith (short walk to Keith Town)
Refreshments: Dufftown

Rolling stock
3 Canadian 'Speeder' vehicles
A selection of freight vehicles for maintenance purposes

Souvenir shop: Keith
On site facilities: Visitor information point is now located at Keith Town station. Information on local accommodation providers, visitor attractions and souvenirs. Woodland walks from Drummuir station and access to the Walled Garden at Drummuir Castle
Period of public operation: Weekends — Easter until end of May and throughout September.

Fridays, Saturdays and Sundays during June, July and August
Special events: Spring and autumn Whisky Festivals, please contact for dates. Santa Specials — in December (please enquire about dates)
Membership details: Membership Secretary, c/o above address
Membership journal: *The Keith & Dufftown Express* — half-yearly

| Miniature Railway | Kerr's Miniature Railway | Angus |

Location: Along the sea front to the west of town
Headquarters: West Links Park, Arbroath, Angus.
Contact: Jill Kerr
Telephone: (01241) 879249/874074
Internet address: *e-mail:* jillkerr@tiscali.co.uk
Web site: www.geocities.com/kmr_scotland
Access by public transport: First ScotRail Arbroath station 1.5 miles; Strathtay Buses route A92
On site facilities: Small shop, the park has toilets, snack bar, etc

Locomotives

Name	No	Builder	Type	Built
Ivor	—	Coleby-Simkins	0-6-0	1972
King George	2005	Bullock	4-6-0	1935
Auld Reekie	9872	Jennings	4-4-2	1936
—	25081	Eastwood	Bo-Bo	1981
—	D7594	Eastwood	Bo-Bo	1994
Firefly	3007	Bullock	0-6-0	1936

Length of line: 10.25 in gauge; 400yd (alongside main line)
Period of public operation: Easter-end of September — weekends (14.00-17.00). All of July and first half of August —

daily 12.00-16.00. Sundays throughout the winter (end September-end March). All times weather permitting
Special events: Halloween and Santa Specials plus other events

| Steam Centre | Leadhills & Wanlockhead Railway | Lanarkshire |

Member: HRA
Situated in the Lowther Hills between Abington and Sanquhar, the society was formed in 1983 to construct and operate a 2ft gauge tourist railway between the villages of Leadhills and Wanlockhead. The track now extends to the old county boundary between Lanarkshire and Dumfriesshire. The highest adhesion worked railway in Great Britain at 1,498ft above sea level. Signalbox built using terracotta bricks from the demolished viaduct at Risping Cleuch, with a variety of pre-Grouping signalling &

telegraph equipment (eg North British Railway lever frame and Caledonian Railway lattice post signal)
Operating society/organisation: Andrew Munro, Leadhills & Wanlockhead Railway, 18C Aurs Drive, Barrhead, Glasgow G78 2LR
Telephone: 0141 580 9133
Internet address: *Web site:* www.leadhillsrailway.co.uk
Main station: Leadhills
Access by public transport: ScotRail trains stop at Sanquhar on Nith Valley Line (approx 10 miles) every 1hr 30min-2 hours. Bus

service (Western Scottish Stagecoach) to Leadhills (please check for times). Nearest motorway — M74 — J14 from south/J15 from north. From A76 take B797 to Leadhills
Length of line: 1 mile
Journey time: Approx 30min round trip
On site facilities: Shop, ticket office, toilets, small museum and picnic tables. Extensive country walks. Also on 'Southern Upland Way'. Scottish Lead Mining Museum at Wanlockhead (1 mile). Guided tour of signalbox and

176

engine shed. Disabled access to shop and toilet

Period of public operation: Saturdays and Sundays 11.00-17.00 Easter to end September; Sundays 11.00-17.00 in October. Plus Good Friday, Easter Monday and Bank Holidays. Group discount 50%
Special events: Steam Fair weekend (usually late July)
Membership details: Simon Lowe, Flat 0/1, Holmlea Road, Glasgow G44 4BL
Society journal: Quarterly

Industrial locomotives

Name	No	Builder	Type	Built
Charlotte	—	O&K	0-4-0T	1913
Elvan	2	M/Rail (9792)	4wDM	1955
Luce	4	R/Hornsby (7002/0467/2)	4wDM	1966
Little Clyde	5	R/Hornsby (7002/0467/6)	4wDM	1966
Clyde	6	Hunslet (6347)	4wDH	1975
Nith	8	H/Clarke (DM1002)	0-4-0DMF	1956
Mennock	10	H/Barclay (LD 9348)	0-4-0DM	1994
—	—	Decauvill (917)	0-4-0T	1917
—	—	Clayton (18190)	4wDM	1978
—	—	Moyse	4wDM	1941

Rolling stock
2 air-braked passenger coaches and guard's van built at Leadhills. 1 air-braked coach chassis built by Talyllyn Railway, with the L&WR completing the bodywork. Assorted permanent way wagons and former industrial stock

Timetable Service — Mull Rail — Isle of Mull

Member: HRA, TT
Scotland's original island passenger railway. The terminal at Craignure is reached by ferry from Oban. The railway timetable links in with most ferry sailings. The journey is one of great beauty running alongside the Sound of Mull with extensive views of Ben Nevis, the Glencoe Hills, the island of Lismore and the mass of Ben Cruachan
Commercial Manager: Graham E. Ellis
Operations Manager: Vacant
Operating society/organisation: Mull & West Highland (NG) Railway Co Ltd, Old Pier Station, Craignure, Isle of Mull PA65 6AY
Telephone/Fax: (01680) 812494/812567
Internet address: *e-mail:* info@mullrail.co.uk
Web site: www.mullrail.co.uk
OS reference: NM 725369
Car park: At Craignure, free
Access by public transport: Caledonian MacBrayne ferry from Oban (40min sail)
On site facilities: Gift shop, car park (free) at Craignure during operational hours
Family ticket: Available (2 adults & 2 children under 16)

Locomotives

Name	No	Builder	Type	Built
Lady of the Isles	—	Marsh	2-6-4T	1981
Waverley†	—	Curwen	4-4-2	1952
—	—	Alcock	4w-4PM	1973
Glen Auldyn	—	Davies	B0-B0 DH	1986
Victoria*	—	Vere	2-6-2T	1993
Frances	—	Vere	B0-B0 DH	1999

†currently at Rudyard Lake Railway
*largest tank engine built for 10.25in gauge

Rolling stock
12 coaches (two with wheelchair accommodation); 3 bogie wagons; 1 4-wheel wagon

Owner
Waverley — The Waverley Group

Length of line: 1.25 miles/10.25in gauge
Public opening: Daily 29 March to 27 October
Facilities for disabled: No steps on railway, two compartments for wheelchairs
Membership details: Friends of Mull Rail, David Crombie, 1 Mulberry Drive, Dunfermline, Fife KY11 8BZ. Tel: (01383) 728652
Membership journal: *Crankpin Journal* — annual

Special facilities: Special trains can be chartered within and outside timetable hours
Special notes: First island passenger railway in Scotland, runs to Torosay Castle and 12 acres of gardens, superb panoramic views of mountains and sea. Group discount available for 20+ pre-booked passengers. Joint Torosay Castle/Mull Rail tickets available at Craigmore station

Paddle Steamer Preservation Society

Member: TT, Heritage Afloat
Paddle steamers: *Waverley* &
Kingswear Castle. Pleasure cruise
ship: *Balmoral*

The Paddle Steamer *Waverley*, the
last sea-going paddle steamer in the
world, was built for the London &
North Eastern Railway in 1946, and
replaced a vessel of the same name
which was sunk off Dunkirk during
May 1940. Sold to the PSPS — a
Registered Charity — in 1974,
Waverley sails on day trips and
afternoon cruises from ports and
piers in most coastal areas and river
estuaries of the United Kingdom,
from Easter until October each year.
Also in the 'fleet' is the traditional
motor cruiser *Balmoral*. The river
paddle steamer *Kingswear Castle*
sails from Chatham Historic

Dockyard on the River Medway
Commercial Director:
Kathleen O'Neil
Operations Director:
Ian McMillan
Headquarters:
Waverley and *Balmoral:*
Waverley Excursions Ltd, Waverley
Terminal, Anderston Quay,
Glasgow G3 8HA
Kingswear Castle:
The Historic Dockyard, Chatham,
Kent ME4 4TQ
On ship facilities: Self-service
restaurants, bars, toilets (disabled
toilets on *Waverley* and *Balmoral*),
souvenirs
Special facilities: *Waverley* and
Balmoral are available for private
hire and party bookings
Membership details: Paddle

Steamer Preservation Society,
PO Box 365, Worcester WR3 7WH
Membership journal:
Paddlewheels — quarterly.
Details of the full programme of
cruises operated by and *Waverley*
and *Balmoral* can be obtained from
the National Booking Office,
Waverley Excursions Ltd, Waverley
Terminal, Anderston Quay,
Glasgow G3 8HA
Tel: 0845 130 4647.
Book online at:
www.waverleyexcursions.co.uk
Further info for *Kingswear Castle:*
Tel: 01634 827648
e-mail: kc@pskc.freeserve.co.uk
Online booking for *Kingswear
Castle:*
www.pskc.freeserve.co.uk

Prestongrange Industrial Heritage Museum

Location: On the B1348 between
Musselburgh and Prestonpans.
OS reference: NT 734737
Operating society/organisation:
East Lothian Museum Service,
Library & Museum Headquarters,
Dunbar Road, Haddington, East
Lothian EH41 3PJ
Telephone: (0131) 653 2904
(Prestongrange Visitor Centre),
(01368) 861954 (Museum Service)
Internet address:
e-mail: info@prestongrange.org
Web site: www.prestongrange.org
Car park: On site
On site facilities: Once part of the
Scottish Mining Museum,
Prestongrange is being developed as
a museum which tells the story of
people and industries in East
Lothian — local coal deposits
encouraged the growth of numerous
other industries such as pottery,
pipe making, soap, glycerine and
brewing
Visitor centre: Changing
exhibitions of local industries.
Displays of local art and crafts —
one-off events, demonstrations,

Industrial locomotives

Name	No	Builder	Type	Built
—	6	A/Barclay (2043)	0-4-0ST	1937
—	17	A/Barclay (2219)	0-4-0ST	1946
Prestongrange	7	G/Ritchie (536)	0-4-2ST	1914
Tomatin	1	M/Rail (9925)	4wDM	1963
—	—*	Hunslet (4440)	4wDM	1952
—	32	R/Hornsby (458960)	4wDM	1962
George Edwards	33	R/Hornsby (221647)	4wDM	1943
—	—	E/Electric (D908)	4wDM	1964

*2ft gauge

Rolling stock
Steam crane, Whittaker No 30, c1890

Special note: The locomotives are stored under cover with no public
access at the time of writing. Visitors wishing to see the exhibits MUST
make arrangements before visiting.

workshops. Cornish beam engine,
installed 1874 to pump water from
the mine. Colliery locomotives
restored by Prestongrange Railway
Society are housed in the Pit Head
Baths
Toilets: Visitor centre
Refreshment facilities: Available
at visitor centre

Public opening: Museum site open
daily throughout the year.
Visitor centre and exhibitions April
to October, 11.00-16.00.
Admission free
Length of line: 400m (standard
gauge). No public rides
Facilities for disabled: Access and
toilet at visitor centre. Access to

powerhouse exhibition, and footpaths along the site
Special events: Events held throughout the season

Contact: For Prestongrange Railway Society — Colin Boyd, 3 Stuart Wynd, Craigmount View, Edinburgh EH2 8XU

Diesel Centre | Royal Deeside Railway | Aberdeenshire

Member: HRA

After 10 years' effort the Society has succeeded in returning passenger services to Deeside, albeit on a limited basis, offering diesel-hauled brake van rides over the 0.25 mile section of track laid so far through the historic Leys estate.

It is hoped to offer more trips in 2007, subject to HMRI approval. More tracklaying is due to take place in 2007 towards Banchory using the diesel railcrane on loan from the Strathspey Railway Co. The RDRPS visitor centre is housed in the two former BR Mk 2 coaches will and continue to be open on weekend afternoons.

The battery-powered 'Sputnik' railcar are now on site, guided tours of which are available by prior request.

Steam power in the form of *Bon Accord* is expected to be on site from late 2007.

The railway is being rebuilt by volunteer members of the Royal Deeside RPS.

Headquarters: Milton of Crathes Craft village

Operating society/organisation: Mr D. Mitchell RE, Chairman, The Royal Deeside Railway Preservation Society, 3 Alder Drive, Portlethen, Aberdeenshire AB12 4WA

Telephone: 01224 782479

Internet address: *Web site:* www.deeside-railway.co.uk

OS reference: NO 914962

Car Parking: Free, on site

Access by public transport: By bus — Stagecoach Bluebird from Aberdeen rail/bus interchange

Locomotives and multiple-units

Name	No	Origin	Class	Type	Built
—	D2134	BR	03	0-6-0DH	1960
—	D9551	BR	14	0-6-0DM	1965
—	79998*	BR	—	DMBS	1956
—	79999*	BR	—	DTCL	1956

†rebuilt with hydraulic drive
*battery-powered multiple-unit

Industrial locomotives

Name	No	Builder	Type	Built
Bon Accord	—*	Barclay (807)	0-4-0ST	1897

*off site for restoration, expected to arrive late 2007

Rolling stock

2 BR Mk 2 coaches, GNSR full brake, GNSR 5-comp lav composite (body only), GNSR 5-comp lav Third (body only), GNSR 5-comp Third (body only), GNSR 4-comp First (body only), GNSR former steam railmotor (body only), LNWR Picnic Saloon (body only), LMS CCT, BR 20-ton brake van, BR 25-ton brake van, ex-LMS wagon underframe, 75ton rail-mounted crane (on loan from Strathspey Railway)

Owners

Bon Accord — the Grampian Transport Museum, on long term loan to Bon Accord Locomotive Society

(railway adjacent to A93). Access by car — from south, A90 to Stonehaven, then A957 (historic Slug Road) to A93 at Crathes; from the west, A93 from Ballater, A980 from Donside to Banchory

On site facilities: Two static display coaches with light refreshments available (seasonal weekend opening)

Length of line: 0.25 mile, 2.75 miles when complete

Public opening: Weekends April-September 13.00-17.00

Special events: Occasional events with transport theme. Santa's Grotto in December. Deeside Steam & Vintage Club annual rally held at Milton, 18/19 August

Membership details: Mr W. Halliday, Membership Secretary, 32 Abbotshall Crescent, Cults, Aberdeen AB15 9JP

Membership journal: *The Queen's Messenger* (quarterly)

Note: Some locomotives and rolling stock undergoing restoration off-site with no public access, please contact for details

Affiliated society: The Bon Accord Locomotive Society, c/o Mr Murray M. D. Duncan, 19 David Street, Stonehaven, Kincardineshire AB39 2AJ

Web site: www.bon-accord.org

Scottish Industrial Railway Centre

Member: HRA, TT, AIM

The Scottish Industrial Railway Centre is based on part of the former Dalmellington Iron Co railway system which was one of the best known industrial railway networks in Britain. Steam worked up until 1978 when the collieries it served in the scenic Doon Valley closed. It is the aim of the centre to preserve part of the railway.

The Centre is operated by the Ayrshire Railway Preservation Group, who also own the former Glasgow & South Western Railway station at Waterside, half a mile from the Centre.

During the winter of 2002/3 the ARPG moved its operations from the former colliery at Minnivey to the Dunaskin Ironworks site at Waterside, and is now based in the former NCB locomotive shed and wagon works there.

Location: 10 miles southeast of Ayr on the A713 to Castle Douglas

Contact address: Scottish Industrial Railway Centre, Dunaskin Ironworks, Waterside, Panta, Ayrshire KA6 7JF

OS reference: NS 438085

Operating society/organisation: Ayrshire Railway Preservation Group

Telephone: ARPG information line (01292) 269260. ARPG Secretary (01292) 313579 (evening & weekends)

Internet address: *e-mail:* agcthoms@aol.com
Web site: www.arpg.org.uk

Length of line: Approx 0.3 mile

Access by public transport: Nearest rail station, Ayr (10 miles). Half hourly Stagecoach bus service from Ayr. Tel: (01292) 613500

On site facilities: Steam-hauled brake van rides (over third mile). Small museum of railway relics and photographs, and souvenir shop

Public opening: To be announced in spring 2007

Membership details: Mr Charles Robinson, 3 Links Crescent, Troon, Ayrshire KA10 6SS

Locomotives

Name	No	Origin	Class	Type	Built
*—	MP228 (12052)	BR	11	0-6-0DE	1949
*—	MP229 (12093)	BR	11	0-6-0DE	1951

*on loan to Caledonian Railway

Industrial locomotives

Name	No	Builder	Type	Built
—	16	A/Barclay (1116)	0-4-0ST	1910
—	8	A/Barclay (1296)	0-6-0T	1912
—	19	A/Barclay (1614)	0-4-0ST	1918
—	8	A/Barclay (1952)	0-4-0F	1928
*Harlaxton	—	A/Barclay (2107)	0-6-0ST	1941
—	10	A/Barclay (2244)	0-4-0ST	1947
NCB No 23	—	A/Barclay (2260)	0-4-0ST	1949
—	25	A/Barclay (2358)	0-6-0ST	1954
—	1	A/Barclay (2368)	0-4-0ST	1955
—	—	A/Barclay (347)	0-4-0DM	1941
—	118	A/Barclay (366)	0-4-0DM	1943
—	7	A/Barclay (399)	0-4-0DM	1956
Lily of the Valley	—	Fowler (22888)	0-4-0DM	1943
—	—	Fowler (4200028)	0-4-0DM	1948
Tees Storage	—	N/British (27644)	0-4-0DH	1959
—	—	R/Hornsby (224352)	4wDM	1943
Blinkin Bess	—	R/Hornsby (284839)	4wDM	1950
Johnnie Walker	—	R/Hornsby (417890)	4wDM	1959
—	—	R/Hornsby (421697)	0-4-0DM	1959
—	107	Hunslet (3132)	0-4-0DM	1944
—	—	Sentinel (10012)	4wDM	1959
—	—	Donnelli (163)	4wDMR	1979

3ft gauge (stored off-site)

—	—	R/Hornsby (256273)	4wDM	1949
—	—	Hunslet (8816)	4wDH	1981

2ft 6in gauge (stored off-site)

—	2	R/Hornsby (183749)	4wDM	1937
—	3	R/Hornsby (210959)	4wDM	1941
—	1	R/Hornsby (211681)	4wDM	1942

Note: Not all standard gauge locomotives are on public display
*on loan to Caledonian Railway

Stock

1 BR Mk 1 TSO, 1 BR Mk 1 BSK, 2 Wickham trolleys; 1 steam crane; various other items

Special notes: For further information and details of special events, please contact the information line (01292) 269620, or the secretary Gordon Thomson (01292) 313579, or write to 8 Burnside Place, Troon, Ayrshire KA10 6LZ

Strathspey Railway

Member: HRA, TT

Scotland's steam railway in the Highlands connects the busy tourist resort at Aviemore to the more traditional highland village of Boat of Garten, famed as one of the few nesting places of the osprey (viewing site 3 miles from station). The golf course here was designed by James Braid, who also designed Gleneagles. Beyond Boat of Garten the scenery changes as the 'strath' opens out giving fine views of the Spey en route to Broomhill. This station appears as 'Glenbogle' in the TV series 'Monarch of the Glen'. Broomhill is approximately 3.5 miles from Grantown on Spey, the railway's ultimate goal

Superintendent of the Line: Laurence Grant

Enquiries: Aviemore Station, Dalfaber Road, Aviemore, Inverness-shire PH22 1PY (SAE for copy of timetable brochure)

Telephone: 01479 810725.

Internet address: *e-mail:* strathtrains@strathspeyrailway.co.uk *Web site:* www.strathspeyrailway.co.uk

Main station: Aviemore. The railway occupies one platform at the main line Aviemore station

Other public stations: Boat of Garten and Broomhill

OS reference: Aviemore NH 898131, Boat of Garten NH 943789

Car parks: Aviemore (Strathspey Railway side of station (off Dalfaber Road) for railway customers only, Boat of Garten and Broomhill

Access by public transport: ScotRail services and express bus to Aviemore. Local service to Boat of Garten

Refreshment facilities: On-train buffet car or facilities on many trains. Picnic tables at Boat of Garten (for use of ticket purchasers). No refreshment facilities on Saturday services

Souvenir shop: Boat of Garten and Aviemore

Depot: Aviemore (not open to public), sidings at Aviemore and Boat of Garten are not open to the public, those at Broomhill are

Locomotives and multiple-units

Name	No	Origin	Class	Type	Built
—†	5025	LMS	5MT	4-6-0	1934
E. V. Cooper, Engineer†	46512	LMS	2MT	2-6-0	1952
—†	828	CR	812	0-6-0	1899
—	D2774	BR	—	0-4-0DH	1960
—	08490	BR	08	0-6-0DE	1959
—†	D5302	BR	26	Bo-Bo	1958
—†	26025	BR	26	Bo-Bo	1958
—*	D5394	BR	27	Bo-Bo	1963
—	D5862	BR	31	A1A-A1A	1962
—	51367	BR	117	DMBS	1959
—	51402	BR	117	DMS	1959
—†	51990	BR	107	DMBS	1961
—	52008	BR	107	DMBS	1960
—	52030	BR	107	DMC	1960
—	54047	BR	114	DTC	1959

Industrial locomotives

Name	No	Builder	Type	Built
—	48†	Hunslet (2864)	0-6-0ST	1943
Cairngorm	9	RSH (7097)	0-6-0ST	1943
Swiftsure	—†	Hunslet (2857)	0-6-0ST	1943
—	60†	Hunslet (3686)	0-6-0ST	1948
Niddrie	6	Barclay (1833)	0-6-0ST	1924
Forth	10*	Barclay (1890)	0-4-0ST	1926
Balmenach	2	Barclay (2020)	0-4-0ST	1936
—	17	Barclay (2017)	0-6-0T	1935
Inveresk	16	R/Hornsby (260756)	0-4-0DM	1950
Inverdon	15§	Simplex (5763)	4wDM	1957
—	14	North British (27549)	0-4-0DH	1956
Queen Anne	20†	R/Hornsby (265618)	4wDM	1948

*not on site

†stored and/or not on public display

§likely to leave during 2007

Locomotive notes: In service: 9, 17, 08490, 51367, 51402, 52008 and 54047. Under restoration: 828, 46512, D5394

Stock

20 ex-BR coaches; 4 ex-LMS coaches; 2 ex-LMS sleeping cars; 1 ex-LNER sleeping car; 1 ex-HR coach (stored at Bo'ness); 1 ex-NBR coach; numerous examples of rolling stock

Owners

6, 17 and 46512 the Highland Locomotive Co Ltd
828 the Scottish Locomotive Preservation Trust Fund
5025 the Watkinson Trust
D5302 and 26025 the Highland Diesel Locomotive Co Ltd
51367 and 51402 the Blue Square Heritage Group
51990, 52008, 52030 and 54047 My Little Sprinter Ltd

visible from the road

Length of line: 10 miles

Journey time: Aviemore-Boat of Garten 15min; Aviemore-Broomhill 45min (outward) 35min, (inward).

Round trip takes approximately 90min

Passenger trains: Steam-hauled services. Aviemore-Boat of Garten/Broomhill. Most Saturdays, unless a special event is taking place, services are run with a 'branch line' set

Period of public operation: 17/18, 21/22, 24/25, 28/29, 31 March; 1, 4-9, 11-15, 18/19, 21/22, 25/26, 28/29 April; 2/3, 5-7, 9/10, 12/13, 16/17, 19/20, 23/24, 26, 28, 30/31 May; daily June to September; 3/4, 6/7, 10/11, 13/14, 17/18, 20/21, 24/25, 27/28, 31 October; 1 November; 27, 31 December; 1/2 January 2008

Special events: Two Train Days — 5/6, 26/27 May, 21/22, 29 July, 5,

12 August; Steam Fair (Boat of Garten) — 21/22 July; Santa Express — 9, 15/16, 22, 24 December

Facilities for disabled: Access possible at Aviemore, Boat of Garten and Broomhill. Please contact in advance for directions and if a party involved

Special notes: First and third class travel available on most trains. Family fares available for third class travel. Special rates/arrangements for parties. Luncheon on the train — Sundays

24 March to 28 October, also on Fridays 1 June until 30 September. Evening diner, the 'Strathspey Highlander', every Wednesday and Friday 1 June until 14 September. Bicycles and dogs carried at a 'flat fee' of £1 — groups must give prior notice (bicycles must not be ridden on platforms or pedestrian pathways)

Membership details: Strathspey Railway Association at above address

Membership journal: *Strathspey Express* — quarterly

The compactness of a large number of narrow gauge locomotives makes it relatively easy to replicate previous designs. In 2007 the revitalised Hunslet Engine Co is building a batch of 0-4-0STs as seen at Bala and Llanberis. In the 'here is one I made earlier' mode is Corris Railway 0-4-2ST No 7 based on an original CR locomotive now on the Talyllyn Railway. *ACB*

Scotland

Wales

Member: HRA, TT

This delightful narrow gauge railway follows the route of the former Bala-Dolgellau Railway, along the shore of Wales' largest natural lake. The railway's headquarters are to be found in the fine old station building at Llanuwchllyn at the south-western end of the line. Do not be deterred by the fact that the railway runs down the opposite shore of the lake to the main road — it is well worth the detour

General Manager: Roger Hine

Headquarters: Rheilffordd Llyn Tegid (Bala Lake Railway) Llanuwchllyn, Bala, Gwynedd LL23 7DD

Telephone: Llanuwchllyn (01678) 540666

Internet address: *Web site:* www.bala-lake-railway.co.uk

Main station: Llanuwchllyn

Other public stations: Llangower, Bala. Request halts at Pentrepiod and Bryn Hynod

OS reference: Llanuwchllyn SH 880300, Bala SH 929350

Car parks: Llanuwchllyn, Llangower and Bala town centre

Access by public transport: Arriva service No 94 to both Bala and

Industrial locomotives

Name	No	Builder	Type	Built
George B	—	Hunslet (680)	0-4-0ST	1898
Holy War	3	Hunslet (779)	0-4-0ST	1902
Alice	3	Hunslet (802)	0-4-0ST	1902
Maid Marian	5	Hunslet (822)	0-4-0ST	1903
Triassic	1270	Peckett (1270)	0-6-0ST	1911
Meirionnydd	11	Severn-Lamb (7322)	Bo-Bo	1973
Chilmark	12	R/Hornsby (194771)	4wDM	1939
Bob Davies	—	YEC (L125)	4wDM	1983
Cernyw	—	R/Hornsby (200748)	4wDM	1940
Lady Madcap	—	R/Hornsby (283512)	4wDM	1949

Locomotive notes: *Holy War, Maid Marian* and *Alice* are in regular use, remainder are on static display
Triassic is being overhauled, *George B* is being re-assembled

Llanuwchllyn (from Wrexham or Barmouth)

Road access: Off the A494 Bala-Dolgellau road

Refreshment facilities: Llanuwchllyn. Large picnic site with toilet facilities by lake at Llangower

Souvenir shop: Llanuwchllyn

Depot: Llanuwchllyn

Length of line: 4.5 miles, 1ft 11.625in gauge

Passenger trains: Llanuwchllyn-Bala. Journey takes 25min in each direction

Period of public operation: 31 March-end of September (except some Mondays and Fridays)

Facilities for disabled: Facilities available on most trains

Special notes: Small parties (10/12) may just turn up, but a day's notice required for larger groups

Family tickets: Available for all round trip journeys

Membership details: Membership Secretary, c/o Llanuwchllyn station

Membership journal: *Llanuwchllyn Express*

Member: HRA

Steam and diesel-hauled rides over 3 miles of branch line

Location: Barry Island Station, Barry Island, South Wales

General Manager: Janet Small

Operating society: Vale of Glamorgan Railway Co

Car park: Large public car park near site

Locomotives and multiple-units

Name	No	Origin	Class	Type	Built
—	2861	GWR	2800	2-8-0	1918
—	4115	GWR	4101	2-6-2T	1936
—	5227	GWR	5205	2-8-0T	1924
—	6686	GWR	5600	0-6-2T	1928
—	44901	LMS	5MT	4-6-0	1945
—	48518*	LMS	8F	2-8-0	1944
—	80150	BR	4MT	2-6-4T	1956
—	92245	BR	9F	2-10-0	1958

OS reference: ST 115667

Access by public transport: Frequent train services from Cardiff to Barry Island for cross-platform interchange (Arriva Valley Lines)

On site facilities: Museum, shop, light refreshments

Public opening: Easter to mid-September (weekends and Bank Holidays), December (tel: 01466 748816 for more details)

Special events: Events include Easter Bunny — 6-9 April; Day out with Thomas — 28/29 April, 5-7 May; Transport Festival — 9/10 June; Rail Ale — 23/24 June; Ivor the Engine — 7/8 July; Day out with Thomas — 21/22, 25, 28/29 July; '60s Weekend — 11/12 August; Diesel Gala — 25-27 August; Waterfront Festival — 1/2 September; Ghost Trains — 28, 31 October; Bonfire Night Shuttle — 5 November; Santa Specials — 2, 8/9, 15/16, 22/23 December; Mince Pie Special — 30 December

Length of line: 3 miles

Facilities for disabled: Barry Island station is all on the level with no steps. Ramp access available for all trains. 100m level walk from ticket office to train. Parking by special arrangement to private car park

Further information: The Chairman, Vale of Glamorgan Railway Co, Barry Island Station, South Wales CF62 5TH

Membership details: Membership Secretary c/o above address

Name	No	Origin	Class	Type	Built
—	08481	BR	08	0-6-0DE	1958
—	D9521	BR	14	0-6-0DH	1964
—	20228	BR	20	Bo-Bo	1966
—	D1725	BR	47	Co-Co	1964
—	51339	P/Steel	117	DMBS	1959
—	51382	P/Steel	117	DMS	1959
—	51655	BR	115	DMBS	1959
—	51677	BR	115	DMBS	1959
—	51919	BR	108	DMBS	1956
—	52048	BR	108	DMCL	1960
—	54279	BR	108	DTC	1959
—	59664	BR	115	TC	1959

Locomotive notes: In store, not on public view, except 5538 on site. *several of the locomotives listed above are expected to be used as a source of parts for 're-creation' projects. The 'Barry 8' are open to the public during the Transport Festival and Waterfront Festival

Industrial locomotives

Name	No	Builder	Type	Built
Pamela	—	Hunslet (3840)	0-6-0ST	1956
Ugly	62	RSH (7673)	0-6-0ST	1950
	7705	RSH (7705)	0-4-0ST	1952
Bill Caddick	—	H/Clarke (1168)	0-6-0DM	1959
—	—	Unilok (2183)		1964
—	—	Hunslet (6688)	0-4-0DH	1968

Stock

BR Mk 1 and Mk 2 coaches, TVR coach No 153, operational steam crane, various freight vehicles

Owners

D9521 the D9521 Locomotive Group
08481, D1725 and DMU vehicles the Barry Railcar Project
20228 Traditional Traction

| Timetable Service | **Brecon Mountain Railway** | Merthyr Tydfil |

A narrow gauge passenger-carrying railway close to Merthyr Tydfil built on part of the trackbed of the former Brecon & Merthyr Railway. Gradually being extended northwards, the railway has some interesting narrow gauge steam locomotives imported from East Germany and South Africa

General Manager: A. J. Hills

Headquarters: Brecon Mountain Railway, Pant Station, Dowlais, Merthyr Tydfil CF48 2UP

Telephone: Merthyr Tydfil (01685) 722988

Fax: (01685) 384854

Locomotives

Name	No	Builder	Type	Built
—	1	Baldwin (15511)	2-6-2	1898
—	2	Baldwin (61269)	4-6-2	1930
Sybil	—	Hunslet (827)	0-4-0ST	1903
Graf Schwerin-Löwitz	—	Arn Jung (1261)	0-6-2WT	1908
Pendyffryn	—	de Winton	0-4-0VBT	1894
Redstone	—	Redstone	0-4-0VBT	1905
—	146*	Henschel	2-8-2	1959
—	—	Brecon MR (001)	0-6-0DH	1987

*former South African Railways locomotive

Stock

Two balcony end 39-seat coaches; 2 balcony end 40-seat coaches; 1 19-seat Caboose; 4 flat cars, crane and tamper, miscellaneous rail-carrying and ballast wagons; Wickham petrol trolley

Wales

Main station: Pant
Car park: Pant station
OS reference: SO 063120
Access by public transport: Bus to Pant Cemetery — half hour frequency from Merthyr bus station. Main line rail service to Merthyr from Cardiff Central
Depot: Pant
Length of line: 5 miles (3.5 miles open for passenger traffic), 1ft 11.75in gauge
Journey time: Return trip approx 65min
Period of public operation: Daily 24 March-4 November, EXCEPT for: 26, 30 March; 2, 16, 20, 27, 30 April; 4, 14, 18, 21, 25 May; 17, 21, 24, 28 September; 1, 5, 8, 12, 15, 19, 22, 26 October

Refreshment facilities: Cafés at Pant and Pontsticill
Special events: Santa Specials — December
Facilities for disabled: Facilities for disabled include ramps, toilets and carriage designed to carry wheelchairs
Special notes: There is no road access to Pontsticill

| Museum | Conwy Valley Railway Museum | Betws-y-coed (Conwy CB) |

Conveniently situated alongside Betws-y-coed railway station, the Museum presents some well-displayed distractions to pass the time including model train layouts to delight both adult and child
Location: Adjacent to Betws-y-coed station
OS reference: SH 796565
General Manager: Mr C. M. Cartwright
Operating society/organisation: Conwy Valley Railway Museum, The Old Goods Yard, Betws-y-coed, Conwy LL24 0AL
Telephone: 01690 710568
Fax: 01690 710132
Car park: On site
Access by public transport: Betws-y-coed main line station
On site facilities: Refreshments in buffet car. Bookshop and model/gift shop in museum foyer, operating train layouts, miniature railway (1.25-miles, 7.25in gauge) steam-hauled. Picnic area. 15in Tramway (operates daily) with 1989-built single-deck bogie tram
Public opening: Daily 10.00-17.30
Facilities for disabled: Access to café, museum and toilets from car park. Toilets are adapted for disabled

Locomotives

Name	No	Builder	Type	Built
Britannia	70000	TMA Engineering (1ft 3in gauge)	4-6-2	1988
Old Rube*	—	Milner Eng	2-8-0	1983
Petunia*	—±	J. Stubbs	0-4-2T	1989
Shoshone*	—	Simkins/Milner	2-8-0	1975
Union Pacific*	—	R. Greatrex	Bo-Bo	1991
Douglas*	—†	P. Frank	2-4-0T	2004
Dragonfly*	—†	P. Frank	2-4-0T	2004
Gwyda Castle*	—	P. Zwicky-Ross/P. Frank	Bo-Bo	2004
—	—§	—	4-6-2	1935

*7.25in gauge
†based on Isle of Man Railway locomotives
§6in gauge Canadian Pacific locomotive, a prize winner at the Model Engineer Exhibition
±on permanent loan

Stock
Standard gauge: 1 GWR fitter's van; 1 LMS 6-wheel van; 1 LNER CCT van; 1 BR Mk 1 coach; 2 SR luggage vans; 1 Pullman coach; 15in bogie tramcar
7.25in gauge: 5 articulated sit-in coaches; 2 twin-set articulated sit-in coaches; 2 sets 3 articulated sit-in open coaches; 4 wagons plus 'self-drive' 0-4-0 'Toby Tram' and 2-4-0 *Billy*. 1 bogie ballast wagon (P. Frank)
15in gauge: 1 wagon

| Railway Centre/Museum | Corris Railway and Museum | Gwynedd |

Member: HRA
In the heart of Wales' 'narrow gauge country', the Corris Railway provides a 50min round trip on the restored section of Mid Wales' first public narrow gauge railway. The Museum, situated in the remaining buildings of Corris station, displays relics, photographs and models of the railway
Location: In Corris village off A487 trunk road. Turn opposite Braichgoch Hotel, five miles north of Machynlleth and 11 miles south of Dolgellau
OS reference: SH 755078
Operating society: The Corris Railway Society, Corris Station Yard, Gwynedd (postal address: Corris, Machynlleth, Powys SY20 9SH)

Telephone: 01654 761303
Internet address:
e-mail: enquiries@corris.co.uk
Web site: www.corris.co.uk
Car park: Adjacent
Access by public transport: Arriva Trains services to Machynlleth. Bus Gwynedd services 2 (Aberystwyth-Dolgellau-Machynlleth), 30 (Machynlleth-Tywyn) and 34 (Machynlleth-Aberllefenni); Dyfi Valley service 530 (Tywyn-Machynlleth-Abergynolwyn)
Catering facilities: Snacks, teas and light refreshments
On site facilities: Souvenir shop, toilets and children's playground; close to Corris Craft Centre and King Arthur's Labyrinth; two miles from Centre for Alternative Technology
Passenger trains: Corris to Maespoeth
Length of line: Three-quarter-mile, 2ft 3in gauge track. Planning permission for a further two miles of track has been granted
Public opening:
(Full details on web site.)
Railway — passenger trains (usually steam-hauled) operate at

Locomotives

Name	No	Builder	Type	Built
Alan Meaden	5	M/Rail (22258)	4wDM	1965
—	6	R/Hornsby (51849)	4wDM	1966
—	7	Winson/Watkins	0-4-2ST	2005
—	8	Hunslet (7274)	4wDM	1973
Aberllefenni	9	Clayton (8045)	4wBE	1974

Locomotive notes: 5, 6 and 7 operational. 7 based on Corris No 4 now Talyllyn No 4 *Edward Thomas*. 8 and 9 undergoing restoration

Stock
3 carriages (4th under construction) , 4 brake vans, 18 works wagons and 5 historic wagons

Owner
8 on loan from the National Mining Museum
9 donated by Winalate Ltd

weekends, Bank Holidays and daily on specified weeks in season leaving Corris hourly 11.00-16.00. Santa Specials 15/16 December. Museum — Open on train operating days
Special trains and Museum openings can be booked by prior arrangement. Please check web site or write for further details
Special events: Race the Train Fun Run — 19 May (provisional); Mini Steam Gala and Teddy Bears ' Picnic, Corris — 4/5 August; Model Railway Exhibition, Machynlleth — 25-27 August
Facilities for disabled: Disabled access carriage on all trains. Access to display area of Museum and shop
Membership details: Membership Secretary, c/o above address

Timetable Service	**Fairbourne Railway**	Gwynedd

Member: Britain's Great Little Railways
Since 1986 this railway has been regauged from 15in to 12.25in and has been transformed by the introduction of new locomotives and rolling stock, a tunnel through the sand dunes, signalboxes, new workshops, a café overlooking the Mawddach estuary. During the main season a two-train service is in operation. A free indoor nature attraction and small museum are open at Fairbourne terminus
Headquarters: North Wales Coast Light Railway Co Ltd, Fairbourne & Barmouth Steam Railway, Beach Road, Fairbourne, Gwynedd LL38 2EX
Telephone: (01341) 250362
Fax: (01341) 250240
Internet address: *e-mail:* fairbourne.railway@btconnect.com
Web site: http://www.fairbournerailway.com

Locomotives

Name	No	Builder	Type	Built
Beddgelert	—	Curwen	0-6-4ST	1979
Yeo	—	Curwen	2-6-2T	1978
Sherpa	—	Milner	0-4-0STT	1978
Russell*	—	Milner	2-6-4T	1985
Lilian Walter†	—	FLW	A1-1AD	1985
Gwril	—	FLW	4wBE	1987
T. J. Thurston	—	Thurston	4-6-2	1948

FLW — Fairbourne Locomotive Works
*built as replica Leek & Manifold *Elaine*, rebuilt to present form 1985 at FLW
†originally built by G&S Engineering in 1961 as 15in gauge *Sylvia*. Rebuilt at Fairbourne in 1985

Stock
18 coaches; 15 freight

Owner
T. J. Thurston is privately owned

Main station: Fairbourne
Other public stations: Golf Halt, Barmouth Ferry Station

OS reference: SH 616128
Car parks: Fairbourne
Access by public transport:

Wales

Above: This 12.25in gauge version of a Lynton & Barnstaple Railway 2-6-2T is a half-scale replica of the type of locomotive that once ran on the original line. A full-size replica is currently under construction at the Boston Lodge Works of the Ffestiniog Railway. *FR*

Below: Built in the USA by the American Steam Locomotive Co (Alco) in 1917, *Mountaineer* is now on the roster of the Ffestiniog Railway. It is seen at Boston Lodge with Snowdonia in the background. *Alan Barnes*

Wales

Fairbourne railway station. Bus Gwynedd service (No 28)
Refreshment facilities: Penrhyn Point café, tea shop on platform at Fairbourne
Souvenir shop: Fairbourne
Depot: Fairbourne
Length of line: 2.5 miles, 12.25in gauge
Passenger trains: A 2.5-mile journey connecting with ferry at Penrhyn Point to Barmouth. 20min single journey. Through tickets to Barmouth (including ferry)

available
Period of public operation: 30 March, 1 April, 6-15, 21/22 April; daily 28 April-13 July (closed on Fridays); daily 14 July-6 September; daily 8-23 September (closed on Fridays); 29/30 September; 6/7, 13/14 October; daily 20-28 October (closed on Fridays); Santa Specials operate 8/9 December
Special events: Friendly Fairbourne Engines — 27-29 May, 22-24 July; RNLI Lifeboat Day— 25 July;

Friendly Fairbourne Engines — 19-21 August; Indian/Darjeeling Day — 26/27 August; Santa Specials — 8/9 December
Membership details: Fairbourne Railway Supporters' Association, c/o 2 Leicester Road, Fleckney, Leics LE8 8BF
Special notes: During inclement weather the service may be restricted or cancelled. Extra trains and special parties by arrangement with the manager

---

Timetable Service	Ffestiniog Railway	Gwynedd

Member: HRA

In many ways, evocative of the early Swiss mountain railways as it climbs high above Porthmadog with some breathtaking views, the railway still operates an interesting variety of locomotives including some unusual Victorian survivors. Passengers have replaced slate as the principal traffic over this former quarry line

General Manager: Paul Lewin
Headquarters: Ffestiniog Railway Co, Harbour Station, Porthmadog, Gwynedd, LL49 9NF
Telephone: Porthmadog (01766) 516000
Fax: 01766 516005
Internet address: Web site: http://www.festrail.co.uk
Main stations: Porthmadog Harbour, Blaenau Ffestiniog
Other public stations: Boston Lodge, Minffordd, Penrhyn, Plas Halt, Tan-y-Bwlch, Dduallt, Tanygrisiau
OS reference: SH 571384
Car parks: Porthmadog, Tan-y-Bwlch, Tanygrisiau, Blaenau Ffestiniog
Access by public transport: Minffordd and Blaenau Ffestiniog main line stations. Porthmadog, Minffordd and Blaenau Ffestiniog served by local buses
Refreshment facilities: Licensed restaurant at Porthmadog, café at Tan-y-Bwlch, refreshments also on most trains
Souvenir shops: Porthmadog, Tan-y-Bwlch, Blaenau Ffestiniog
Museum: Interesting artefacts in

Locomotives

Name	No	Builder	Type	Built
Princess	1	G/England (199/200)	0-4-0STT	1863
Prince	2	G/England	0-4-0STT	1863
Palmerston	4	G/England	0-4-0STT	1863
Welsh Pony	5	G/England (234)	0-4-0STT	1867
Earl of Merioneth	—	FR	0-4-4-0T	1979
Merddin Emrys	10	FR	0-4-4-0T	1879
David Lloyd George	12	FR	0-4-4-0T	1992
Taliesin	—	FR	0-4-4T	1999
Moelwyn	—	Baldwin (49604)	2-4-0DM	1918
Lilla*	—	Hunslet (554)	0-4-0ST	1891
Blanche	—	Hunslet (589)	2-4-0STT	1893
Linda	—	Hunslet (590)	2-4-0STT	1893
Britomart*	—	Hunslet (707)	0-4-0ST	1899
Mountaineer	—	Alco (57156)	2-6-2T	1917
Livingston Thompson†	3	FR	0-4-4-0T	1886
Harlech Castle	—	B/Drewry (3767)	0-6-0-DH	1983
Ashover	—	Hibberd (3307)	4wDM	1948
Moel Hebog	—	Hunslet (4113)	0-4-0DM	1955
Mary Ann	—	M/Rail (596)	4wDM	1917
Criccieth Castle	—	FR	0-6-0DH	1995
The Colonel	—	M/Rail (8788)	4wDM	1943
Diana	—	M/Rail (21579)	4wDM	1957
Stefcomatic	—	Matisa (48589)	2-2-0DH	1956
Vale of Ffestiniog	—	Funkey	Bo-Bo	1968
Moel-y-Gest	—	Hunslet (6659)	0-4-0DM	1965

*privately owned
†on loan to National Railway Museum

Stock
32 bogie coaches; 8 4-wheel coaches; 4 brake vans, plus numerous service vehicles

Spooner's Bar, Porthmadog
Depot: Boston Lodge
Length of line: 13.5 miles, 1ft 11.5in gauge
Passenger trains: Porthmadog-Blaenau Ffestiniog

Period of public operation: Daily 24 March to 4 November, limited winter service
Special events: Interactive IV Weekend — 5-7 May (drive, fire, ride on the locomotives); 175th

Anniversary Celebrations — 28 May. Other events being planned, please visit our web site for details
Facilities for disabled: Porthmadog and Blaenau Ffestiniog easily accessible for wheelchairs.

Limited facilities on trains for disabled in wheelchairs by prior arrangement
Special facilities: Tan-y-Bwlch station is a registered location for civil/wedding ceremonies. Special Functions

department handles private train bookings — phone for details
Membership details: Ffestiniog Railway Society (see above address)
Membership journal: *Ffestiniog Railway Magazine* — quarterly

---

Timetable Service — Great Orme Tramway — Conwy

Member: HRA
A cable-hauled street tramway to the summit of the Great Orme is operated as two sections involving a change halfway. Opened to the public in July 1903, it includes gradients as steep as 1 in 3.9
Location: Great Orme Tramway, Victoria Station, Church Walks, Llandudno LL30 1AZ
OS reference: SH 7781
Operating society/organisation: Conwy County Borough Council, Property Services, Library Buildings, Mostyn Street, Llandudno LL30 1JP
Telephone: (01492) 879306

Internet address: *e-mail:* tramwayenquiries@conwy.gov.uk
Web site: www.greatormetramway.com
Car park: Approximately 100yd from Lower Terminal or adjacent to Summit Terminal
Access by public transport: Good
On site facilities: Shop
Exhibits for viewing: There are exhibits displayed at the Halfway station and a small exhibition (free)
Period of public operation: March to end of October (daily) 10.00-18.00 (17.00 March and October). Trams run every 20min.
Can be subject to change

Special notes: The only remaining cable-hauled street tramway in Britain. 1 mile long rising to 650ft (3ft 6in gauge)
Stock: 4 tramcars each seating 48, built 1902/3
Family tickets: Available, along with joint tickets for Great Orme Mine — Bronze Age Heritage Centre
Facilities for disabled: The tramway has limited disabled access and is unsuitable for the wheelchair-bound, although wheelchairs can be folded away in the tramcars

---

Timetable Service — Gwili Railway (Rheilffordd Gwili) — Carmarthenshire

Member: HRA, TT
Runs alongside the River Gwili on part of the former Carmarthen-Aberystwyth line. Attractions include a fully restored signalbox and historic station building. Extension to Danycoed opened in April 2001. A 7.25in gauge miniature railway and a riverside picnic site at Llwyfan Cerrig.
Headquarters: Gwili Railway Co Ltd, Bronwydd Arms Station, Bronwydd Arms, Carmarthen, SA33 6HT
Telephone: Carmarthen (01267) 230666
Internet address: *e-mail:* company@gwilirailway.co.uk
Web site: www.gwili-railway.co.uk
OS reference: Bronwydd Arms SN 417239
Llwyfan Cerrig SN 405258,
Main station: Bronwydd Arms
Other public station: Llwyfan

Locomotives

Name	No	Origin	Class	Type	Built
—**	D2178	BR	03	0-6-0DM	1962

Industrial locomotives

Name	No	Builder	Type	Built
Trecatty	—	R/Hornsby (421702)	0-6-0DM	1959
Olwen	—	RSH (7058)	0-4-0ST	1942
Welsh Guardsman	71516	RSH (7170)	0-6-0ST	1944
Nellie	02101	YEC(2779)	0-4-0DE	1960
Victory	—	A/Barclay (2201)	0-4-0ST	1945
Sir John†	—	Avonside (1680)	0-6-0ST	1914
*Swansea Jack**	—	R/Hornsby (393302)	4wDM	1955
*Haulwen†**	—	V/Foundry (5272)	0-6-0ST	1945

Stock
8 ex-BR Mk 1 coaches; 1 ex-BR griddle car; 1 ex-BR Mk 3 sleeper; 1 ex-TVR coach (built 1891); 1 Booth diesel-hydraulic crane; 1 ex-GWR 'Mink' van; 2 ex-GWR Fruit D; 1 ex-GWR Crocodile; 1 GWR Bloater; 2 ex-GWR Loriot D; 3 GWR Toad brake vans; 2 GWR bogie bolster wagons; 1 SECR parcels van; 2 SR parcels vans; 1 SR bogie parcel van; 1 LMS 20-ton brake van; 1 LNER open wagon; 2 LNER vans; 2 Army vans; 6 BR open wagons; 2 BP tank wagons; 3 open wagons

Cerrig, Danycoed
Car park: Bronwydd Arms (free) (not 6-9 April, 27-29 October when Park & Ride from Carmarthen must be used)
Access by public transport: Carmarthen railway station, then First Cymru services (Info Line: 0870 608 2306)
Refreshment facilities: Bronwydd Arms
Souvenir shop: Bronwydd Arms
Depot: Bronwydd Arms, stock also kept at Llwyfan Cerrig
Length of line: 2.5 miles
Passenger trains: Bronwydd Arms-Llwyfan Cerrig-Danycoed, approximately 1 hour service
Period of public operation: 6-9 April; 6/7, 27-31 May; 3, 6, 10, 17, 20, 27 June; 4, 8, 11, 15, 18, 22, 25, 27 July; 1-3, 5, 8-10, 12, 15-17, 19,

22-24, 26/27, 29-31 August; 2, 9, 16, 23, 30 September; 27-29 October; 8/9, 15/16, 20-24 December
Public opening: Trains leave Bronwydd Arms at 11.15, 12.30, 14.00, 15.15 and 16.30 on most operating days (except Sundays in June and September — 11.15, 12.45, 14.15, 15.45). A more frequent service operates in December
Facilities for disabled: Access to stations and trains

Owners
*The Railway Club of Wales
** Caerphilly Railway Society
†Vale of Neath Railway Society
†*National Museum of Wales Industrial & Maritime Museum in care of Caerphilly Railway Society

Special events: Day out with Thomas — 6-9 April, 27-29 October; Jazz Trains — 12 May, 23 June; Santa Specials — 8/9, 15/16, 20-24 December, details: Booking Hotline 01267 238213
Special notes: Family tickets available
Special facilities: Trains may be hired for special events, tour parties, birthdays, etc. Driver experience days — 5, 19 May

---

Timetable Service
Llanberis Lake Railway (Rheilffordd Llyn Padarn)
Gwynedd

Member: HRA

A narrow gauge passenger-carrying railway starting next to the historic Dinorwic Quarry workshops (now part of the National Museum of Wales) and running along the shores of the Llanberis lake using the trackbed of the former slate railway line to Port Dinorwic. Excellent views of Snowdonia and good picnic spots along the line

General Manager: David Jones
Headquarters: Llanberis Lake Railway, Gilfach Ddu, Llanberis, Gwynedd LL55 4TY
Telephone: Llanberis (01286) 870549
Internet address: *e-mail:* info@lake-railway.co.uk
Web site: www.lake-railway.co.uk
Main station: Padarn Park station/Gilfach Ddu
Other public stations: Cei Llydan and Llanberis (village)
OS reference: SH 586603
Car park: Padarn Park station/Gilfach Ddu
Refreshment facilities: Padarn Park station/Gilfach Ddu
Souvenir shop: Padarn Park station/Gilfach Ddu, Llanberis station

Industrial locomotives

Name	No	Builder	Type	Built
Elidir	1	Hunslet (493)	0-4-0ST	1889
Thomas Bach/Wild Aster	2	Hunslet (849)	0-4-0ST	1904
Dolbadarn	3	Hunslet (1430)	0-4-0ST	1922
Topsy	7	R/Hornsby (441427)	4wDM	1961
Twll Coed	8	R/Hornsby (268878)	4wDM	1956
—	—	R/Hornsby (425796)	4wDM	1958
Garrett	11	R/Hornsby (198286)	4wDM	1939
—	18	M/Rail (7927)	4wDM	1941
Llanelli	19	R/Hornsby (451901)	4wDM	1961
Una*	—	Hunslet (873)	0-4-0ST	1905

*not part of the railway's motive power stock. Housed at the adjacent slate museum and can sometimes be seen working demonstration freight trains

Stock

Length of line: 2.5 miles, 1ft 11.5in gauge
Journey time: approx 60min
Passenger trains: Gilfach Ddu-Llanberis-Penllyn-Gilfach Ddu The half mile extension from Gilfach Ddu to Llanberis village is now open
Journey time: Return trip approx 60min
Period of public operation: Tuesdays in February and early March, and daily February half term week. Sundays to Thursdays in March and October. Sundays to Fridays, April to September.

Tuesdays in November and early December. Also Saturdays June, July and August. Family tickets available, under 3s free
Special events: Santa trains in December
Facilities for disabled: Level approaches throughout shop, café and to train. Special toilet facilities provided. Specially adapted carriage for wheelchair users
Marketing names: Rheilffordd Llyn Padarn Cyfyngedig (Padarn Lake Railway Ltd); Llanberis Lake Railway

190

Wales

Great Western Railway No 6430 was built in 1937 and is normally resident on the Llangollen Railway. It is seen here with a GWR autocoach in tow whilst on loan to the Gwili Railway. *Alan Barnes*

Wales

Member: HRA, TT

The line, which is presently 7.5 miles long, is situated in the picturesque Dee Valley and follows the River Dee for much of its route. It affords good views of the dramatic Welsh countryside between Llangollen and Carrog the latter station having been reached in 1996. In that year the railway was the winner of the Ian Allan 'Independent Railway of the Year' award. In 2002 the section between Glyndyfrdwy to Carrog was the venue for BBC 2's Timewatch re-enactment of the Rainhill Trials using the replica locomotives *Rocket*, *Sans Pareil* and *Novelty*, whilst 2003 saw the award-winning renovation of Berwyn Viaduct. This included the reinstatement of the cantilevered platform extension, the original having been removed by British Railways in the early 1960s. Last year the extensive

Locomotives and multiple-units

Name	No	Origin	Class	Type	Built
—	2859	GWR	2800	2-8-0	1918
—	3802*	GWR	2800	2-8-0	1938
—	5199	GWR	5101	2-6-2T	1934
—	5532	GWR	4575	2-6-2T	1928
—	5538	GWR	4575	2-6-2T	1928
—	5643	GWR	5600	0-6-0PT	1937
—	6430+	GWR	6400	0-6-2T	1925
Betton Grange	6880§	GWR	'Manor'	4-6-0	
—	7754	GWR	5700	0-6-0PT	1930
Foxcote Manor	7822	GWR	'Manor'	4-6-0	1950
—	47298	LMS	3F	0-6-0T	1924
Magpie	44806	LMS	5MT	4-6-0	1944
—	80072	BR	4MT	2-6-4T	1954
—	03162	BR	03	0-6-0DM	1960
—	13265	BR	08	0-6-0DE	1956
—	D8142	BR	20	Bo-Bo	1966
—	25313	BR	25	Bo-Bo	1966
—	37240	BR	37	Co-Co	1964
Mirlees Pioneer	37901	BR	37	Co-Co	1963
—	46010	BR	46	1Co-Co1	1961
Oribi	D1566	BR	47	Co-Co	1962
—	50416	Wickham	109	MBS	1958
—	50447	BRCW	104	DMBS	1957

restoration of Llangollen station was completed with assistance from the Heritage Lottery fund. Work is proceeding to complete the reinstatement of signalling at Carrog this year and progress continues to be made for the eventual restoration of the railway to the town of Corwen, 2.5 miles west of Carrog, where a new terminus will be constructed

Location: Llangollen station is situated alongside the River Dee at the junction of Abbey Road (A542) with Castle Street/Mill Street (A539). Traffic from the A5 should turn off at the traffic lights into Castle Street (A539).

Chairman: Gordon Heddon

Operating company: Llangollen Railway plc

Headquarters/principal station: Llangollen Railway Trust Ltd, The Station, Abbey Road, Llangollen, Denbighshire LL20 8SN (both organisations)

Telephone:
General enquiries: 01978 860979 (office hours).
Talking Timetable: 01978 860951 (24hr).
Santa booking: 01978 860979 (1 October to 24 December).

Fax: 01978 869247

Internet address: *E-mail:* llangollen,railway@btinternet.com
Web site: http://www.llangollen-railway. co.uk

OS reference: SJ 214422

OS reference: SJ 214422

Car park: Llangollen (Market St) and Mill St; Carrog — station car park on B5437 off A5 west of Llangollen

Access by public transport:
By rail: Ruabon (5 miles) on Shrewsbury-Chester line, then by bus
By bus: Regular service runs Monday-Saturday and less frequently on Sundays. Enquiries: Traveline Cymru 0870 608 2 608

Station information:
Llangollen — Toilets (inc disabled and baby changing, souvenir shop, cafe
Berwyn — Tea room open on summer weekends
Deeside Halt — Trains call by request only, please inform guard or give a clear signal to driver to be picked up (please see timetable

Name	No	Origin	Class	Type	Built
—	50454	BRCW	104	DMBS	1957
—	50528	BRCW	104	DMC	1957
—	51118†	Gloucester	100	MBS	1957
—	51618	BR	127	DMBS	1959
—	51907	BR	108	DMBS	1960
—	54490	BR	108	DTC	1960
—	55513±	BR	141	DMS	1984
—	55533±	BR	141	DMSL	1984
—	56097†	Gloucester	100	DTCL	1957
—	56171	Wickham	109	DTC	1958
—	56456	Cravens	105	DMBS	1958

*expected to return to South Devon Railway during 2007
+expected to return to Lakeside & Haverthwaite Railway during 2007
§new build by 6880 Bretton Grange Project to create 81st member of class
†currently at Midland Railway — Butterley for restoration
±currently out based for use at Midland Railway — Butterley

Industrial locomotives

Name	No	Builder	Type	Built
Eliseg	—	Fowler (22753)	0-4-0DM	1939
Jennifer	—†	H/Clarke (1731)	0-6-0T	1942
Jessie	—	Hunslet (1873)	0-6-0ST	1937
Darfield No 1	—†	Hunslet (3783)	0-6-0ST	1953
Austin No 1	—†	Kitson (5459)	0-6-0ST	1932
—	68072	Vulcan (5309)	0-6-0ST	1945
—	391•	YEC (2630)	0-6-0DE	1959
—	398•	YEC (2769)	0-6-0DE	1959
—	D2892	YEC/BTH (2782)	0-4-0DE	1960
—	D2899	YEC (2854)	0-6-0DE	1961
Davy	—	E/Electric (1901)	0-6-0DE	1951

†expected to be away on hire for 2007
•on five year loan from Wilmott Bros, Ilkeston

Stock: *coaches, capprox 45 in total including* — Service sets of Mk 1 stock, 4 BR suburban coaches (3 off site); 1 LNER Thompson lounge car; 1 LNER Thompson brake coach; 2 GWR autocoaches; 1 GN brake, etc, some under restoration

Stock: *wagons, approx 50 including* — 2 Bolster wagons; 3 GWR Toad brake vans; 1 BR(E) brake van; 4 BR ballast wagons; 1 BR Presflow wagon; 1 GWR 'Fruit D'; 2 GWR Tube wagons; 1 Esso tank wagon; 1 Shell tank wagon plus various other items of freight stock

Stock: *maintenance* — Cowans 50-ton breakdown crane ARD96718 ex-Laira; 1 Matisa track recording machine; 1 Trackmaster light shunting vehicle; O&K road-railer

Owners
2859 and 5532 the Llangollen Railway GW Locomotive Group
3802 the GW 3802 Ltd
5199 the 5199 Project
5643 the Furness Railwa Trust
7754, 13265, *Jennifer* and *Austin No 1* the Llangollen Railway Trust Ltd
7822 the Foxcote Manor Society
80072 the 80072 Steam Locomotive Co Ltd
03162 the Wirral Borough Council
All DMUs the Llangollen Railcar group
All main line diesel fleet (except 37901) plus *Davy* the Llangollen Diesel Group
Remainder are privately owned

for specific services)

Glyndyfrdwy — Toilets, tea room open on pak weekends

Carrog — Car and coach park (free), toilets with disabled access and tea room (closed Mondays except for special events, also from Christmas to end january)

Length of line: 7.5 miles

Passenger trains: Llangollen-Carrog

Period of public operation: 3/4, 10/11, 16-18, 24-31 March; 1-15, 17-22, 24-26, 28/29 April; 1-3 May; daily 5 May to 14 October; 16-18, 20 October to 4 November; 1/2, 8/9, 15/16, 20-24, 26-31 December; 1 January 2008.

Special events: Spring Diesel Gala — 16-18 March; Steel, Steam & Stars Steam Gala — 20-22 April (more info on www.6880gala.co.uk); Murder Mystery Train* — 12 May; Railcar Gala — 9/10 June; Murder Mystery Train* — 16 June, 21 July; Day out with Thomas — 4-12 August; Autumn Steam Gala — 15/16 September; Autumn Diesel Gala — 5-7 October; Day out with Thomas — 20-28 October; Santa Specials* — 1/2, 8/9, 15/16, 20-24 December; Mince Pie Specials — 26 December to 1 January 2008. Events marked * must be pre-booked

Driver experiences: The railway offers a varied programme of footplate and railway experience courses from early spring through to late autumn, ranging from the basic Summer Evening Ramble to the more advanced all-day railway experience. Cources are available on Steam and diesel locomotives as well as DMUs for both individual and group bookings. A brochure is available from Llangollen station and early booking is recommended

Special facilities: The Robertson Suite at Llangollen is licensed for civil/wedding ceremonies. Train hire available for receptions

Facilities for disabled: Special passenger coach for wheelchairs, toilet facilities at llangollen and Carrog

Membership details: The Membership Secretary, Llangollen Railway Trust Ltd, c/o above address

Membership journal: *Steam at Llangollen*

Special note: For safety reasons visitors to the railway are not permitted access to locomotive yard, engine shed or workshop unless accompanied by a qualified member of the Llangollen Railway

---

Museum — Penrhyn Castle Industrial Railway Museum — Conwy

Member: HRA

A collection of historic industrial steam locomotives, both standard and narrow gauge, displayed in Penrhyn Castle, a well-known National Trust property in the area regularly open to visitors

Location: Llandegai, near Bangor. One mile east of Bangor on the A5

OS reference: SH 603720

Operating society/organisation: National Trust, Penrhyn Castle, Industrial Railway Museum, Llandegai, Nr Bangor LL57 4HN

Telephone: Bangor (01248) 353084

Internet address: *Web site:* www.nationaltrust.org

Car park: Within castle grounds

Access by public transport: By rail: Bangor (3 miles). Bus: Arriva Cymru 5, 6, 7 and 67, 5X

On site facilities: The castle is open to the public, and contains a gift shop. Light refreshments are available, hot meals are available between 12.00 and 14.30

Public opening: Daily (except Tuesdays) late March-end October. July/August — 10.00-17.00. Other months —11.00-17.00. Last admission 30min before closing

Facilities for disabled: Access to castle and museum

Special notes: For those interested in stately homes the castle is well worth a visit. The entrance fee covers both the castle and the railway exhibits housed in the castle courtyard. Ruston Hornsby locomotive *Acorn* can be seen operating on some occasions during opening times. For exhibits not on display please ask a member of museum staff for assistance. Reduced entry fee for grounds and railway museum

Industrial locomotives

Name	No	Builder	Type	Built
Kettering Furnaces No 3	—	B/Hawthorn (859)	0-4-0ST	1885*
Watkin	—	de Winton	0-4-0VBT	1893*
Fire Queen	—	Horlock	0-4-0	1848†
Hawarden	—	H/Clarke (526)	0-4-0ST	1899
Vesta	—	H/Clarke (1223)	0-6-0T	1916
Charles	—	Hunslet (283)	0-4-0ST	1882§
Hugh Napier	—	Hunslet (855)	0-4-0ST	1904§
—	1	Neilson (1561)	0-4-0WT	1870
Haydock	—	Stephenson (2309)	0-6-0T	1879
Acorn	—	R/Hornsby (327904)	0-4-0DM	1948

*3ft gauge
†4ft gauge
§1ft 10.75in gauge

Stock

10 narrow gauge rolling stock exhibits from the Padarn/Penrhyn system. The small relics section includes a comprehensive display of railway signs and model locomotives in the upper stable block

Pontypool & Blaenavon Railway

Member: HRA

The historic Blaenavon site, complete with its railway installations and locomotives, can easily be included in a visit to Big Pit Mining Museum

Location: Just off the B4248 between Blaenavon and Brynmawr. Signposted as you approach Blaenavon

OS reference: SO 237093

Operating society/organisation: Pontypool & Blaenavon Railway Co (1983) Ltd, Council Offices, 101 High Street, Blaenavon NP4 9PT

Telephone/Fax: (01495) 792263

Internet address: *e-mail:* railwayoffice@aol.com
Web site: www.pontypool-and-blaenavon.co.uk

Car park: Adjacent to railway terminus

On site facilities: Light refreshments and souvenir shop on train

Public opening: Weekends and Bank Holidays (except Good Friday) 15 April to 1 October, daily 20-25 August, plus Wednesdays 1, 8, 15 August.

Trains run every half hour from Furnace Sidings station from 11.30-16.30.

Santa trains run every half hour 11.00-15.30.

Return journey time about 17min

Note: All services will be either DMU or diesel-locomotive hauled except 11/12 August

Special events: Easter Bunny Specials — 8/9 April; Teddy Bears' Picnic — 6/7 May; Lucky Dip Specials — 27/28 May; Father's Day Specials — 17 June; Model Railway Show — 23/24 June; Diesel Gala — 28/29 July; Ivor the Engine — 11/12 August (steam service); DMU — 20-25 August; Fifth Grand Transport Rally —

Locomotives

Name	No	Origin	Class	Type	Built
—	2874	GWR	2800	2-8-0	1918
—	3855	GWR	2884	2-8-0	1942
—	4253	GWR	4200	2-8-0T	1917
—	5668	GWR	5600	0-6-2T	1926
Bickmarsh Hall	5967	GWR	'Hall'	4-6-0	1937
—	9629	GWR	5700	0-6-0PT	1946
—	51351	P/Steel	117	DMBS	1959
—	51397	P/Steel	117	DMS	1959
—	51942	BR	108	DMCL	1960
—	52044	BR	108	DMCL	1960
—	54270	BR	108	DTCL	1960
—	50632	BR	108	DMCL	1960
—	59520	P/Steel	117	TC	1959
—	60117	BR	205	DMBS	1957
—	60828	BR	205	DTC	1957

Industrial locomotives

Name	No	Builder	Type	Built
Harry	—	Barclay (1823)	0-4-0ST	1926
Tom Parry	—	Barclay (2015)	0-4-0ST	1935
—	8	RSH (7139)	0-6-0ST	1944
Llanwern	104	E/Electric (D1249)	0-6-0DH	1968
—	106	E/Electric (D1226)	0-6-0DH	1971
—	RT1	Fowler (22497)	0-6-0DM	1938
Ebbw	17	Hunslet (7063)	0-8-0DH	1971
—	14	H/Clarke (D615)	0-6-0DH	1938
—	DL16	H/Clarke (D1387)	0-4-0DH	1968
Panteg No 1	—	Sentinel (10083)	0-6-0DH	1961

Stock

10 ex-BR Mk 1 coaches, 4 ex-GWR coaches, 3 ex-LSWR coaches, 1 ex-LMS sleeper, 23 other vans, china clay, coke and tank wagons

Owners

Class 108s the Gwent 108 Group

26/27 August; Blues and Jazz Special — 6 October; Santa Specials (steam) — 1/2, 8/9, 15/16, 22/23 December. New Year DEMU Specials — 29/30 December Please visit web site for up-to-date information.

Special notes: The railway incorporates the former mineral/LNWR passenger lines running through Big Pit. Both north and southward extensions are being considered. Service currently operates between Furnace Sidings platform and Whistle Inn platform. The railway runs near to the Garn Lakes — ideal for picnics after a train ride

Membership details: c/o above address, or call at 'The Railway Shop', Broad Street, Blaenavon

Rheilffordd Eryri — Welsh Highland Railway (Caernarfon)

Timetable Service | Gwynedd

Member: HRA

The Welsh Highland Railway Construction Ltd has been incorporated to reconstruct much of the original WHR line. The new northern terminus is at Caernarfon, with reopening to Porthmadog anticipated by 2009

General Manager: Paul Lewin

Headquarters: Ffestiniog Railway Co, Harbour Station, Porthmadog LL49 9NF

Telephone: Porthmadog (01766) 516000

Fax: 01766 516005

Internet address: *Web site:* http://www.festrail.co.uk

Main station: Caernarfon

Other public station: Bontnewydd, Dinas, Waunfawr, Plas y Nant, Snowdon Ranger, Rhyd Ddu

OS reference: SH 481625

Car parks: Caernarfon

Access by public transport:
Caernarfon is served by local buses. The station at Bangor is served by Virgin and Arriva Trains (Wales). There is a regular bus service between Bangor and Caernarfon

Depot: Dinas

Length of line: 12 miles, 1ft 11.5in gauge

Passenger trains: Caernarfon-Rhyd Ddu

Future extensions: Rhyd Ddu-Porthmadog

Locomotives

Name	No	Builder	Type	Built
—	K1	B/Peacock (5292)	0-4-0+0-4-0	1909
—**	133	S. F. Belge (2683)	2-8-2	1953
—**	134	S. F. Belge (2684)	2-8-2	1953
*Millennium/ Mileniwm**	138	B/Peacock (7863)	2-6-2+2-6-2	1958
—*	140	B/Peacock (7865)	2-6-2+2-6-2	1958
—*	143	B/Peacock (7868)	2-6-2+2-6-2	1958
—*§	87	Cockerill (3267)	2-6-2+2-6-2	1936
Castell Caernarfon	—	Funkey	Bo-Bo	1968
Upnor Castle	—	Hibberd (3687)	4wDM	1954
Conway Castle	—	Hibberd (3831)	4wDM	1958

*former South African Railways NGG16 class locomotives
**former South African Railways NG15 class locomotives
†not on site
§undergoing restoration at Ffestiniog Railway's Boston Lodge works
The above locomotives may not be on site. Ffestiniog Railway Co locomotives may operate some services

Stock

12 bogie coaches, 1 brake van (goods), numerous service vehicles

Period of public operation: Daily 25 March-4 November, limited winter service

Facilities for disabled: Limited facilities on trains for disabled in wheelchairs by prior arrangement

Refreshments: A refreshment trolley is available on most trains. Snowdonia Parc Hotel is situated at Waunfawr station serving a large selection of snacks, meals and real ale

Souvenir shop: There is a new enlarged gift shop at Caernarfon

Special event: 'Rail Ale' Beer Festival — 12/13 May; 'Join-in' Weekend — 9/10 September

Membership details: Welsh Highland Railway Society (see above address)

Membership journal: *Snowdon Ranger* — quarterly

Rhyl Miniature Railway

Steam Centre | Denbighshire

Member: Britain's Great Little Railways

The miniature railway operating around the Marine Lake at Rhyl is among the oldest 15in gauge railways in the world. Its origins go back to 1911, and on peak days you can ride on the same train that visitors in 1920 would have found

Operating society/organisation:

Rhyl Steam Preservation Trust

Location: Marine Lake, Wellington Road, Rhyl, Denbighshire

Internet address: *Web site:* www.rhylminiaturerailway.co.uk

Trust secretary: Simon Townsend

Postal address: 10 Cilnant, Mold, Flintshire CH7 1GG

Telephone: 01352 759109

OS reference: SN 072124

Length: Approx 1 mile (1ft 3in gauge)

On site facilities: Car park

Access by public transport: Approx 1 mile from Rhyl main line station, buses to Towyn and Abergele pass by

Period of public operation: Operation (steam) Bank Holiday Sundays and Mondays, every Sunday from mid-June to early September, every Thursday and

Saturday during school holidays; all weather permitting from 13.00 or earlier. Also diesel haulage on other days during summer school holidays
Special event: Grand Gala Weekend — 26-28 May, to coincide with the opening of new station building and museum
Membership details: Friends of Rhyl Miniature Railway, details from 01745 339477, newsletters twice a year

Locomotives

Name	No	Builder	Type	Built
Joan	101	Barnes	4-4-2	1920
Billy	106	Barnes	4-4-2	1934
—	44	Cagney	4-4-0	c1910
Clara	—	Guest & Saunders LE	0-4-2DM (SO)	1961
—	—	Lister	4wDM	1938

Rolling stock: 5 bogie 'cars de luxe' built in the 1910s and a similar vehicle built in 2001, 2 Cagney bogie coaches built c1904. Ballast wagon

Owners
Billy Rhyl Town Council

Timetable Service	**Snowdon Mountain Railway**	Gwynedd

Member: HRA
The only public rack and pinion railway in the British Isles, opened in 1896, this bustling line climbs the slopes of Snowdon to the café at the top
General Manager: Alan Kendall
Engineering Manager: Sam Reeves
Commercial Manager: Vince Hughes
Marketing Manager: Jonathan Tyler
Headquarters: Snowdon Mountain Railway, Llanberis LL55 4TY
Telephone: 0870 450 0033 (advance bookings available via telephone)
Fax: (01286) 872518
Internet address: *e-mail:* info@snowdonrailway.co.uk *Web site:* www.snowdonrailway.co.uk
Main station: Llanberis
Other public stations: Summit, also Clogwyn/Rocky Valley when Summit is inaccessible
OS reference: SH 582597
Car park: Llanberis
Access by public transport: Bangor railway station then by bus, either direct, or alternatively via Caernarfon. Snowdon Sherpa Services to/from Beddgelert and Betws-y-coed stop outside the station
Refreshment facilities: Llanberis
Souvenir shops: Llanberis
Depot: Llanberis
Length of line: 7.5km, 800mm gauge
Passenger trains: Llanberis-

Locomotives

Name	No	Builder	Type	Built
Enid	2	SLM (924)	0-4-2T	1895
Wyddfa	3	SLM (925)	0-4-2T	1895
Snowdon	4	SLM (988)	0-4-2T	1896
Moel Siabod	5†	SLM (989)	0-4-2T	1896
Padarn	6	SLM (2838)	0-4-2T	1922
Ralph	7*	SLM (2869)	0-4-2T	1923
Eryri	8*	SLM (2870)	0-4-2T	1923
Ninian	9	Hunslet (9249)	0-4-0DH	1986
Yeti	10	Hunslet (9250)	0-4-0DH	1986
Peris	11	Hunslet (9305)	0-4-0DH	1991
George	12	Hunslet (9312)	0-4-0DH	1992

All steam locomotives were built by Swiss Locomotive Works, Winterthur
All diesel locomotives were built by Hunslet Engine Co, Leeds
†currently out of service
*currently stored out of service (boilerless)

Stock
8 closed bogie coaches; 1 bogie works car; 1 4-wheel open wagon; a 3-car diesel-electric railcar set built 1995 by HPE Tredegar (fleet Nos 21, 22, 23 [Works Nos 1074/5/6])

Clogwyn. Journey time approx 45min. Departures from Llanberis at 30min intervals subject to passenger demand. Round trip approx 2hr
Period of public operation: Daily 31 March-first week of November inclusive subject to winter maintenance. Please visit web site for updated opening times
Group bookings: Bookings for groups of 15 or more can be taken in advance. Please call 0870 450 0033 for special rates
Summit redevelopment: Due to rebuilding to the Summit facility, all trains in 2007 will be terminating at Clogwyn (3/4 distance up Snowdon). Please note

there is a partial fare for the return journey to Clogwyn
Facilities for disabled: Those requiring wheelchair access should please telephone in advance to discuss their particular requirements. Disabled parking is available and there are suitable toilet facilities in both Llanberis station and the Summit. Only officially registered support dogs can travel on the trains
Special notes: Trains depart subject to weather conditions and passenger demand. If weather conditions become severe on Snowdon trains will terminate at Rocky Valley (5/8 distance up Snowdon).

Swansea Vale Railway

Member: HRA

The Swansea Vale Railway operates over a 1.5 mile section of the former Midland Railway route between Swansea and Brecon, on what was one of the oldest tramroads in South Wales. Passenger services ceased completely in 1950, and by 1968 the last section of the line between Six Pit and the Docks had been closed

Charity No: 1012356

Location/headquarters: Swansea Vale Railway, Upper Bank, Pentrechwyth, Swansea SA1 7DB

Telephone: 01792 461000

Internet address: *e-mail:* swanseavalerailway@thersgb.co.uk *Web site:* www.swanseavalerailway.co.uk

Main stations: Nantyffin, Nantyffin Road, Llansamlet, Swansea.

Llansamlet is situated 2 miles north of the City of Swansea, opposite Comet store

Other stations: Cwm Halt and Upper Bank Junction (awaiting development)

OS reference: Nantyffin — SN 683969, Upper Bank Junction — SN 668953

Length of line: 2 miles

Car parks: Free car parks at Six Pit Junction and Upper Bank Works at owner's risk

Access by public transport: By train — Llansamlet (approx 20min walk). By bus — ring Traveline Cymru (0870 608 2608), ask for Nantyffin station (opposite new Comet store), Llansamlet. To visit workshops ask for Upper Bank, Pentrechwyth

Refreshment facilities: On train on operating days only (snacks and hot & cold drinks)

Souvenir shop: On train souvenir on operating days. The society also has a shop selling railway memorabelia, model railway equipment and books in High Street

Locomotives and multiple-units

Name	No	Origin	Class	Type	Built
	03141	BR	03	0-6-0DM	1960
—	51134	BR	116	DMBS	1958
—	51135	BR	116	DMBS	1958
—	51147	BR	116	DMS	1958
—	51148	BR	116	DMS	1958
—	55026	P/Steel	121	DMBS	1960
—	59445	BR	116	TS	1959
—	59490	P/Steel	117	TCL	1960

Industrial locomotives

Name	No	Builder	Type	Built
Llantarnam Abbey	—	Barclay (2074)	0-6-0ST	1939
—	—	Hunslet (3829)	0-6-0ST	1955
Mond	1	Peckett (1345)	0-4-0ST	1914
—	2	N/British (27914)	0-4-0DM	1961
—	—	R/Hornsby (200792)	4wDM	????
Lady Natasha	—	R/Hornsby (200793)	4wDM	????
—	—	R/Hornsby (312433)	4wDM	1951

Stock: *coaches:* 1 BR Mk 2 BSK

Stock: *wagons:* 1 GWR brake van 'Toad', 1 BR brake van, 3 4-wheel tar tanks (ex-NCB), 3 LMS 12-ton mineral wagons, 1 BR 'Gane A' bogie bolster, 1 GWR 'Mink' 10-ton van, 3 GWR 10-ton vans, 1 10-ton open, 2 GWR 'Tunney' wagons, 1 LNER low-fit, GWR Pooley van, BR 13-ton single bolster wagon

Stock: *cranes:* Smith-Rodley 4-wheel steam crane, Cowans & Sheldon LMS rail-mounted hand crane

Owners

DMUs the Llanelli & District Railway Society
Llantarnam Abbey the Llantarnam Abbey Locomotive Association
Mond SULSOC
Rustons) — private owners
Smith-Rodley crane — privately owned
03141 the Dean Forest Diesel Association

Arcade, Swansea, open most weekdays and Saturdays (Tel: 07973536246 [mobile])

Depot: Upper Bank Works

Facilities for disabled: Nantyffin Road station has a wheelchair ramp, and each train carries awheelchair ramp for access from platforms

Period of public operation: The workshops are not currently open to the public, though special arrangements for guided tours may be made by telephoning the depot in advance

Operating days: Due to major

tracklaying/improvement operations, public services are currently suspended until further notice

Membership details: Iain Pearce, 18 Sketty Avenue, Sketty, Swansea SA20TE.
Tel: 01792 428 721

Membership journal: *Vale News*

Steam & Diesel hire: For special parties, school or society outings and educational visits

Driver training experience courses: On steam or diesel multiple-unit

Talyllyn Railway

Member: HRA, TT

The very first railway in the country to be rescued and operated by enthusiasts, the line climbs from Tywyn through the wooded Welsh hills past Dolgoch Falls to Nant Gwernol. The trains are hauled by a variety of veteran tank engines, all immaculately maintained by the railway's own workshops at Tywyn Pendre

Managing Director: David Mitchell

Traffic manager: David Leech

Headquarters: Talyllyn Railway Co, Wharf Station, Tywyn, Gwynedd LL36 9EY

Telephone: Tywyn (01654) 710472

Fax: (01654) 711755

Internet address: Web sites: www.talyllyn.co.uk www.ngrm.org.uk

Main station: Tywyn Wharf

Other public stations: Tywyn Pendre, Rhydyronen, Brynglas, Dolgoch Falls, Abergynolwyn, Nant Gwernol

OS reference: SH 586005 (Tywyn Wharf)

Car parks: Tywyn Wharf, Dolgoch, Abergynolwyn

Access by public transport: Tywyn main line station. Bus Gwynedd services to Tywyn

Refreshment facilities: Tywyn Wharf, Abergynolwyn hot and cold snacks available. Picnic areas at Dolgoch Falls and Abergynolwyn.
   Railway adventure children's playground at Abergynolwyn station

Souvenir shops: Tywyn Wharf, Abergynolwyn

Museum: Tywyn Wharf

Depot: Tywyn Pendre

Length of line: 7.25 miles, 2ft 3in gauge

Passenger trains: Tywyn-Nant Gwernol

Period of public operation: Sundays in March. Daily 25 March to 3 November, 26 December-1 January 2008

Journey times: Tywyn-Nant Gwernol — single 55min, return 2hr 15min

Special events: Tom Rolt Vintage Rally — 27/28 May; Children's

Locomotives

Name	No	Builder	Type	Built
Talyllyn	1	F/Jennings (42)	0-4-2ST	1865
Dolgoch	2	F/Jennings (63)	0-4-0WT	1866
Sir Haydn	3	Hughes (323)	0-4-2ST	1878
Edward Thomas	4	K/Stuart (4047)	0-4-2ST	1921
Midlander	5	R/Hornsby (200792)	4wDM	1940
Douglas/Duncan	6	Barclay (1431)	0-4-0WT	1918
Tom Rolt*	7	Barclay (2263)	0-4-2T	1949
Merseysider	8	R/Hornsby (476108)	4wDH	1964
Alf	9	Hunslet (4136)	0-4-0DM	1950
Bryneglwys	10	Simplex (101T023)	0-4-0DM	c1985

Locomotive notes: In service — Nos 1, 2, 3, 4, 6 and 7
*virtually a new locomotive rebuilt from the original at Pendre Works

Stock

13 4-wheel coaches/vans; 10 bogie coaches; 45 wagons

Narrow Gauge Museum, Tywyn

Name	No	Builder	Type	Built
Dot	—	B/Peacock (2817)	0-4-0ST	1887
Rough Pup	—	Hunslet (541)	0-4-0ST	1891
—	2	K/Stuart (721)	0-4-0WT	1902
Jubilee 1897	—	M/Wardle (1382)	0-4-0ST	1897
George Henry	—	de Winton	0-4-0T	1877
—	13	Spence	0-4-0T	1895
Nutty*	—	Sentinel (7701)	0-4-0VB	1929

Various wagons and miscellaneous equipment
*not currently on site

Duncan Day* — 31 May; Talyllyn Have-a-Go Gala — 6-8 July; Victorian Week — 29 July-2 August; Race the Train (limited service) — 18 August; Murder Mystery Train — 22 (Wed) August; Land Rover Rally — 26 August; *Duncan's* Special Children's Day — 23* August; Carol Train (7pm) — 16 December; Santa Specials — 16, 22-24 December.
*Thursdays

Talyllyn Vintage Train: The TR is probably alone in still being able to run its complete original passenger train dating from the 1860s, and invites you to enjoy this unique experience, travelling in original coaches behind an original locomotive. The train will depart at 11.00 on Thursdays 14, 28 June, 12 July and 6, 13, 20 September, featuring photographic opportunities and guided tour. Advance booking is advised. Small supplement payable

Family tickets: Available

Facilities for disabled: No problem for casual visitors, advance notice preferred for groups. Access to shop, museum and cafeteria possible at Tywyn and Abergynolwyn. Disabled toilet facilities at Tywyn and Abergynolwyn. Limited capacity for wheelchairs on trains

Special notes: Parties, private charter trains and footplate experience days by arrangement. Children under 5 years of age free. Great Little Trains of Wales discount card accepted

Membership details: L. & J. Garvey (TRPS), 2 Brynmair, Tywyn, Gwynedd LL36 9AG

Membership journal: *Talyllyn News* — quarterly

Marketing names: One of the Great Little Trains. The first preserved railway in the world

Member: HRA

The line at Henllan was part of an extensive network of railways that spread through the valleys of west Wales in the mid-19th century. Originally laid in broad gauge, before being relaid to standard gauge. After the closure of commercial operations, the narrow gauge line was laid by enthusiasts

Operating society/organisation: Teifi Valley Railway, Henllan Station, Nr Newcastle Emlyn SA44 5TD

Telephone: (01559) 371077

Internet address: *Web site:* www.teifivalleyrailway.com

Main station: Henllan

Other public stations: Forest Halt, Pontprenshitw, Llandyfriog

Car park: Henllan (on B4334)

OS reference: SN 358407

Access by public transport: BR station — Carmarthen (14 miles). Bus service 461 to Henllan or 460

Refreshments: Henllan

Souvenirs: Henllan

Length of line: 2 miles (2ft gauge)

On site facilities: Children's play areas, woodland waterfall, nature trails, crazy golf and crazy quoits, picnic area, plus quarter-mile 7.25in gauge miniature railway. Display of narrow gauge freight wagons

Depot: Henllan (not open to public)

Facilities for disabled: All facilities including portable steps and wide door for wheelchairs in two coaches

Period of public operation: Daily 1 April to 31 October (EXCEPT 26/27 April; 3/4, 10/11, 17/18 May; 8, 15, 22, 29 June; 6, 13 July 6/7; 13/14, 20/21 September)

Special events: Halloween (evening trains), Santa Specials in December. Please contact for further details

Special notes: Pay once only and ride all day

Membership details: Teifi Valley Railway Society, c/o Henllan station

Membership journal: *Right Away* — quarterly

Industrial locomotives (2ft gauge)

Name	No	Builder	Type	Built
Alan George	—	Hunslet (606)	0-4-0ST	1894
Sgt Murphy	—	K/Stuart (3117)	0-6-2T	1918
Sholto	—	Hunslet (2433)	4wDM	1941
Simon	—	M/Rail (7126)	4wDM	1936
Sammy	—	M/Rail (605)	4wDM	1959

Industrial locomotive (standard gauge)

Name	No	Builder	Type	Built
Swansea Vale No 1*	—	Sentinel (9622)	4wVBTG	1958

Owners

*The Railway Club of Wales

Member: GLTW

This narrow gauge railway offers a 23-mile round trip from Aberystwyth to Devil's Bridge providing spectacular views which cannot be enjoyed by road. At Devil's Bridge there are walks to the Mynach Falls and Devil's Punch Bowl. Many artists have been inspired by the magnificence of Devil's Bridge and the Rheidol Valley

General Manager: N. Thompson

Headquarters: Vale of Rheidol Railway, The Locomotive Shed, Park Avenue, Aberystwyth SY23 1PG

Telephone: (01970) 625819

Fax: (01970) 623769

Internet address: *Web site:* www.rheidolrailway.co.uk

Locomotives

Name	No	Origin	Ex-BR Class	Type	Built
Owain Glyndwr	7	GWR	98	2-6-2T	1923
Llywelyn	8	GWR	98	2-6-2T	1923
Prince of Wales	9	GWR	98	2-6-2T	1924
—	10	Brecon MR (002)	98/1	0-6-0DH	1987

Stock

16 bogie coaches; 1 4-wheel guard's van; 14 wagons for maintenance use; 1 inspection trolley

The following locomotives are stored on the railway pending restoration and future display

Name	No	Builder	Type	Built
—	4	Decauville (1027)	0-4-0T	1926
Kathleen	—	de Winton	0-4-0VBT	1877
—	6	Fowler (10249)	0-6-0T+T	1905
—	21	Fowler (11938)	0-4-2T	1909
—	23	Fowler (15515)	0-6-2T	1920
Margaret	—	Hunslet (605)	0-4-0ST	1894
—	31	Mafei (4766)	0-8-0T	1916

Main station: Aberystwyth
(adjacent to main line station)
Other public stations: Devil's
Bridge, Rhiwfron, Rheidol Falls,
Aberffrwd, Nantyronen, Capel
Bangor, Glanrafon, Llanbadarn
OS reference: SN 587812
Car parks: Aberystwyth, Devil's
Bridge
Access by public transport:
Aberystwyth main line station, and
bus services to Aberystwyth
Refreshment facilities:
Aberystwyth (not railway owned),
Devil's Bridge (not railway
operated)

Name	No	Builder	Type	Built
—	—	H/Clarke (D564)	4wDM	1930
—	—*	R/Proctor (50823)	4wPM	1918
—	—	K/Stuart (3114)	0-4-0ST	1918

*metre gauge
Also Henschel bogie tender (11854/25 of 1917)

Souvenir shop: Aberystwyth
Depot: Aberystwyth (not open to
the public)
Length of line: 11.75 miles, 1ft
11.75in gauge
Journey time: Single 1hr, return
3hr
Passenger trains: Aberystwyth-

Devil's Bridge
Period of public operation:
Daily 3 April to 27 October, with
some exceptions in April, May,
June, September and October

(Timetable service) **Welsh Highland Railway — Porthmadog** (Gwynedd)

Member: HRA, GLToW, Star-
Attractions
The Welsh Highland Railway Ltd
operates services at the south-
western end of the old Welsh
Highland line and has its base in
the bustling holiday town of
Porthmadog. The company is
developing an exciting project to
enhance visitor facilities at the
Gelert's Farm site. Extension to
Pont Croesor is now under way.
  The WHR is very much a family
orientated attraction and adults
have the opportunity to purchase a
footplate pass
Location: Tremadog Road,
Porthmadog, immediately adjacent
to main line railway station and
opposite the Queen's Hotel
OS reference: SH 571393
Operating society/organisation:
Welsh Highland Railway Ltd,
Tremadog Road, Porthmadog,
Gwynedd LL49 9DY
Telephone:
Porthmadog: 01766 513402
24hr information line: 0870 321
2402
Out of hours phone: 01766 513402
Internet address: e-mail:
info@.whr.co.uk
Web site: www.whr.co.uk
Car park: Free — overflow car
park opposite the railway; this is
council owned, with the usual
charges, and includes
accommodation for coaches
Catering facilities: 'Russells'
supplying a range of

Locomotives

Name	No	Builder	Type	Built
Moel Tryfan	—	Bagnall (3023)	0-4-2T	1953
Gelert	—	Bagnall (3050)	0-4-2T	1953
—	—	Baldwin (44699)	4-6-0T	1917
Russell	—	Hunslet (901)	2-6-2T	1906
Karen	—	Peckett (2024)	0-4-2T	1942
Glaslyn	1	R/Hornsby (297030)	4wDM	1952
Kinnerley	2	R/Hornsby (354068)	4wDM	1953
Cnicht	36	M/Rail (8703)	4wDM	1941
Katherine	9	M/Rail (605363)	4wDM	1968
—	4	M/Rail (605333)	4wDM	1963
—	5	Hunslet (6285)	4wDM	1968
—	3	R/Hornsby (370555)	4wDM	1953
Jonathon	6	M/Rail (11102)	4wDM	1959
—	7	Hunslet (7535)	4wDM	1977
—	10	R/Hornsby (481552)	4wDM	1962
—	11	Hunslet (3510)	4wDM	1947
Beddgelert*	NG120	S. F. Belge	2-8-2	1950
Snowdonia/Eryri†	60	August 23 Works	0-6-0DM	1977
—†	69	August 23 Works	0-6-0DH	1980
—†	58	August 23 Works	0-6-0DH	1980
—	—	Barclay (554)	4wDH	1970
—	—	Barclay (555)	4wDH	1970
—	—	M/Rail (22237)	4wDM	1965
Kathy	—	H/Barclay (LD 9350)	0-4-0DM	1994
Emma	—	H/Barclay (LD 9346)	0-4-0DM	1994

*ex-South African Railways Class NG15 (may not be on site for all of
2007)
†ex-Polish State Railways class LYD2,
August 23 Works is situated in Romania

Locomotive notes: Gelert, 60, Glaslyn and Kinnerley will operate the 2007
service with a visiting steam locomotive for the summer. Ex-World War 1
Baldwin locomotive currently on display will be reconstructed as the
famous WHR No 590

Stock
Passengers will have the opportunity to travel in the historic 'Gladstone'

Wales

201

adult/children's meals and light refreshments

Access by public transport: Arriva Trains Wales to adjacent Porthmadog station. National Express Buses 200yd. Bus Gwynedd services 1, 2, 3, 97, 98, 99, 99a, S96, S97

On site facilities: Souvenir and railway book/video shop, disabled toilet facilities, information boards, footplate passes and extended shed tours. Steam driver experience courses available

Length of line: Traeth Mawr extension opens this year providing 1.5 mile (3 mile return). 60cm gauge. Porthmadog (WHR) to Traeth Mawr via Pen-y-Mount

Passenger trains: Porthmadog-Traeth Mawr. Return journey approx 40min incorporating works tours. Steam-hauled Bank Holidays, most weekends and daily from mid July to end of August and durimg Easter week. May week and

coach; other replica Welsh Highland coaches in the course of construction. Rebuilt 1923 Hudson 'Toastrack' coach will be in service. Coach 3 now converted into disabled access coach

October half term (all other trains are diesel hauled)

Family tickets: Available, 2 adults + 2 children

Tickets: Your ticket enables you to travel all day and includes the guided, interactive hands-on shed tour in each journey. 3-in-1 ticket available covering both WHR (Porthmadog) and WHR (Caernarfon) together with the Ffestiniog Railway

Period of public operation: Daily 1 April to 30 September; 6/7, 13/14, 20-28 October. Trains run 10.30, 11.45, 13.30, 14.30, 15.30, 16.30 (the 16.30 does not run in September and October)

Special events: Polish Super Power Day — 6 April; Easter Bunnies — 8 April; Narrow Gauge and Industrial Gala — 5-7 May; Polish

Super Power Weekend — 19/20 May; Teddy Bears' Picnic — 2/3 June; Wild West Weekend — 16/17 June; Polish Super Power Weekend — 30 June/1 July; Pirates' Treasure Hunt — 14/15 July; Jack the Station Cat book signing — 26/27 August; Polish Power Weekend — 8/9 September

Facilities for disabled: Toilet, ramp and provision on train, wheelchairs provided. Disabled passengers can be accommodated without prior notice

Membership details: Membership Secretaries, R. & P. Hughes, 2 Clos Sulien, Llanbadarn, Aberystwyth, Ceredigion SY23 3GF. Instant membership available at the shop

Membership journal: *The Journal* — quarterly

Welshpool & Llanfair Light Railway

Member: HRA

There is a decidedly foreign atmosphere to the trains over this line. The steam locomotive collection embraces examples from three continents, and the coaches are turn-of-the-century balcony saloons from Austria or 1950s bogies from Hungary. The line follows a steeply graded route (maximum 1 in 24) through very attractive rolling countryside, and is rather a gem in an area too often missed by the traveller heading for further shores

General Manager: Terry Turner

Headquarters: Welshpool & Llanfair Light Railway Preservation Co Ltd, The Station, Llanfair Caereinion SY21 0SF

Telephone: Llanfair Caereinion (01938) 810441

Fax: (01938) 810861

Internet address: *Web site:* www.wllr.org.uk

Main station: Welshpool (Raven Square)

Locomotives

Name	No	Builder	Type	Built
The Earl	1	B/Peacock (3496)	0-6-0T	1902
The Countess	2	B/Peacock (3497)	0-6-0T	1902
Monarch	6	Bagnall (3024)	0-4-4-0T	1953
Chattenden	7	Drewry (2263)	0-6-0DM	1949
Dougal	8	Barclay (2207)	0-4-0T	1946
Sir Drefaldwyn	10	S. F. Belge (2855)	0-8-0T	1944
Ferret	11	Hunslet (2251)	0-4-0DM	1940
Joan	12	K/Stuart (4404)	0-6-2T	1927
SLR No 85	14	Hunslet (3815)	2-6-2T	1954
Orion	15	Tubize (2369)	2-6-2T	1948
Scooby	16	Hunslet (2400)	0-4-0DM	1941
TSC No 175	17	Diema	0-6-0DM	1978
CFI 764.423	18	Resita (1128)	0-8-0T	1954
CFI 764.425	19*	Resita	0-8-0T	1954

*being overhauled in Romania and due to enter service during 2007

Locomotive notes: Locomotives expected in service 2007 — *The Earl, The Countess,* SLR No 85. *Joan* is currently undergoing overhauled at Llanfair. Some locomotives may not be accessible by the public

Stock

1 replica of original W&LLR Pickering carriage; 6 ex-Zillertalbahn coaches; 4 ex-Sierra Leone coaches, 2 Hungarian State Railway coaches, 6 W&LLR wagons; 8 ex-Admiralty wagons; 2 ex-Bowater wagons; 1 Wickham trolley

Other public stations: Castle Caereinion, Sylfaen, Llanfair Caereinion
OS reference: SJ 107069
Car parks: Llanfair Caereinion, Welshpool (both free)
Access by public transport: Main line station at Welshpool, one mile from Raven Square. Arriva buses from Shrewsbury, Oswestry and Newtown to Welshpool
Refreshment facilities: Light refreshments at Llanfair Caereinion. Picnic areas at Welshpool and Llanfair
Souvenir shops: Welshpool, Llanfair Caereinion
Depot: Llanfair Caereinion
Length of line: 8 miles, 2ft 6in gauge

Note: Not all of the vehicles are in service and some are stored in areas not accessible by the public. A second Pickering replica is expected to enter service during the latter half of 2007

Passenger trains: Welshpool-Llanfair Caereinion
Period of public operation: Weekends Easter to October. Daily in school holidays, plus some other days in June, July and September
Special events: Vintage Weekend — 23/24 June; Steam Gala — 1/2 September; Santa trains — 15/16, 22/23 December
Facilities for disabled: Specially adapted coaches for wheelchairs. Please phone in advance. Easy access to shops. Disabled toilet facility at Welshpool and Llanfair

Membership details: David Barker, 458 Oxford Road, Gomersal, Cleckheaton, West Yorks BD19 4LB
Membership journal: *The Journal* — quarterly
Marketing name: Llanfair Railway
Special notes: Open balcony coaches — travel right next to the engine at the front of the train. Or see the line rolling away behind the back end!

Returned to service in 2006 after a comprehensive rebuild was this former Tasmanian Railways Garratt. Built by Beyer-Peacock, Manchester in 1909, K1 was originally preserved by its manufacturers before moving to the Ffestiniog Railway. Following a number of years as a static exhibit it entered traffic on the Rheilffordd Eryri over the Super Power Weekend in September 2006. K1 is seen taking water at Caernarfon, having worked a shuttle service from Dinas. *ACB*

Channel Islands & Isle of Man

Alderney Railway

Channel Islands

In 1997 the Alderney Railway was 150 years old, having opened on 14 July 1847. Queen Victoria was the only passenger until 1980
Location: Alderney, Channel Islands
Operating society/organisation: Alderney Railway Society, PO Box 75, Alderney, Channel Islands
Telephone: (01481) 822978
Internet address: *Web site:* www.alderneyrailway.com
Car park: Yes
Access by public transport: Aurigny Air Services from Southampton
Location: Station at Braye Road (tickets & souvenirs)
Public opening: Weekends and Bank Holidays, Easter to end of September
Special events: Alderney Week

Industrial locomotives

Name	No	Builder	Type	Built
Elizabeth	—	Vulcan (D2271)	0-4-0DM	1949
Molly 2	—	R/Hornsby	0-4-0DM	1958

Stock
4 Wickham cars
2 Goods wagons
2 ex-London Underground 1956 Stock tube cars (locomotive-hauled)
2 Wickham flats

August. Easter Egg Specials on Easter Sunday. Santa Specials, Saturday before Christmas
On site facilities: Miniature railway (7.25in gauge), quarter-mile circuit operates at Mannez in connection with standard gauge line
Length of line: 2 miles
Facilities for disabled: No, but train crew will always help wherever possible
President: Frank Eggleston
Chairman: Anthony le Blanc (tel: 01481 822978)
Notes: Engine shed at Quarry. Wickham 'train' operates in low season; *Elizabeth* and tube cars in high season and Easter

---

Great Laxey Mine Railway

Isle of Man

The railway was opened on 25 September 2004 and is a reconstruction of the surface section of the former Great Laxey Mine tramway which was used to haul wagon loads of ore from inside the mine and onto the former ore washing and dressing floors at Laxey. The railway runs beneath the main Laxey to Ramsey road — the longest railway tunnel on the Island

Locomotives

Name	No	Builder	Type	Built
Ant	—	GNS	0-4-0WT	2004
Bee	—	GNS	0-4-0WT	2004

GNS — Great Northern Steam Ltd, Darlington, based on original 1877 design by Stephen Lewin, Poole,

Rolling stock
2004-built passenger vehicle, 6 replica ore wagons dating from 2000

Contact: Andrew Scarffe
Operating company: Laxey & Lonan Heritage Trust, West Lynne, Mateland Drive, Laxey, Isle of Man IM4 7N4
Telephone: 01624 861706 (there is no direct telephone on the railway)
Car park: Available in nearby Laxey
Main station: Valley Gardens, Laxey

Access by public transport: A few minutes' walk from Laxey station on the Manx Electric Railway and bus stop of the route 3 Douglas to Ramsey service
On site facilities: No refreshment facilities on site, but café and public house nearby
Length of line: 0.25-mile, 1ft 7in gauge
Public opening: Saturdays and

bank holidays Easter until end of September, 11.00-16.30
Facilities for disabled: Unable to carry wheelchair-bound passengers, though Valley Gardens are accessible
Membership details: From above address

Steam Centre | Groudle Glen Railway | Isle of Man

Location: Groudle Glen Railway, Isle of Man
Officer in charge: Tony Beard
Operating company: Groudle Glen Railway Ltd (managed by the Isle of Man Steam Railway Supporters' Association) of 29 Hawarden Avenue, Douglas, Isle of Man IM1 4BP
Telephone: (01624) 622138 (evenings); (01624) 670453 (weekends)
Car park: Yes
Access by public transport: Manx Electric Railway (Groudle Hotel)
On site facilities: Sales shop
Length of line: 0.75-mile, 2ft gauge
Public opening: Easter Sunday and

Locomotives

Name	No	Builder	Type	Built
Dolphin	1	H/Hunslet (4394)	4wDM	1952
Walrus	2	H/Hunslet (4395)	4wDM	1952
Sea Lion	—	Bagnall (1484)	2-4-0T	1896
Annie	—	Booth/GGR	0-4-2T	1998
Polar Bear	—	BEV (556801)	2-B-2	2004

Monday, Sundays May to September (11.00-16.30); Tuesday evening services August (19.00-21.00); Wednesday evening services July/August (19.00-21.00); Santa Trains — December (11.00-15.30)
Facilities for disabled: Due to the line's location, those who are disabled will have some difficulty. It is

suggested that they telephone for advice
Further information and membership details: From above address
Membership journal: *Manx Steam Railway News* — quarterly

Timetable Service | Isle of Man Railway | Isle of Man

Member: HRA
The 3ft gauge Isle of Man Railway is a survivor of a system which previously also operated from Douglas to Peel and Ramsey. Almost continuous operation since 1873 makes it one of the oldest operating railways in the British Isles. The majority of the track was completely renewed between 2002 and 2004 including the provision of platforms at intermediate stations and the installation of automatic level crossings along the line. It runs for over 15 miles between Douglas and Port Erin through the island's rolling southern countryside.

Locomotives

Name	No	Builder	Type	Built
Loch	4	B/Peacock (1416)	2-4-0T	1874
Fenella	8	B/Peacock (3610)	2-4-0T	1894
G. H. Wood	10	B/Peacock (4662)	2-4-0T	1905
Maitland	11	B/Peacock (4663)	2-4-0T	1905
Hutchinson	12	B/Peacock (5126)	2-4-0T	1908
Kissack	13	B/Peacock (5382)	2-4-0T	1908
Caledonia	15	Dubs & Co (2178)	0-6-0T	1885
Viking	17	Schottler (2175)	0-4-0DH	1958
Ailsa	18	Hunslet (22021)	4wDM	1994

Locomotive note: All operational, all other rolling stock stored off the line

On display in museum at Port Erin

Name	No	Builder	Type	Built
Peveril	6	B/Peacock (1524)	2-4-0T	1875
Mannin	16	B/Peacock (6296)	2-4-0T	1926

The line is owned and operated by the Isle of Man Government
Head of Railways: M. P. Ogden
Railway Engineer: G. F. Lawson
Headquarters: Department of Tourism & Leisure — Public Transport Division, Transport Headquarters, Banks Circus, Douglas, Isle of Man IM1 5PT
Telephone: Douglas (01624) 662525
Fax: (01624) 663637
Main station: Douglas
Other public stations: Port Soderick, Santon, Ballasalla, Castletown, Colby, Port St Mary and Port Erin

Rolling stock
16 coaches, 20 runners, 1 van, 2 open wagons, 1 well wagon, 1 track tamping machine

Car parks: Douglas, Ballasalla, Castletown, Port St Mary and Port Erin
Access by public transport: Isle of Man Transport bus to main centres
Refreshment facilities: Port Erin and Douglas
Souvenir shops: None
Museum: Port Erin
Depot: Douglas
Length of line: 15.5 miles, 3ft gauge

Passenger trains: Douglas-Port Erin
Period of public operation: Beginning of April to end October. Please contact for timetable information
Facilities for disabled: Level access throughout Douglas and Port Erin stations including refreshment area. Carriages able to carry wheelchairs, ramps provided. Advance notice helpful

---

Timetable Service — Manx Electric Railway — Isle of Man

Member: HRA
The 3ft gauge Manx Electric Railway is a unique survivor of Victorian high technology. A mixture of railway and tramway practice, it was built in 1893 and was a pioneer in the use of electric traction. It illustrates an example of a true electric interurban line. Two of the original cars are still in service making them the oldest tramcars still in operation on their original route in the British Isles. After leaving Douglas, the railway passes the Groudle Glen Railway before reaching the charming village of Laxey, for the Snaefell Mountain Railway. The line continues over some of the most breathtaking coastal scenery in the island before reaching its terminus at Ramsey nearly 18 miles from Douglas.

The line is owned and operated by the Isle of Man Government
Head of Railways: M. P. Ogden
Railway Engineer: G. F. Lawson
Headquarters: Department of Tourism & Leisure — Public Transport Division, Transport Headquarters, Banks Circus, Douglas, Isle of Man IM1 5PT
Telephone: Douglas (01624) 662525
Fax: (01624) 663637
Main stations: Douglas (Derby Castle), Laxey and Ramsey
Other public stations: Groudle, Dhoon Glen, Ballaglass and numerous wayside stops

Motor cars

Nos	Type	Seats	Body	Built
1, 2	Unvestibuled saloon	34	Milnes	1893
5, 6, 7, 9	Vestibuled saloon	32	Milnes	1894
16	Cross-bench open	56	Milnes	1898
19-22*	Winter saloon	48	Milnes	1899
26	Cross-bench open	56	Milnes	1898
32, 33	Cross-bench open	56	UEC	1906
34	Engineer's Car	—	IoMT	2004

*22 rebodied 1991, McArd/MER

Trailers

Nos	Type	Seats	Body	Built
36, 37	Cross-bench open	44	Milnes	1894
40, 41, 44	Cross-bench open	44	EE Co	1930
42, 43	Cross-bench open	44	Milnes	1903
45-48	Cross-bench open	44	Milnes	1899
49-51, 53, 54	Cross-bench open	44	Milnes	1893
56*	Cross-bench open	44	ERTCW	1904
57, 58	Saloon	32	ERTCW	1904
59	Special Saloon	18	Milnes	1895
60	Cross-bench open	44	Milnes	1896
61, 62	Cross-bench open	44	UEC	1906

*rebuilt as disabled access trailer in 1993

Note: Other rolling stock stored off the line

Car parks: Douglas, Laxey, Ramsey (nearby)
Access by public transport: Isle of Man Transport buses to main centres. Douglas Corporation Horse Tramway to Derby Castle in summer
Depots: Douglas and Ramsey
Refreshment facilities: Laxey in summer
Length of line: 17.5 miles, 3ft gauge
Passenger service: Douglas-Ramsey
Period of public operation: Beginning of April to end October. Please contact for timetable information
Special notes: Folded wheelchairs can be carried. Please notify in advance. One trailer with disabled access used on advance request

Snaefell Mountain Railway

Member: HRA

The 3ft 6in gauge Snaefell Mountain Railway is unique. It is the only electric mountain railway in the British Isles. Almost all the rolling stock is original and dates back to 1895. The railway begins its journey at the picturesque village of Laxey where its station is shared with the Manx Electric Railway. The climb to the summit of Snaefell (2,036ft) is a steep one and the cars travel unassisted up gradients as severe as 1 in 12. From the summit, the views on a clear day extend to Wales, Scotland, England and Ireland.

The line is owned and operated by the Isle of Man Government

Head of Railways: M. P. Ogden

Railway Engineer: G. F. Lawson

Trams

Nos	Type	Seats	Body	Built
1-4, 6	Vestibuled saloon	48	Milnes	1895
5 (rebuild)	Vestibuled saloon	48	MER/ Kinnin	1971

Headquarters: Department of Tourism & Leisure — Public Transport Division, Transport Headquarters, Banks Circus, Douglas, Isle of Man IM1 5PT

Telephone: Douglas (01624) 662525

Fax: (01624) 663637

Main station: Laxey

Other public stations: Bungalow, Summit

Car parks: Laxey, Bungalow (nearby)

Access by public transport: Manx Electric Railway or Isle of Man Transport bus to Laxey

Depot: Laxey

Refreshment facilities: Laxey, Summit

Souvenirs shops: None

Length of line: 4.5 miles, 3ft 6in gauge

Passenger service: Laxey-Snaefell summit

Period of public operation: Beginning of April to end of September. Please contact for timetable information

The bulk of the Isle of Man Steam Railway fleet is made up of Beyer Peacock 2-4-0Ts. This view was taken at Douglas. *ACB*

Channel Islands & Isle of Man

Northern Ireland

Downpatrick & County Down Railway

Member: HRA

The railway museum is the only preserved Irish standard gauge (5ft 3in) railway operating in Ireland. It is a representative of the former Belfast & County Down railway terminus in Downpatrick, which closed in 1950, two years after being taken into state ownership

Location: The Railway Station, Market Street, Downpatrick, Co Down BT30 6LZ

OS reference: J483444

Operating society/organisation: Downpatrick & County Down Railway Society

Telephone: 077 9080 2049

Internet address: *Web site:* www.downrail.co.uk

Car park: Free parking adjacent to station

Access by public transport: A regular service is operated by Ulsterbus from Belfast Europa bus centre (next to Great Victoria Street railway station).
Tel: (028) 9032 0011

Refreshment facilities: Buffet carriage open on operating days

On site facilities: Souvenir shop, toilets

Length of line: 4 miles open to public traffic. Current terminus: King Magnus's Halt. Track was extended southwards to Ballydugan and north to a new station at Inch Abbey

Public opening: Special events (see below) and weekends 16 June-9 September

Journey time: 45min return journey from Downpatrick town to Downpatrick Loop Platform and King Magnus's Halt and Inch Abbey

Special events: St Patrick's Day

Diesel locomotives and multiple-unit

Name	No	Origin	Class	Type	Built
W. F. Gillespie OBE	E421	CIE	421	C	1962
—	E432	CIE	421	C	1962
—	G611	CIE	611	B	1962
—	G613	CIE	611	B	1962
—	G617	CIE	611	B	1962
—	RB3	BRE-Leyland	—	4wDM	1981

Name	No	Origin	Class	Manufacturer	Type	Built
—	712	CIE	–	Wickham (8919)	4wDH	1962

Steam locomotives

Name	No	Builder	Type	Built
—	1*	O&K (12475)	0-4-0T	1934
—	3	O&K (12662)	0-4-0T	1935

*at Railway Preservation Society at Whitehead for overhaul

Rolling stock

2 CIE Brake open standards (Nos 1918 & 1944); CIE Travelling Post Office (No 2978); 1 CIE Brake open standard generating steam van (No 3223); CIE Buffet open standard (No 2419); NIR '70' class railcar brake open standard intermediate (No 728); B&CDR 'Royal Saloon' (No 153); B&CDR 1st/2nd composite (No 152); B&CDR 3rd open (ex-railmotor); B&CDR 6-wheeled 2nd (No 154); B&CDR 6-wheeled brake 3rd (No 39); GS&WR 3rd open (No 836); GSWR 6-wheeled brake first (No 69); Ulster Railway Family Saloon (No 33); GNR 6-wheeled third, M&GW full brake c1900; 4 LMS (NCC) parcels vans; 2 LMS (NCC) open wagon; LMS (NCC) brake van; CIE closed van; 2 GNR closed vans; GNR brake van; GSWR ballast hopper; GSWR ballast plough; LMS (NCC) steam crane; 2 private oil company tankers, CIE track inspection vehicle No 712; selection of carriage and wagon underframes for internal use

Owners

712, G611 and G617 the Irish Traction Group
G613 and M&GW full brake privately owned
RB3 is owned by Translink
E421 and E432 the Downpatrick & County Down Railway Society

Specials — 17 March; Easter Egg Specials — 8, 10 April; May Day Specials — 7, 28 May; Halloween Ghost Trains — 27/28 October; Santa Specials — 8/9, 15/16, 22/23 December

Facilities for disabled: Toilets, shop, platform and trains accessible for disabled

Membership details: The

Membership Secretary,
Downpatrick & County Down
Railway Society, The Railway
Station, Downpatrick, Co Down
BT30 6LZ

Timetable Service — Giant's Causeway & Bushmills Railway — Co Antrim

The GC&BR was opened in 2002 using the stock of the former Shane's Castle Railway on the last two miles of the site of the Portrush to Giant's Causeway electric tramway closed in 1949. The line runs between Bushmills and the Giant's Causeway with its charming views along the River Bush, and spectacular vistas across the sea to Donegal

Location: The railway links the distillery (open to visitors) in the village of Bushmills to the entrance of the Giant's Causeway. Follow the signs to either Bushmills or the Giant's Causeway and the railway is clearly signposted. Car parking is dedicated to railway passengers at both Bushmills and the Giant's Causeway

Operating organisation: Giant's Causeway & Bushmills Railway, Giant's Causeway Station, Runkerry Road, Bushmills, Co Antrim, Northern Ireland BT57 8SZ

Industrial locomotives

Name	No	Builder	Type	Built
Tyrone	1	Peckett (2264)	0-4-0T	1904
Rory	2	Simplex (102T016)	4wDH	1976
Shane	3	Barclay(2281)	0-4-0T	1949

Telephone: (028) 2073 2594 (information line)
Telephone/Fax: (028) 2073 2844
Internet address: *e-mail:* infogcbr@btconnect.com
Web site: www.freewebs.com/giantscauseway railway
OS reference: 943437 (Irish Grid)
Access by public transport: Nearest Translink railway stations are Portrush (5 miles), Coleraine (7 miles). Various bus routes (including an open topped vehicle on fine days in the summer) operate from either or both, depending on the route. For timetables either contact Translink enquiries on (028) 9066 6630 or www.translink.co.uk

Length of line: 2 miles, 3ft gauge
On site facilities: Souvenir shop, toilets and picnic tables at Giant's Causeway station. Free parking at both stations for railway passengers
Passenger trains: Bushmills-Giant's Causeway
Public opening: Usually St Patrick's Day (17 March) and daily at Easter. Daily during July and August.
Note: Trains will operate at other times for advance party bookings in excess of 20 persons
Facilities for disabled: Access avaiable at Giant's Causeway station and Bushmills platform. One coach has been adapted for wheelchair use

Steam Centre — Railway Preservation Society of Ireland — County Antrim

Members: HRA, TT
The RPSI was formed in 1964, making it one of the older preservation societies in these islands. It has always specialised in main line steam operations, and runs an intensive summer programme of trips out of both Belfast and Dublin. The main maintenance base is situated at Whitehead, 15 miles north of Belfast on the NIR route to Larne Harbour. Here not only are the traffic locomotives shedded but the locomotive shed is also used for heavy maintenance; currently the society is completing the full

rebuilding of its sixth boiler 'in-house'. A large engineering workshop has just been constructed for the Locomotive Department, with the 100-year-old overhead crane which was originally in the Belfast & County Down Railway Locomotive Erecting Shop at Queen's Quay in Belfast. This workshop which will undertake all heavy engineering for the Society is currently being fitted out. A large carriage shed is also on site where traffic vehicles are maintained and coaches are fully rebuilt. There are also heavy lifting facilities on site, and access may occasionally be

limited for safety reasons when these are in use. Annual operations commence with 'Easter Bunny' trains out of Belfast, usually on Easter Monday. In May the 'International Railtour' is the main event, a three day steam extravaganza. During June there are main line trips out of both Belfast and Dublin, including a Midsummer Barbecue train and a Musical Special. July and August see the 'Portrush Flyers' from Belfast to Portrush and back, around 180 miles of main line steam, as well as the 'Sea Breeze' excursions from Dublin to Rosslare and back, covering 205 miles. During June, July and August there are steam train rides on site at Whitehead on Sunday afternoons, and at the end of July there will be an Open Day in conjunction with the Whitehead Community Association when not only will there be train rides but also at least two locomotives will be in steam and there will be access to the workshop areas. The season usually ends with further excursions in September to Rosslare and Whitehead, and Halloween shuttles between Belfast and Whitehead. November sees the operation of a Santa Special to Derry out of Belfast, before the Santa Specials out of both capital cities

Location: Whitehead Excursion Station, Co Antrim, Northern Ireland

Operating society: Railway Preservation Society of Ireland, Castleview Road, Whitehead, Carrickfergus, Co Antrim BT38 9NA

Telephone/fax:
From UK (028) 2826 0803.
From Eire (01) 280 9147

Internet address: *e-mail:* rpsitrains@hotmail.com
Web site: www.steamtrainsireland.com

Car park: Public car parking is readily available adjacent to the Society premises, with a further large car park less than 5min walk away on the sea front. Both car parks are normally free

Access by public transport: Northern Ireland Railways or Ulsterbus to Whitehead

On site facilities: Souvenir shop (operating days only)

Public opening: Visitors welcome most weekends. Site not open during the week (except public holidays) or when main line trains are operating from Whitehead or Belfast. Special opening for parties, or in the evening, may be arranged by telephoning in advance

Locomotives

Name	No	Origin	Class	Type	Built
Merlin	85*	GNR(I)	V	4-4-0	1932
—	131**	GNR(I)	Q	4-4-0	1901
Slieve Gullion	171†	GNR(I)	S	4-4-0	1913
—	4	LMS (NCC)	WT	2-6-4T	1947
—	184†	GS&WR	J15	0-6-0	1880
—	186§	GS&WR	J15	0-6-0	1879
—	461††	D&SER	K2	2-6-0	1922
Lough Erne	27	SL&NCR	Z	0-6-4T	1949
Eagle	101	NIR	DL	Bo-Bo	1969
Falcon	102	NIR	DL	Bo-Bo	1969

Industrial locomotives

Name	No	Builder	Type	Built
Guinness	3	H/Clarke (1152)	0-4-0ST	1919
R. H. Smyth	3	Avonside (2021)	0-6-0ST	1928
—	23	Planet (3509)	0-4-0DM	1951
—	1	R/Hornsby	0-4-0DM	1954

*on loan from Ulster Folk & Transport Museum
**frames and boiler only
†awaiting restoration
††undergoing restoration
§returned to traffic in 2004

Stock

The Society also owns some 20 operational coaches, normally divided between Whitehead and Dublin. Further coaches are awaiting restoration and a small number of freight wagons are also preserved, as well as a steam crane. A serious fire due to vandalism a couple of years ago destroyed several vehicles, and any rebuilding is likely to be some years in the future at best. The Society has purchased a variety of Mk 2 coaches which are undergoing major overhaul and six of which returned to traffic in 2004 with two more to follow over the next year. The Society's secondary maintenance base is at Mullingar, Co Westmeath, but there is **no** access to the public.

Special notes: The RPSI is noted for its main line excursions and traditional rolling stock. For details: RPSI Railtours, Box 171 Larne BT40 1UU (9x4 SAE please).

Facilities for disabled: Please note that wheelchair facilities can be provided on trains, with advance notice if possible. A dedicated coach for carrying wheelchairs operates out of Whitehead on Belfast-based trains. Wheelchair access around the workshops at Whitehead is possible, but difficult, and advance warning is requested of any visitors who may need special facilities

Membership details: Membership Secretary, 148 Church Road, Newtownabbey, Co Antrim BT36 6HJ

Future developments: Completion of a new heavy engineering workshop is planned, as well as a projected extension to the Carriage Shed and additional stores and maintenance areas, and there are further developments in the pipeline which will hopefully improve access. Additional locomotive and coach restoration is proposed.

Member: HRA

Forty-five acres are devoted to the Transport Galleries. Permanent exhibitions include the earliest forms of transport, horse-drawn vehicles, bicycles, motor cars and the Museum's *Titanic* exhibition.

The Irish Railway Collection is displayed in an award-winning purpose-built gallery — the largest Transport Museum gallery in Ireland.

The collection features *Maedb* — the largest locomotive run in Ireland. The display includes narrow gauge and standard gauge rolling stock, locomotives, carriages, goods wagons, railcars and railbuses along with memorabilia

Location: Ulster Folk & Transport Museum, Cultra, Holywood

Operating organisation: Ulster Folk & Transport Museum, Cultra, Holywood BT18 0EU

Telephone: (028) 9042 8428

Fax: (028) 9042 8728

Internet address: *Web site:* www.magni.org.uk

Access: By car or bus the museum is about 7 miles from Belfast city centre on the A2 Belfast-Bangor road. You can also reach the museum by train

Car park: Extensive free parking

On site facilities: Shops, toilets, tea room

Opening times: All year round; opening times vary with season, check with the museum for details

Locomotives (5ft 3in)

Name	No	Origin	Class	Type	Built
—	93	GNR(I)	JT	2-4-2T	1895
—	30	BCDR	I	4-4-2T	1901
Dunluce Castle	74	LMS(NCC)	U2	4-4-0	1924
Maedb	800	GSR	B1A	4-6-0	1939
—	1	R/Stephenson (2738)	—	0-6-0ST	1891
Merlin*	85	GNR(I)	V	4-4-0	1932
—	1	GNR(I)	—	Railbus	1932

*on loan to Railway Preservation Society of Ireland at Whitehead

Locomotives (narrow gauge)

Name	No	Origin	Class	Type	Built
Blanche	2	CDRJC	5A	2-6-4T	1912
Kathleen	2	CLR	—	4-4-0T	1887
Phoenix	11	CVR	—	4wD	1928
—	20	Industrial	—	0-4-0	1905
—	2	Industrial	—	0-4-0	1907

Stock

1 Dublin, Wicklow & Wexford Railway coach; 1 Dundalk, Newry & Greenore Railway coach; 1 Midland & Great Western Railway directors' saloon (ex-private vehicle); 1 Electric tramcar of Bessbrook-Newry Tramway; 2 trams from Giant's Causeway Tramway, Great Northern Railway Ireland Fintona tram, Great Northern Railway Ireland Hill of Howth electric tramcar, 1 Cavan-Leitrim Railway coach; 2 County Donegal Railway railcars; 1 County Donegal Railway directors' coach; 1 County Donegal Railway trailer coach (bodywork ex-Dublin & Lucan Railway coach); 1 Giant's Causeway (P&BVR) saloon trailer; 1 Castlederg & Victoria Bridge Tramway 1st/3rd coach; 1 County Donegal Railway 7-ton open wagon, 3 Belfast trams, 1 Belfast trolleybus, 1 Belfast double-deck bus. Extensive collection of cars, motorcycles, bicycles, commercial vehicles, horse-drawn vehicles, fire-fighting equipment and industrial railway vehicles

Republic of Ireland

Cavan & Leitrim Railway

Restoration work commenced in June 1993 and to date some half-mile of line has been rebuilt, water tower and engine shed refurbished and new workshops and carriage shed constructed. The ultimate objective is to rebuild a further 5.75 miles of line to Mohill

Location/headquarters: The Narrow Gauge Station, Dromod, Co Leitrim, adjacent to the Irish Rail station

General Manager: Michael Kennedy

Telephone/Fax: 071-9638599

Internet address:
e-mail: info@irish-railway.com
Web site: www.irish-railway.com

Main station: Dromod

Car park: Dromod terminus

Access by public transport: Rail service to Dromod (Irish Rail) on the Dublin-Sligo line. Bus Eireann and Ulsterbus routes also call at Dromod

Refreshment facilities: Tea room open by arrangement. Full meals available at nearby bars

Souvenir shop: Dromod

Length of line: Half-mile (3ft gauge)

Museum: Large collection of locomotives, rolling stock, road vehicles and aircraft, many still awaiting restoration

Period of public operation: Closed 23 December to 2 January, otherwise every Saturday, Sunday and Monday. Diesel trains run on demand

Special events: Vintage Rally — 6 May; Halloween Ghost Train — 31 October;

Locomotives

3ft gauge

Name	No	Builder	Type	Built
Dromod	1	K/Stuart (3024)	0-4-2ST	1916
Nancy*	1	Avonside (3024)	0-6-0T	1908
Dinmor	F511	Fowler (3900011)	4wDM	1947
—	LM11	Ruhrthaler (1082)	4wDM	1936
—	9	M/Rail (115U093)	4wDH	1970
—	LM350	Simplex (60SL748)	4wDM	1980
—	LM91	R/Hornsby (371962)	4wDM	1952
—	LM131	R/Hornsby (379086)	4wDM	1955
—	LM87	R/Hornsby (329696)	4wDM	1952
—	LM131	R/Hornsby (382809)	4wDM	1955
—	LM260	Deutz (57841)	0-4-0DM	1965
—	LM180	Deutz (57122)	0-4-0DM	1960
—	LM186	Deutz (57132)	0-4-0DM	1960
—	—	Hunslet (6075)	4wDM	1961

*Nancy under restoration at Alan Keef Ltd, Ross on Wye

5ft 3in gauge

Name	No	Builder	Type	Built
—	SZA 979	Scammel lorry	2-2wDM	1959

2ft gauge

Name	No	Builder	Type	Built
—	D5	H/Hunslet (2659)	4wDM	1942
—	1	H/Hunslet (7340)	4wDM	1940
—	2	H/Hunslet (7341)	4wDM	1940
—	3	H/Hunslet (7341)	4wDM	1943
—	LM198	R/Hornsby (398076)	4wDM	1954

1ft 10in gauge (Ex Guinness locomotives)

Name	No	Builder	Type	Built
—	22	Spence	0-4-0T	1912
—	31	Planet (3446)	4wDM	1950
—	36	Planet (3447)	4wDM	1950
—	26	Planet (3255)	4wDM	1948

Railcars

Name	No	Builder	Type	Built
—	*5	Drewry Car (1945)	4wDMR	1927
—	C11	Bord na Móna	4wDMR	–
—	C42	Wickham (7129)	4wPMR	1955
—	C47	Bord na Móna	4wPMR	1958

Santa Trains — 9, 16, 23
December
Contact address: The Cavan &
Leitrim Railway Co Ltd, Station
Road, Dromod, Co Leitrim,
Republic of Ireland

Name	No	Builder	Type	Built
—	C56	Wickham (7681)	4wPMR	1957
—	W6/11-4	Wickham (9673)	2-2-0PM	1964

*built as 5ft 3in gauge inspection car for Great Southern Railway, regauged
in 1994
C42 used as unpowered p-way trolley

Rolling stock
Tralee & Dingle coaches 47C (6T), 45C (7T), 48C (8T) and 44C (10T) all
built 1890; Great Northern Railway (Ireland) AU345 built 1955 as motor
bus. Alan Keef-built No 13, (built 1997)
GNR Gardiner Bus No 389, built Dundalk 1951

Museum	County Donegal Railway Restoration Society	County Donegal

Member: HRA
Old Station House opened as a
permanent Railway Museum &
Heritage Centre from Easter 1995.
There are numerous outside exhibits
ranging from *Drumboe* to a garden
railway. Inside attractions include a
video-viewing room, railway
pictures and railway memorabilia
Location/Headquarters: Old
Station House, Tírconaill Street,
Donegal Town, Co Donegal, Ireland
Telephone: (00353-7497 [from
UK]) (07497 [from Ireland]) 22655
Fax: (00353-7497 [from UK])
(07497 [from Ireland]) 23843
Internet address: *e-mail:*
rrailway@gofree.indigo.ie
Web site:
http://cdrrs.future.easyspace.com/
Contacts: Anne Temple
Public opening: October-May

Locomotives

Name	No	Origin	Class	Type	Built
Drumboe*	5	CDR	5	2-6-4T	1907

*undergoing restoration at RPSI, Whitehead

Stock
1 CDR brake/third coach No 28
1 CDR railcar No 14
1 CDR trailer No 5
1 CDR combined goods/cattle and horse van (247 of 1893)
1 goods van

Viewing of all rolling stock is by arrangement only

Monday-Friday 09.00-16.00 (closed
weekends). June-September
Monday-Saturday 09.00-17.00,
Sunday 14.00-17.00
Membership details: From above
address
Membership journal: *The Phoenix*

Special notes: Outline planning
permission has been received for a
3/4-mile-long line from the station
to Gorrelks crossing

Steam Centre	Cumann Traenach na Gaeltacht Láir	County Donegal

This stretch of track has been laid
on the formation of the Fintown-
Glenties line. The railway runs
along the shore of Lough Finn and
it is planned to have a dual ride,
out by rail and return by boat. The
rolling stock presently used
consists of an ex-mining Simplex
locomotive with three turn of the
century (19th/20th) passenger
tramcars from Charleroi (Belgium)
Location/headquarters: Fintown

Locomotives

Name	No	Builder	Type	Built
—	LM77	R/Hornsby (329680)	4wDM	1952
—	—	M/Rail (102T007)	4wDM	1974

Railcar

Name	No	Origin	Class	Type	Built
—	18	CDRJC	—	Diesel railcar	1940

Rolling stock
3 Belgian tramcars

Republic of Ireland

Railway Station, Fintown, Co Donegal, Eire
Manager: Anne-Marie Bonner
Main station: Fintown Station
Car park: Located at station area
Access by public transport: Local buses
Refreshment facilities: Local café at top of station lane
Souvenir shop: Located at station area
Length of line: 2.5 miles (3ft gauge)

Museum: Not in operation but a collection of antiquated farm machinery is being restored
Period of public operation: June — Monday/Friday 13.00-16.00, Sunday 13.00-17.00; July-September — Monday/Friday 11.00-17.00, weekends 1.00-18.00. Departures from Fintown every half hour
Special events: Halloween Ghost Train, Santa Specials in December
On site facilities: Toilet, it is also

hoped to have a playground in operation
Membership details: Bernadette McGee, (Membership Secretary), c/o above address
Membership journal: *An Mhuc Dhubh* — annually

Irish Steam Preservation Society

Steam Centre | County Laois

Member: HRA, NTET
Location: Stradbally Hall, eight miles from Athy, six miles from Portlaoise (on N80 road).
Telephone: 00353 502 25444 (from UK)
Internet address: *Web site:* www.irishsteam.ie
Access by public transport: Irish Rail train to Athy or Portlaoise. Kavanagh's Bus Portlaoise-Stradbally-Athy-Carlow (Monday-Saturday), also Bus Eireann Waterford-Kilkenny-Stradbally-Portlaoise-Athlone (one daily service including Sunday)
On site facilities: 3ft gauge railway
Catering facilities: None on site but town centre quarter-mile away

Industrial locomotives

Name	No	Builder	Type	Built
—	2	Barclay (2264)	0-4-0WT	1949
Nippy	—	Planet (2014)	4wDM	1936
—	4	R/Hornsby (326052)	4wDM	1952

Stock
1 passenger coach; 2 ballast wagons; 1 brake van

Length of line: 1km
Public opening: Please contact for details
Special notes: This is the longest established heritage railway in Ireland, now in its 36th year. Please contact Rally Secretary, ISPS, Bunnacrannagh, Timahoe Road,

Stradbally, Co Laois for further details or telephone above number or visit web site. All trains will be operated by a veteran diesel locomotive, pending repairs to the steam locomotive

---

Irish Traction Group

Museum | County Tipperary

Member: HRA
The Irish Traction Group was formed in 1989 with the objective of preserving at least one of each class of diesel locomotive to have operated on the Irish railway system. The ultimate aim of the Group is to restore its collection of locomotives to full main line standard
Location: The former goods store adjacent to Carrick-on-Suir railway station

Locomotives/Railcar

Name	No	Origin	Class	Manufacturer	Type	Built
—	1	NIR	DH	E/Electric (D1266)	6wDH	1969
—	A3R	CIE	001/A	M/Vickers (889)	Co-Co	1955
—	A39	CIE	001/A	M/Vickers (925)	Co-Co	1956
—	B103	CIE	101/B	BRCW (DEL22)	A1A-A1A	1956
—	226	CIE	201/C	M/Vickers (972)	Bo-Bo	1957
—	C231	CIE	201/C	M/Vickers (977)	Bo-Bo	1957
—	G601	CIE	601/G	Deutz (56119)	4wDH	1956
—	G611	CIE	611/G	Deutz (57225)	4wDH	1962
—	G616	CIE	611/G	Deutz (57227)	4wDH	1962
—	G617	CIE	611/G	Deutz (57229)	4wDH	1962
—	712	CIE	–	Wickham (8919)	4wDH	1962

Republic of Ireland

Operating society/organisation:
Irish Traction Group, 31 Hayfield Road, Bredbury, Stockport, Cheshire SK6 1DE, England
Telephone: 07713 159869 (Mon-Sat 09.00-18.00 only)
Car park: Available in station goods yard
Access by public transport:
Infrequent train service. Services operated by Bus Eireann from Dublin, Limerick and Waterford
Facilities: Toilets on IE station. Site is located quarter-mile from town centre

Notes:
A3R and A39 are stored at IE Inchicore Works
G611 and G617 currently on loan to Downpatrick & Co Down Railway
C231 is stored at IE Inchicore Works
712 is currently on loan to Downpatrick & Co Down Railway
1 is currently stored at the premises of Beaver Power Ltd, Merthyr Tydfil. South Wales

Special events: Operation of railtours over IE/NIR systems
Opening times: Premises not open to the public, locomotives B103 and G601 are both stabled outside

---

Timetable service	Tralee & Blennerville Steam Railway	County Kerry

The Tralee & Blennerville Steam Railway is Europe's most westerly line and as part of the former Tralee & Dingle Light Railway (1891-1953) it has folklore and tradition stretching back over 100 years. The railway links the town of Tralee with Blennerville on the coast
Location: Tralee (Ballyard) station is situated near the Aqua Dome, Blennerville station is adjacent to the windmill, 1 mile to the west of town on the main road to Dingle (N86)
Headquarters: Tralee & Blennerville Steam Railway, Tralee, Co Kerry, Republic of Ireland
General Manager: Nora Teahon
Telephone: 35366 7121064 (from UK)
Internet address: *e-mail:* blenmill@eircom.net
Web site: www.tdlr.org.uk

Locomotives
3ft gauge

Name	No	Builder	Type	Built
—	5*	Hunslet (555)	2-6-2T	1892
—	LM92L	R/Hornsby (371967)	4wDM	1954

*an original Tralee & Dingle Railway locomotive

Rolling stock
A selection of passenger coaches and works wagons

Car park:
At Tralee (Ballyard) station. Blennerville Windmill car park
Access by public transport:
By rail service to Tralee (Irish Rail).
By air to Kerry airport (10 miles) (car hire available).
By Bus Eireann to Tralee
Refreshment facilities: Restaurant at Blennerville in windmill complex
Length of line: 3km (3ft gauge)

Period of public operation: Daily June to September (subject to confirmation)
Passenger service: Trains operate from Blennerville 10.30-16.30 (17.30 in July and August); from Tralee at 11.00-17.00
Facilities for disabled: Toilets and wheelchair access, museum and catering facilities available at Blennerville windmill

---

Timetable Service	Waterford & Suir Valley Railway	Co Waterford

This heritage narrow gauge railway follows over 6km of the route of the abandoned Waterford-Dungarvan line. The line runs mostly along the picturesque banks of the River Suir between Kilmeadan and Waterford City. It offers views of the Mount Congreve Gardens and the recently discovered site of a Viking settlement at Woodstown. This is an area rich in history and only

Industrial locomotives

Name	No	Builder	Type	Built
—	LM179	Deutz (57121)	0-4-0DM	1960
—	LM183	Deutz (57127)	0-4-0DM	1960
—	—	M/Rail (60SP382)	4wDM	1969

Stock
Two carriages built specially for the railway. The steel coaches have approximately two thirds of the accommodation in open toastrack seating, the remainder being an enclosed saloon, accessed from an end veranda

accessible by train
Location: Kilmeadan station, Kilmeadan, Co Waterford on the R680.
Contact: Maria Kyte, Business Development Manager, Waterford & Suir Valley Railway Co, Kilmeadan Station, Kilmeadan, Co Waterford
Telephone: 00353 (0) 51 384058
Internet address: *e-mail:* info@wsvrailway.ie
Web site: www.wsvrailway.ie
Charity number: CHY 13857
Access by public transport: Suirway bus service to Kilmeadan (schedule can vary)
Access by road: Kilmeadan is

10km outside Waterford City on the Cork Road, N25. From the Waterford/Cork road take the R680 towards Portlaw/Carrick-on-Suir for 13.km. The entrance to Kilmeadan station is on the left
Length of line:
6km, 3ft gauge railway.
Round trip approximately 40min
Catering facilities: Coffee shop at station
Souvenir shop: Kilmeadan
Car parking: On site
Length of track: 6km of track laid from Kilmeadan to Carriganore. The summer schedule will provide for a 12km round trip on the 6km of track

Public opening: Provisional schedule for 2007 is Easter to September — Monday to Saturday 11.00-16.00, and Sundays 12.00-17.00
Special events: Halloween Ghost Trips — October; Santa Trips — December. Please contact for dates
Special facilities: Children's birthday parties (ride and refreshments).
Gift vouchers available for tickets, special events, Friends membership
Facilities for disabled: Train carriages accessible to wheelchairs, ticket office, shop and toilets

Steam Centre — West Clare Railway (The Percy French Line) — County Clare

Originally closed in 1961, the new railway currently operates over 1.5 miles of original trackbed located at the triangular junction of Moyasta. The station house survives and contains a museum. During 2007, the track is to be extended towards Kilkee and the 1892 steam locomotive *Slieve Callan* (now restored) will be operating from May onwards. Percy French who wrote his song 'Are ye right there, Michael' about the railway made the line particularly famous. Footplate experience courses are available from September
Location/headquarters: West Clare Railway, Moyasta Junction, Kilrush, Co Clare, Republic of Ireland
Telephone: 00353 (0) 65 905 1284

Locomotives

Name	No	Builder	Type	Built
Slieve Callan	5*	Dübs (2890)	0-6-2T	1892
—	101L	RFS	4wDH	1989

*an original West Clare Railway locomotive

Rolling stock
2 carriages, with extra vehicles currently under construction

Internet address: *Web site:* www.westclarerailway.com
Chief Executive: Jackie Whelan
Access by public transport: On National Route N67 between Kilrush and Kilkee
Main station: Moyasta Junction
Car park: Located beside station
Length of line: 1.5 miles (3ft gauge), currently being extended
On site facilities: Refreshment coach beside station. Museum in

Station House. Engine shed and facilities beside car park
Period of public operation: Daily all year round. Steam days at weekends and by special arrangement
Facilities for disabled: Fully fitted including wheelchair access to all areas
Membership details: Membership Secretary, c/o above address

Heritage Railway Association

www.heritagerailways.com

Company Limited by Guarantee and not having a share capital.
Registered in England No 2226245
(Registered Office: 2 Littlestone Road, New Romney, Kent TN28 8PL)
President: Dame Margaret Weston DBE
Vice Presidents: Ian Allan OBE, Allan Garraway MBE, Brian Simpson

Friends of HRA Membership Secretary:
Ian Leigh, 206B Crowfield House, North Row, Milton Keynes, MK9 3LQ.
E-mail: ian.leigh4@btinternet.com

Corporate Membership Secretary:
Steve Wood, 15 Croftlands Drive, Ravenglass, Cumbria CA18 1SJ
Tel: 01229 717080 (weekends)
E-mail: woodsysteve@hotmail.com

Members of the Heritage Railway Association

UK Affiliate Members (not in the main part of the book)

Association of Community Rail Partnerships: Dr P. Salvenson, The Rail and River Centre, Canalside, Slaithwaite Civic Hall, Huddersfield HD7 5AB

Brookes No 1 Locomotive Co: Mr D. R. C. Moncton, 10 Blenheim Terrace, Woodhouse Lane, Leeds LS2 9HX

Edmondson Ticket Printing Co: Braehead Halt, Main Street, Forth, Lanark ML11 8HA

English Welsh & Scottish Railways: Mr P Johnson, Loco Engineer, Toton TNMD, Toton Sidings, Long Eaton, Nottingham NG10 1HA

Europe Railway Heritage Trust: Frank Cooper, York House, Clamp Gate Road, Fishtoft, Boston PE21 0RY

R. E. V. Gomm Ltd: Mr M. J. Tyler, Jayesco Works, 31 Commercial Street, Birmingham B1 1RJ

Guild of Railway Artists: Mr F. Hodges, Chief Executive Officer, 45 Dickins Road, Warwick CV34 5NS

Gullane plc: Mathew Way, Maple House, 149 Tottenham Court Road, London W1T 7NF

Lloyd's Railway Society: Mr Douglas Cooper, 24 Yew Tree Road, Southborough, Tunbridge Wells, Kent TN4 0BA

Locomotive Club of Great Britain: Mr R. L. Patrick, 8 Wolviston Ave, Bishopgate, York YO1 3DD

LocoRH200 DE No 424839: Mr B. Cunningham, 20 Ladybrook, Chapel Park, Newcastle upon Tyne

Marsh (UK) Ltd: Mr A. J. C. Brown, No 1, The Marsh Centre, London EC1 8DX

Rannoch Station Visitor Centre: Normanhurst Enterprises Ltd, 9 Burscough Street, Ormskirk, Lancs L39 2EG

Transport Trust: 202 Lambeth Road, London SE1 7JW

Westinghouse Signals Ltd: Helen Webb, PO Box 79, Pew Hill, Chippenham, Wiltshire SN15 1ND

Overseas Affiliate Members

Australian Railway Historical Society: Mr R. Jowett, New South Wales Division, 67 Renwick St, Redfern, NSW 2016, Australia

Puffing Billy Railway: Mr Mel Elliot, PO Box 451, Belgrave, Victoria 3160, Australia

Stoomscentrum Maldegem: Rik Degruyter, De Streep 19, B-8340 Damme-Sysele, Belgium

Stoompoorlijn Dendermonde-Puurs: Mr Jaak Serckx, Station Baasrode Noord, Fabrieksstraat 118, B-9200, Baasrode, Belgium

Additional Corporate Members not listed in the main part of the book

Aln Valley Railway Society:
Mr S. Manley, Alnwick Station, Alnwick, Northumberland NE66 2NP

Altrincham Electric Railway Preservation Society:
Mr A. D. Macfarlane, 25 Prestbury Avenue, Timperley, Altrincham, Cheshire WA15 8HY

Battle of Britain Locomotive Preservation Society:
Les Mitchell, 30 Hilton Way, Sible Hedingham, Essex CO9 3JW

Bridgend Valleys Railway:
Mr J. Leach, 10 Y-Wern, Bettws, Bridgend, Mid Glamorgan CF32 8RR

Britain's Great Little Railways: Mr M. B. Beevers, 64 Bullar Road, Southampton SO18 1GS

Britannia Locomotive Society:
Mr A. Sixsmith, 6 Vermont Grove, Peterborough PE3 6BN

Bulleid Society Ltd:
Mr A. J. Fry, 28 Houndean Rise, Lewes, Sussex BN7 1EQ

Caerphilly Railway Society Ltd: Mr A. Smith, 51 Worcester Crescent, Newport NP9 7NX

Camelot Locomotive Society: Mr P. W. Gibbs, 13 Clarendon Road, High Wycombe, Bucks HP13 7AW

Class 40 Preservation Society: Martin Walker, c/o Beaver Sports (YOMO) Ltd, Flint Street, Fartown, Huddersfield HD1 6LG

Class 45/1 Preservation Society: Mr N. Burden, 97 Richmond Park Crescent, Handsworth, Sheffield S13 8HF

Class 56 Group: Tim Dawe, 1 Stanley Avenue, Sutton Coldfield B75 7EQ

Cornish Steam Locomotive Preservation Society Ltd:
Mr M. Orme, 3 Jubilee Terrace, Goonhavern, Truro, Cornwall TR4 9JY

Cravens Heritage Trains:
James Deacon, 43 Ashpole Furlong, Loughton, Milton Keynes MK5 8ED

Darlington Railway Preservation Society:
Mr M. Bentley, 64 Dimsdale View East, Porthill, Newcastle-under-Lyme ST5 8HL

Dean Forest Locomotive Group:
Mr J. S. Metherall, 15 Sudbrook Way, Gloucester GL4 4AP

Darjeeling Himalayan Railway Society:
Mr P. K. Jordan, Lime Tree Lodge, Thorpe Road, Mattersley, Doncaster DN10 5ED

Deltic Preservation Society: Nigel Paine, 49 Woodgate Road, Wootton Fields, Wootton, Northants NN4 6ET

Devon Diesel Society Ltd: Steve Squires, 15 Springfield, Acle, Norfolk NR13 3JW

Diesel and Electric Group:
Mr J. E. Cronin, The Old Goods Shed, Williton Station, Williton, Somerset TA4 4RQ

Diesel Unit Preservation Associates Ltd:
Mr M. Cornell, 24 Ashbury Drive, Marks Tey, Colchester, Essex CO6 1XW

Dolgarrog Railway Society:
Mr P. Smith, 84 Gorlan, Conwy LL32 8RR

East Essex Locomotive Preservation Society:
Mr R. Moore 7 Woodbine Grove, Enfield, Middx EN2 0EA

Eastleigh Railway Preservation Society Ltd:
Neil Kearns, 38 Arundel Road, Boyatt Wood, Eastleigh, Hants SO50 4PQ

Eden Valley Railway Trust:
Ms G. Boyd, 1 Victoria Road, Barnard Castle, Co Durham DL12 8HW

EPB Preservation Group: Mr R. Baines, 73 Woodhurst Avenue, Petts Wood, Orpington, Kent BR5 1AT

Firefly Trust: Mr S. Bee, 9 Shenstone, Lindfield, West Sussex RH16 2PU

The Flour Mill: Mr W. A. Parker, Stowe Grange, St Briavels, Lydney, Glos GL15 6QH

Foxcote Manor Society:
Mr G. Heddon, 31 Lordsmill Road, Shavington, Crewe, Cheshire CW2 5HB

Gloucester Railcars Trust Ltd:
Mr M. Hancocks, Stanton Barn, Park Lane, Two Dales, Matlock, Derbyshire DE4 2FB

Glyn Valley Tramway Group:
David Norman, 4 Yew Tree Court, Gresford, Wrexham LL12 8ET

Great Western Heritage Trust:
Stephen Atkins, Dowsers Cottage, 25 High Street, Meysey Hampton, Glos GL7 5JT

GWR 813 Preservation Fund:
Mr P. Goss, 23 Hatchmere, Thornbury, Bristol BS35 2EU

Haig Colliery Mining Museum: John Greasley, Haig Colliery Mining Museum, Solway Road, Kells, Whitehaven, Cumbria CA28 9BG

Hampshire & Sussex Units Preservation Society:
Mr C. Dann, 48 Hollybrook Park, Bordon, Hants GU35 0DL

Hastings Diesels Ltd:
Mr J. White, The Rail Engineering Centre, Bridgeway, St Leonards on Sea, East Sussex TN38 8AP

Heaton Park Electric Tramway: Roger Morris, 38 Wolsey Road, Sale, Cheshire M33 7AU

Holden F5 Steam Locomotive Trust: Steve Cooper,
4 Dukes Close, North Weald, Nr Epping, Essex
CM16 6DA

Hull & Barnsley Railway Stock Fund:
Mr A. E. Hallman, 6 Chequerfield Court, Pontefract,
West Yorkshire WF8 2TQ

Kingdom of Fife Railway Association (The):
Jim Rankine, 'Lairg', Haughmill Lane, Windygates,
Fife KY8 5DH

Lambton No 29 Syndicate:
Mr J. M. Richardson, 509 Westgate Apartments, York
YO26 4ZF

Lancashire & Yorkshire Railway Preservation Society:
Mr E. Ring, PO Box 3593, Newport Pagnall
MK16 9ZJ

*Lincolnshire Coast Light Railway Historical Vehicles
Trust:*
Mr H. L. Goy, 12 Giles Street, Cleethorpes
DN35 8AE

Llanelli & Mynydd Mawr Railway: Martin Doe,
16 Melrose Avenue, Penylan, Cardiff CF23 9AR

LMS Carriage Association: David Winter,
42 Tandlewood Park, Royton, Oldham OL2 5UZ

Locomotive Owners Group (Scotland) Ltd:
Mr H. Stevenson, 28 Hazeldean Avenue, Bo'ness,
West Lothian EH51 0NJ

London & North Western Society: Mr R. J. Williams,
3 Chieveley Court, Emerson Valley, Milton Keynes
MK4 2DD

Lynton & Barnstaple Light Railway: Mr D. Hill,
8 Long Lakes, Williton, Taunton, Somerset TA4 4SR

Maid Marian Locomotive Fund: Mr H. Johns,
139 Stoops Lane, Doncaster DN4 7RG

Market Drayton Railway Preservation Society:
Glyn Rowe, Shakeford Mill House, Hinstock, Market
Drayton, Shropshire TF9 2SP

Maunsell Locomotive Society:
Mr J. S. Pilcher, 312 Riverside Mansions, Garnett
Street, Wapping, London E1 9SZ

Merchant Navy Locomotive Preservation Society Ltd:
Howard G. Reynolds, 4 Ash Grove, Liphook, Hants
GU30 7HZ

Merseyside Tramway Preservations Society:
Robert Jones, 103 Grove Road, Wallasey, Merseyside
CH45 3HG

Midsomer Norton Station Project:
John Baxter, 12 Huxley Close, Shrewsbury SY2 6JR

Modern Railway Society of Ireland: Mr D. Brian
King, 4 York Avenue, Whitehead, Co Antrim,
N. Ireland BT38 9QT

Moseley Railway Trust: Dr John Rowlands,
10 Braxfield Court, St Annes Road West, St Annes on
Sea, Lancs FY8 1LQ

NER 1903 Electric Autocar Trust: Stephen Middleton,
Rose Lea House, 23 Brunswick Drive, Harrogate
HG1 2QW

North Eastern Locomotive Preservation Group:
Mr C. Hatton, 20 Sorrell Court, Marton,
Middlesbrough TS7 8RZ

North Gloucestershire Railway Co Ltd:
Mr R. H. Wales, 'Wellesbourne', Oakfield Street,
Tivoli, Cheltenham, Gloucestershire GL33 8HR

Ongar Railway Preservation Society: Mr B. Ayton,
75 Highland Road, Nazeing, Essex EN9 2PU

Princess Royal Locomotive Trust Ltd:
Mr George Bailey, The Gables, Whitecross,
Hallatrow, Bristol BS39 6ER

Railway Vehicle Preservations Ltd:
Mr Gordon Maslin, 14 Lawson Avenue, Stanground,
Peterborough PE2 8PA

Red Rose Society:
Mr G. Jones, Astley Green Colliery Museum, Higher
Green Lane, Astley, Tyldesley, Manchester M29 7JB

Royal Gunpowder Mills Waltham Abbey:
John Bowles, 9 Humber Road, London SE3 7LS

Salisbury Steam Locomotive Preservation Trust:
Mr E. J. Roper, 33 Victoria Road, Wilton, Salisbury,
Wiltshire SP2 0DZ

Scottish Locomotive Preservation Trust Fund:
Mr J. Shepherd, 29 Earlspark Avenue, Glasgow
G43 2HN

Shipley Glen Tramway: Mr R. Freeman, 19 Ashfield
Drive, Baildon, Shipley BD4 3GA

Sir Nigel Gresley Locomotive Preservation Trust Ltd:
Peter Travis, 26 Cheltenham Gardens, Halifax,
West Yorks HX3 0AN

Southern Electric Group:
Mr B. Cakebread, 41 The Drive, Shoreham by Sea,
West Sussex BN43 5GD

Southern Locomotives Ltd:
Mr S. Troy, 16 Arcadia Road, Istead Rise, Meopham,
Kent DA13 9EH

Southwold Railway Society (The):
Mr J. Bennett, 1 Barnaby Green, Southwold, Suffolk
IP15 6AP

Stanier 8F Locomotive Society Ltd: Mr G. Moon,
5 Orchid Fields, St Christopher's Way, Burnham on
Sea, Somerset TA8 2NU

Steam Power Trust '65:
Mr A. R. Thompson, The Station House, Penshaw,
Houghton le Spring DH4 7PQ

Stephenson Locomotive Society: Mr B. F. Gilliam,
25 Regency Close, Chigwell, Essex IG7 5NY

Stratford on Avon, Broadway Railway Society:
Mr G. Turner, Manor Lodge, Penelope Gardens,
Manor Road, Wickhamford, Evesham, Worcs
WR11 6SG

Suburban Electric Railway Association:
Mr R. Davidson, 6 Coombfield Drive, Darenth,
Dartford, Kent DA2 7LQ

Underground Railway Rolling Stock Trust:
Mr D. C. Alexander, 13 Irvine Drive, Stoke
Mandeville, Aylesbury HP22 5UN

Urie Locomotive Society:
Mr A. Ball, 'Lavenham', Adams Lane, Selborne,
Alton, Hants GU34 3LJ

Wainwright 'C' Preservation Society:
Mr N. W. DeMaid, Flat 2, The Old Stable House,
Bromley, Kent BR1 3JF

Weardale Railway Trust:
Mr G. Chatsfield, Stanhope Station, Bondisle, Bishop
Auckland, Co Durham DL13 2YS

Western Locomotive Association: Mr H. Coates,
5 Rake End Court, Ridware, Rugeley, Staffs
WS15 5RW

Worcester Locomotive Society Ltd: Mr A. T. Dowling,
9 Queens Court, Ledbury, Herefordshire HR4 9DN

1857 Society: Mr G. West, 21A Broad Street,
Brigtown, Cannock, West Midlands WS11 3DA

4247 Ltd: Mr N. Powles, Station House, Station Road,
Lower Heyford, Oxon OX6 3PD

48624 Locomotive Soc: Keith Godley, 11 Cobnar
Drive, Newbold, Chesterfield S41 8DD

6201 Princess Elizabeth Society Ltd: Mr A. Harries, 1
Ormerod Close, Sandbach, Cheshire CW11 4HA

35006 Locomotive Co Ltd: Mr G. Chidley,
102 Anfield Court, Russell Terrace, Leamington Spa
CV31 1HD

*71000 Duke of Gloucester Steam Locomotive Trust
Ltd:* D. J. Brown, 11 Stirling Close, Woolston,
Warrington WA1 4DW

8E Railway Association: Mr A. Ashurst, 149 St Mary
Street, Latchford, Warrington, Cheshire WA4 1EL

LM2MT 46464 Trust: Mr I. Hopley, The Carmyllie
Pilot Co Ltd, 6 Ninian Place, Portlethen AB12 4QW

Applicant Organisations

Amman Valley Railway Society

Bury Port & Gwendraeth Railway Co Ltd

Colne Valley Railway Preservation Society

*Denbigh & Mold Junction Railway Heritage Centre
Trust*

Gawr Valley Railway

Gwendraeth Valley Railways Co Ltd

Lincolnshire Coast Light Railway

Threlkeld Museum

Waverley Route Heritage Association

Wisbech & March Bramley Line

45163 Ltd

Britain's Great Little Railways

Brookside Miniature Railway: (see main section)

Dragon Miniature Railway:
Mr B. Lomas, Wyevale Garden Centre, Otterspool,
Marple, Cheshire SK6 7HG

Eastleigh Lakeside Railway: (see main section)

Exmoor Steam Railway: (see main section)

Fairbourne Railway (see main section)

Haigh Hall Railway: Mr T. Sharratt, Haigh Hall
Country Park, Haigh, Wigan, Lancs WN2 1PE

Little Giant Railways: Merton Hill Railway, Merton
Abbey Mills, London SW19 2RD

Moors Valley Railway (see main section)

Mull Rail (see main section)

Perrygrove Railway: (see main section)

Road, Rail & Waterway: Mr J. Shackell, 27 Witney
Road, Duckington, Witney, Oxon OX8 7TX

Rudyard Lake Railway: (see main section)

Shibden Miniature Railway: Shibden Park, Listers
Road, Halifax, W. Yorks HX3 6XG

Swanley New Barn Railway:
Mr P. Jackson, New Barn Lane, Swanley, Kent

Weston Miniature Railway:
Mr R. Bullock, Marine Parade, Weston-super-Mare,
Somerset

INDEX

HERITAGE RAILWAYS
2007

80136

NATIONAL TIMETABLE OF
SCHEDULED SERVICES

Price £1.50

Heritage Railways Timetable and Directory

This timetable has been produced by *Railways Illustrated* and Ian Allan Publishing Ltd and was printed by Ian Allan Printing Ltd of Hersham, Surrey.

NOTES TO THE TIMETABLE

Throughout the Timetable, the 24 hour clock is used.

Days of operation are shown. Timetable information is also provided.

Many trains have on board refreshment facilities. These are not shown herein as availability may vary according to staffing conditions and seasons of the year.

For details of Wine and Dine, Thomas the Tank Engine, Santa Specials and other out-of-the-ordinary facilities, please enquire of the appropriate railway company for details.

Telephone and fax number, postal address and www. address (website) of each railway operator is shown at the head of each entry so that specific enquiries can be made direct.

The entries are mostly in alphabetical order but in some cases there has been a slight variation to meet space requirements.

DISCLAIMER

This timetable has been compiled from information received from operating companies and is believed to be accurate. However, neither the publisher nor HRA accept any responsibility for any loss, damage or delay which may be caused by variances between this brochure and actual operations or any other cause.

Where there are exceptions to the normal operations of running, dates are shown in *italics* and throughout the timetable **Santa Specials** are denoted by the letters SS. © Ian Allan Publishing Ltd 2007

MARKS OF QUALITY

Some railways excel in certain fields, and in this timetable special merit markings are applied as has been thought appropriate. The symbols represent individual quality; a double symbol represents excellence. Winner in the 2006 Ian Allan Independent Railway of the Year Awards are highlighted.

	Award winner 2006		Interesting Rolling Stock		On-board catering
¶¶	On-shore catering		Interesting Engines	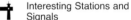	Interesting Stations and Signals
	Big Engines	WC	Loos		Views from the train

HERITAGE RAILWAY OF 2006

Congratulations to

West Somerset Railway adjudged by this Heritage publication as:

Heritage Railway of the Year 2006

on the basis of its great progress in all departments.

Apart from dispensing merit marks for specific aspects of the various heritage railways we are awarding 1, 2 and 3 stars to those railways that are particularly worthy of recognition.

★★★ stars go to leading companies who offer professional service in all departments.

★★ stars go to the best of the rest.

★ star goes to the up-and-coming.

Cover image: BR Standard Class 4MT No 80136 at Bishops Lydeard on the West Somerset Railway. *Alan C. Butcher*

AVON VALLEY RAILWAY

0117 932 5538

Bitton Station, Bath Road, Bitton, Bristol BS30 6HD

Fax: 0117 932 5935 Web: www.avonvalleyrailway.org

Trains run on **January** 1 and 2; **March** 18; **April** 1, 6-18, 22, 28 and 29; **May** 5-7, 12, 13, 20 and 26-31; **June** 1, 3, 9, 10, 16, 17 and 24; **July** 1, 8, 14, 15, 21, 22, 28, 29 and 31; **August** 1, 2, 4, 5, 7-9, 11, 12, 14-16, 18, 19, 21-23 and 25-30; **September** 1, 2, 8, 9, 16, 23 and 30; **October** 6, 7, 14, 21 and 28; **December** 30, with **SS** on **November** 25; **December** 1-3, 8, 9, 15, 16 and 22-24.

Timetable: Trains leave Bitton at 11.00, 12.15, 13.30, 14.45, 16.00 via Oldland and Avon Riverside. The overall journey time is 1 hour and there is a special timetable on certain days, details of which can be obtained by phoning.

BALA LAKE RAILWAY

01678 540666

The Station, Llanuwchllyn, Gwynedd LL23 7DD

Fax: 01678 540535 Web: www.bala-lake-railway.co.uk

Trains run daily from **March** 31 to **September** 30 *EXCEPT April 2, 16, 20, 23, 27 and 30; May 4, 11, 14, 18, 21 and 25; June 4, 8, 11, 15, 18, 22, 25 and 29; September 3, 7, 10, 14, 17, 21, 24 and 28*, then on **October** 2, 3, 9, 10 and 23-25 with **SS** on **November** 8 and 9.

Timetable: Standard service provides for departures from Llanuwchllyn at 11.15, 12.50, 14.25, 16.00. Intending passengers are recommended to contact for timetable details in October.

BATTLEFIELD LINE

01827 880754

Shackerstone Station, Leicestershire CV13 6NW

Fax: 01827 881050 Web: www.battlefield-line-railway.co.uk

Trains run on **April** 6-11, 14, 15, 21, 22, 28 and 29; **May** 5-7, 12, 13, 19, 20 and 26-28; **June** 2, 3, 9, 10, 16, 17, 23, 24 and 30; **July** 1, 4, 7, 8, 11, 14, 15, 18, 21, 22, 25, 28 and 30; **August** 1, 4, 5, 8, 11, 12, 15, 18, 19, 22, 25-27 and 29; **September** 1, 2, 8, 9, 14-16, 22, 23, 29 and 30; **October** 6, 7, 13, 14, 20, 21, 27 and 28, with **SS** on **November** 24 and 25; **December** 1, 2, 8, 9, 15, 16, 22-24, 29 and 30.

Timetable: Normal service provides for departures from Shackerstone at 12.00, 13.20, 14.40, 16.00 arriving at Shenton 20 minutes later. Return departures are at 12.35, 13.55, 15.15, 16.35. There is a special timetable in respect of Santa Specials.

BLUEBELL RAILWAY

01825 720800

Sheffield Park, Uckfield, East Sussex TN22 3QL

Fax: 01825 720804 Web: www.bluebell-railway.co.uk

Timetable: Please contact for details.

BODMIN & WENFORD RAILWAY

01208 73666

General Station, Bodmin, Cornwall PL31 1AQ

Fax: 01208 77963 Web: www.bodminandwenfordrailway.co.uk

Trains run on **February** 10; **March** 14, 18, 21, 24, 25 and 28; **April** 1-15, 17, 18, 21, 22, 24, 25 and 29; **May** 1, 2, 5-9, 13, 15, 16, 20, 22, 23 and 26-31, daily from **June** 1 until **September** 30, then on **October** 3, 7, 10, 14, 17, 20-28 and 31; **November** 7; **December** 26, 27, 29 and 30, with **SS** on **December** 1, 2, 8, 9, 15, 16 and 22-24.

BO'NESS & KINNEIL RAILWAY

01506 825855/822298

**Scottish Railway Preservation Society,
17-19 North Street, Bo'ness EH51 0AQ** Fax: 01506 828766 Web: www.srps.org.uk

Trains run on **March** 31; **April** 1, 6-9, 14, 15, 21, 22, 28 and 29; **May** 5-7, 12, 13, 19-21, 26 and 27; **June** 2, 3, 5, 9, 10, 12, 16, 17, 19, 23, 24, 26 and 30; daily from **July** 1 until **August** 26; September 1, 2, 8, 9, 15, 16, 22, 23, 29 and 30; **October** 6, 7, 13, 14, 20, 21, 27 and 28; **December** 30 and 31 with **SS** on **December** 1, 2, 8, 9, 15, 16, 22 and 23.

Timetable: Standard timetable provides for departure from Bo'ness at 11.00, 12.15, 13.45, 15.00, 16.15 returning from Birkhill at 11.35, 12.42, 14.20, 15.35, 16.40. Journey time 17 minutes each way. Augmented timetable operates on certain dates. Please check for details.

BRECON MOUNTAIN RAILWAY

Pant Station, Merthyr Tydfil CF48 2UP 01685 722988

Fax: 01685 384854   Web: www.breconmountainrailway.co.uk

Trains run from **March** 24 until **November** 4 *EXCEPT March* 26 and 30, *April* 2, 16, 20, 23, 27 and 30; *May* 4, 14, 18, 21 and 25; *September* 17, 21, 24 and 28; *October* 1, 5, 8, 12, 15, 19, 22 and 26; then **SS** on **December** 1-23.

Timetable: Trains leave Pant at 11.00. 12.15, 13.30, 14.45, 16.00.

BURE VALLEY RAILWAY

Aylsham Station, Norwich Road, Aylsham, Norfolk NR11 6BW   01263 733858

Fax: 01263 733814   Web: www.bvrw.co.uk

Trains run on **January** 1 and 2; **February** 10-18; **March** 3, 4, 10, 11, 17, 18, 24, 25 and 31; daily from **April** 1 until **September** 30, **October** 6, 7, 13, 14 and 20-28; **December** 27-31 with **SS** on **November** 25 and **December** 1, 2, 8, 9, 12, 14-16 and 18-24.

Timetable: Early season departure from Alysham at 11.00 and 14.15 arriving at Wroxham at 11.45 and 15.00. Returning from Wroxham at 12.15 and 15.30. Journey time 45 mintues each way.
During the shoulder weeks trains leave Alysham at 10.05, 11.35, 12.45, 14.15 and 15.25 and in the high season there are departures from Alysham at 09.25, 10.05, 11.35, 12.45, 14.15, 15.25 and 16.35.

CALENDONIAN RAILWAY (BRECHIN) LTD

The Station, 2 Park Road, Brechin, Angus DD9 7AF   01356 622992

Web: www.caledonianrailway.com

Trains run on **April** 7 and 8; **May** 5-7 and 27; **June** 17; **July** 7, 8, 14, 15 and 21; **August** 4, 18, 24 and 25; **September** 2, **SS** on **December** 9, 15, 16, 22 and 23.

Timetable: Please contact for details.

CHASEWATER RAILWAY

Chasewater Country Park, Pool Road, Nr Brownhills, Staffs WS8 7NL   01543 452623

Trains run on **January** 7, 14, 21 and 28; **February** 4, 11, 18, 24 and 25; **March** 4, 11, 18 and 25; **April** 1, 7-9, 15, 22 and 29; **May** 5-7, 13, 20, 26-28 and 30; **June** 3, 10, 16, 17, 20, 24, 27 and 30; **July** 1, 4, 7, 8, 11, 15, 18, 21, 22, 25, 28 and 29; **August** 1, 4, 5, 8, 11, 12, 15, 18, 19, 22, 25-27 and 29; **September** 1, 2, 8, 9, 15, 16, 22, 23, 29 and 30; **October** 7, 14, 20, 21 and 28; **November** 4, 11, 18 and 25; **SS** on **December** 1, 2, 8, 9, 15, 16, 22 and 23.

Timetable: Limited services during January and February. Trains run approximately every hour from Brownhills West returning from Chasetown 35 minutes later.

CHINNOR & PRINCES RISBOROUGH RAILWAY

Chinnor Station, Station Road, Chinnor, Oxon OX39 4ER   01844 353535

Web: www.cprra.co.uk

Trains run on **March** 18 and 25; **April** 1, 6-9, 15, 22 and 29; **May** 5-7, 13, 20, 27 and 28; **June** 3, 10, 17, 24, 29 and 30; **July** 1, 7, 8, 14, 15, 21, 22, 28 and 29; **August** 4, 5, 11, 12, 18, 19 and 25-27; **September** 2, 9, 16, 23, 29 and 30; **October** 7, 14, 21 27 and 28; **December** 29 and 30 with **SS** on 2, 8, 9, 15, 16, 22 and 23.

Timetable: Please contact for further details.

CHURNET VALLEY RAILWAY

The Station, Cheddleton, Staffordshire Moorlands ST13 7EE   01538 360522

Fax: 01538 361848   Web: www.churnet-valley-railway.co.uk

Trains run on **January** 2, 7, 13, 14, 21 and 28; **February** 10, 11, 13 and 14; **March** 4, 11, 18 and 25; **April** 2, 6-9, 11, 15, 22, 28 and 29; **May** 5-7, 13, 20, 26-28 and 30; **June** 1-3, 9, 10, 16, 17, 23, 24 and 29; **July** 1, 4, 7, 8, 11, 14, 15, 18, 21, 22, 25, 28, 29 and 31; **August** 1, 4-6, 8, 11-13, 15, 18-20, 22, 25-27 and 29; **September** 1, 2, 8, 9, 15, 16, 22, 23, 29 and 30; **October** 7, 14, 21 and 24; **December** 30, with **SS** on **December** 1, 2, 5, 8, 9, 12, 15, 16, 19 and 22-24.

Timetable: Round trip Constall to Froghall at 10.30, 11.50, 13.10, 14.30, 15.50 and departures from Froghall at 11.07, 12.27, 13.47, 15.07, 16.27. Travel time 13 minutes between Froghall and Consall and 7 minutes from Consall to Cheddleton and vice versa.

CLEETHORPES COAST LIGHT RAILWAY 01472 604657

Lakeside Station, Kings Road, Cleethorpes, North East Lincs, DN35 0AG

Fax: 01472 291903   Web: www.cleethorpescoastlightrailway.co.uk

Timetable: Train service starts at 10.30 from Lakeside and trains run at approximately half-hourly intervals. Travel time 15 minutes.

COLNE VALLEY RAILWAY

Castle Hedingham, Halstead, Essex CO9 3DZ   **01787 461174**

Fax: 01787 462254   Web: www.colnevalleyrailway.co.uk

Trains run on **March** 4, 11, 18 and 25; **April** 1, 3-12, 14, 15, 22 and 28-30; **May** 5, 6, 13, 20 and 26-31; **June** 2, 3, 9, 10, 12-14, 16, 17, 19-21, 23 and 24; **July** 1, 7, 8, 14, 15, 22-26, 28, 29 and 31; **August** 1, 2, 4, 5, 7-9, 11, 12, 14-16, 18, 19, 21-23 and 25-30; **September** 1, 2, 8, 9, 16, 23, 26, 27, 29 and 30; **October** 2-4, 6, 7, 14, 21, 23-25 and 28; with **SS** on **December** 2, 8, 9, 15, 16 and 21-24.

Timetable: There is no standard pattern of train services but various events are held focusing on steam operation, diesel operation, educational visits and wine and dine trains.

CORRIS RAILWAY

Corris Railway Museum, Station Yard, Corris, Machynlleth,   **01527 5421580**
Powys SY20 9SH   Web: www.corris.co.uk

Trains run on **April** 6-9, 14, 15, 22 and 29; **May** 5-7, 13, 20 and 26-28; **June** 2, 3, 10, 17 and 24; **July** 1, 7, 8, 14, 15, 21, 22 and 28-31; **August** 1-5, 11, 12 and 18-27; **September** 1, 2, 9, 16, 23 and 30; **October** 27 with **SS** on **December** 15 and 16.

Timetable: Passengers board the train at Corris only, departing at 11.00, 12.00, 13.00, 14.00, 15.00, 16.00. The round trip takes 50 minutes.

CRICH TRAMWAY VILLAGE

Crich, Matlock, Derbyshire DE4 5DP   **01773 854321**

Fax: 01773 854320   Web: www.tramway.co.uk

Trams run daily from **February** 10-25 from 10.30 until 16.00. **Weekends** in **March** from 10.30 to 16.00. Daily from March 31 until **October** 28 from 10.00 to 17.30. **Weekends** from **November** to **December** 16 from 10.30 to 16.00.

DEAN FOREST RAILWAY

Forest Road, Lydney, Gloucestershire GL15 4ET   **01594 843423**

Web: www.deanforestrailway.co.uk

Trains run on **March** 18; **April** 1, 6-9, 12-15, 22 and 29; **May** 5-7, 13, 20, 26-28 and 31; **June** 1-3, 6, 9, 10, 13, 16, 17, 20, 23, 24, 27 and 30; **July** 1, 4, 7, 8, 11, 14, 15, 18, 21, 22, 24-26, 28, 29 and 31; **August** 1, 2, 4, 5, 7-9, 11, 12, 14-16, 18, 19, 21-23 and 25-31; **September** 1, 2, 5, 8, 9, 12, 15, 16, 19, 22, 23, 26, 29 and 30; **October** 7, 14, 21, 24, 27, 28 and 31; **December** 29-31 with **SS** on **December** 8, 9, 15, 16 and 22-24.

Timetable: All trains call at intermediate stations Lydney Town 5 minutes, St Mary's 9 minutes after leaving Norchard. Departures from Norchard at 11.10, 13.18, 14.49, 16.19 arriving at Lydney Junction 12 minutes after leaving Norchard. Trains leave Lydney Junction at 11.40, 13.44, 15.14, 16.41.

DIDCOT RAILWAY CENTRE

Didcot, Oxfordshire OX11 7NJ   **01235 817200**

Fax: 01235 510621   Web: www.didcotrailwaycentre.org.uk

The Centre is open at weekends throughout the year and daily during **July** and **August**. Also on **February** 10-18; **March** 2; **April** 2-6 and 9-13, **May** 7 and 28-31; **June** 1 and 25-29; **September** 3; **October** 5; **December** 27, 28 and 31, with **SS** on **December** 8, 9, 14-16 and 21-24.

Timetable: Opening time March to October 10.00-16.00 extended to 17.00 on steam days. Last admission 30 minutes before closing but allow at least two hours for a visit especially on a steam day.

EAST SOMERSET RAILWAY

Cranmore Station, Shepton Mallet, Somerset BA4 4QP   **01749 880417**

Fax: 01749 880764   Web: www.eastsomersetrailway.com

Timetable: Please contact for details.

EAST KENT RAILWAY
Station Road, Shepherdswell, Kent CT15 7PD **01304 832042**

Web: www.eastkentrailway.com

Trains run on **March** 18; **April** 6-9, 15, 22 and 29; **May** 5-7, 13, 20 and 26-28; **June** 3, 10, 17 and 24; **July** 1, 8, 15, 22, 28 and 29; **August** 4, 5, 11, 12, 18, 19 and 25-27; **September** 2, 9 and 16; **October** 27 and 28, with **SS** on **December** 8, 9, 15, 16 and 21-24.

Timetable: Standard service provides for departures from Shepherdswell at 11.30, 12.45, 14.00, 15.15. Round trip takes 37 minutes.

EAST LANCASHIRE RAILWAY
Bolton Street Station, Bolton Street, Bury, Lancs BL9 0EY **0161 764 7790**

Fax: 0161 763 4408 Web: www.east-lancs-rly.co.uk

Trains run on **January** 1, 6, 7, 13, 14, 20, 21, 27 and 28; **February** 3, 4, 10, 11, 17, 18, 24 and 25; **March** 3, 4, 10, 11, 17, 18, 24, 25 and 31; **April** 1, 4-15, 21, 22, 28 and 29; **May** 2-7, 9-13, 16-20, 23-28, 30 and 31; **June** 1-3, 6-10, 13-17, 20-24 and 27-30; **July** 1, 4-8, 11-15, 18-22 and 25-29; **August** 1-5, 8-12, 15-19, 22-27 and 29-31; **September** 1, 2, 5-9, 12-16, 22, 23, 29 and 30; **October** 6, 7, 13, 14, 20, 21, 27 and 28; **November** 3, 4, 10, 11, 17, 18, 24 and 25; **December** 26 with **SS** on **December** 1, 2, 8, 9, 15, 16 and 21-24.

Timetable: Basic service provides for departures from Bury Bolton Street at 10.00, 11.45, 14.00, 15.45. Travel time Bury Bolton Street to Rawtenstall 32 minutes. Return trains from Rawtenstall run at 10.50, 12.35, 14.50, 16.30. This service is considerably augmented at weekends and bank holidays. Intending passengers are advised to check timetable arrangements before travelling.

EMBSAY & BOLTON ABBEY STEAM RAILWAY
Bolton Abbey Station, Bolton Abbey, Skipton, N. Yorks BD23 6AF 01756 710614

Fax: 01756 710720 Web: www.embsayboltonabbeyrailway.org.uk

Timetable: Standard timetable provides for departures from Embsay at 10.30, 12.00, 13.30, 15.00, 16.30 (4 March to 27 October) and from Bolton Abbey at 11.10, 12.40, 14.10, 15.40, 17.00 (4 March to 27 October only). Journey time, one way, 15 minutes. Round trip 70 minutes. All trains call at Holywell Holt 5 minutes after departing from Embsay and 10 minutes after departing from Bolton Abbey.
Intending passengers should check by telephone/website which days are actually operating.

EXBURY GARDENS RAILWAY
 023 8089 1203
Exbury Gardens, Exbury, Nr Southampton, Hampshire SO45 1AZ

Fax: 023 8089 9940 Web: www.exbury.co.uk

Trains run daily from **March** 17 until **November** 6.

FAIRBOURNE RAILWAY
Beach Road, Fairbourne, Gwynedd LL38 2EX **01341 250362**

Fax: 01341 250240 Web: www.fairbournerailway.com

Trains run on **February** 10-15, 17 and 18; **March** 31; **April** 1, 6-15, 21, 22 and 28-30; daily from **May** 1 until **September** 23, *EXCEPT May 4, 11, 18 and 25*; **June** 8, 15, 22 and 29; **July** 6 and 13; **September** 7, 14 and 21, then on **September** 29 and 30; **October** 6, 7, 13, 14, 20-25, 27 and 28, with **SS** on **December** 8 and 9.

Timetable: Normal service provides for departures from Fairbourne at 11.15, 13.45, 15.30 and from Barmouth at 11.45, 14.15, 16.00. The service augmented in the peak with trains running every 40 minutes in both directions.

FFESTINIOG RAILWAY
Harbour Station, Porthmadog, Gwynedd LL49 9NF **01766 516000**

Fax: 01766 516005 Web: www.festrail.co.uk

Trains run on **January** 1, 5, 7-11, 13, 15-17, 19, 20, 22, 23, 25, 26 and 31; **February** 1, 7, 8, 10, 23 and 28; **March** 1, 7, 8, 14, 15, 17, 18, 21, 22, 24 and 25, then daily from **March** 27 until **November** 4.

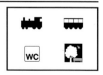

Timetable: Two trains per day operate in the off peak augmented to a more or less hourly service in the peak months. All trains call at intermediate stations Tan-y-Bwlch 40 minutes after leaving Porthmadog.

FOXFIELD STEAM RAILWAY
PO Box 1967, Stoke-on-Trent, Staffordshire ST4 8YT   **01782 396210**
Fax: 01782 396210   E-mail: enquiries@foxfieldrailway.co.uk   Web http://foxfieldrailway.co.uk

Timetable: Please contact for details.

GARTELL LIGHT RAILWAY
Common Lane, Yenston, Templecombe, Somerset BA8 0NB   **019630 370752**
Fax: 01963 373915   Web: www.glr-online.co.uk

Trains run on **April** 9; **May** 7 and 28; **June** 24; **July** 29; **August** 5, 12, 19, 26 and 27; **September** 30; **October** 28, with **SS** on **December** 15 and 16.

Timetable: Standard service operates every 45 minutes throughout the day and in the high season every 15 minutes from 10.30 until 16.30 inclusive. Return journey time 23 minutes.

GLOUCESTERSHIRE WARWICKSHIRE RAILWAY
The Railway Station, Toddington, Glos GL54 5DT   **01242 621405**
Web: www.gwsr.com

Trains run on **March** 3, 4, 10, 11, 17, 18, 24, 25, 30 and 31; **April** 1, 3-12, 14, 15, 21, 22, 28 and 29; **May** 3, 5-7, 10, 12, 13, 17, 19, 20, 24 and 26-31; **June** 1-3, 6, 7, 13-17, 20, 21, 23, 24, 27, 28 and 30; **July** 1, 4, 5, 7, 8, 11, 12, 14, 15, 18, 19, 21, 22, 24-26, 28, 29 and 31; **August** 1, 2, 4, 5, 7-9, 11, 12, 14-16, 18, 19, 21-23 and 25-30; **September** 1, 2, 4-6, 8, 9, 13, 15, 16, 20, 22, 23, 27 and 29-30; **October** 6, 7, 13, 14, 20, 21, 23-25; 27 and 28; **November** 3, 4, 10, 11, 18, 24 and 25; **December** 26-31, with **SS** on **December** 1, 2, 8, 9, 15, 16 and 22-24.

Timetable: The normal timetable service provides for departures from Toddington at 10.30, 11.30, 13.00, 14.15, 15.15, 16.35. All trains call intermediately at Winchcoombe 9 minutes after leaving Toddington and most trains provide a service to Cheltenham Race Course which is reached 31 minutes after leaving Toddington. Returning trains leave Cheltenham at 11.15, 12.15, 14.00, 15.00, 16.00, 17.20. Train times vary during the season and intending passengers are advised to check which timetable is in operation before travelling.

GOLDEN VALLEY LIGHT RAILWAY
c/o Butterley Station, Ripley, Derbyshire DE5 3QZ   **01773 747674**
Fax: 01773 570721   Web: www.gvlr.org.uk

Trains run on **March** 3, 4, 10 and 11-31; **April** 1, 6-15, 21, 22, 28 and 29; **May** 5, 6, 12, 13, 19, 20 and 26-31; **June** 1-3, 9, 10, 16, 17, 23, 24 and 30; **July** 1, 7, 8, 14, 15, 21 until **August** 31; **September** 1-3, 8, 9, 15, 16, 23 and 30; **October** 6, 7, 13, 14, 20, 21, 27 and 28; **November** 3.

Timetable: **Trains** leave Butterley Park station at 11.50, 12.30 and every three-quarters of an hour until 16.15. Return journey 25 minutes.

GREAT CENTRAL RAILWAY
Great Central Road, Loughborough, Leicestershire LE11 1RW   **01509 230726**
Fax: 01509 239791   Web: www.gcrailway.co.uk

Trains run on **January** 6, 7, 13, 14, 20, 21, 27 and 28; **February** 3, 4, 10, 11, 17, 18, 24 and 25; **March** 3, 4, 10, 11, 17, 18, 24, 25 and 31; **April** 1, 6-9, 14, 15, 20, 21, 27 and 28; **May** 5-7, 12, 13, 19, 20, 23, 26-28 and 30; **June** 2, 3, 5-7, 9, 10, 12-17, 19-21, 23, 24, 26-28 and 30, daily during **July** and **August**, *EXCEPT July 2, 6, 9, 13;* then on **September** 1, 2, 5, 8, 9, 12, 14-16, 19, 22, 23, 26, 29 and 30; **October** 6, 7, 13, 14, 20, 21, 27, 28 and 31; **November** 3-5, 10, 11, 17 and 18; **December** 25-31, with **SS** on **November** 24 and 25, **December** 1, 2, 8, 9, 15, 16 and 18-24.

Timetable: Standard service provides for departures fromf Loughborough Central at 11.00, 13.00, 15.00, 19.30 and from Leicester North at 11.45, 13.45, 15.45, 20.50. Journey time 28 minutes in each direction. The services augmented at most weekends providing for a more or less hourly service from 09.30 to 20.45 from Loughborough Central. Intending passengers are recommended to check train times by telephone.

GREAT ORME TRAMWAY
Victoria Station, Church Walks, Llandudno LL30 2AZ   **01492 879306**

Fax: 01492 879781   Web: www.greatormetramway.com

Trams run from **March** 17-31 from 10.00-17.00, from **April** 1 until **September** 30 from 10.00-18.00 and from **October** 1 until **November** 4 from 10.00-17.00.

Frequency: Every 20 minutes – on the hour, twenty past and twenty to the hour (trams are able to run every 10 minutes during the peak season).

Journey time: The journey is split into two sections: lower section and upper section. Each section takes approximately 8-10 minutes to complete. Passengers then have to change at the Halfway Station, where there is a tramway exhibition and a chance to view into the Winding House, before boarding the tram to the summit.

GROUDLE GLEN RAILWAY
29 Hawarden Avenue, Douglas, Isle of Man IM1 4BP   **01624 622138**

E-mail: tbeard@manx.net

Trains run on **April** 8 and 9; **May** 6, 13, 20 and 27; **June** 3, 10, 17 and 24; **July** 1, 4, 8, 11, 15, 18, 22, 25, 29 and 31; **August** 1, 5, 7, 8, 12, 14, 15, 19, 21, 22 and 26; **September** 2, 9, 16, 23 and 30; **December** 26 with **SS** on **December** 16, 22 and 23.

Standard service operates between 11.00 and 16.30 and **SS** between 11.00–15.30.

Please contact for further details.

GWILI STEAM RAILWAY
Bronwydd Arms Station, Bronwydd, Carmarthen SA33 6HT   **01267 238213**

Web: www.gwili-railway.co.uk

Trains run on **April** 6-9; **May** 5-7, 12, 19 and 27-31; **June** 3, 6, 9, 13, 17, 20, 23 and 27-29; **July** 4, 8, 11, 15, 18, 22, 25 and 29; **August** 1-3, 5, 8-10, 12, 15-17, 19, 22-24, 26, 27 and 29-31; **September** 2, 9, 16, 23 and 30; **October** 27-29 with **SS** on **December** 8, 9, 15, 16 and 20-24.

Timetable: Please contact for details.

HAYLING SEASIDE RAILWAY
20 Jasmond Road, Cosham, Portsmouth PO6 2SY   **02392 372427**

E-mail: haddock@jasmond.fsnet.co.uk   Web: www.easthaylinglightrailway.co.uk

Timetable: Please contact for details.

ISLE OF MAN   **01624 663366**
Dept of Tourism & Leisure – Railways, Transport Headquarters, Banks Circus, Douglas, Isle of Man IM1 5PT

Fax: 01624 663637   Web: www.iombusandrail.info

Timetable: Please contact for details.

ISLE OF WIGHT STEAM RAILWAY   **01983 882204**
The Railway Station, Havenstreet, Isle of Wight PO33 4DS

Fax: 01983 884515   Web: www.iwsteamrailway.co.uk

Trains run on **January** 1, **March** 18, 22, 25 and 29; **April** 1-15, 19, 22, 26 and 29; **May** 2, 3, 5-7, 9, 10, 13, 15-17, 20, 22-24 and 26-31; **June** 1-7, 10-14, 17-21, 24-28 and 30; daily from **July** 1 until **September** 30 *EXCEPT September 17, 21, 22, 24 and 28; October 4, 7, 11, 14, 18 and 20-28*, with **SS** on **December** 2, 8, 9, 15, 16, 19-24, 26 and 27.

Timetable: Services start at approximately 11.00 with trains running to Wootton and then returning by Smallbrook Junction back to Havenstreet and vice versa. Return journey approximately one hour. Various times are available and intended passengers should contact for details or turn up at Havenstreet where trains leave in both directions.

KEIGHLEY & WORTH VALLEY RAILWAY

Haworth Station, Keighley, West Yorkshire BD22 8NJ　　　**01535 645214**

Fax: 01535 647317　Web: www. kwvr.co.uk

Trains run on **January** 1, 6, 7, 13, 14, 20, 21, 27 and 28; **February** 3, 4, 10, 11, 17, 18, 24 and 25; **March** 3, 4, 10-18, 24, 25 and 31; **April** 1-15, 21, 22, 28 and 29; **May** 5-7, 12, 13, 19, 20 and 26-31; **June** 1-3, 9, 10, 16, 17, 19-21, 23, 24, 26-28 and 30; **July** 1, daily from **July** 7 to **September** 2, then **September** 8, 9, 15, 16, 22, 23, 29 and 30; **October** 6, 7, 12-14, 20, 21 and 26-28; **November** 3, 4, 10, 11, 17, 18, 24 and 25; **December** 26-31 with SS on **December** 1, 2, 8, 9, 15, 16, 22 and 23.

Timetable: In the high season trains run approximately every three-quarters of an hour from Oxenhope and Keighley. During the off peak five trains operate per day. Please check details at any station at which all trains stop. Haworth 5 minutes after leaving Oxenhope, Oakworth 8 minutes, Damems 13 minutes and Ingrow 16 minutes.

KEITH & DUFFTOWN RAILWAY

Dufftown Station, Dufftown, Banffshire, Scotland AB55 4BA　　**01340 821181**

Web: www.keith-dufftown.org.uk

Timetable: Trains operate sporadically between April and September with three services daily leaving Dufftown at 11.20, 14.00, 15.50. Round trip from Dufftown to Keith Town is approximately one-and-a-half-hours.

KENT & EAST SUSSEX RAILWAY

Tenterden Town Station, Station Road, Tenterden, Kent TN30 6HE 0870 06006074

Fax: 01580 765654　Web: www.kesr.org.uk

Timetable: Please contact for details.

KIRKLEES LIGHT RAILWAY

Park Mill Way, Clayton West, Near Huddersfield HD8 9XJ　　　**01484 865727**

Fax: 01484 866333　E-mail: www.kirkleeslightrailway.com

Trains run April 6-10, 28 and 29; **May** 19 and 20; **June** 23 and 24; **July** 20 and 21; **August** 18, 19 and 31; **September** 1, 2, 15 and 16; **October** 27 and 28; **SS** operates on **November** 24 and 25; **December** 1, 2, 8, 9, 15, 16 and 22-24.

Timetable: Please contact for details.

LAKESIDE & HAVERTHWAITE RAILWAY CO LTD

Haverthwaite Railway, Ulverston, Cumbria LA12 8AL　　　**01539 531594**

Web: www.lakesiderailway.co.uk

Trains run on **March** 24, 25 then daily from **March** 31 until **October** 28, again on **November** 3 and 4; with **SS** on **December** 1, 2, 8, 9, 15 and 16.

Timetable: Trains leave Haverthwaite at 10.40, 11.50, 13.00, 14.05, 15.10, 16.15, 17.20 (peak season only). All trains call at Newby Bridge 12 minutes after leaving Haverthwaite and arrive at Lakeside 18 minutes after leaving Haverthwaite. Return journey departs Lakeside at 11.15, 12.30, 13.35, 14.40, 15.45, 16.50, 17.48 (peak season only).

LAUNCESTON STEAM RAILWAY

01566 775665

St Thomas Road, Launceston, Cornwall PL15 8DA　　**www.launcestonsr.co.uk**

Trains run on **April** 6-13, daily from **May** 27 until **September** 21, *EXCEPT June 2, 9, 16, 23 and 30; July 7, 14, 21 and 28; August 4, 11, 18 and 25; September 1, 8 and 15.*

Timetable: Launceston depart 11.00, 11.50, 12.45, 14.00, 14.45, 15.35, 16.30 returning from Newmills 20 minutes later. Trains also stop by request at Hunt's Crossing.

LEIGHTON BUZZARD RAILWAY

Page's Park Station, Billington Road, Leighton Buzzard LU7 4TN01525 373888

Fax: 01525 377814　Web: www.buzzrail.co.uk

Trains run on **March** 11, 18 and 25; **April** 1, 4, 6-9, 11, 15, 22 and 29; **May** 5-7, 13, 20, 26-28 and 30; **June** 3, 6, 10, 13, 17, 20, 24 and 27; **July** 1, 4, 8, 11, 15, 18, 22, 25, 29 and 31; **August** 1, 4, 5, 7, 8, 11, 12, 14, 15, 18, 19, 21, 22 and 25-27; **September** 2, 8, 9, 16, 23 and 30; **October** 6, 7, 14, 21, 24 and 28; **November** 11; **December** 26-28 with SS on **December** 1, 2, 5, 8, 9, 12, 15, 16, 19, 23 and 24.

Timetable: Trains run from Page's Park to Stonehenge Works at frequent intervals during the day. Travel time is 25 minutes each way. Round trip takes approximately 70 minutes.

LLANBERIS LAKE RAILWAY

Rheilffordd Llyn Padarn, Llanberis, Gywnedd, Wales LL55 4TY   01286 870549

Fax: 01286 870549   Web: www.lake-railway.co.uk

Trains services operate on **January** 30; **February** 6, 11-25 and 27; **March** 6, 13, 20-22 and 27-29; then daily from **April** 1 until **October** 31, *EXCEPT April 14, 21 and 28; May 12 and 19; September 8, 15, 22 and 29; October 5, 6, 12,13, 19 and 20,* then on **November** 1, 2, 4, 6, 13, 20 and 27; **December** 5, 11 with **SS** on **December** 8, 9, 15, 16 and 18.

Timetable: Trains operate from Gilfach Ddu (Llanberis 11.10) at 11.00 until late afternoon. Please check which service operates on day of travel. In the high season trains run approximately half-hourly. Round trip from Gilfach Ddu to Llanberis takes 1 hour 20 minutes.

LLANGOLLEN RAILWAY

The Station, Abbey Road, Llangollen, Denbighshire LL20 8SN   01978 860979

Fax: 01978 869247   Web: www.llangollen-railway.co.uk

Trains run on **January** 1, 7, 14, 21 and 28; **February** 4, 10-18, 24 and 25; **March** 3, 4, 10, 11 and 16-18, daily from **March** 24 until **November** 4. *EXCEPT April 16, 23, 27 and 30; May 4; June 3; October 15 and 19; November 2;* then on **December** 1, 2, 8, 9, 15, 16, 20-23 and 26-31.

Timetable: Please contact for details.

MANX ELECTRIC RAILWAY

01624 663366

Dept of Tourism & Leisure – Railways, Transport Headquarters, Banks Circus, Douglas, Isle of Man IM1 5PT

Fax: 01624 663637   Web: www.iombusandrail.info

Timetable: Please contact for details.

MIDDLETON RAILWAY

The Station, Moor Road, Hunslet, Leeds LS10 2PQ   0113 271 0320

Web: www.middletonrailway.org.uk

Trains run on **March** 31; **April** 1, 7-9, 15, 21, 22, 28 and 29; **May** 5, 6, 12, 13, 19, 20, 26 and 27; **June** 2, 3, 9, 10, 16, 17, 23, 24 and 30; **July** 1, 7, 8, 14, 15, 21, 22, 28 and 29; **August** 1, 4, 5, 8, 11, 12, 15, 18, 19, 22, 25, 26 and 29; **September** 1, 2, 8, 9, 15, 16, 22, 23, 29 and 30; **October** 7, 14, 21, 27 and 28; **November** 4, 11, 18 and 25; **December SS** on 1, 2, 8, 9, 15, 16 and 22-24.

Timetable: Please contact for details.

MID-HANTS RAILWAY (Watercress Line)

The Railway Station, Alresford, Hampshire SO24 9JG   01962 733810

Fax: 01962 735448   Web: www.watercressline.co.uk

Trains run on **January** 1, 6, 7, 13, 14, 20, 21, 27 and 28; **February** 3, 4, 10, 11, 13-15, 17, 18, 20-22, 24 and 25; **March** 2-4, 10, 11, 17, 18, 24, 25 and 31; **April** 1, 6-15, 21, 22 and 28-30; **May** 5-10, 12, 13, 15-17, 19, 20, 22-24 and 26-31; **June** 1-3, 5-7, 9, 10, 12-14, 16, 17, 19-21, 23, 24, 26-28 and 30; **July** 1, 3-5, 7, 8, 10-12, 14, 15, 17-19, 21, 22, 24-26 and 28-31, daily during **August, September** 1, 2, 4-6, 8, 9, 11-13, 15, 16, 18-23, 29 and 30; **October** 6, 7, 13, 14 and 20-28; **December** 26 and 29-31 with **SS** on **December** 1, 2, 8, 9, 15, 16 and 21-24.

Timetable: Normal timetable offers departures from Alton at 10.50, 11.55, 12.50, 13.55, 14.50, 15.55. Departures from Alresford 11.00, 11.43, 13.00, 13.43, 15.00, 15.43. Journey time 34 minutes.

MIDLAND RAILWAY – Butterley

Butterley Station, Ripley, Derbyshire DE5 3QZ   01773 747674

Fax: 01773 570721   Web: www.midlandrailwaycentre.co.uk

Trains run on **January** 1, 7, 14, 20, 21, 27 and 28; **February** 3, 4, 10-18, 24 and 25; **March** 3, 4, 10, 11, 18, 25 and 31; **April** 1-15, 21, 22, 28 and 29; **May** 5-7, 10, 12, 13, 19, 20 and 26-31; **June** 1-3, 9, 10, 14, 16, 17, 21, 23, 24, 28 and 30; **July** 1, 5, 7, 8, 12, 14, 15 and 21-31; daily throughout **August, September** 1-3, 6, 8, 9, 13, 15, 16, 23 and 30; **October** 6, 7, 13, 14 and 20-28; **November** 3, 4 and 11; **December** 27-31 with **SS** on **November** 17, 18, 24 and 25; **December** 1, 2, 6, 8, 9, 13, 15, 16 and 20-24.

Timetable: Trains leave Butterley at 10.30, except in off-peak. First departure is 11.15, return journey time approximately 45 minutes, 4 trains a day normally but this is augmented to 10 on peak dates.

MID-NORFOLK RAILWAY
The Railway Station, Station Road, Dereham, Norfolk NR19 1DF 01362 690633
Fax: 01362 698487   Web: www.mnr.org.uk

Timetable: Please contact for details.

MULL RAIL
Old Pier Station, Craignure, Isle of Mull, Argyll PA65 6AY   01680 812494
Fax: 01680 300595   Web: www.mullrail.co.uk

Trains run daily from **March** 29 until **October** 27 inclusive.

Timetable: During the high season trains run approximately every half-hour from 11.10 until 17.00. During off peak there are 4/5 trains per day. Please contact for up-to-date information.

NENE VALLEY RAILWAY
Wansford Station, Stibbington, Peterborough PE8 6LR   01780 784444
Fax: 01780 784440   Web: www.nvr.org.uk

Trains run on **January** 1, 7, 14, 21 and 28; **February** 4, 10, 11, 13-15, 17, 18, 21 and 25; **March** 3, 4, 11, 17, 18, 25 and 31; **April** 1, 4, 6-12, 14, 15, 21, 22, 27 and 28; **May** 5-7, 12, 13, 16, 19, 20, 23 and 26-31; **June** 1-3, 6, 8-10, 13, 16, 17, 20, 23, 24, 27, 29 and 30; **July** 1, 3, 7, 8, 11, 14, 15, 18, 21, 22, 24-29 and 31; **August** 1-5, 7-12, 14-19 and 21-31; **September** 1, 2, 8, 9, 15, 16, 19, 22, 23, 26, 29 and 30; **October** 5-7, 13, 14, 20, 21, 23-25, 27 and 28 with **SS** on **December** 1, 2, 5, 8, 9, 12, 15, 16, 19 and 21-24.

Timetable: Standard service provides for departure from Wansford at 11.00, 12.45, 14.30. Journey time from Wansford to Peterborough 25 minutes and Peterborough to Wansford 26 minutes. All trains call at Ferry Meadows and Orton Mere. The service is augmented from time to time and intending passengers are recommended to contact for details.
Trains go via Yarwell Junction though passengers cannot leave or join the train there. All trains call at Ferry Meadows (35) minutes and Orton Mere (40) minutes after leaving Wansford and Orton Mere (6) minutes and Ferry Meadows (11) minutes after leaving Peterborough NV.

NORTHAMPTON & LAMPORT RAILWAY
Pitsford & Brampton Station, Pitsford Road, Chapel Brampton,
Northampton NN6 8BA   01604 820327   Web: www.nlr.org.uk

Trains run every Sunday and bank holidays March to October. Hourly service augmented to 45 minutes at bank holidays. Please contact railway for further details and special events.

NORTH YORKSHIRE MOORS RAILWAY
Park Street, Pickering, North Yorkshire YO18 7AJ   01751 472508
Fax: 01751 476970   Web: nymr.co.uk

Trains run on **January** 1-3; **February** 11-25; **March** 4 and 11, daily from **March** 17 until **November** 4, then on **November** 10, 11, 17, 18, 24 and 25; **December** 27-31 with **SS** on **December** 1, 2, 8, 9, 15, 16 and 20-23.
Timetable: Varies from day to day and it is recommended that intending passengers check with Pickering to see which is operating on their intending day of travel. All trains call at Levisham 20 minutes and Grosmont 30 minutes after leaving Pickering. Passengers should allow two-and-a-half hours for return journey.

PAIGNTON & DARTMOUTH STEAM RAILWAY
Queens Park Station, Torbay Road, Paignton, Devon TQ4 6AF   01803 555872
Fax: 01803 664313   Web: www.paignton-steamrailway.co.uk

Trains run daily from **April** 1 until **October** 28 *EXCEPT April 23, 25, 27 and 30; May 2, 4, 9 and 11; October 1, 3, 5, 8, 10, 12, 15, 17 and 19*, then with **SS** on **December** 2, 8, 9, 15, 16, 22, 23 and 24.
Timetable: Trains call at Goodrington 5 minutes and Churston 15 minutes after leaving Paignton and arrive at Kingswear 30 minutes after leaving Paignton. Kingswear departures are at 11.15, 13.00, 15.15, 17.00. The journey time for a single trip is 30 minutes. The company operates a ferry service between Kingswear and Dartmouth connecting with the train service.

PEAK RAIL

Matlock Station, Matlock, Derbyshire DE4 3NA　　　　　　**01629 580381**

Fax: 01629 760645　　Web: www.peakrail.co.uk

Trains run on **January** 2, 7, 14, 21 and 28; **February** 4, 11, 14, 15, 18 and 25; **March** 3, 4, 11, 18, 25 and 31; **April** 1, 6-9, 14, 15, 21, 22, 28 and 29; **May** 5-7, 12, 13, 19, 20 and 26-29; **June** 2, 3, 6, 9, 10, 13, 16, 17, 20, 23, 24, 27 and 30; **July** 1, 4, 7, 8, 11, 14, 15, 18, 21, 22, 25, 28 and 29; **August** 4, 5, 7, 8, 11, 12, 14, 15, 19, 21, 22 and 25-29; **September** 1, 2, 5, 6, 8, 9, 12, 13, 15, 16, 22, 23, 29 and 30; **October** 6, 7, 13, 14, 20, 21, 24, 25, 27, 28 and 31; **November** 4, 11, 18 and 25; with **SS** on **December** 1, 2, 8, 9, 15, 16, 22 and 23.

Timetable: Please contact for details.

The POPPY LINE (The North Norfolk Railway)

Sheringham Station, Sheringham, Norfolk NR26 8RA　　　　**01263 820800**

Fax: 01263 820801　　Web: www.nnr.co.uk

Trains run on **January** 1-3; **February** 3, 4, 10-18, 24 and 25; **March** 3, 4, 10, 11, 17, 18, 24, 25 and 31; and daily from **April** 1 until **October** 28, *EXCEPT* April 16 and 23; **May** 4, 11 and 18; **October** 5, 12 and 15 then on **November** 3, 4, 9, 10, 17, 18, 24 and 25; **December** 29-31 with **SS** on **December** 1, 2, 8, 9, 15, 16, 20-24 and 26-28.

Timetable: Please contact for details.

RAVENGLASS & ESKDALE RAILWAY

Ravenglass Station, Ravenglass, Cumbria CA18 1SW　　　　**01229 717171**

Fax: 01229 717011　　Web: www.ravenglass-railway.co.uk

Trains run on **January** 1, 2 and 3; **February** 3, 4, 10, 11 and 17-25; **March** 3, 4, 10 and 11 then daily from **March** 17 until **October** 28; **November** 3, 4, 10, 11, 17 and 18; **December** 1, 2, 8, 9, 15, 16, 22, 23 and 26-31.

Timetable: Three different timetables operate during the season with first trains leaving Ravenglass at 10.30 (earlier service at peak periods). Services operate normally on approximately hourly basis with additional trains in the high season and four trains a day only in off-peak. Intending passengers should enquire which services are available.

ROMNEY, HYTHE & DYMCHURCH RAILWAY

New Romney Station, New Romney, Kent TN28 8PL　　　　**01797 362353**

Fax: 01797 363591　　Web: www.rhdr.org.uk

Trains run on **January** 1, 7, 14, 21 and 28; **February** 3, 4, 10-18, 24 and 25; **March** 3, 4, 10, 11, 17, 18, 24, 25 and 31, daily from **April** 1 until **October** 28, *EXCEPT October* 15-19, then on **December** 29-31 with **SS** on **December** 1, 2, 8, 9, 15, 16 and 20-24.

Timetable: Please contact for details.

SEATON TRAMWAY

Harbour Road, Seaton, Devon EX12 2NQ　　　　　　**01297 20375**

Fax: 01297 625626　　Web: www.tram.co.uk

Trams run on **January** 20; **February** 4 and 10-25; **March** 3, 4, 10, 11, 17, 18, 24, 25 and 31 then daily from **April** 1 until **October** 31; **November** 1-4, 10, 11, 17, 18, 24 and 25; **December** 1, 2, 8, 9 and 15; with **SS** on **December** 16 and 22-24.

Timetable: Trams run from Seaton at frequent intervals from 10.00 and call at Colyford in each direction. Journey time approximately 20 minutes each way.

SEVERN VALLEY RAILWAY

01299 403816

The Railway Station, Bewdley, Worcs DY12 1BG　Fax: 01299 400839　www.svr.co.uk

Trains run on **January** 6, 7, 13, 14, 20, 21, 27 and 28; **February** 3, 4, 10-18 , 24 and 25; **March** 3, 4, 10, 11, 17, 18, 24, 25 and 31; **April** 1-15, 21, 22, 28 and 29, daily from **May** 5 until **September** 30, then on **October** 6, 7, 11-14 and 20-28; **November** 3, 4, 10, 11, 17, 18, 24 and 25; **December** 26-31, with **SS** on **December** 1, 2, 8, 9, 15, 16, 19-23.

Timetable: Aprart from January and February trains run approximately every hour and the single trip to Kidderminster and Bridgnorth takes 69 minutes. Similarly from Bridgnorth to Kidderminster. All trains call at Bewdley, Arley, Highley and Hampton Loade.

SITTINGBOURNE AND KEMSLEY LIGHT RAILWAY

PO Box 300, Sittingbourne, Kent ME10 2DZ
0871 222 1568
Web: www.sklr.net

Trains run on **April** 1, 6-9, 15, 22 and 29; **May** 6, 7, 13, 20, 27, 28 and 30; **June** 3, 10, 17 and 24; **July** 1, 7, 8, 15, 22, 25 and 29; **August** 1, 5, 8, 12, 15, 19, 22, 25-27 and 29; **September** 2, 9, 16, 23, 29 and 30; with **SS** on **December** 1, 2, 8, 9, 15, 16, 22, 23 and 26.

Timetable: Trains leave Sittingbourne hourly from 13.00 until 16.00. Journey time 15 minutes. In the high season additional trains run hourly from 11.00.

SNAEFELL MOUNTAIN RAILWAY

01624 663366
Dept of Tourism & Leisure – Railways, Transport Headquarters, Banks Circus, Douglas, Isle of Man IM1 5PT
Fax: 01634 662637   Web: www.iombusandrail.info

Timetable: Please contact for details.

SNOWDON MOUNTAIN RAILWAY

Llanberis, Caernarfon, Gwynedd LL55 4TY
01286 873470
Fax: 01286 872518   Web: www.snowdonrailway.co.uk

Daily Service from **mid-March** to **October** 31 (subject to weather conditions). There is no fixed timetable. Due to development of the Summit building trains will be running only to Clogwyn. For up-to-date information see website.

SOUTH DEVON RAILWAY

The Station, Buckfastleigh, Devon TQ11 0DZ
0845 345 1420
Fax: 01364 642170   Web: www.southdevonrailway.org

Trains run on **January** 1 then daily from **March** 24 until **October** 28; **November** 3; **December** 30 and 31 with **SS** on **December** 2, 8, 9, 15, 16, 20 and 23.

Timetable: Trains leave Buckfastleigh at 10.45, 12.15, 14.15, 15.45 returning from Totnes at 11.30, 13.00, 15.00, 16.30. Journey time 30 minutes. Timetable is augmented in August with trains every 45 minutes.

SOUTH TYNEDALE RAILWAY

The Railway Station, Alston, Cumbria CA9 3JB
01434 381696
Talking Timetable: 01434 382828   Web: www.strps.org.uk

Trains run daily from **March** 31 to **April** 15, then **April** 21, 22, 28 and 29; **May** 5-7, 12, 13, 19, 20 and 26-31; **June** 1-3, 5, 7, 9, 10, 12, 14, 16, 17, 19, 21, 23, 24, 26, 28 and 30; **July** 1, 3, 5, 7, 8, 10, 12 and 14-31, daily during **August**, **September** 1, 2, 4, 6, 8, 9, 11, 13, 15, 16, 18, 20, 22, 23, 25, 27, 29 and 30; **October** 6, 7, 13, 14, 20, 21, 23, 25, 27 and 28; with **SS** on **December** 8, 9, 15, 16 and 21-23.

Timetable: Trains leave Alston at 10.45 and then at more or less hourly intervals until 16.15.

SPA VALLEY RAILWAY

West Station, Royal Tunbridge Wells, Kent TN2 5QY
01892 537715
Web: www.spavalleyrailway.co.uk

Trains run on **January** 1; **April** 5-9, 12-15, 21, 22, 28 and 29; **May** 5-7, 12, 13, 19, 20, 26-28 and 31; **June** 1-3, 7, 9, 10, 14, 16, 17, 21, 23, 24, 28 and 30; **July** 1, 5, 7, 8, 12, 14, 15, 19, 21, 22, 26, 28 and 29; **August** 2-5, 9-12, 16-19, 23-27, 30 and 31; **September** 1, 2, 8, 9, 15, 16, 22, 23, 29 and 30; **October** 6, 7, 13, 14, 19-21 and 25-28; **December** 29-31; with **SS** on **December** 1, 2, 8, 9, 15, 16 and 20-24.

Timetable: Standard timetable provides for trains leaving Tunbridge Wells West at 10.30, 11.45, 13.15, 14.30, 15.45, 17.00, returning from Groombridge at 11.05, 12.20, 13.50, 15.05, 16.20, 17.30. Journey time is 16 minutes and all trains call at intermediate station High Rocks. The late season timetable provides for departure from Tunbridge Wells West at 11.00, 12.15, 14.15, 15.30, returning from Groombridge at 11.35, 12.50, 14.50, 16.05.

STRATHSPEY RAILWAY

Aviemore Station, Dalfaber Road, Aviemore PH22 1PY　　　　**01479 810725**

Web: www.strathspeyrailway.co.uk

Trains operate on **March** 17, 18, 24, 25 and 31; **April** 1, 4-9, 11-15, 18, 19, 21, 22, 25, 26, 28 and 29; **May** 2, 3, 5-7, 9, 10, 12, 13, 16, 17, 19, 20, 23, 24, 26-28, 30 and 31; daily from **June** 1 until **September** 30, then on **October** 3, 4, 6, 7, 10, 11, 13, 14, 17, 18, 20, 21, 24, 25, 27, 28 and 31; **November** 1 with **SS** on **December** 9, 15, 16 and 22-24.

Timetable: Standard service provides for departures from Aviemore at 10.30, 11.30, 12.30, 13.30, 14.45, 15.40, 16.25, 17.15 and from Broomhill at 10.30, 11.30, 12.30, 13.30, 14.45, 15.40, 16.30. All trains call intermediately at Boat of Garten 15 minutes after leaving Aviemore. The round trip journey time is 95 mintues. Broomhill serves Nethybridge and Dulnain Bridge and is located off the A95 trunk road approximately 3 ½ miles south of Grantown on Spey.

SWANAGE RAILWAY

Station House, Swanage, Dorset BH19 1HB　　　　**01929 425800**

Fax: 01929 426680　　E-mail: davidagreen@orange.net　　Web: www.swanagerailway.co.uk

Trains run on **January** 1; **February** 17-25; **March** 3, 4, 10, 11, 17, 18, 24, 25 and 31, daily from **April** 1 until **October** 28, then on **November** 3, 4, 10, 11, 17, 18, 24 and 25; **December** 26-31 with **SS** on 1, 2, 8, 9, 15, 16 and 22-24.

Timetable: The standard timetable provides for departures from Swanage at 09.50, 11.10, 12.30, 13.50, 15.10, 16.30 and from Norden Park & Ride at 10.30, 11.50, 13.10, 14.30, 15.50, 17.10. On Fridays from April 6 to September 28 additional diesel departures at 18.10, 19.10, 20.10, 22.00, 23.00. All trains call at Herston, Harmans Cross and Corfe Castle. Journey time for a single trip 23 minutes. Normal round trip approximately 63 minutes. During August trains run approximately every 40 minutes.

TALYLLYN RAILWAY

Wharf Station, Tywyn, Gwynedd LL36 9EY　　　　**01654 710472**

Fax: 01654 711755　　Web: www.talyllyn.co.uk

Trains run on **January** 1; **February** 10-22; **March** 4, 11 and 18; daily from **March** 25 until **November** 3 then on **December** 26-31.

Timetable: All trains call at intermediate stations: Rhydyronen (12) and Dolgoch Falls (31) minutes after leaving Tywyn and at Dolgoch Falls (10) and Rhydyronen (25) minutes after leaving Abergynolwyn. Standard timetable is augmented during peak season. Trains run approximately hourly from 10.10 to 16.10 depending on timetable in operation.

TEIFI VALLEY RAILWAY

Henllan Station, Henllan, Newcastle Emlyn, Ceredigion SA44 5TD　01559 371077

Fax: 01559 371077　　E-mail: elizabeth.perry1@tesco.net　　Web: www.teifivalleyrailway.com

With some exceptions, which should be checked, trains run on most days between May and October. Trains run from 11.00 and 12.00 and hourly from 13.30-16.30.

VALE OF GLAMORGAN RAILWAY COMPANY

Barry Island Station, Romanswell Road, Barry, Vale of Glamorgan　01446 748816

Fax: 01446 749018　　Web: valeglamrail.co.uk

Trains run between May and October and usually on an hourly basis. Last train at 16.15 from Barry Island.

VALE OF RHEIDOL RAILWAY

Park Avenue, Aberystwyth, Ceredigion SY23 1PG　　　　**01970 625819**

Fax: 01970 623769　　Web: www.rheidolrailway.co.uk

Timetable: Provides for departure at 10.00 and 14.00 from Aberystwyth arriving at Devil's Bridge one hour later. Returning at 12.30 and 16.00 from Devil's Bridge. Augmented services in August and certain specific dates providing additional trains at 12.15 and 14.45 from Aberystwyth.

WELSH HIGHLAND RAILWAY (PORTHMADOG)

Tremadog Road, Porthmadog, Gwynedd LL49 9DY

Tel: 01766 513402　　Fax: 01766 513402　　Web: www.whr.co.uk

Trains run on **February** 11, 12, 17 and 18, daily from **April** 1 until **September** 30, then **October** 6, 7, 13, 14 and 20-28.

Timetable: Trains depart from Porthmadog at 10.30, 11.45, 13.30, 14.30, 15.30, 16.30 (the 16.30 does not run in February, September and October).

WELLS & WALSINGHAM LIGHT RAILWAY

Wells-next-the-Sea, Norfolk NR23 1QB

01328 711630

Web: www.wellswalsinghamrailway.co.uk

Trains run daily from **April** 1 until **October** 31 with departures fromf Wells at 10.30, 12.00, 14.00, 15.30 and from Walsingham at 11.15, 12.45, 14.45, 16.15. Augmented service operates in August with departures from Wells at 10.15, 11.45, 13.30, 15.00, 16.30 and from Walsingham at 11.00, 12.30, 14.15, 15.45, 17.15. There is a limited service in October and early autumn with departures from Wells at 11.00, 12.45, 14.30 and from Walsingham at 11.45, 13.30, 15.15. The journey time in each direction is 30 minutes.

WELSH HIGHLAND RAILWAY (CAERNARFON)

Harbour Station, Porthmadog, Gwynedd LL49 9NF

Tel: 01766 516000   Fax: 01766 516005   Web: www.festrail.co.uk

Trains run on **January** 1; **February** 10, 11, 13-15, 17, 18, 20-22, 24 and 25, daily from **March** 24 until **November** 4, *EXCEPT October 1, 5, 8, 12, 15 and 19,* then on **November** 10, 11, 17, 18, 24 and 25; **December** 1, 2, 8, 9 and 26-31, with **SS** on **December** 15, 16, 22 and 23.

The timetable varies during the season and enquiries should be made regarding specific journeys. Journey time between Caernarfon and Rhyd Ddu is 65 minutes each way and the round trip takes approximately 2 hours 30 minutes. Trains call at intermediate stations Dinas and Waufawr 15 and 30 minutes respectively after leaving Caernarfon. Normal off-peak service of 2 trains a day and high season 4 trains a day.

WELSHPOOL & LLANFAIR LIGHT RAILWAY

The Station, Llanfair Caereinion, Powys SY21 0SF

01938 810441

Fax: 01938 810861   Web: www.wllr.org.uk

Trains run on **March** 31; **April** 1-15, 21, 22, 28 and 29, **May** 5-7, 12, 13, 19, 20 and 26-31; **June** 1-3, 5-7, 9, 10, 12-14, 16, 17, 19-21, 23, 24, 26-28 and 30; **July** 1, 3-5, 7, 8, 10-12, 14, 15, 17-19 and 21-31, daily during **August**, **September** 1, 2, 4-6, 8, 9, 11-13, 15, 16, 22, 23, 29 and 30; **October** 6, 7, 13, 14 and 20-28, with **SS** on **December** 15, 16, 22 and 23.

Timetable: Normal services provides for departures from Welshpool at 11.15, 14.15, 17.00 and from Llanfair Caereinion at 09.45, 13.00, 15.45. Journey time 50 minutes single.

WEST LANCASHIRE LIGHT RAILWAY

Station Road, Hesketh Bank, Nr. Preston, Lancs PR4 6SP

01772 815881

Fax: 0845 130 3777   Web: www.westlancs.org

Trains run on **April** 1, 6, 8, 9, 15, 22 and 29; **May** 6, 13, 20 and 27; **June** 3, 10, 17 and 24; **July** 1, 8, 15, 22 and 29; **August** 5, 11, 12, 19, 26 and 27; **September** 2, 9, 16, 23 and 30; **October** 7, 14, 21 and 28; with **SS** on **December** 16, 22 and 23.

Timetable: Sundays and bank holidays, Easter to October 31 trains depart from Becconsall at 12.00 arriving Delph at 12.05. Round trip 15 minutes. Trains run every 20 minutes.

HERITAGE RAILWAYS AWARD WINNER 2006

WEST SOMERSET RAILWAY

The Railway Station, Minehead, Somerset TA24 5BG

01643 704996

Fax: 01643 706349   Web: www.west-somerset-railway.co.uk

Trains run on **February** 17, 18, 20-22, 24 and 25; **March** 3, 4, 10, 11, 17, 18, 20-25, 27-29 and 31, daily from **April** 1 until **November** 1, *EXCEPT April 16, 20, 23, 27 and 30; May 4, 11, 14, 18 and 21; October 8, 12, 15 and 19* then on **December** 27-31 with **SS** on **December** 1, 2, 7-9, 15, 16, 22 and 24.

Timetable: Four different timetable services operate during the season and prospective travellers are recommended to check as the service does not follow a set pattern. First trains start mid-morning from Minehead and Bishops Lydeard with last trains leaving Minehead and Bishops Lydeard late afternoon. Most services operate throughout the line from Minehead and Bishops Lydeard and vice versa although some trains in the off peak season run between Minehead and Williton. Journey time is 1 hour 45 minutes in each direction. There are normally 4 or 5 trains a day with services augmented in the high season to 6 trains a day.

All trains call at intermediate stations: Dunster (6), Blue Anchor (14), Washford (23), Watchet (32), Williton (43), Stogumber (54) and Crowcombe (64) minutes after leaving Minehead and at Crowcombe (15), Stogumber (23), Williton (35), Watchet (44), Washford (52), Blue Anchor (60) and Dunster (67) minutes after leaving Bishops Lydeard.

INDEX TO TIMETABLES

* Narrow Gauge Railway.   † 2006 Heritage Railway of the Year Award Winner.

The scene at Weybourne on the Poppy Line in early Spring 2006 as London, Brighton & South Coast Railway No 662 prepares to return to Sheringham. The locomotive, restored at Bressingham Steam Experience, was operating some of its first passenger trains since returning to steam. *ACB*